THE MARILYN SCANDAL

The True Story

Sandra Shevey

ARROW BOOKS

To my parents, Hy and Alice Shevey
whose fortitude has been an inspiration

Arrow Books Limited
62–65 Chandos Place, London WC2N 4NW

An imprint of Century Hutchinson Limited

London Melbourne Sydney Auckland
Johannesburg and agencies throughout
the world

First published in Great Britain by Sidgwick & Jackson 1987
Reprinted 1987 (twice)
Arrow edition 1989

© 1987 by Sandra Shevey

This book is sold subject to the condition that it shall
not, by way of trade or otherwise, be lent, resold,
hired out, or otherwise circulated without the pub-
lisher's prior consent in any form of binding or cover
other than that in which it is published and without a
similar condition including this condition being imposed on the subsequent purchaser.

Photoset in Linotron 202 Bembo by
Rowland Phototypesetting Limited
Bury St Edmunds, Suffolk

Printed and bound in Great Britain by
Anchor Press Ltd, Tiptree, Essex
ISBN 0 09 960760 3

Contents

List of Illustrations

Acknowledgements

The idea to write a book which revealed the Marilyn Monroe I came to know through the reminiscences of close friends began in 1972. I wish to thank Sheila MacRae, in particular, for sharing her memories with me. In addition, I wish to thank Maureen Stapleton and Henry Ephron for their extremely candid observations; Joan Copeland for the lighter side of Monroe; Norman Rosten for sharing the tremendous well-spring of love and affection he has for her; Jack Cardiff and Roy Baker – two Englishmen who appreciate her 'genius'; John Springer and Rupert Allan, the kind of press agents who are heaven-sent; James Bacon for sharing his memories and affection; Billy Travilla for his co-operation; Jan Sterling for sharing with me her trenchant observations on American politics; the British Film Institute for the use of its screening facilities and the extreme helpfulness of their staff; Jane Smith for arranging private viewing facilities in other instances; Whitey Snyder for having granted an interview although he had previously said he would never give another one (and for memories that go back a long way with Monroe); Joshua Logan for granting an interview when he was unwell; Stanley Rubin for both lunch and anecdotage; and Robert Slatzer for sharing his confidences. I also wish to express my devotion to editors Don Feitel (now deceased) and Dick Kaplan, without whose guidance there never would have been a first article, let alone a first book; and Robert Smith, whose belief in me and this project sustained me. I also wish to thank the staff at the Beverly Sunset Hotel who took messages and were helpful above and beyond what they had to do during the few weeks I stayed there whilst doing research. Bless you all! Love, Sandy.

1
The Woman Behind the Myth

A friend once observed of Marilyn Monroe: 'She's camp!' It is partly true, which is why I never used to like her. But in coming to an appreciation I have found that the glitzy aspects of her appeal were an adjustment to the Hollywood of the fifties which derided female sex and in consequence created a Marilyn who was at times a parody of herself.

The aim of this book is neither to pass along the myth of Marilyn as an object of veneration, since I believe that all myths – particularly supremacy myths – are psychologically dangerous icons of assimilation; nor to blame (and disparage) the actress because of the way the myth was misused by the very medium she sought to exploit. Rather, the intention is to present a balanced picture of a very human lady – someone who had enormous talent, drive, ambition, youth, sexuality and ego, and whose genius for self-realization allowed her to use her talents to launch a 'product' that was marketable worldwide. Why and how Marilyn failed to survive in a society which was fast becoming depersonalized, unisex and collectivist in outlook, underscored by rigid human and technological controls, is in essence the tragedy of Monroe that I will consider.

Like many lovers, Hollywood was neither doting nor protective. Fickle and soul-destroying, jealous and contemptuous, it mocked her attempts to commercialize those aspects of herself which she considered to be marketable. Her success predictably stupefied executives who tried to copy her and failed. 'She was just too beautiful and too talented to survive,' observes Joshua Logan, who directed Monroe in *Bus Stop*. 'They couldn't forgive her both beauty and talent.' In the years Monroe spent as starlet and then superstar, she had little peace, enjoyed the confidence of few, was used by many, and generally elicited feelings of ambiguity in both friends and lovers.

An American original, brassy, sassy and camp, she was a self-made performer of tremendous honesty, wit and romanticism – offbeat and conventional almost simultaneously. She was given to excesses; could love prodigiously – sometimes more than one man at a time (never completely letting go); and adored fantasy (catered for it) whilst at the same time perceiving the reality of things underneath. She worshipped Gable, but didn't sentimentalize him the way Arthur Miller did in his *Misfits* dedication: 'To the man who did not know how to hate.' Largely self-educated, she was propelled toward self-improvement of body and mind: a devotee of both Method and psychoanalysis. Both have been cited as having been detrimental in their effect on her, yet their success can be seen in the depth of her latter film work. By then, Marilyn's comprehension of sophisticated ideas was remarkable; even Miller admitted that she could say a great deal in a single glance.

Her tastes were eclectic, even in men. And although John Kennedy was *not* on her renowned list of Sexy Men, many of those that were, including Miller, Montand, Brando, Sinatra, Wallach and Laughton, succeeded in being 'seduced'. She was absolutely immune to prejudice. She was not lesbian, but she had among her friends people of all sexual persuasions. Her racial and religious attitudes were also fair. She was a Jewish convert, but considered herself to be an 'atheist Jew'.

Rapaciously inquisitive, her intelligence matured at an astonishing pace. Both a zealous Democrat and a keen citizen, she followed politics and corresponded with Lester Markel, then editor of the *New York Sunday Times*, often complaining to him about news coverage and the lack of prominence given to some important stories. It is also worth noting the little known fact that Roxbury, Connecticut, where Monroe was resident in 1960, nominated her as an alternate delegate to the Democratic convention, indicating that those who knew and loved her took her very seriously indeed.

For the most part, however, she was misunderstood. 'The starlet was derided whilst the superstar was vilified,' observes a friend.

Never properly acknowledged as homicide, her appalling death is still an unexplained mystery. Robert Kennedy (then Attorney General), admitted to having entered her flat with Monroe's analyst on the afternoon of 4 August 1962 because, in his own words, 'She had been bothering my brother'*, leaving us to wonder at the role he might have played in the tragedy. Still officially regarded as suicide by the Los Angeles District Attorney's office, the case remains closed despite efforts by some to instigate an investigation to look into why her analyst, Dr Greenson, paying what was described as a routine house call (for which the estate was later billed), came, together with Robert Kennedy, bearing a hypodermic needle loaded with tranquillizer.

Despite the widespread suggestion of foul play, Los Angeles society, government officials, police officers, film studio personnel, Hollywood columnists and medical practitioners all choose to give credence to the suicide theory, citing Marilyn as having a wanton self-destructive personality. This book will attempt to show that far from being a suicidal type, Marilyn survived

* *A Hero for Our Times*, Ralph Martin, p. 404.

several calculated attempts to undermine her physical and mental equilibrium.

Rejected and vilified, her body lay unclaimed for days on a slab in the city morgue, with only a name tag for a talisman knotted around her big toe. Both Miller and DiMaggio were contacted, but neither of them made an immediate effort to redeem the body. *Misfits* producer Frank Taylor asked Monroe's makeup man, Whitey Snyder, to do it, but since the deed necessitates the willingness to undertake certain financial obligations he, like the others, was reluctant and it remained for the Monroe estate to make the formal claim. DiMaggio generously donated a bronze crypt costing $800. The funeral costs, however, were charged to the estate.

When it came to the reading of the will, it was discovered that there was very little capital left, which prevented beneficiaries from receiving anything until months, sometimes years, later. Royalty payments, however, have since buoyed the cash flow, making bequests in some cases much larger than expected. It would be heartening, I am sure, for Marilyn to learn that Dr Marianne Kris' bequest upon her death was donated to the Anna Freud Centre in Hampstead, London, a psychiatric clinic for gifted children. What she wouldn't have appreciated is the current squabbling promoted by Lee Strasberg's second wife and widow, Anna, who is trying to stop all further payments to the centre. Anna Strasberg married Lee after his wife Paula's death following Marilyn's demise.

Some of those prominent in Monroe's life have also since died: her psychiatrist Dr Ralph Greenson, actor/friend Peter Lawford, John and Robert Kennedy, press agent Arthur Jacobs, director George Cukor, drama coaches Lee and Paula Strasberg, business partner Milton Greene and lawyer Frank Delaney. For the rest, little has changed. They practise in the same places the same way, availing others of their considerable talents and skills. Lawyer Milton Rudin, press agent John Springer, press agent Rupert Allan, internist Dr Hyman Engelberg, producer Henry Weinstein and press agent Patricia Newcomb are all very much alive; Newcomb is still active in the film industry.

Years after her death, the myth of Monroe persists – a projection of the best (and worst) fantasies of us all. In *Hollywood 1950s*, Adrian Turner promotes the diabolical side of Monroe: '. . . [her] body was voluptuous and ridiculous, her face a blank negative on which male fantasies of rape and impotency were printed. She was projected as an icon, but only dimly comprehended the meaning, possibilities and dangers . . . The strain was too much and she killed herself in 1962 . . .'

During her lifetime she was accused of some horrible things. Rumours of her lesbian 'tendencies' were circulated by her former husband DiMaggio in an attempt to get her to drop her divorce action. That she was a nymphomaniac, truant and notoriously late are other 'legends' that have grown up around Monroe, all of which will be examined in this book.

Robert Slatzer, whose brief marriage to Monroe was annulled at the behest of Fox chief Darryl Zanuck, explains the perversity of DiMaggio's insinuations and the effect they had on Monroe. 'She started seeing a psychiatrist,' he says simply. While I will deal with this saga in detail later, it is worth noting briefly that Monroe's friend, Sheila MacRae, also mentioned her obsession with therapy to me. She never stated explicitly whether the sex scandal catapulted her into therapy, but she confirmed that it was during this time that Marilyn began seeing a succession of analysts, observing that none seemed to offer any reassurance or satisfaction.

It is with the help of people like Sheila MacRae that I have come to understand Marilyn, and it should be acknowledged, too, that the observations of another friend, actress Maureen Stapleton, have also assisted me. Stapleton, a prominent New York Actors Studio member, knew Monroe following her move to the city in 1955 and was privy to the intimacies of the courtship with playwright Arthur Miller, Monroe's third husband. They also worked together on a scene from *Anna Christie*, which by all accounts was remarkable, and succeeded in convincing incredulous Actors Studio members that Studio Director Lee Strasberg's praise of Monroe and Marlon Brando as the greatest actors of their time was not misplaced. Stapleton talked at length about Monroe's inferiority and how it was exploited. ('When she married Arthur, she told him: "People will laugh. It is not too late to back out."') She could also be very aloof, and whilst DiMaggio has always boasted that he scored with her on the first date, Stapleton insists it was some time before Miller really got to first base.

I also learned about Monroe's temperament – her rashes, hysteria, retching and other neuroses which could be triggered by tension or confrontation. They say she went white when faced with the slightest hint of obscenity. Hardly the response of a nymphomaniac.

It is Monroe folklore that she was notoriously truant and often late in getting to the set. There is rarely any film in which she starred (and I am referring now to the days when she already was a superstar) where she was not asked to apologize to the entire cast for some breach in behaviour. True to form, more than twenty-five years on, I.A.L. Diamond, who scripted *Some Like It Hot* – the film Monroe finished in spite of courting a miscarriage – still asserts that she was bossy, bitchy and brassy. 'She was superior to those who could not fight back,' he told me in a recent interview. Among other things, Diamond recalled the famous incident when Marilyn, having been given a curtain call by the assistant director, told him (since she wasn't ready) in common terms to drop dead.

The incident made front-page headlines when Billy Wilder (the director) referred to it in print as an example of Monroe's ego, calling her, in consequence, 'the meanest woman in Hollywood'. But why the fuss? Monroe never made any attempt to have him removed from the set. How many superstars tolerate insubordination from inferiors? When Brando comes on to a set he hibernates in his dressing room for hours, sometimes days, until he is ready to shoot. The sad truth is that Monroe, even at the height of her career, never had the respect due a superstar. She was always plain old Marilyn: Fox's ageing sexpot.

In reality Monroe was the consummate professional allowing herself a minimum of recuperation between films. Her truancy was related to illness – often pregnancy – although she was sickness-prone, having a constitution whose delicacy is well noted. The lapses during *Something's Got to Give*, from which Fox fired her, were due to some *bona fide* physical ailment. Since she had had one miscarriage whilst filming *Some Like It Hot*, believing it was her professional duty to finish the film, Monroe felt, and understandably so, that the studio owed her some indulgence on *Something's Got to Give*. Unfortunately, Fox did not agree and they made no effort to suspend production. Co-star Dean Martin, whose company was producing the film, had a commitment which dovetailed the scheduled completion of the picture and there could be no postponement without losing him. Fox therefore replaced Monroe with Lee Remick and filed a lawsuit against her.

Monroe was never secure in the hands of practitioners supposedly committed to her welfare. Her lawyer, a top-flight Hollywood attorney, should have been able to solve the problems at Fox, but he failed and Monroe was put both into financial limbo and emotional turmoil. She was devastated by the Fox firing, since she had grossed over $250,000,000 for the studio, only a fraction of which she had seen herself. She had recently purchased a modest Spanish bungalow in the middle-class neighbourhood of Brentwood (a house less posh by far than Jayne Mansfield's Beverly Hills mansion, a Fox star of much less stature), and falling behind in mortgage payments, had to borrow $5,000 from Robert Slatzer – a rather embarrassing episode at the superstar juncture of her career.

She fared badly with doctors, too. The completion of *Misfits* and *Let's Make Love* back to back, coupled with the breakup of her marriage to playwright Arthur Miller, catapulted Monroe into a state of emotional exhaustion. She asked Dr Marianne Kris, her New York analyst of some years, to arrange hospitalization for a few weeks of rest and recuperation, but instead found herself committed under restraint into Payne-Whitney, an institution for the mentally highly disturbed, where patients are watched and accommodation is little better than a padded cell. It was only through the efforts of DiMaggio that after three days Monroe was released and transferred to the Columbia Presbyterian Medical Center where she remained for three weeks. The Payne-Whitney episode not only proved insufferable for Marilyn – it was something she never stopped talking about – but worse, it damaged her credibility at the studio, where she was now written off as a nut case, having always been considered borderline because it was known that her mother, Gladys Baker (a negative film cutter in the thirties and forties), had been in a mental institution for the major part of her life.

Like most people whose livelihood depends on beauty, Monroe did what she had to do without complaint. I was quite amazed to discover the great many physiological changes she had undergone to achieve her universally accepted good looks. Monroe was always an obliging and patient victim, until demands became petty and unremitting, driving her into neurosis about the tiniest wrinkle or flaw. Joshua Logan relates as early as *Bus Stop* (1956) how Monroe would spend hours in front of the mirror, noticing something that wasn't quite right about her physiognomy. At the time of her death, she wouldn't leave the house for any meeting or party without makeup man Whitey Snyder and hairdresser Agnes Flanagan to prepare her. (Her cosmetic bills during those last months were enormous.) Her replacement by a younger actress (Lee Remick) in *Something's Got to Give* completely obliterated whatever confidence she had managed to muster and along with daily visits to the analyst there was an appointment made (and cancelled) with a Beverly Hills plastic surgeon to examine some minor injury to her nose. (Marilyn had earlier had plastic surgery on her nose and chin and it has been hinted that, like Judy Garland, she wore a latex bridge to widen the cinematic effect of her profile. Her makeup man, Snyder, does not, however, confirm it as being true.) Ironically, footage from *Something's Got to Give*, included in a BBC documentary, looks wonderful. Monroe is radiant. But it has also been suggested that use was made both of filters and an Obie spot to make Monroe appear younger.

I approach Monroe's relationship with President John Kennedy with some trepidation, but I do so to refute claims that she was a one-night stand, a VIP call girl, or the mistress to both brothers. I will also discuss Robert Kennedy's involvement in her death, citing reasons why I believe that it was not suicide. Many think it was a crime which warranted prosecution and one which could even have been premeditated.

The weekend Monroe spent at Lake Tahoe was, it has been suggested, a precedent for suicide. Kitty Kelley supports this in *His Way*, her biography of Sinatra. '. . . Marilyn Monroe tried to commit suicide there but she managed to contact the Cal-Neva operator in time to be rushed to the hospital to have her stomach pumped. (A few days later, in Los Angeles, she died of another overdose.)' And yet the story is contradicted by Monroe biographer Fred Guiles who writes: 'Those few who knew Marilyn's secret were *horrified*. While friends were told that Marilyn had gone for a long weekend in Lake Tahoe, she was secretly hospitalized on 20 July in Cedars of Lebanon Hospital . . . A surgical termination of pregnancy was decided upon . . .'

Not inherently destructive, but psychologically oppressed, Monroe's final days have been described as abysmal. An unremitting fear of being compromised made her suspicious of anyone soliciting employment in her domicile. 'In other ways, too, her behaviour grew bizarre,' said Jet Fore, the Fox press agent whose relationship with Marilyn dates back to 1946 when she first came to the studio. 'She'd ring me from a public booth. She was paranoid about her telephone being tapped.' The phone tap was later validated, Monroe's flat having been bugged by private eye Bernard Spindel in an attempt to get something on the Kennedys to use against the Attorney General in his battle with the Teamsters. But since the eavesdrop was accomplished, according to the BBC, using a long-range 'bug', the only way that she could possibly have been aware of any invasion of privacy was by hearing or seeing things said privately made public. (In other words, there was no actual plant in the house.) It is stranger still that the telephone records for the months she had been dogging the Kennedys in Washington, Palm Springs and Hyannisport mysteriously disappeared. Copies were later released to columnist James Bacon when it was discovered they had been confiscated by the police at the command of Robert Kennedy (then Attorney General) who presumably alleged at the time of her death that she was a security risk.

Did Marilyn intend to hold a press conference to embarrass the Kennedys politically? Legend cites her as a security risk, in possession of a diary detailing important

political secrets. Press agent Newcomb denies the existence of any such diary. And Bobby Kennedy, in his
moment of truth, failed to mention it in an important
police deposition, although the widely preemptive
powers he evoked on that fatal night imply it was the
impression he wished to convey.

My own thinking is that it was a red herring, introduced to justify the use of political imperatives to cope
with a situation which had become a personal embarrassment to the Kennedys. It is quite amazing that despite
his bizarre involvement in the last few hours of her
life that not only was Robert Kennedy never publicly
investigated but he mounted a successful primary campaign to get the Democratic presidential nomination and
would assuredly have got it had he not been assassinated.
Even if Marilyn had disclosed the nature of her relationship with Jack Kennedy (which the press knew about
anyway and kept mum) there is no indication at the time
that anybody was willing to tell tales. John Kennedy has
remained a hero inviolate for many years after his death:
out of bounds for some segments of the US media.

Any suggestion of an affair between Robert and Marilyn is ludicrous: any true insight into Monroe's character
and temperament precludes her finding his advances
appealing, since she was, at the time, not only sleeping
with his brother but also carrying his child. The insin-
uation that she was sleeping with both boys bitterly
confirms the lie that she was promiscuous. Monroe's
feelings for John Kennedy were innocent, selfless and
loving; there is much evidence to suggest that in the
early stages of their relationship his for her were the
same. That he should have behaved so shabbily in
the final episode was deeply regrettable and very unfair.

Whilst Arthur Miller seemed unable to forgive his
wife's indiscretions during her lifetime (or perhaps what
he couldn't forgive was sharing her love with a man
of John Kennedy's stature, wit and intelligence), he is

paradoxically able to commiserate with her in death. Many of the metaphorical observations he makes in *After the Fall* and *Misfits* help us to understand the woman's complexity. I do not believe it is accidental that during their marriage she gave some of her best screen performances.

Joseph Mankiewicz told me when I asked about the casting of Monroe in *All About Eve* that she died at the right time: 'she was old, fat and unwanted.' True, when she died a new prototype was emerging. Monroe was a symbol of a dying femininity (open and voluptuous), the necessity for which had long since ceased to exist and, of which, perhaps, she was the last brilliant incarnation. Society had moved into a unisex era. *That* is the message of *Misfits*. Who's to say Monroe would not have weathered the storm? She had talent and had she been given half a chance her dramatic abilities could have been unsurpassed. 'She could have made it with a little luck,' Miller was quoted as having said following her death.

I find it vastly dismaying that of all the people I interviewed protesting affection and regard for Monroe, no one at the time spoke up on her behalf and challenged the mockery of an investigation into her death. And yet – I daresay – the whole town knew what went on that night. Those who didn't actually cover for the Kennedys – and there were a great many who did – did so in effect by remaining silent. And even now I am sure in their hearts they believe they did the right thing. There is something more than a little corrupt about people reputing to disavow considerations of family and class who rally round the flag once the alarm has been sounded. I think that must be what director George Cukor meant when he said: 'Power. Money. In the end it was too much.'

Some have called it a conspiracy of silence – a sort of cabalist community ritual – voodoo – when there is an unspoken general feeling of ill-will mounted against a

person because of something about them that is alien.
Makeup man Whitey Snyder and dresser Marge Plecher
confirm Monroe perceived evidence of witchcraft. Just
before the Kennedy denouement that morning, or the
day before, she received in the post a stuffed animal.
There was no card – nothing with it. But something
about it made her behave strangely, fingering it mysteriously as if she perceived it was an omen.

One of the greatest legends of the twentieth century,
Marilyn Monroe's life is a combination of forces. What
I have tried to do is to present events objectively: allowing the reader to draw their own conclusions about the
kinds and degrees of malevolence involved.

2
The Brothers Kennedy

Poet Norman Rosten is right: when Marilyn Monroe returned to the west coast of America in the autumn of 1961 after a seven-year absence, it was the final act. There would be a year and a half interlude before her death, but in that time all the things which could go wrong for her would, and John Huston's remark, after the completion of *Misfits*, that 'In a while she'll either be dead or in a mental institution' would prove to be prophetic.

The Miller marriage, the unquestionable climax of Monroe's life, was over – ended by a Juarez divorce in January 1961 (which coincided with John Kennedy's presidential inauguration). The perennial student, Monroe was always looking for a father figure, and in hindsight Miller will be remembered as her most devoted and reassuring professor. But he had found someone else: an Austrian photographer (Inge Morath) who he had met on *Misfits* and who he married about the time Monroe moved into the bungalow she had purchased in Brentwood. ('I can't imagine buying a house alone,' Marilyn said at the time. 'But why can't I? I have always been alone.')

Putting together the pieces after the end of her whirl-wind affair with the French actor Yves Montand ('She didn't know what hit her,' says a friend, 'when Montand

upped and went back to his French wife'), Monroe
enjoyed a few consolatory dates with Marlon Brando,
José Bolaños (a Mexican diversion) and Frank Sinatra
(who, according to reports, grew quite serious). The
only suitor (I believe) to have given Monroe not diamonds, but emeralds, Sinatra has been quoted as saying
his solicitude sprang simply from the desire to get the
lady out of the house. Nevertheless, there was a vague
but persistent hope on Monroe's part that he might
propose, although she told friends Norman and Hedda
Rosten that she believed he still was in love with his first
wife, Nancy, and always would be. In any event, the
weekends aboard his yacht, or at the Sands Hotel in Las
Vegas (where he was performing) were convivial, and
gave Marilyn the chance to meet other members of
the Rat Pack such as Dean Martin whose production
company, Claude, put together the deal on her last film,
Something's Got to Give. ('She must have been high on
Sinatra,' says a friend, 'to have signed to do that film.')
Certainly it wasn't a huge success when Leo McCarey
directed the 1940 version, *My Favourite Wife*, and there
was no indication that the Nunnally Johnson update
would make it work any better. Even when the film was
revamped as *Move Over Darling* for Doris Day in 1963,
it failed to become a box-office hit. Sinatra's sudden
announcement of an engagement to Juliet Prowse, however, even though it lasted only for a couple of weeks,
put a damper on any marriage plans Monroe herself
might have envisaged and she resumed seeing Joe
DiMaggio.

But the real distraction occupying Monroe's thoughts
during those final months was John Kennedy, whose
ardour had persisted throughout her marriages both to
DiMaggio and Miller, and showed no signs of diminishing upon her return to California, where he openly
escorted her as his mistress. According to Robert Slatzer,
DiMaggio was infuriated by the attention Kennedy

lavished upon Marilyn, and it seems probable that the Kennedy flirtation also rankled with Miller, who was known to be prone to jealousy, and it is conceivable that Kennedy may have been responsible for their marital breakup. The first signs of trouble in paradise between Monroe and Miller were said to have been detected during their honeymoon in England where Marilyn was filming *The Prince and the Showgirl*. Whitey Snyder, Monroe's makeup man, told me that when Miller returned from a trip he had made to the USA, something in his feelings for Marilyn had changed. 'Something was different. I don't know what,' says Snyder. 'But he had changed. And it very much upset Marilyn.'

Much has been written about Miller's diary entry referring to how his first wife had let him down, and how now Marilyn had too; that he was beginning to believe Olivier was right and that she was a troublesome bitch; and that the only person he could really love was his daughter, Jane. Miller, it is said, deliberately left open the diary so that Marilyn could read the selected passage: its contents so shocked her that she fell to pieces and was only stuck together for the film's completion by the appearance on the set of her analyst, Dr Marianne Kris, who had to be flown in from New York. It seems likely that the origins of Miller's resentment (intensified by his problems with Congress) derived from gossip he had overheard about his wife's infidelity with John Kennedy before, during and after their marriage.

Sammy Davis Jr has been quoted as saying that during Miller's absences Monroe was having an affair with a photographer friend of his. One possible candidate is Milton Greene, then vice-president of Marilyn Monroe Productions. But it is unlikely, and I think the real cause of jealousy was the Kennedy affair, which Miller must have got wind of in Washington. 'How could he have *not* known?' asks a gossip. 'It was so out in the open.' That Monroe chose Kennedy's inauguration (January

1961) to obtain her Mexican divorce from Miller is also significant, perceiving as she did the symbolism in everything around her. Was she implying that Kennedy, if he had indeed said something had been proven right about Miller – that in the end he was disloyal? While filming *Misfits*, Marilyn found a draft of Miller's *After the Fall* which he had left lying around and, once again, she became hysterical. She also saw a diary he had been keeping about their marriage – observations about her set down from the day they were wed.

John Kennedy was not the communist-baiter his brother Robert was (Bobby observed a day of mourning when Senator Joseph McCarthy passed away), but, even so, he might have felt (and told Marilyn) that it was inappropriate for Arthur Miller to have publicly proposed marriage to her whilst being investigated by Congress. Monroe's press agent Rupert Allan, a former naval commander, never really forgave Miller for his conduct at the time of the hearings and even now says: 'I don't like the way he behaved before Congress, nor do I sympathize with the way he dragged Marilyn into it. He was in hot water politically. What better an out but to marry the all-American girl?' Monroe later confided to Allan, when the marriage began to wind down, that she had been put off by the publicity attending the proposal. 'He told them [the public] before he told me,' she remarked. Although surely at the time it was a mere formality, as they had been seeing each other secretly since Monroe's move into New York City in 1955 and Miller had already completed the Nevada residency requirement necessary to obtain a divorce from Mary Miller, his wife of fifteen years, at the time of the hearings.

The 'inaugural' divorce from Miller also signalled the tempering of her infatuation with intellectuals. 'It's what is going on emotionally between two people that is important,' she told Richard Meryman in a *Life* magazine interview. Kennedy was the man of her dreams, and although she held out no hope of marrying him, Monroe was, for a period of eight successive years, content to be John Kennedy's mistress. She has been given little recognition by Kennedy biographers but the reality of the matter was that upon her return to the West Coast in the summer of 1961, Marilyn Monroe was *de facto* a Kennedy. 'We had explained the ground rules to her: about the need for discretion in these matters. She assented, saying that she understood and willingly complied,' says a member of the Kennedy clan, razing any doubt that Monroe was anything amounting to a passing fancy. Columnist James Bacon, a Kennedy insider, told me in a recent interview that he knew about Marilyn's affair with Jack Kennedy for years. 'But I didn't dare use it. The only columnist to turn the other cheek was Walter Winchell: he never sat on a story. And he came as close as anybody to blowing the lid off the relationship which led to her death,' he says. 'JFK was completely open about the romance, but the press out of respect for his position kept it quiet. Let's face it: Jack Kennedy was our most romantic President.'

According to Bacon, Kennedy and his wife had an understanding and in all the years he knew Kennedy (first as a Congressman, then as a Senator and finally as President) Bacon never knew him to appear on the West Coast with Jackie. (Mrs Kennedy occupied herself with yachting in the Mediterranean or fox hunting in Virginia when she wasn't fulfilling her rigorous schedule of events as First Lady.) 'When he came west,' says Bacon, 'he would use the Bing Crosby house in Palm Springs' (which because it was cut into the side of a mountain, and had only two other houses nearby, was extremely secure).

The persistence of the 'Bobby' rumour is explained by Bacon as a smokescreen used to discredit Marilyn's involvement with John Kennedy. 'I never heard her talk about Bobby, but boy! she sure was open about her affair with John.' Having seen Marilyn and Bobby together at a party given by Peter Lawford, Bacon observes: 'There didn't seem to be any relationship between Bobby and Marilyn at all. Marilyn would follow him around. She was wearing horn-rimmed glasses and was carrying a notebook and whenever Bobby said anything about civil rights or whatever Marilyn took it down. I thought it was strange at the time. But Marilyn always had a kooky sense of humour.'

She also had a tremendous sense of romance, and it must have been gratifying for her to watch her lover rise from US Senator to President within the span of a few years. She was utterly dazzled. Had anyone tried to talk sense to her, pointing out that the Kennedy affair endangered not only her marriage to DiMaggio but that to Miller, too, would she (could she) have listened?

Two significant examples of Monroe's romanticism give us insight into her character. The first harkens back to the days when she was being courted by DiMaggio. Despite being a famous actress she was only receiving a nominal salary from Fox and could not afford to buy really nice clothes. When she was in Niagara Falls filming *River of No Return* she rang up her friend Ceil Chapman and asked to be outfitted in something special because she wanted to impress DiMaggio who was then in New York. While by that time she had ample evidence of his affection, it is telling that she still wanted to do something that would give him pleasure. The second anecdote concerns her first meeting with Miller in 1951 when she was filming *As Young As You Feel*. Elia Kazan was directing something on the same lot and during a break for lunch brought Arthur Miller round to meet Marilyn. They looked for her but she had disappeared. The director said that she was on a sound stage which wasn't being used and that 'the kooky girl often goes over there to be alone'. When Kazan and Miller found her, Marilyn was jumpy and crying. Apparently she had seen Kazan with Miller on the set and had run off embarrassed at the thought of actually getting to meet someone who had been a hero of hers for years. Rupert Allan recalls that when he did his first interview with Marilyn, after she had filmed *Asphalt Jungle*, there was a photograph hanging on her wall of three men, two of them were Kazan and Miller.

There is not as much on record about Marilyn's first encounter with Kennedy in 1954 at a party given by Charles Feldman. He was quoted, however, as having said that what people admired in him, he admired in Monroe: optimism, energy and determination. Given Kennedy's propensity for understatement, that was quite a grand compliment. Following their meeting, Marilyn confided to Robert Slatzer that Kennedy was everything DiMaggio was, and also what he was not — '"both athletic and smart", she said,' recalls Slatzer. Kennedy in his turn told Slatzer that he thought Marilyn was 'a fine human being and a vastly underrated actress'. (Kennedy had been a fan for years, and Monroe's 'Golden Dreams' nude calendar had a prominent place on his wall.)

Anthony Summers confirms that Monroe's affair with Kennedy started as early as 1954 and quotes Arthur James, a friend of Marilyn's from the late forties. 'They sometimes drank at the Malibu Cottage' (a beachfront haunt of some of the most famous Hollywood names) 'or walked hand in hand on the shore near the Malibu pier,' says James. Their trysts, according to him, often took place at the Holiday House Motel in Malibu, which was owned by the Dudley Murphys, friends of both Marilyn and Jack. The lovers would also frequently use Peter Lawford's place — the old Louis B. Mayer beach house on the Malibu gold coast in Santa Monica. (Lawford was at the time married to the President's sister, Patricia, although they later divorced.) That Lawford's

role was that of a kind of 'pimp' was confirmed by an
interview his last wife, Deborah Gould, gave to the BBC
in which she alluded to his collaboration in removing
from Monroe's flat anything linking her with the Kennedys. Peter and Pat divorced following JFK's assassination and it is generally thought that Pat Lawford (who
had been a close friend of Marilyn) felt badly about her
husband's actions in connection with Marilyn's death.

Whilst he was a Senator, Kennedy had far fewer
security restrictions than when he became President and,
at the time, Lawford's house was ideal. Later on it proved
too accessible and Monroe found the Secret Service
men intrusive. Columnist Earl Wilson quotes her as
complaining about 'those damned Secret Service men
. . . always hovering around . . . they got to be a real
pain in the ass!'

According to Wilson, Kennedy was probably the first
White House nudist. He apparently loved to sit around
naked and he and Marilyn would visit the nude beaches
at Malibu – Monroe wearing a dark wig and Kennedy
donning a beard, sunglasses and a baseball cap.

The couple also saw a great deal of each other in New
York, where Marilyn kept a flat on East 57th Street
which she obtained after the formation of Marilyn
Monroe Productions and which she retained during the
Miller marriage as a *pied-à-terre*. Kennedy favoured the
Hotel Carlyle on East 76th Street as his New York base
and had a duplex decorated all in white. When he became
President, Kennedy insisted that Secret Service men be
excluded from the premises, and that the Washington
mail pouch, delivered daily, be left downstairs at the
desk.

Since most of their dates were casual – at the desert
(in Palm Springs) or the beach (in Malibu), Monroe
didn't need to fuss about her appearance. Consequently
Kennedy didn't suffer too much from Monroe's notorious lateness. There was one occasion when he met it

headlong, however, and although he realized it stemmed from insecurity, his displeasure, although momentary, was severe. Kennedy had arranged to host a private dinner party at the Carlyle, and an escort was despatched to fetch Marilyn. When the escort arrived at the 57th Street flat he found her in utter disarray. She was in a complete dilemma about what dress to wear, what wig and what makeup. It was a typical Monroe scene. 'She spent hours staring at herself in the mirror and then, after a while, decided to re-do her face,' the escort reveals. 'She tried on three black wigs, chose one, tried on and rejected three dresses, finally accepted the fourth and was ready to go one and a half hours late. When they arrived, the President was uncharming. "I can't believe this really happened. You ruined this whole dinner party. The food's spoiled. Everything's cold." The President pouted for about two or three minutes; then he looked at the beautiful white dress she was wearing, and he melted.'

Any doubts about the nature of the relationship between Marilyn and Kennedy are dispelled by Sheilah Graham: 'Early in August, while waiting for the *Something's Got to Give* film to resume, Marilyn . . . visited her friends, the Dudley Murphys, at their Holiday House Motel overlooking the ocean in Malibu. Marilyn loved the beach and was also a constant visitor to the Pat and Peter Lawford home in Santa Monica . . . All the Kennedys liked Marilyn, and she would play with the Lawford children and be quiet and content . . .'

Monroe was Kennedy's DuBarry, his Hamilton; even, some maintain, his Swanson – a reference to the actress Gloria Swanson, whom Jack's father, Joseph Kennedy, took as a mistress, maintaining her in a style comparable to that of his wife Rose. Openly consorting *à trois*, they all sailed to Europe aboard the *Queen Mary* in adjoining compartments. 'Believe it or not, Marilyn was family,' confirms a friend. 'But the press protected Kennedy.

They wouldn't print a word about it.' Columnist Sidney Skolsky agrees. 'In a society that boasts of freedom of the press no reporter, including myself, dared to write about Marilyn Monroe's affair with John Kennedy.'

It was an inside story and one which many did not then, as now, want to believe. Like it or not, however, when she died, Monroe had reached a new plateau of socializing – her friends occupying the highest strata of American society. Amongst her closest friends was Kennedy's sister Patricia (Lawford), whose humour had an infectious and exhilarating effect upon Monroe. Often they'd all go to Vegas to catch Sinatra, Dean Martin or Sammy Davis Jr who would be there performing. On occasion Davis would act as a beard for the President, squiring Marilyn to some event or other. Often they'd use President Kennedy's plane, *The Caroline*, to go to Tahoe or Palm Springs, Marilyn smuggling herself aboard wearing yet another dark wig. 'They were both easy to like,' says Earl Wilson. 'They both enjoyed a drink. They were both privileged characters.'

The significance of Marilyn's acceptance as 'one of the family' should not be discounted. 'At first I thought it was a joke,' observes a Kennedyite. 'But then I saw it was for real. Marilyn and Jack together. At a political function. Was he in earnest going to divorce Jackie?'

In mid-November 1961, a year into his Presidency, Kennedy returned to Los Angeles to elicit continuing support amongst Democrats for what he hoped would be a second term. Two hundred of Hollywood's most affluent Democrats had crowded into the Beverly Hilton Hotel's Escoffier Room to meet the man in person. 'Marilyn was there in the room with him,' recalls an observer. 'I had heard stories about them, and it came as no particular surprise . . . I spoke to her, too, and thought her a beauty – she was in a skin-tight white dress – but empty-headed was how I thought of her that evening . . .'

Perhaps it was the public appearance of Monroe with Kennedy, but something sent Jacqueline Kennedy's fur flying and the White House rafters shaking over what she perceived to be public ridicule of her First Lady image. Democrat Jan Sterling, who worked the campaign in California for many years, offers her own insights into Kennedy's relationship with his wife. 'I think that they had an understanding,' she told me in an interview, 'that he could do anything, so long as he didn't make her look cheap.' If Kennedy was considering a second term (as it appears that he was), he could not afford to create a scandal. And if public recognition of Marilyn was tantamount to a risk of scandal, then Kennedy would have to re-evaluate his relationship with Monroe.

The popular picture of Jacqueline Kennedy as an aloof, elegant lady is deceptive. On more than one occasion she is known to have put an end to Jack's affairs. Monroe was preceded in his affections by a similar type of girl. (Curiously, for all his sex appeal, Jack Kennedy was attracted to offbeat women. His fascination for Marilyn had probably as much to do with her appealing quality of tentativeness as it did with her body measurements.) Ralph Martin also refers to another affair with 'the girl with the snapping eyes', which began before Kennedy met Jackie and carried over into his marriage. Apparently the affair finished when Jackie found out about it and determined to bring it to a halt.

It is possible that the same fate befell Marilyn once word of their affair had drifted back to Washington. 'Jackie,' a friend told me, 'was mercurial. She would remain silent about Jack's philandering, and then all of a sudden, she would lay down the law.' In this instance, she made her position perfectly clear by announcing that she would not attend the Madison Square Garden $1,000-per-head birthday fundraiser due to be held on 19 May. If Monroe goes, I do not, was the implication.

True to form, Jackie went fox hunting in Virginia, leaving her husband to cope with an affair which by then was doomed to extinction.

Perhaps wifely objections would have carried less weight had Kennedy not been diverted by a new romantic interest. 'A very attractive, medium-blonde, half-serious girl with a mysterious hidden quality' is how historian Martin describes Mary Meyer, an ideal Kennedy type who came into Kennedy's life at the opportune moment, causing someone to speculate that perhaps she was 'a Monroe decoy'. Their relationship began shortly after Monroe's death and continued until Kennedy's assassination a year later. Ironically, Miss Meyer was also the victim of an assassin's bullet the following year.

Any flagging interest on Kennedy's part at this juncture was largely unknown to Monroe, who was busily making preparations to entertain him at the birthday gala which was being planned by Democratic Party Chairman Arthur Krim, President of United Artists, the company which released *Misfits*. Jean Louis the designer for *Misfits* and *Something's Got to Give*, who had also been a Columbia staff designer in the forties when he fitted Marilyn for the costumes she wore in *Ladies of the Chorus*, was recruited by Marilyn to come up with something special for the occasion. 'I always thought that she was cute,' he admits, 'but I never thought of her as being this cute.' The costume Jean Louis created was almost transparent (probably *peau-de-soie*), fashioned with lots of net and covered with rhinestones. (The stones were hand-sewn, smaller ones replacing the original larger ones which were found to be too heavy.) Jean Louis remembers fitting Marilyn in her Brentwood house which had three bedrooms (in addition to a solar or sun room in the patio area), one of which Marilyn had transformed into a fitting room encased in glass. (She was shy and felt uncomfortable being fitted at the studio.) Although Monroe was, in James Bacon's word, 'built like a statue', she wanted her round, voluptuous breasts to appear pear-shaped and therefore asked designers to stitch beads in the appropriate areas. Jean Louis recalls that he was not told what the dress was for, but discovered the truth when a call came through one afternoon from Hyannisport.

Marilyn planned to leave for New York a couple of days early in order to rehearse the 'Happy Birthday' song she had been asked to sing. When the new Fox production chief got wind of her plans, however, word came down that she risked her job, since *Something's Got to Give* was already behind schedule having been delayed because Marilyn had picked up a 'flu bug in Mexico, which lingered into production, causing additional delays. Marilyn was also pregnant and beset by fears of miscarrying. Having lost one baby while filming *Some Like It Hot*, she was being particularly careful not to jeopardize her chances this time around. That the child was Kennedy's is almost certainly true, although the rumour was discounted even by Monroe's closest friends.

Getting leave to appear at the gala proved as difficult as obtaining a Russian exit visa: the studio position being that if she was well enough to fly to New York to perform at Madison Square Garden, she was well enough to report to work. Monroe's rejoinder was that she had promised the Democrats and, more importantly, she wanted to surprise the President. Astutely she pointed out to Fox how much free publicity would be generated by her appearance. Nonetheless the situation proved demoralizing, co-star Dean Martin (having also been invited and having declined) quipped: 'I told them I had to work.' Producer Henry Weinstein argued with her to remain (hinting that by going she risked being fired). Forced into concocting an adolescent excuse, she told him that she had her period and couldn't work. (Monroe's menstrual cramps have been the subject of much speculation, co-star Robert Mitchum having once diagnosed their intensity as having to do with the way she was built; Gable, when working on *Misfits* also observed her intense suffering and inability to perform when menstruating.) Weinstein's response was: 'But why didn't she have a period last month?'

Weinstein, although he owned a couple of theatres on the East Coast, came to Hollywood via TV and theatre and was a novice to films. Prior to producing *Something's Got to Give* (for Dean Martin's Claude Productions) he had only one other film credit at Fox (*Tender is the Night*). It was Dr Greenson, Monroe's analyst, who introduced them; Marilyn liking Weinstein and agreeing to work with him, which in view of his inexperience in films makes it all the more ironic that he failed to appreciate her grasp of the PR potential that would be generated by her appearing at the gala. (Weinstein is now, twenty-five years on, a story executive at Cannon Films.)

The gala was the brainchild of Richard Adler, Kennedy's favourite Broadway producer, who was responsible for such brilliant musicals as *The Pajama Game* and *Damn Yankees* (a story about a baseball player named Joe who gets involved with a hag transformed into a sex queen). The aim was to pay off campaign debts by hosting a JFK birthday bash for 20,000 people at $1,000 per head; included in the package were Ella Fitzgerald, Harry Belafonte, Henry Fonda and Marilyn Monroe warbling 'Happy Birthday'.

On Thursday afternoon Marilyn set off, having earlier breezed in and out of a story conference with George Cukor (the director), Walter Bernstein (the writer) and Weinstein. Bernstein was assigned to 'doctor' the original Nunnally Johnson script, which Marilyn had liked but which the studio felt needed 'punching up' (there had been six or seven other writers on the project before Bernstein). 'Lee Strasberg says it needs jokes!' Monroe chirped as she sped past the men having just been given a vitamin shot by the studio physician. When Bernstein objected, she replied: 'Don't be such a *writer*.' His impression of Marilyn, then verging on her thirty-sixth year, was that she had more energy than he had imagined, but that she did not seem particularly attractive – not, at least, in the scarf, blouse and capri pants that obscured her fabulous figure.

Monroe's appearance at the birthday gala was, in short, vulgar. Everything about it was wrong, and yet, in spite of that, her performance was enormously appealing. Firstly, the effect of having been ill and then being buoyed on vitamins was visible in the way Monroe seemed to strain in her delivery of the 'Happy Birthday' song. Then, her outfit was wrong: the wig was awful (it didn't seem to fit right) and the dress was too revealing (her body had, after all, matured). The worst part about it, however, was the change compared with the light, airy, effortless ebulliency of Monroe performing 'Diamonds Are a Girl's Best Friend'. (At that stage of her life her hair hadn't been frazzled from bleaching, and her figure still looked good in scanty clothes.)

The performance, which lasted all of ten minutes, drained Monroe and it took her two and a half hours to recover before appearing at John Kennedy's Carlyle reception. Anyone who believes that this lady with the quirky nervous system could have done a Broadway show every night simply should have observed the effect of the brief Madison Square Garden appearance.

Arriving at the party in the very same gown she had worn on stage (referred to by the actress herself as 'skin and beads'), all that appeared to be holding her up was willpower. (Marilyn's aversion to lingerie was discovered accidentally one night by John Kennedy. Seated beside her at dinner, he ran his hand up her thigh, only to discover that she wasn't wearing any knickers. 'I wouldn't go much further,' she winked. Kennedy reddened visibly.) The Carlyle penthouse was aglow with festivity: it was, by anybody's standards, the duplex of duplexes with one of the most spectacular views of New York City, giant picture windows, a white phone under the bed, and absolute privacy. Monroe's escort for the evening was Arthur Miller's father, Isadore, with whom Marilyn remained in close touch following the divorce. Whirling him across the room to be introduced to President Kennedy, Monroe lapsed into a song-and-dance routine – something about the man coming to this country as an immigrant and now meeting the President. Ironically, the immigrant saga, whilst true of some, was not valid for Isadore Miller, since he was born into relative wealth, his own father having been a successful New York merchant. The vagaries of American economics placed the Millers in reduced circumstances, however, giving rise to Isadore's own father's complaints that megacapitalism was driving out small businessmen and that rapacious consolidation by families such as the Texas Hunts was ruining free enterprise. It is these very sentiments that Miller articulates in *Death of a Salesman*.

Adlai Stevenson said of Monroe that night: 'I do not think I have seen anyone so beautiful in my life.' Later, when writing to a friend, he noted: 'My encounters, however, were only after breaking through the strong defences established by Robert Kennedy, who was dodging around her like a moth and a flame.'

If she was the last to arrive she was the last to leave, notes historian Martin. But James Haspiel, then a fan and now an important Monroe scholar, disagrees, and reveals that he was waiting outside Marilyn's apartment building when she returned from the party, and that the hour was quite early – 4 a.m. Consequently it may be inferred that whatever 'big surprise' Monroe had intended for Kennedy that night had been greeted without enthusiasm. According to Hollywood manager Al Rosen, gossip suggested that 'It was over. Kennedy was through with her. When she arrived at the Carlyle, she was put on a plane with a one-way ticket back to Los Angeles.'

The rejection proved devastating and while perhaps she hoped that things could be sorted out that summer when Jack Kennedy was due to come West, she began feeling increasingly insecure, particularly when Kennedy declined to accept her telephone calls, fobbing her off on to Bobby. 'Bobby was always very sympathetic,' his secretary recounted when discussing Monroe with Anthony Summers. The constancy and doggedness of Monroe's calls to the Justice Department, the White House and Hyannisport during June, July and August 1962, are revealed by her telephone bills, which were confiscated at the time of her death, but surfaced later on when James Bacon obtained copies. The persistency of the calls suggests a panic whose origins almost certainly derived from the fact Marilyn was pregnant, a theory supported by the fact that following the abortion on 20 July there was only one final call (lasting 8 minutes) made to the Justice Department.

Hoping, of course, for palpable manifestations of John Kennedy's affection, not to mention preparations to be made for the prospective new arrival, Monroe must have been utterly distracted when he failed to respond. It is quite clear that for neither of them was the affair an overnight fling, and I suspect, in addition, that the possibility of having children was acceptable, all of which makes Jack Kennedy's behaviour very peculiar indeed.

Struggling to complete *Something's Got to Give*, Monroe's mental health deteriorated along with her physical condition. Firstly, as a result of taking time off (without permission) she was fired by Fox. Secondly, her regular analyst, Greenson, had accepted a speaking engagement in Europe and his replacement refused to renew Monroe's sleeping tablet prescription, triggering symptoms of forced withdrawal. Thirdly, she had discovered she was pregnant and hadn't the faintest notion of what to do. She wanted a child desperately, having sacrificed previous chances either by abortion (it is alleged that this is what triggered the final breach in the DiMaggio marriage, Darryl Zanuck having convinced Monroe that women lose their shapes after having children), or miscarriage (often resulting from strenuous manoeuvres in the course of filmmaking).

How awful it must have been for Monroe, herself illegitimate, to have been left high and dry by her own lover, particularly since she must have believed in some measure that she had triumphed over those marginal social origins. But the truth, succinctly put by Summers was that: 'the Kennedy brothers finally realized the folly of associating with Monroe . . .'

In the five weeks preceding her death, Marilyn would not be seen again with either Kennedy brother, although she spent much of the time in the company of Peter and Pat Lawford whose conviviality was immensely cheering. (Peter's boyish crush on Marilyn prevailed over the years, having first been ignited when she was a 24-year-old starlet and he was a contract player at MGM.) Although an adoring sister, Pat was uncomfortably caught in the middle of a situation which remained intensely volatile and it is testimony to her fondness for Marilyn that she passed along confidential telephone numbers enabling Marilyn to contact the Kennedy brothers on the weekend of 4 August when Bobby was in northern California.

That weekend Kennedy arrived in northern California with his family to fulfil a speaking engagement before the American Bar Association, followed by a vacation which was long overdue. The Kennedys were guests at the Bates' ranch in Gilroy, California, although Bobby also kept a suite at the St Francis Hotel in San Francisco for business meetings. Monroe, it is claimed, both telephoned the hotel and made an excursion to the Bates' ranch. The latter seems unlikely, but there must have

been something in the lady's behaviour to have alarmed
Bobby Kennedy sufficiently to make a trip to Los
Angeles on the weekend of 4 August 1962.

The extent of Monroe's mental instability that summer is revealed in an incident that occurred when she
was a house guest at the Lawfords'. '. . . One night I
woke up . . . it was dawn,' Peter recalled. 'I saw a figure
standing on the balcony. It was Marilyn . . . tears were
streaming down her face. Pat by then had woken, too,
and we brought her in and talked to her.'

On 20 July Marilyn was secretly hospitalized in Cedars
of Lebanon Hospital for four days for a surgical termination of pregnancy. 'Those few who knew Marilyn's
secret were horrified,' says Fred Guiles, Monroe's biographer. The rest of her friends were told that Marilyn
had gone for a long weekend to Lake Tahoe. She summoned the façade of jollity, but the operation had left her
desperately weak, and when designer William Travilla
bumped into her at the Frascati restaurant in Beverly
Hills on 3 August, the Friday before she died, he found
her 'pale, thin and lifeless'. He says: 'I couldn't believe
it was the Marilyn I knew, the Marilyn of *Gentlemen
Prefer Blondes* and *The Seven Year Itch*. All the natural
buoyancy was gone. She didn't even look the same. It
was a different girl.'

Travilla recounts the incident, becoming emotional as
the memory of Marilyn twenty-five years ago looms
back to haunt him. 'My partner and I were having dinner
with three of our buyers and somebody pointed to a gal
in the room wearing a white turban and said: "It looks
like Marilyn." I said: "Yeah, with makeup she could
look like Marilyn." I thought nothing else about it, and
then I heard the giggle. And I said: "Marilyn's here." I
generally do not tablehop but when it is Marilyn, I do.
I excused myself and went over to the table. Marilyn
was seated with her New York group – Peter Lawford
and his wife' (actually press agent Pat Newcomb) 'and

(I think) Lawford's manager. She looked at me as if she didn't know who the hell I was. I was embarrassed. I was hurt. Then she said: "Billy, Billy. Meet Peter Lawford and so forth. How do you do?" I was angry and deeply hurt. I thought: 'I think I'll write her a letter. She's got her little New York group around her and she is forgetting that there are some people who love and adore her. I thought: you are not going to treat me like that. She had cut off the whole world out here. I was going to write to her and tell her off. The next day I heard that she was dead. I am glad I never wrote that letter. I would never have forgiven myself.'

Kennedy's break with Monroe was uncharacteristically and unnecessarily brutal since the affair had lasted eight years. She was his acknowledged mistress; almost certainly the mother of his love child; and doubtless his best unpaid supporter in the world, rallying and cheering him on in the political arena. (Never mind that the Madison Square Garden appearance had cost her job.) So what propelled him to behave so outrageously towards Marilyn? Kennedy had had other mistresses where the parting of the ways had been infinitely more amicable. Historian Martin cites the case of one girl who got oil wells as a going-away present. Marilyn didn't want money, however. She never did, although she was always short of cash. What she wanted was an explanation and that, presumably, is what occasioned Bobby Kennedy's visit to her flat on 4 August.

3
Crime Without Punishment

What kind of people were the Kennedy brothers? How ruthless? How monstrous? How ambitious? The Monroe saga summons up images of ancient Rome: of Nero, Claudius and Caligula.

The kind of premeditation necessary to effect such a crime without there being any public outcry and the kind of conspiracy there would have to have been to preclude any prosecution, not to mention the silence of the press until long after the principals were all dead, suggests awesome power.

Democrat Jan Sterling witnessed Kennedy egomania during the Democratic convention in Los Angeles in 1960, the first time in forty years that it had been held in the city. 'I was among those that wanted Adlai Stevenson to be our candidate,' says Sterling. 'Stevenson had run (and lost) in 1956 but we hoped that this time it would be different,' she adds. 'Jack Kennedy, however, was taking no chances at being turned down again as his running mate, and the campaign that he had been mounting over the past four years got into full swing during nomination week.' The question the Kennedy political machine put to the delegates was: Do you want to win the upcoming election? Do you want jobs to go home to? Then vote for Jack Kennedy. 'It was disgusting,' says Sterling. 'They had girls and booze. They got the delegates so sauced I don't think they knew what they were doing. I tried to tell the people of California. I am a Jewish convert. I got all the Hadassah ladies together, and asked Drew Pearson (the columnist) to tell them what he knew about the Kennedys. But it didn't help. Kennedy got the California delegates on the first ballot, and, in consequence, a lot of the other states went his way, too.' Her verdict on the Kennedys: 'They play to win. Their father taught them young: "You want to win. Win. Do anything you have to do to win." That was their credo.'

Even so, it is difficult to envisage Jack Kennedy as part of a subterranean plot to murder Marilyn Monroe. The events that transpired on 4 August 1962 most probably were a combination of Bobby's ineptitude, exacerbated by Monroe's mounting hysteria at her inability to find an amicable solution. ('Marilyn could be very annoying,' says a friend.) Bobby was probably the worst possible man for the job having on a previous occasion been reprimanded by his brother for his treatment of the mobsters. 'John Kennedy did not object to Robert's investigation of the Teamsters' Union or of organized crime, but he did frequently object to his brother's methods, because there seemed to be a possibility that some of his tactics were themselves illegal (and equally as dangerous as those he was fighting). Often innocent people were being hurt along with the guilty.'*

There have been many accounts of the events of 4 August, most of them conflicting. Dr Greenson reported having seen the deceased at about 5.15 p.m. because she was unable to sleep, and yet Bobby Kennedy told the police in a deposition that he and Greenson had made the house call principally because, in Kennedy's words, 'she was bothering my brother'. Kennedy was seen arriving, by some neighbourhood ladies playing cards,

* *Sinatra's Women*, Gerry Romero.

in a Mercedes or Cadillac. He had been once before to
Monroe's house under friendlier circumstances on 27
June, having first met the actress at his brother's birthday
party gala on 19 May. (Although it may seem strange
that they had not met before, the fact is the Kennedy
brothers led very independent lives.) The acquaintance-
ship was rekindled at a dinner party given by Peter
Lawford for Bobby when he was in town discussing
with Fox producer, Jerry Wald, the film possibilities for
his novel about racketeering entitled *The Enemy Within*.
Monroe warmed to his boyish charm. He was, after all,
her lover's brother, and as a friendly gesture she invited
him round to see her new house – to show off the
exposed timber beams and Mexican tiling of which she
was most proud.

On this trip, however, a minimum of small talk was
made, Kennedy coming straight to the point: stop
bothering John. Whatever else was said – whatever accusations and recriminations uttered – we shall never
know. What we do know is that whatever went on
between Robert Kennedy and Marilyn inflamed an
already aggravated situation to the extent that, according
to Kennedy, 'she clawed at him when he held her so that
the doctor could inject a tranquillizer'. There must have
been decided resistance by Monroe, since the autopsy
report (which allegedly was doctored to play things
down) indicates that there was evidence of violence to
the body and that the thigh areas, in particular, showed
marked discolouration and bruising.

Monroe apocrypha makes no mention at all of Bobby
Kennedy's appearance at the house on 4 August. The
accepted sequence of events begins with Marilyn arising
before Newcomb (still asleep in the third bedroom).
There is some equivocation as to whether or not for
lunch Monroe ate an omelette (or a burger) and what
the subject of an argument with Newcomb had been
about. By all accounts Lawford (with whom they had

dined the previous evening) had invited them both to supper on Saturday night (4 August). Marilyn wanted instead to spend the evening with the Kirk Douglases (Pat Lawford was out of town and Peter was cutting up a bit in her absence, inviting girls to the party – girls whom Monroe referred to as 'hookers'). It is noteworthy that both as friend and press agent, Newcomb appears to have been in contention with Monroe about a number of matters, and, yet, their relationship sustained, however fraught. In contrast, the Kirk Douglases were bed-rock Hollywood: nice wholesome family-type people whose parties were given in the grandest style, and with whom it was smart to mingle since it was with such leading men as Douglas that Monroe could (if she had lived) done some fine film work. 'They were waiting and waiting and were very disappointed when Marilyn didn't show up,' says Jan Sterling, who had also been asked to spend the evening with the Douglases.

Because of Monroe's highly emotional condition, Greenson, it is claimed, asked Newcomb to leave. Housekeeper Eunice Murray, who had been shopping from 2–4 p.m., returned and was present during the Greenson visit, but said nothing at the time about Bobby Kennedy being at the house and would not do so until an interview she gave in 1985. It is worth noting that Mrs Murray, although working for Monroe in the capacity of housekeeper, had been a psychiatric nurse and was recommended for the post by Dr Greenson. Marilyn was unhappy with her – not because she distrusted her, but because she felt uncomfortable being herself in the woman's presence, and regarded Mrs Murray as too austere and judgmental. (Prior to her death Monroe had spoken to her black maid about coming back.)

Newcomb most certainly left the house, since Bullets Durgom (business manager) told me that she had popped in at the party Peter Lawford was hosting to tell them that Marilyn would not be coming to dinner. In his book *Coroner to the Stars*, Los Angeles coroner Dr Thomas Noguchi, who was dismissed and then reinstated as Los Angeles Chief Medical Examiner, relates testimony of an 8 p.m. telephone call Peter Lawford made to Marilyn. 'He had telephoned her because she was supposed to join [him] and friends for a poker game and then dinner. His wife, Patricia, was on Cape Cod at the Kennedy compound. According to Lawford, Monroe's voice was slurred. She said she couldn't come to dinner that night. Then she added words that were chilling: "Say good-bye to Pat, say good-bye to the President. Say good-bye to yourself because you've been a good guy."'

But it wasn't a telephone call that Lawford made. Instead he made tracks over to the Monroe residence as speedily as possible. At least that is what Lawford's wife, Deborah Gould, told the BBC in an interview. The lady recounts how during their own brief marriage (Lawford died shortly thereafter) he had confessed to her what really happened. 'He told me,' she says, 'that he had gone to Monroe's house to clear away anything that might incriminate the Kennedys.'

Former wife of PR man Arthur Jacobs, president of the firm that represented Monroe, Natalie Jacobs says that Arthur was at the scene hours before the crime was reported to the police, summoned 'to fudge the press'. Jacobs left the concert he and Natalie were attending at the Hollywood Bowl, as he received a note from Pat Newcomb saying that Marilyn was dead. (Newcomb, however, says that she wasn't aware of the tragedy until early the following morning when she broke down in tears.)

Jack Clemmons, the first police officer to arrive on the scene, who has since been fired from the police force and is now working in the construction business, recalls that Greenson told him they first had to call the PR people. Robert Slatzer says that he was personally told that Fox VIPs, lawyers and security police were there in tandem with Monroe's press agents and Kennedy's people: all of whom were anxious to eliminate any Kennedy connection with Monroe.

Internist Dr Hyman Engelberg told the police that he arrived on the scene shortly after Dr Greenson at 3.50 a.m. A highly respected Beverly Hills practitioner who treated Monroe for a period of about four years, he is surprisingly resilient for a man who has been the focus of attention for twenty-five years. 'For a while people thought that Ralph [Greenson] and I had done it,' he says, himself the victim of physical brutality when a couple of members slammed him against the lockers of the Beverly Hills Tennis Club, where he had gone to play tennis the Sunday morning, 5 August, following the tragedy. Screenwriter Henry Ephron recounts: 'A couple of us slammed Engelberg against the lockers. We were so angry.' He pauses. 'Greenson? You tell me he's dead. I am glad. I hated that bastard.'

Having previously declined to be interviewed, Engelberg breaks his vow of silence, talking briefly about what he remembers of the death scene twenty-five years ago. What did she look like? How was the body lying? Was she naked or covered up? His voice registers a kind of horrible stupefaction that sends shivers up your spine: it also tells you that his unconscious prohibits articulation of the horrific death scene.

According to Engelberg, by the time he examined Marilyn *rigor mortis* had discoloured one side of the body, placing the time of death early on Saturday evening, since it takes six to eight hours for discolouration to set in. It is said that when people die under certain circumstances that their faces remain contorted in the expression registered at the time of death. Had Monroe been given an overdose (under her armpit which would minimize detection, particularly after a couple of hours when the needle mark would have disappeared) and had

she been an unwilling victim, her face would have frozen
into a look of panic.

Stories vary as to whether there was any attempt made
to save Monroe's life, although I think it reasonable to
assume that there was, since this would account for the
story of her being taken by ambulance to hospital in the
hope that she would regain consciousness. The hospital
in question is reputed to be Santa Monica, where a
Schaefer Ambulance driver claims to have rushed
Monroe into its emergency room where she was pro-
nounced dead upon arrival.

The nuts and bolts of the story hold together only,
however, if we assume that the greatest latitude had been
taken within police powers, and the only way that such
latitude could have been taken was if the directive had
come from the Attorney General in person. Why else
would the hospital have released a dead body not into
police custody but to civilians? The conspiracy theory
postulates that the body was returned to the house and
placed on the bed in a position to suggest suicide, the
hand draped over the telephone in a theatrical gesture
designed to suggest a cry for help.

If, as according to the testimony of those who saw
her at 3.30 a.m. on 5 August, *rigor mortis* had already set
in, there was no way Monroe could have been alive at
8 p.m. on 4 August 1962. Those who say they spoke to
her in the early evening – Joe DiMaggio Jr, Lawford and
Jeanne Carmen (a neighbour) say that her voice sounded
slurred. Was someone therefore doing a Monroe impersonation (Marilyn's voice was easily imitated)? Or were
these phone calls intercepted?

For the official version of Marilyn's death – that she
ingested either accidentally or on purpose a fatal overdose of barbiturates – to hold up it must be assumed that
Dr Greenson left Marilyn at 7 p.m. heavily tranquillized;
that in the intervening hours she spoke to the friends
whose conversations with her we have already noted;

and that she wilfully swallowed the entire contents of several bottles of pills found empty by her bedside, including Seconal, chloral hydrates and Nembutals.

This theory makes credible Jeanne Carmen's assertion that Marilyn called her desperate to locate a quantity of sleeping tablets. The question then becomes: so why were no barbiturate traces found in Marilyn's stomach? One could argue that although there were no traces of drugs in the stomach lining, there might have been traces detected in the intestines, had the intestines been properly examined which they were not. However, ingestion of an overdose in the intestines would also have left traces of dye in the stomach lining area.

The lone voice of dissent is that of former LAPD Sergeant Jack Clemmons, the first officer at the Monroe house the night she died. The version he was told is both standardized and accepted by both biographers and law enforcement agencies. Dr Greenson left Monroe's residence at about 7 p.m. on 4 August 1962. Pat Newcomb was not around, leaving Mrs Murray alone to attend to Marilyn. Monroe supposedly retired at about 8 p.m. (chatting on the telephone until late into the evening). At about midnight Mrs Murray got up to go to the bathroom. She noticed a light under Monroe's door. (The story was changed when Mrs Murray later said she had awakened at 3 a.m., the disquieting artifact then being a telephone cord lying loose in the hallway.) The door to Marilyn's room was locked. (She feared burglars, and had once been accosted by a policeman in burglar drag when she lived in a furnished room in the San Fernando Valley.) Mrs Murray peered through Monroe's bedroom windows – the drapes had not been drawn – and saw Monroe's taut body lying on the bed. She called Dr Greenson, who hurried over and broke a window to gain access into the room. Dr Hyman Engelberg was also called, as were the police.

Having been through it a thousand times, Clemmons

agreed to recount once again the circumstances of his
visit to Monroe's Brentwood residence on Sunday morning, 5 August 1962. In his capacity as Acting Watch
Commander for the West Los Angeles Patrol Division,
Sergeant Clemmons was the first police officer to arrive
at the death scene, having responded to a call the station
had received at 4.25 a.m. Clemmons recalls that Mrs
Murray was using the washing machine while he was
there. He also observed that the housekeeper looked
'scared'; that her regular medical doctor looked very
'remorseful' and was quiet; and that the psychiatrist 'had
a smirk on his face and didn't look natural to him'.

Twenty-five years on, Clemmons continues to maintain that 'it was the most obvious murder I ever saw.
Everything was staged. The body was rigid and artifici-
ally placed. It did not look like a position you would die
in (Monroe was lying face down in what is commonly
known as the "military position" – her hand grabbed
the telephone receiver). When I asked why, if the body
was discovered by Mrs Murray at midnight (later
changed to 3 a.m.) it took them three hours to call the
police? Greenson told me that they had to get permission
from the publicity department before they could call
anybody,' says Clemmons. (It has been suggested that
the delay allowed Bobby Kennedy time to helicopter
out of town, but there are also sources who claim that
he popped in at Peter Lawford's beach party that evening
before joining his family at the Bates' ranch at Gilroy in
northern California where on Sunday morning, at 9.30
a.m., he attended Mass in the parish church.) Adds
Clemmons: 'Greenson never admitted what we know
to be true, on account of the Kennedy deposition, to
having injected Monroe – even accidentally. Why didn't
he admit it? Why – if it was an accident? Why the lies?
And why that amount of time?'

The death certificate and the coroner's report both
confirm death by suicide, although Dr Noguchi was

severely criticized and even subsequently fired (later to be reinstated) over allegations of professional misconduct. Although he found high barbiturate levels in the blood-stream, he did not examine the intestines, so that there was no record of any trace of drugs in the stomach. His examination also failed to disclose needle marks (which we know from the Kennedy deposition must have and did exist), though possibly they had disappeared by the time Dr Noguchi did the autopsy. His failure to examine the colon, however, meant he was unable to speculate as to whether death might have been caused by suppository which must have been used for so much drug to have been found in the body.

In *Finding Marilyn: a Romance* David Conover describes his own interview with Sergeant Jack Clemmons. 'Marilyn did not stretch out to die on her crumpled sheet from taking a fatal overdose of Nembutals. No trace of drugs was found in her stomach, only in the liver and blood.' The former Police Sergeant also told Robert Slatzer that he believes Marilyn was murdered by some-one she knew and trusted, who administered the drug by suppository or injection into the bloodstream. 'He was shocked to high heaven by the official conclusion of suicide,' says Slatzer. Clemmons also alleged that the original homicide reports were changed, evidence disappeared, and the police chief rushed to Washington to see Bobby Kennedy.

Former deputy coroner at the time, Lionel Grandison, was quoted in the *Los Angeles Sunday Mirror* on 22 April 1979 as saying that 'in spite of his reluctance, his superiors had forced him to sign the death certificate on the 36-year-old movie star, which said that on 5 August 1962, she had taken a fatal overdose of forty-seven Nembutals.' He now admits that the investigation was a farce.

Press agent John Springer (the other half of the partner-ship which represented Monroe, Springer helming the East Coast office of Jacobs–Springer Associates) recalls having first heard of the death by telephone. (It was Springer who had set up the last *Life* magazine interview conducted by Richard Meryman who said that she came across as cynical. The tapes from the interview, played on the *Life* magazine television tribute in 1986, confirm that she sounded cynical on tape, too.) 'I was away for the weekend. We were going to the Harkness' place in Round Hill (Va.). She had this new dance group which she was supporting and she had them there for the weekend. I got called at 8 a.m. on Sunday morning (I had been up until 4 a.m. on Saturday night). It was my vice-president who said: "John, Marilyn is dead." So I had to get a train and get back to New York to fly out to the Coast with Lee and Paula Strasberg to attend Marilyn's funeral. Arthur Jacobs and I were trying to work out Marilyn's funeral and Joe DiMaggio took over and said, "So and so cannot be invited. So and so I will personally kick out." A lot of people's feelings were badly hurt because they were not invited, but that was Joe's decision.'

Marilyn's makeup man Whitey Snyder, who did attend the funeral (he was a pallbearer with Joe), recalls that he had been rung by Frank Taylor (producer of *Misfits*) a few days before enquiring about who would claim the body. 'I don't know why nobody did it. I didn't even know about it until they called me from New York. I don't know why DiMaggio didn't do it. Maybe it was because it's expensive. You have to pay for certain things.'

Whilst most of the big stars are buried at the Forest Lawn Mortuary, a hideous tract of manicured landscape in Burbank, Monroe is neatly tucked away at the Westwood Mortuary in a small graveyard where Wilshire Boulevard intersects with Westwood, and where the Monroes have been buried for generations. Although Monroe was a foster child and ward of Los Angeles County, she was by no means rootless. The family,

probably Anglo-Spanish in origin, dates back to the
beginnings of the California state, which was settled by
the Sepulvedas and other Spanish families of noble birth.
(Monroe is a genuine family name: an offshoot of the
main branch, and linked with American President James
Monroe.) The physical changes wrought on Marilyn
over the years obliterate any trace of Latin ancestry, but
those who remember her when she was a starlet confirm
she was more Latin than Nordic.

DiMaggio paid for the $800 casket of ornamental
bronze (which Monroe would probably have hated,
since she always said how much she disliked the carved
Italian decor of their Doheny Drive flat). Joe DiMaggio
Jr's appearance in uniform added a militaristic touch to
the proceedings. It was as if Eva Peron had passed
on; doubtless Marilyn would have objected, since she
despised anything that smacked of fascism.

The funeral arrangements were made by DiMaggio
in tandem with Inez Melson (Marilyn's manager for a
short time and West Coast executrix of the estate) and
Bernice Miracle (Monroe's half-sister, who bears an
uncanny resemblance to Doris Day, who played Marilyn's role in *Something's Got to Give* in *Move Over Darling*). A decidedly private affair, only twenty-four were
admitted, the chosen few including Dr and Mrs Greenson; friends the Kargers; drama coaches Lee and Paula
Strasberg; Marilyn's dressing room team; masseur Ralph
Roberts; lawyer Milton Rudin; and Pat Newcomb.
There were no stars, although Sinatra, along with Ella
Fitzgerald and Sammy Davis, tried to muscle their way
in with security people. Patricia Lawford had flown out
from the East Coast, but both she and Peter were barred.
None of her New York friends such as Maureen Stapleton, Montgomery Clift, the Wallachs or the Rostens
were present either. Arthur Miller was conspicuously
absent. Rupert Allan, James Bacon, Tennessee Williams,
Clifton Webb, Travilla, Judy Garland, Jack Cole and

Gary Cooper were also excluded. All press were barred, too, but for Walter Winchell, which is perversely appropriate since it was to him that DiMaggio gave the lesbian story when he and Marilyn divorced in 1954. Winchell waved in Larry Schiller, which is odder still, since the man had no real relationship with Monroe but for shooting those awful nudes which make her appear plastic and brittle. Even today Whitey Snyder is angry at the way DiMaggio dominated the proceedings. 'I was a pallbearer with Joe. He wouldn't allow that many people into the chapel,' he complains. 'Mitzi Gaynor and her husband wanted to come. She said they would have done anything to come.' (Why, one wonders, when it has been documented that they didn't get on, and that Monroe believed Gaynor had mocked her when they worked together on *There's No Business Like Show Business*?) Adds Whitey: 'People who wanted to be there, legitimately wanted to say farewell, couldn't come in because of DiMaggio.'

Whilst the private service was being conducted inside the chapel, outside there was pandemonium, and a crowd of 500 spectators and sixty private and city policemen. Lee Strasberg delivered the eulogy. Carl Sandburg was asked and declined, saying that he did not really know Monroe well enough, which seems odd since on a great number of occasions he was quite eloquent about her wistful combination of youth and sagacity. However, knowing Monroe as well as he did, Strasberg was by far the better choice. He paid homage to Marilyn saying: 'In her own lifetime . . . she created a myth of what a poor girl from a depressed background could attain. For the entire world she became a symbol of the eternal feminine. But I have no words to describe the myth and the legend. I did not know this Marilyn Monroe. We gathered here today knew only . . . a warm human being, impulsive and shy, sensitive and in fear of rejection . . .'

The service, intentionally non-denominational, was nevertheless suffused in religious pomp far too ceremonious for Monroe's taste. She would probably have preferred a simpler ceremony with Rabbi Robert Goldberg of Roxbury, Connecticut (with whom she studied Judaism) giving the reading. Instead, the Reverend A.J. Soldan of the non-denominational Village Church of Westwood conducted the service. He called Marilyn Monroe 'a grand, great woman whose death caused a wave of sorrow to be felt by millions'. The service included readings from the 23rd Psalm; the 14th chapter of the Gospel of St John and excerpts from the 139th and 46th Psalms, and the Lord's Prayer; culminating in music from Tchaikovsky's *Andante Cantabile* and *Symphony No.6 Pathétique* and 'Yip' Harburg's 'Over the Rainbow'.

A tragedy felt around the world, Marilyn Monroe's death was covered on the front pages of all major publications worldwide. Of the 36-year-old superstar whose metamorphosis from lamb into lioness astonished even herself, *Time* magazine wrote: 'Marilyn Monroe's unique charisma was the force that caused distant men to think that if only a well-intentioned, understanding person like me could have known her, she would have been all right. In death, it has caused women who before resented her frolicsome sexuality to join in the unspoken plea she leaves behind – the simple, noble wish to be taken seriously . . .'

New York Times film critic Bosley Crowther, a fan of Monroe's from way back, threw his own laurel on the grave: '. . . the Monroe personality, as established and developed over the years, was that of a generous young woman, healthy, good-humoured, full of warmth and eager for honest self-improvement, despite intellectual limitations and crudities. It was a highly potential personality, apt for satire as well as farce, and open, it seemed, for extension to drama and tragedy.' The *New*

York Times was one of the first newspapers to have declared that Monroe was, in spite of the image, anything but the empty-headed heroine she created with brilliance. Crowther went on to say: 'Indeed it appeared from the appealing and poignant performance that Miss Monroe gave in *Bus Stop* . . . and from some of her . . . tender scenes in her last picture *Misfits* . . . that she was headed for stronger creations than those earlier comedies.'

Richard Meryman's *Life* interview paid its own homage by quoting Monroe in her own words. 'It might be a kind of a relief to be finished. It's sort of like you don't know what kind of a yard dash you're running, but then you are at the finish line and you sort of sigh – you've made it! But you never have. You have to start all over again.'

At the start of the next work day most people settled back into their old routines. Those closely involved with her on a professional level had other clients who required looking after, although Pat Newcomb virtually vanished after the funeral and remained at the Kennedy Hyannisport compound for several months. When she surfaced she was frequently to be found, when unavailable at the office, at Hyannisport. Jack Kennedy went ahead with his planned trip West the week following, but only stayed a brief time, returning to Washington where he was often photographed with his wife and child. He was shot dead the following year.

Although Monroe grossed over $250 million for Fox, she saw only a small share of that money. She was living on what amounted to peanuts, and what little she had was being rapidly depleted by mortgage payments (she had taken a $35,000 mortgage on a house which cost $77,500), analyst's bills (charged at the rate of $50 for 1½ hours per day) and bills from her hairdresser and the makeup man.

Initially believed to have been valued at $1 million,

the estate was solvent at $82,000 at the time of Monroe's death. It was not until 1969 that residual payments created any kind of cash flow, allowing beneficiaries to see any real money in terms of their bequests. Administrated by New York attorney Aaron Frosch and Los Angeles surrogate Inez Melson, the will prepared the previous year provided for the following bequests: $10,000 to half-sister Bernice Miracle and secretary May Reis; $5,000 to close friends Norman and Hedda Rosten for the education of their daughter Patricia; personal effects and clothing to Lee Strasberg; $5,000 per year for the institutionalized care and maintenance of her mother, Gladys Baker; and $2,500 per year for the wife of her drama coach, Mrs Michael Chekhov. Dr Marianne Kris as the contingent beneficiary was required to donate her share to the psychiatric institution of her choice. Any additional earnings following these instructions were to be divided among Reis (25 per cent not to exceed $40,000), Kris (25 per cent) and Strasberg (50 per cent).

So what was the public consensus about Monroe from those who worked with her? Director Billy Wilder said she had 'Flesh impact which is rare. Clara Bow had it. So did Jean Harlow and Rita Hayworth. It was worth a week's torment to get three luminous minutes on the screen.' On another occasion, however, Wilder said: 'It was worth waiting two hours – but six!' Screenwriter Nunnally Johnson, a somewhat reluctant convert to Monroe, said: 'You can't talk to it. It can't talk to you. All you can do is stand back and be awed by it. It is a phenomenon of nature, like Niagara Falls or the Grand Canyon.' Joshua Logan, director of *Bus Stop* said: 'She was the most unappreciated woman in the world.' Director Henry Hathaway, in spite of his reputation for being a misogynist, adored Monroe: 'You don't have to hold an inquest to find out who killed Marilyn Monroe. Those bastards in the big executive chairs killed her.'

It is Arthur Miller's remark, however, that prevails

as perhaps the best example of the phony solicitude surrounding her death. 'If she was simple, it would have been easy to help her. She could have made it with a little luck.'

Joseph Mankiewicz, in whose film *All About Eve* she came to prominence years later, is fatalistic. 'She died at the right time – she was old, fat and unloved.' Huston, who directed her in both *Asphalt Jungle* and *Misfits*, agrees: within a few years she would either have died or been institutionalized.

But was Monroe washed up, and was it inevitable that *Something's Got to Give* would be the film which finished her?

4
Something 'Had' Got to Give

In 1955 Marilyn walked out on Fox and went to New York where she formed her own production company with photographer Milton Greene as vice-president.

The break with Fox, for which some say she was never forgiven, turned out to be a protracted negotiation lasting an entire year. It began, however, innocently enough, with Monroe going on suspension when she refused to do *Heller in Pink Tights* with Frank Sinatra as she considered the film to be low in content. Having by then wed Joe DiMaggio, she agreed to come back to do *There's No Business Like Show Business*, another film she did not rate highly but which she agreed to do because the studio had purchased for her the film rights to the theatrical comedy *The Seven Year Itch*, to be directed by Billy Wilder. In the interim Fox drew up a new contract, not substantially different from the old one, but which gave Monroe a little more money. Meanwhile, Monroe, in the throes of completing *The Seven Year Itch*, on which the rushes were fabulous, was told by Fox what her next project was to be, *How to Be Very, Very Popular*, yet another comedy low in content and which she consequently rejected. It was at this juncture, seeing Fox had no intention of offering her high quality material, that Marilyn fled to New York. There Milton Greene and his lawyer Frank Delaney prepared a seven-year non-exclusive Fox contract which required Marilyn to do four films for Fox at $100,000 per picture, but left her free to take additional freelance assignments. *Something's Got to Give* was the third of the four pictures and one which Monroe wanted quickly to complete so that negotiations could begin for a new contract in parity with the $1 million per picture being paid to Elizabeth Taylor.

All of which gives us the background for a very important point. The screenwriters for the two films *Heller in Pink Tights* and *How to be Very, Very Popular* (made with Sheree North, who was groomed as Monroe's replacement, and Betty Grable, who was brought back on a one-off deal, her contract having been terminated shortly after *How to Marry a Millionaire*) were Walter Bernstein and Nunnally Johnson, which wouldn't mean very much except that it is they whose joint developmental efforts conceived the shooting script for *Something's Got to Give* – the film which Monroe never finished but which instead finished her. Johnson and Monroe were not exactly strangers. He had fashioned her role in *We're Not Married* 'to take advantage of her body' and also wrote the part of Pola in *How to Marry a Millionaire* 'to play up her physical assets'. Perhaps that was the problem. After *How to Marry a Millionaire*, Marilyn said: 'I hadn't the slightest idea of what I was supposed to have been doing.' Over the years Johnson's opinion of Monroe changed from loathing to tolerance to appreciation. But his first reaction is worth noting. 'Marilyn made me lose all sympathy for actresses. In most of her takes she was either fluffing lines or freezing. She didn't bother to learn her lines. I don't think she could act her way out of a paper script. She had no charm, delicacy or taste. She's just an arrogant little tail switcher who's learned to throw sex in your face.'

Precisely why Fox chose Johnson to revamp the 1940 Cary Grant–Irene Dunne film *My Favourite Wife* (directed by Leo McCarey), or why in fact they chose to re-make it at all, is one of the great mysteries of the motion picture industry. *Something's Got to Give* was to be made in Technicolor – Monroe's contract stipulated that all her films were to be made in colour – and the plot dealt with a woman presumed dead whose husband remarries only to discover that his first wife is very much alive. Monroe was to play the returned dead wife, Dean Martin the husband, and Cyd Charisse, the second wife. George Cukor was to be the director (he had worked with Marilyn before on *Let's Make Love*). Whilst Cukor was a brilliant stage director, whose period films in the thirties and forties are some of the greatest ever made, he really did not have any idea how to use Monroe. *Let's Make Love* was not a box-office success, nor was it likely that *Something's Got to Give* would be either, but Monroe was undoubtedly too exhausted to go another round with Fox over what her next project would be. Although the 1955 contract drawn up by Greene's lawyer Frank Delaney gave her director and script approval, together with approval of cameramen, makeup and wardrobe people, she did *not* have screenwriter approval.

Johnson's account of how he was assigned the task of updating the remake is quite witty. ' "I don't think there is very much I would change," he told Fox executives. "We don't want very much changed. Just a word here and there." "And for that you're paying me a fee?" I asked incredulously. "We want to remake the picture. Just update it where you feel it needs it," they told me. Which is what I did.'

Talking Marilyn into doing it was something else again. Johnson asked her to join him for a drink at the Beverly Hills Hotel Polo Lounge – the most ostentatiously Hollywood place in Hollywood – where over three bottles of champagne, according to Johnson's account, they had a jolly old time. Marilyn read and approved the script only to discover that Johnson (for tax purposes) could not remain in Los Angeles. Since director Cukor wanted a writer on the set there was no alternative but to hire another writer. 'I told [the producer] Henry Weinstein,' says Johnson, 'you can do what you want. But let me tell you something. You've only done one picture here [*Tender is the Night*]. You get a director a writer on the set and no matter what he tells you, you've lost the picture. It won't be yours any more, because he will tell the writer what to write.'

Johnson's prophesy proved correct. The new writer (Walter Bernstein) redeveloped the character of Ellen, the first wife, in a way that was unacceptable to Monroe. Instead of being whimsical and shy, she became a Bette Midler-type comedienne hotly pursuing the husband. Monroe wanted it to appear as if they met accidentally, and then he fell for her before discovering she was his first wife. She was also unhappy with the way Cyd Charisse's character was being made desirable, since she felt that it undermined the original concept. Monroe is also alleged to have objected to the colour of Charisse's hair which was to be honey-blonde. She is purported to have quipped: 'Her unconscious wants it blonde.' In consequence the producer, rather unnecessarily, also darkened the housekeeper's hair. Marilyn was concerned, too, that the children should respond naturally to her as their real mother, although it was not yet known to them that she was, and this too caused difficulties.

Scheduled to start in early April, the film did not get underway until later that month, and then there were numerous production delays due to a virus that Monroe picked up in Mexico (where she bought a lot of junk furniture, too short of money to purchase any really nice stuff). Doubtless Kennedy's rejection, the love child which almost certainly was his and about which she was undecided whether to abort, and Miller's remarriage to Morath all contributed to an instability that once again had producers shaking their heads unsure of whether the film would ever get finished. Not surprisingly, Marilyn was absolutely miserable on the set and had to work herself into the right frame of mind to come to the studio. Typically awakening at 5 a.m., the lapses this time round had nothing to do with time spent in makeup or wardrobe. Here she was often seen retching at the studio gate before she even set foot on to the set.

Henry Weinstein has subsequently implied, at least to Anthony Summers, that Monroe, fearing replacement by a younger actress, effectively propositioned him. Monroe was often a dinner guest of Weinstein, and according to television producer Lucy Jarvis (another guest) she was shy and winsome despite her stature. 'She never took it for granted that she was a *femme fatale* which, I think, made her all the more fatal.'

Abraham Ribicoff, then US Secretary of Health, Education and Welfare, met Monroe at one of these parties, and in a recent interview with me recalled that he found her agreeably intelligent and deeply compassionate. 'I was in Los Angeles to generate support of the government's programme to maintain welfare funding for orphans and foster children, and was scheduled to give a talk at the Dorothy Chandler Pavilion. Marilyn told me that she was a welfare child, and began telling me about some of the problems she had encountered and how poorly she had been treated and in consequence why she supported the government's proposals. She asked if she could come to the lecture. "You know, I could wear a dark wig," I remember her saying. But she rang next morning and apologised. She couldn't come. Her psychiatrist had ruled against it.'

In view of her willingness to work with a newcomer, Weinstein's uncompromising behaviour towards Monroe is all the more reprehensible. According to columnist Sidney Skolsky, 'A group in the studio barber shop, putting [Weinstein] on, said Marilyn would give him a tough time, being late, missing a day of shooting, making it a rough assignment. "That doesn't go with me," answered Henry. "She steps out of line and I'll have her fired."' It appears that the friendly, convivial persona which encouraged Monroe originally into believing that they could work well together, changed once production began. Firstly, Weinstein allowed Cukor to make repeated script changes, sending around the revised draft to Monroe's house at about 10 p.m. after having already had her learn the lines of the previous draft. Did they want to get her off the picture? Susan Strasberg, whose mother Paula had been Monroe's coach, says yes. 'Mother told me that they did, and that they were making things particularly difficult so that Marilyn would either quit or be fired. She said they wanted to see Marilyn replaced.'

Replaceable? Monroe? 'She was always being treated as a novice,' a friend observed, 'bullied and bossed about mercilessly. Things were never done for her convenience, always for the other person's whether it was a fitter or a stagehand.' Years after she was already a big star, she was required to come for costume fittings at 8 a.m. During filming of *Something's Got to Give* producer Weinstein rang Marilyn after she missed the session. 'She was comatose,' he relates. Although she was obviously lucid enough to have mumbled something, for this is the occasion she is supposed to have propositioned Weinstein with the words: 'There's only one bed. Where will you sleep?'

The rumour about replacing Monroe with a younger actress gathered apace when Lee Remick was asked to go for costume fittings for the role. Monroe understandably felt betrayed. 'They think I'm awful – for doing nothing,' she told Lena Pepitone (the lady who kept house for her in New York). 'I'd like really to give them something to get mad about.' Sensing the mounting ill will towards her on the set, she was also moved to confide in friends: 'They all hate me.' Apparently not paranoia, since, after her death, Walter Bernstein has gone on record as having said that the situation was fraught from the beginning. The remark was occasioned by a BBC documentary investigation into the circumstances surrounding the events of 4 August and in this context David 'Buck' Hall, the assistant director on *Something's Got to Give*, was prominently mentioned. Bernstein has said that the friction between them was extreme but Hall was not removed and the effect was to exacerbate Monroe's mental instability.

Prior to starting work on *Something's Got to Give*, Monroe had been committed to Payne-Whitney, a New York hospital for highly disturbed mental patients, a mistake only rectified when DiMaggio, through his money and power, managed to get her transferred to the Columbia Presbyterian Medical Center where she spent three weeks. Although at Payne-Whitney for only three days, news of her committal reached studio walls, confirming the view of Fox executives that Monroe was as nutty as her mother. When I interviewed Joe Mankiewicz in 1986 and suggested that I thought Monroe deserved better than she got, he shouted: 'She got everything her little illiterate heart could desire. Where did she get her ideas from – her mother?'

After the Payne-Whitney episode, Monroe's relationship with Paula Strasberg deteriorated. She had written a note to Lee and Paula beseeching them to intervene but they did nothing. Paula continued, however, to coach Marilyn and Cukor, unlike other directors, having known Paula from before, did not object to her presence on the set. Perhaps Marilyn interpreted the concession as an indication of conspiracy. Whatever, this is one film where she and Strasberg had a decided lack of cohesive vision. Paula would query a perfectly good take, fearing that Marilyn wouldn't like it because the camera had favoured Dean Martin. There were other things they argued about, too. Paula began making changes to the script unacceptable to Marilyn. There was also the fact that she had approved the set – a plastic mockup of Cukor's gaudy mini Versailles mansion high up in the Hollywood Hills.

Then, too, at roughly the same time, a woman claiming to have been Marilyn's lover was paid a lot of money by Fox to keep silent. That the studio gave in to such outrageous blackmail must have infuriated Monroe, further increasing her sense of demoralization.

It is possible, even probable, that both the Payne-Whitney episode and the lesbian payoff confirmed the minds of her enemies that she was a nut case. By the same token it justified in others the aggression that they already felt. Consequently if Marilyn was paranoid, she had good reason to be. (Cukor incidentally is mentioned in *Hollywood Babylon* as a Hollywood gay. Why they say he was a 'woman's director' confounds me. I always found him savagely aggressive – cruel and caustic.) Nunnally Johnson, observing the oil and water combination, wrote: 'Most of those young actresses always think the director is God, and he [Cukor] was changing all these things. It shot [Marilyn] right down to the bottom, to the point where she wouldn't get out of bed. She was terrified. She dreaded Cukor. He terrified her, and he loathed her. He told me so.'

Marilyn's press agent Rupert Allan thinks that although Cukor's patience lasted during *Let's Make Love*, by the time they got to *Something's Got to Give* the honeymoon was over. 'He was doing artsy-craftsy junk which was not for Marilyn. She shouldn't have worked with Cukor. He didn't understand her and she didn't understand him. He had a sharp humour and wit – she was afraid of him.'

Whatever Monroe perceived his feelings about her to be, and however paranoid those perceptions were thought to have been, Cukor publicly confirmed the worst suspicions as true in an interview he gave after her death. He told Gavin Lambert: 'I think [Marilyn] was quite mad, subject to bad advice and beyond the reach of communication. I had no real communication with her at all. You couldn't get at her. She was very concerned about a lot of rather pretentious things (she'd done a lot of shit-ass studying) and I'd say, "But Marilyn, you're so accomplished. You do things that are frightfully difficult to do." She had this absolute unerring touch with comedy . . . She acted as if she didn't quite understand why it was funny. Which is what made it so funny. She could also do low comedy pratfalls and things like that – but I think her friends told her it wasn't worthy of her.'

Of her technique (which after nearly twenty years in the business remained deliciously unformulated) Cukor says: 'She either couldn't or wouldn't control herself. She wouldn't match things – you know, when you have a cigarette in one scene, and when you cut to the close shot, you can't not have the cigarette. She simply couldn't be bothered with this. And she couldn't sustain scenes. She'd do three lines and then forget the rest . . . You would have to shoot it piecemeal.'

There is nothing which more encapsulates Marilyn as a child of Hollywood than the birthdays which she enjoyed on the set of whatever film she was shooting. They were, for her particularly, a tradition. Perhaps because Monroe was, in effect, an orphan, her childhood having been spent in foster homes where she had been mistreated, it was almost a precedent that on 1 June a birthday cake would be wheeled on to the set, cast and crew gathering round to sing 'Happy Birthday'. Screenwriter I.A.L. Diamond who goes back with Marilyn to the days when, as a starlet, she was filming *Let's Make It Legal* (1950), recalls the fuss which was made on that occasion: 'They brought a cake on to the set between takes and everybody sang "Happy Birthday". It was very sweet. In those days she used to come to the studio wearing no makeup and with her hair in curlers. She was pretty in a natural, unaffected way.'

Twelve years later, Marilyn's thirty-sixth birthday party was a very different story. 'The atmosphere was tense,' writes Sheilah Graham, 'but following the usual custom, they had a party on the set for her with a birthday cake and thirty-six candles and congratulations from her co-star Dean Martin and Henry Weinstein, the producer, and George Cukor, the director, and the rest of the cast and crew. It was a brief ceremony, and afterwards Marilyn walked out to the chauffeur-driven limousine provided by the studio', which later that evening transported her, not to some hot spot where she could relax and dine with friends, but to a benefit for muscular dystrophy at Chavez Ravine baseball park. The birthday party, usually a source of joy, had not been reassuring and Marilyn told a friend: 'They gave me a party, but they sure didn't mean it. They wanted me out. I could tell.'

A viral relapse prompted correspondence with the studio on Monday 4 June. By the end of the week she had been fired. Did Fox want her out? Were they looking for an excuse? Maybe so, though probably the real reason Monroe was fired by Fox, the studio for which she had grossed $250 million, had as much to do with Marilyn as it did with the campaign being waged at the time against the big stars who were bankrupting the studios because of production delays. In fairness, the finger could have been pointed at Elizabeth Taylor, paid $1 million to do *Cleopatra*, which went horrendously over budget. It was Marilyn who was singled out as the scapegoat. Two hundred employees working the *Something's Got to Give* set lashed out at her in an advert they took in one of the Hollywood trade newspapers, while *The Hollywood Reporter* ran an editorial on 13 June 1962 scolding actors who wanted to be a law unto themselves, regardless of the expense they might cause others.

When asked by *Life* reporter Richard Meryman how

many people rallied round when she had been fired,
Monroe replied: 'None.' In fairness that is not completely true. Both Nunnally Johnson and Jean Negulesco
(the director of *How to Marry a Millionaire*) were supportive, intervening on her behalf with Peter Levathes, the
newly appointed Fox production chief. (Levathes is now
counsel to a Washington law firm.) 'When I read in the
papers that Peter Levathes . . . was going to take Marilyn
out of the picture,' says Johnson, 'I sent him a cable: "If
you're going to take anyone off of this picture, hadn't
you better first decide who brings people in, George
Cukor or Marilyn Monroe?"'

Apparently, Johnson's message got through to Levathes, because he made an appointment to meet with
Negulesco, telling him: 'The New York people have
decided to have the Monroe picture roll again – with
you as the new director.' 'Levathes was a tall, dark
man, nervous and with the faraway look of a man with
responsibilities beyond his understanding or ability,'
recalls Negulesco.

Having seen the rushes, which were sensational
(portions of the uncompleted film were shown in the
BBC documentary), it was decided that the film would
resume with Marilyn and she would be reinstated. The
Fox executives met with Marilyn at her Brentwood
house (Monroe having been coiffed and made up for the
occasion), where she had invited them to lunch. 'Her
lawyer Milton Rudin was there,' says Levathes. 'We had
re-done the script to proceed. She was happy to come
back to work. We planned several followup meetings.
We already had material on film. I gave her more money
than the contract called for, since some months had
passed in between. She told me she wasn't well, and that
she had been distracted by other things. She was a bright,
sensitive lady. People are creating untrue fantasies about
her. She was due to return to work the Monday following the weekend that she died.'

It has been said of Monroe that she singlehandedly introduced America to the New Wave – a European term referring to an impressionist approach to film making. Up against both studio (which sought to dispense formula sex) and directors (most of whom, in Marilyn's era, were misogynists) Monroe nevertheless overcame the system sufficiently to get her viewpoint across. Her arguments for greater sexual freedom, however, were at best perceived by small-minded moguls as 'cheeky', whilst the Legion of Decency wrote her off as morally subversive and comically derisive of sex (their approach dovetails that of today's hard-line feminists). Her honest intention was to create an image of femininity that was more real to her and in consequence, to other women, too. Antistylized, antitheatrical portrayals were her trademark, and lest anyone proclaim that they were merely the result of poor technique, I would suggest they look again at those marvellous *mise-en-scènes* from *The Seven Year Itch* (air grate), *Some Like It Hot* (seduction) and *Misfits* (horses) before making any further disparaging remarks. It is ironic that Darryl Zanuck, failing to grasp the slightest hint of Monroe's New Wave potential, perversely tried following her death to get with it. Juliette Greco and Bella Darvi were lame attempts by Zanuck to capitalize on New Wave, and Fox ultimately fell back upon a formula of big pictures altered to accommodate the modern idiom.

Larry Schiller, who shot the 'nude swim' in *Something's Got to Give*, praises Monroe's remarkable talent for translating into cinema the visual aspects of still photography. In short, Monroe was the ultimate pinup, but a pinup who turned the tables by exchanging cheesecake for eroticism. 'She probably knew more about her talent than the people who were directing her,' he says. 'Her insecurities only made her better because she never took anything for granted. She had an incredible way of handling the still camera because she was in command of it . . .'

From all accounts, however, the circumstances surrounding the shoot were such that the whole thing turned into a circus. (The outdoor photographs taken weeks later by George Barris on the golden Malibu sands and at Lawford's Santa Monica beach house, which were among the last ones of Marilyn, are far more representative of what Schiller calls 'Monroe's command of the camera'.) The plasticity of the Cukor set, the 'will-she-or-won't-she-disrobe antics' (encouraged by press agent Newcomb) and the behaviour of photographers anxious to catch that extra bit of ass succeeded in creating an ugly atmosphere. According to biographer Fred Guiles: '. . . Schiller and Woodfield realized immediately the excitement of what was happening – the first absolutely nude shots of Marilyn Monroe in fourteen years. [Both] men were crouched low so the splashing water about Marilyn would not obscure what they were after.' In other words, it was a desperate attempt to revitalize a dreary film.

It is typical of Monroe's belief in and understanding of the power of PR that during the months after being fired, she spent time fulfilling newspaper and magazine requests for interviews. Working with Marilyn at the time was Patricia Newcomb, whose role with the actress began as a replacement for Rupert Allan, Marilyn's regular press agent. His assessment of Newcomb, now a big mogul at MGM, was that 'she was a curious person. One of her walls was covered with photographs of Dean Martin and every time she'd have a row with Arthur Jacobs she'd come back and slam the door and poor Dean Martin's photos would wind up on the floor.' Columnist James Bacon describes Newcomb as 'ingratiating. That's how I will always remember Pat. She had this ability to make herself indispensable to Elizabeth [Taylor] or Marilyn [Monroe].' Allan agrees: 'Pat was made for those days. She was the kind of PR person that stars loved to have around; who could handle everything; give them advice on everything. She had lots of "in" knowledge about all the other stars.'

There had always, however, been tension between Marilyn and Newcomb, harking back to the days of *Bus Stop*. 'I do not think that they could have been friends for much longer,' says Allan, who when he had to depart for Europe had been dubious about assigning Pat as his replacement, as at the time of the *Bus Stop* saga Marilyn had said: 'I never want to see or hear from that woman again.' 'She did something that was reprehensible,' adds Allan. 'But when I had to find a temporary replacement (since I would be gone for a couple of weeks) I asked Marilyn if she'd mind taking a call from Pat? When I got back from Europe, I couldn't believe it. Pat had moved in so fast. When I returned and put in a call to Marilyn she said to me: "Why are you calling Marilyn? I just talked to her this morning." I got so angry that I said: "If I wanted to talk to you Pat I would have asked you to call her." Newcomb was very jealous and very possessive of Marilyn . . . One afternoon Pat called me and asked if I was free that night. When I arrived there had been a fight about something. Pat had created an issue out of jealousy. It was a strange thing. Pat didn't want to wear her mink if Marilyn was going to wear hers and so on. It was dumb, unprofessional behaviour on the part of Pat Newcomb.'

And yet the very last, and one of the best, interviews given by Monroe had been arranged by Newcomb with John Springer in New York – the Richard Meryman *Life* magazine interview. 'It was to be a big major interview,' recalls Springer, 'with Dick Meryman. I remember bringing Marilyn to meet Dick and his researcher to decide whether or not she'd go along with it at the old Savoy Plaza Hotel. We were very late by the time we got there. The researcher had had a few drinks and was saying: "All right, now I'm going to be your best friend. This woman completely turned off Marilyn. (She later told me: "I don't have a best friend and if I did it wouldn't be her.") She was not going to do the interview, except through me, and since I trusted Meryman (and the girl was no longer involved) I convinced her to do it.'

Aside from Meryman's parenthetical comments about arriving at 10 a.m. and being told by the housekeeper that Monroe was still asleep, the *Life* feature (which ran after her death) captured the essence of Marilyn in those final days. There is a poignancy to some of the comments – a hardness underlying the humour which seems to be forced gaiety. Her thoughts and free associations on a variety of topics, are quoted below:

On Money: 'There aren't really any kind of monuments or museums . . . nobody left anything behind, they took it, they grabbed it and they ran – the ones who made the billions of dollars, never the workers.'

On Lateness: 'Gable said about me, "When she's there, she's there. All of her is there! She's there to work."'

On Sexuality: 'I feel that beauty and femininity are ageless and can't be contrived, and glamour – although the manufacturers won't like this – cannot be manufactured . . . I think that sexuality is only attractive when it's natural and spontaneous . . . It's a pity so many people despise and crush this natural gift.'

On Fame: 'I now live for my work and the few relationships with the few people I can really count on . . . I've always known [fame] is fickle. If it goes by . . . it's something I experienced, but it's not where I live.'

But it was in the *Redbook* interview that she told the world what she thought of Arthur Miller. Monroe was blamed for the fact that he had produced little during their marriage; even the Russians issued a statement about how she had ruined him getting from him what she could and then ruthlessly discarding him. Her reply would have shocked both the Russians and the House on Un-American Activities. 'I know the man. I lived with the man. He is no communist!' – an allusion, undoubtedly, to the parsimony for which Miller was noted during the years they were married, and which was totally at odds with the idea of a collective spirit.

Prior to her death, Marilyn had come full circle. She had achieved international success at every level and at every level had found it lacking. Her viewpoint was considerably different when she first set foot at Fox in 1946, a skinny, unkempt girl whose teeth protruded, whose hair was mousy brown, and whose features looked as if they had been thrown together in a great hurry. Yet at the same time she was someone whose dreams of stardom were grandiose and whose determination to make those dreams come true was formidable.

5

The Conception:
Myth and Anti-Myth

Before there was the Myth, before there was the Anti-myth, there was only the cry of a newborn baby girl christened Norma Jeane in honour of Norma Talmadge, a silent screen actress and favourite of the infant's mother. (It is ironic that Norma Jeane's first Hollywood protector would be Fox founder Joseph Schenck, once married to Norma Talmadge.)

Circumstances surrounding the 1 June 1926 birth of the baby who one day would grow up to become Marilyn Monroe were not auspicious, since when her mother entered Los Angeles General Hospital she had recently been deserted by her second husband, Edward Mortensen, and the two children by her first marriage to Mr Baker were being looked after, with her consent, by his relatives in Kentucky. It was generally believed that Norma Jeane was the result of Gladys Baker's relationship with a co-worker at the Consolidated Film Industries lab where she was employed, though Stanley Gifford did not accept parental responsibility nor contribute to the office fund circulated to assist Gladys in paying hospital costs.

Much maligned in the volumes of books which have been written about Monroe, Gladys Baker was not always the mental incompetent she has been made out to be. Before suffering her breakdowns, she was a brilliant film cutter, as ambitious as her daughter; why else would she have allowed her children to be raised by relatives while she struggled along in a career which to others seemed thankless at best? She was wilfully independent, trying as best she could to sort out for herself some measure of self-support, rather than becoming financially dependent upon the opposite sex. However, possessing both greater modesty and humility than Norma Jeane, it never occurred to her to confront Gifford or Mortensen with paternity demands. In short, Baker was a woman who knew her place and in this respect she was perfectly cast for her role in the Hollywood of the Depression era which advanced an ethos supporting exploitation of workers by bosses. (Unions only came into existence in Hollywood in the thirties.)

Remembered in her prime as a tough, driving section supervisor of five female employees who cut negative for the major Hollywood studios – Columbia, RKO and MGM among them – Mrs Baker is one of many executives whose energies were dissipated in the belief that their contribution to the company was greater than any responsibility to themselves or their families. If Mrs Baker lived, breathed and sweated film during those interminable night shift hours, she dreamed of film all day, filling her newborn baby's ears with shop talk about the glamorous stars whose films she cut, conveying in both tone and attitude the awe she held for those on the other side of the creative line – the above the line personnel, the stars, the bosses, the directors, the writers and the producers. It was this myth of Hollywood, passed along to the young Norma Jeane, which became the basis for Marilyn Monroe's existence.

It is this naïve idealism which kept Baker in mental institutions for most of her adult life; and whilst it could be argued that as a State ward she was getting back from the country but a little of what she deserved, the reality of heaping financial responsibility upon Monroe's shoulders (it having been discovered that she was a Fox contract player and therefore salaried) begs the issue; for it purges the government of any responsibility for purveying a self-consuming work ethic. The irony of Monroe's assimilation of the credo which damned her own mother is that despite the heights she reached – and they were Olympian – she was forever (in the eyes of the bosses) falling short of what they believed she was capable of doing.

Following the birth of her third child, Mrs Baker (who declined to use her second husband's name, even though they were married in a civil ceremony) rented a room in Hawthorne, a desolate, bible-belt community in southern California close to her mother's place which had been let to an insurance salesman and his wife whilst her mother was in India. In describing the two women, Marilyn always said that she resembled her grand-mother, considering her to be the prettier of the two. But descriptions of Gladys Baker reveal more than a passing resemblance to Faye Dunaway, except that she was a redhead with bright blue eyes.

Gladys retained her room in town close to the film lab where she worked, and boarded her daughter in Hawthorne, paying a small amount for her upkeep to a middle-aged couple called Ida and Wayne Bolender, remembered by Marilyn later on with wry affection as 'religious fanatics'. (The financial burden was assumed by the State when Marilyn was aged three, Mrs Baker having had the first of a series of breakdowns following her own mother's death from which she never fully recovered.) Marilyn remained with the Bolenders until she was seven, and during this time absorbed enough of the asceticism of their lifestyle to reject evangelism in her adult life. When actress Jane Russell, Marilyn's *Gentlemen Prefer Blondes* co-star, and a practising evangelist tried to encourage her to attend prayer groups she met with little success.

Prior to being placed in an institution (and probably also during release periods) Gladys brought the child to the furnished room she let in Hollywood near to the film lab where she worked. These times together must have been special, for in later years Marilyn recalled how the two of them would amble about the streets of Beverly Hills bedazzled by the posh homes belonging to the rich and famous. Occasionally, Gladys would bring her daughter along to the lab where she worked, and Marilyn would often recount the memory of the awful smell (something akin to glue) of wet film negative. Whilst it has been suggested that Marilyn showed little sympathy or concern for her mother, the facts of the matter do not support this. Firstly, Marilyn's will provides generously for her mother for the duration of her life. (Mrs Baker not only survived her daughter but is still alive and resident, when last we checked, in Florida.*) Secondly, during her mother's protracted committal in mental hospitals, Marilyn visited her regularly, often bringing gifts of clothing and sweets. All her dearest friends were introduced to Mrs Baker at least once. That Marilyn was publicly humiliated and forced to assume financial responsibility for her mother's care in a private sanitarium when she herself was earning a mere pittance as a Fox starlet is a cruelty which seems quite harsh and very unnecessary.

During one of her brief releases from hospital, Gladys Baker bought a bungalow near to the Hollywood Bowl concert area – the site where years later Marilyn's press agent Arthur Jacobs received a note alerting him to her death – with the intention of raising her seven-year-old daughter. The plan depended upon letting the house to

---

* It is rumoured that she died in 1984, although the author has not received documentation of her death.

an English couple who had immigrated to America, whilst keeping for themselves two small rooms. The man was actor George Arliss's stand-in; his wife, a 'dress' extra often used as a walk-on in drawing-room comedies. The rooms were sparsely furnished, but there was a luxurious white piano once owned by Frederic March which Mrs Baker had purchased as a showpiece. When they lost the house, and the piano was sold off, it became one of Marilyn's obsessions to find the instrument. Years later she discovered it at an auction and bought it.

Any hopes of establishing a family life, however, were dashed when the English couple abruptly announced plans to return to Britain, the husband having lost his job as Arliss's stand-in. (During the interval Marilyn is reputed to have adopted an English accent, which she lost shortly thereafter.) The disaster thoroughly undermined whatever stability Baker had mustered, precipitating another breakdown and committal into hospital.

Like her mother, Marilyn was made a ward of Los Angeles county, and was placed by the authorities in a series of foster homes in the hope that a suitable adoption could be arranged. 'But no one seemed interested in adopting me permanently,' Monroe said years later. 'I've often wondered about this,' noting parenthetically that adoption had been discouraged by the authorities in view of what they regarded as her family history of mental instability. 'I was known amongst county authorities as a "mental case",' she remarked to an interviewer long after she was an established star. The truth is, however, that even in her most deranged moments, Mrs Baker never once considered the option of offering her daughter up for adoption.

One might surmise from this that Marilyn knew she was loved and any guilt which might have developed about the relationship with her mother came from the publicity campaign master-minded by the Fox Studio

which ostensibly wrote off the woman as dead. The
press item conjured up about 'her mother being unwell
for some time' implied that she had died shortly after
Marilyn's birth, sufficiently confusing the press so as to
preclude any pursuit of family matters. Her father was
reported as having died in a car accident. (Curiously, in
correspondence with actor Tom Ewell, Monroe's *Seven
Year Itch* co-star, I discovered that the myth prevails:
like many others he labours under the misconception
that Gladys Baker died shortly after Marilyn's birth.)

So why does the dead mother myth refuse to die?
Years after it was announced to the world that Marilyn's
mother was being cared for by the State in a publicly-
funded sanitarium, there were still those who preferred
to falsify her origins. These are the same people who, in
blatant disregard of the facts, refuse to believe either the
truth about her affair with Jack Kennedy or the strange
circumstances surrounding her death.

The truth about her mother came out when Monroe
was filming Fritz Lang's *Clash by Night* at RKO where
her mother had been a cutter. (She was loaned to RKO
for the purpose of playing an offbeat dramatic role in a
working-class drama about San Francisco cannery
workers.) It is possible that someone had remembered
Baker or that Marilyn herself talked openly about the
association. In any event, a wire service reporter got
wind of it, checked his facts, and blasted it over the front
pages of every newspaper in America. There was a
scandal and Monroe was accused of being remiss as a
daughter and was compelled (at an inauspicious career
juncture) to assume the financial burden of her mother's
care in a private rest home.

Marilyn's early childhood reads like a chapter from
Dickens set in America in the thirties and forties. A
victim of religious fanatics, drunkards, child beaters, the
odd child molester, and the spongers who used the
county allotment to feed themselves while the ward went

without, the best that can be said of these experiences is that Marilyn might have used them in creating film characterizations noted for their reality. One family of religious fanatics attended church three times on Sundays, Sunday school every Wednesday night, and of course, nightly tent revival meetings. 'Dancing, smoking, movies and playing cards were considered "works of the devil". To to go a movie was a sin. Every night I was told I would wake up in hell,' Marilyn recounted years later.

In another place, the woman of the house lost her pearl necklace and accused Marilyn of having stolen it. Another time she received a birthday gift of fifty cents, which the family confiscated. Then there was the family boasting of three generations of women (the grandmother had known Buffalo Bill and used to delight Marilyn with stories about her frontier past). One day one of the kids tore her dress. Marilyn was blamed and soon after was transferred elsewhere. Another family lost her a role in the Christmas play, as they feared being embarrassed by her limited acting abilities. When she was allowed to appear in an Easter play, she failed to drop her tunic (she was the black spot on a white Cross) and the family asked that she be removed. Another couple described her as strange; Marilyn later recalled having overheard them talking about '. . . that . . . quiet little girl. She makes me nervous. Let's get her out of here.'

At age nine, Marilyn was placed at the Los Angeles County Orphanage where she remained for two years. The building was not far from the RKO. Her confinement there has been recognized by Monroe historians as being among the most traumatic years of her early life. Most biographers note that the accommodation was little better than a reformatory since all wards were not only uniformly dressed but forced to wear heavy platform shoes. Years later Marilyn recounted how that

at nights, when all the kids were asleep, she'd perch in
the dormitory window sill and look across at the RKO
water tower, with RKO in big letters and lights shining
like a Hollywood premiere. '"My mother used to work
there," I'd whisper. "Some day I'd like to be a star
there."'

Existence as a State ward was something which caused
Monroe great chagrin. Years later she still remembered
how she was compelled to wash dishes for five cents per
month – exploitation she recounted in conversations
with Senator Abraham Ribicoff whose campaign to improve the welfare conditions of State wards she zealously
supported. Columnist James Bacon relates an early interview where Monroe summoned up the experience of
being alone at the orphanage during Christmas time.
Given its proximity to the orphanage, the RKO Studios
adopted a paternalistic attitude, inviting the youngsters
over for Christmas Day, filling them with sweets and
screening in the evening a film suitable for children.
Recalls Bacon: 'Marilyn brought tears to my eyes on
Christmas Eve 1951. We were in the dressing room
talking. She said, "It's funny here working at RKO
because I can remember one Christmas when I lived at
the orphanage (a few blocks from here). There were lots
of kids. We didn't get any presents, since the county was
paying for our welfare. I felt very depressed. I walked
outside and looked up at the RKO water tower. Suddenly I noticed somebody standing beside me. It was
one of the children offering me an orange."'

The circumstances which placed the adolescent
Monroe in no less than twelve different foster homes
allowed her to cope with the idiosyncrasies and prejudices of the many different kinds of people she was later
to meet professionally. Sometimes, the prejudices could
be diametrically opposed to each other (this is indeed
something which plagued her later life and while other
biographers minimize its importance, I suspect that

maintaining concurrent relationships with people on both the Left and the Right of the political spectrum could not help but prove emotionally disorientating).

Monroe would later blame these years for producing a battery of emotional problems emanating from ridicule and rejection, including a stutter (which she never really lost); rashes, colds, vomiting, and other psychosomatic ailments.

It was in early 1938 that the gods intervened, placing Marilyn in the care of her mother's friend Grace Goddard, husband 'Doc' (a divorcee) and their three kids (his by a previous marriage) in a small house in West Van Nuys, a Los Angeles suburb characterized by flatness, used-car lots and fast-food chains. Conscious of her child's loathing for life as a county ward, Mrs Baker prevailed upon her close friend and former Columbia Picture colleague (the film studio head librarian) to try to sort out some suitable alternative for her daughter. Initially the situation at the Goddards proved amicable, Grace using the county stipend to enrol the girl in classes for acting, singing and dancing, for which Marilyn had shown an aptitude. Things became fraught, however, when 'Doc', who liked a bit of a tipple, entered Marilyn's room drunk and gave her a sloppy smooch. The next day she was packed off to live with Grace's Aunt Ana Lower, a widowed lady of sixty-five whose influence over the girl was to be considerable and with whom Marilyn kept in contact for ten years until the lady's death in 1948 when Marilyn was well on her way to becoming an international superstar. When she died, Marilyn was moved to remark that she was 'the dearest, sweetest and most unselfish woman I have ever known. She had very little herself but what she had she shared with others. She became a true mother to me – the only touch of mother love I had ever known . . . when Aunt Ana died, I felt the first poignant grief I had ever known.'

Although Grace Goddard remained her legal guardian,

Marilyn physically moved in with Ana, into a large new house in a wealthy Los Angeles suburb known as Westwood near to the Mormon Temple (a massive Los Angeles landmark in the Byzantine style), although Ana herself was a practising Christian Scientist. In the typical way she had of assuming the characteristics of whatever environment in which she lived, during the years spent with Aunt Ana Marilyn became a regular churchgoer and practitioner of the lifestyle advanced by the Christian Science leader Mary Baker Eddy. Later, during the years spent among the Jewish converts in Hollywood, she worshipped in a Catholic church and when she migrated to New York and began mixing with the Jewish intellectuals who became her friends she converted to Judaism. A superb exponent of any and all faiths, it should be noted that the manner in which she catered for any discipline or religion was devotional, extracting the highest moral values from the ethic, but there was never anything remotely approaching fanaticism or bias about the manner or method of practice.

Living in West Los Angeles allowed Marilyn for the first time to enter the world of the upwardly mobile middle-class. No longer did she mingle with the kids of film cutters and other craft personnel. Westwood was the sanctuary of business managers, lawyers, agents and publicists whose kids arrived at University High School in chauffeured Rolls-Royces. It is ironic that the house which Marilyn bought when she attained superstar status was in this very neighbourhood, although by that time it must have seemed very pedestrian indeed and Marilyn had wanted to purchase something spectacular overlooking the Pacific Ocean.

The move into Westwood had another benefit: it placed the teenager in close contact with *Dallas* actor Howard Keel (probably before he became an MGM contract player), remembered by Marilyn as 'Harry'. Marilyn had a passionate schoolgirl crush on him, but

25-year-old Keel responded rather coolly to Marilyn's advances, patronizingly patting her on the head after she had hung around all afternoon to glimpse him. (He probably kicked himself years later for passing up the opportunity.)

The instability which was to plague Marilyn's later life reared its ugly head again shortly after she had settled into Aunt Ana's residence when her legal guardian, Grace Goddard, announced plans to depart for West Virginia, where 'Doc' had accepted a job offer. Accepting the post meant legal termination of guardianship, once again placing Marilyn in the hands of the Fates. What was to become of her?

Whether Ana was too old or unwilling to assume guardianship, or whether she was unable to keep Marilyn without receipt of a State stipend (which had been turned over to her in the past by the Goddards), or whether 'Doc' couldn't have sought a job promotion within the perimeters of California State, the reality is that when it came down to a decision, the consensus among the Goddards and Aunt Ana was, not surprisingly, inherently selfish. Their goal became to find Marilyn a suitable husband and they didn't have to look further than James Dougherty – the boy-next-door, literally! Dougherty lived with his parents in a small bungalow in back of the Goddards. Athletic, church-going, and hardworking (he was a Lockheed Aircraft day labourer) he was considered by the Goddards to be a tremendous catch envisaged originally for their own daughter, Beebe, but then for Marilyn when it was acknowledged that she had caught his eye.

The reaction of the young Monroe to the marriage says a lot about her emotional maturity – the sagacity which poet Sandburg referred to as 'the wisdom beyond her years'. She never forgave Grace Goddard for fixing for her what she considered to be a loveless marriage. It was the first of many betrayals which Marilyn would experience in her lifetime: her response always being the same – outrage, hurt and disappointment at being badly used by people for whom she cared. The reality of what a Christian marriage meant occurred to Monroe in an almost Marxist sense; she disliked the marital domination imposed upon women by their husbands as regards conjugal rights, money, decisions, and career pursuits. It is amusing to contemplate the lady who was often portrayed later as a nymphomaniac enquiring of Aunt Ana if there was any way that she and Dougherty could remain platonic friends. Dougherty, faced with her hesitation, misinterpreted it as sexual shyness: 'She was terrified of being alone with me – later I learned she asked Grace Goddard if she could be married and "just friends" with her husband.'

Marilyn was equally dubious about the guidelines for her wifely role – was she expected to quit high school (which she was) in order to devote herself to housework? Monroe was forty years ahead of her time in asking such questions. In an account of her first marriage she had said: 'When I was aged fifteen, it was arranged for me to marry James Dougherty in a simple ceremony with the idea that it would provide me with a home and a husband. My husband and I lived in a small bungalow court. I wanted to finish high school but I discovered that school and marriage don't mix. We were *poor*. So naturally my job was to keep house on a strict budget.'

It appears that Dougherty was a typical, old-fashioned chauvinist who considered Marilyn, for all her loveliness, something of a private possession, scoffing at her dreams of pursuing a film career. 'I used to confide in my husband my childish dreams of becoming an actress,' she related to an interviewer. 'He'd laugh and assure me I'd never make it.' Dougherty himself was movie-star handsome: tall (6ft 2in), strapping and athletic. At age eighteen he had graduated from Van Nuys High School (where he was a classmate of Jane Russell) and had taken a job as a Lockheed Aircraft labourer (where Robert Mitchum was a mate before he became an actor). (Russell and Mitchum both later co-starred with Monroe in major films.)

Squashing the myth that prior to stardom Marilyn was plain looking, her face disproportionately large for her body, columnist Earl Wilson recounts a conversation about Monroe between Dougherty and Robert Mitchum (who co-starred with Marilyn in *River of No Return*). 'Mitchum says that while working at Lockheed he got to know a fellow toiler named James Dougherty, who annoyed him slightly because he was so happy with life. Mitchum was silent and brooding about making plane parts that were useless, but Dougherty came in every day with his lunch, a cold egg sandwich that his "old lady" had prepared for him at home that morning. Mitchum was so moody he couldn't eat – and especially not a cold egg sandwich. "Your old lady makes you the same sandwich every day?" Mitchum asked sourly. "You ought to see my old lady!" Dougherty said,' producing a photo of a young nubile Marilyn stark naked.

The marriage took place in Westwood on 19 June 1942, three weeks after Marilyn's sixteenth birthday, at the home of one of Dougherty's buddies. The service was performed by the Reverend B.H. Lingenfalter, of the Christian Church of Torrence. The site was chosen primarily because of the winding staircase into the central hall which Marilyn could descend as the wedding march was played. She looked astonishingly lovely, and wore a gown of white eyelet lace hand-sewn by Aunt Ana. Included in the wedding party were the Doughertys, the Bolenders, Aunt Ana, and brothers, sisters, friends and classmates of Jim and Marilyn. The Goddards wired their love and regrets from West Virginia. Gladys, having relapsed, was committed to a sanitarium in the San

Francisco Bay area and unable to attend the ceremony.

The next time Marilyn saw her mother was during a modelling assignment with Hungarian photographer Andre De Dienes which took them to Washington and Oregon in the north-west. At the time, Mrs Baker was living in an old hotel in the centre of Portland, in a depressing bedroom on the top floor. The reunion was fraught, Mrs Baker's concern for her daughter's welfare was clearly apparent, but at the same time, it was obvious she could barely cope with her own instability. '[Marilyn] put on a cheerful front,' recalls Andre. 'She had unpacked the presents we had brought: a scarf, scent, and chocolates. They stayed there on the table. A silence ensued. Then Mrs Baker buried her face in her hands and seemed to forget all about us. It was distressing. She had obviously been released from hospital too soon.' It may also have been that for a careerist such as she was, having attained a top management position as a supervising editor, not to be able to function in that role was both a disappointment and a humiliation. What is more, she had no family life, as she had been abandoned by two husbands (and possibly her lover), and her children had been taken from her – the last one (Marilyn) a reminder of everything she had gained and lost.

There is another very touching account of a brief reunion during the time that Marilyn and Dougherty were separated, Jim having been shipped overseas with the Merchant Marines when America entered the Second World War. Whilst pursuing freelance modelling assignments, Marilyn often used a spare room at Aunt Ana's. It was, in essence, a single unit separated from the main house which provided her with a certain measure of privacy. It was here that Mrs Baker lived with Marilyn during one brief release from hospital. Marilyn was then enrolled in a grooming course at Emmeline Snively's Blue Book Modelling Agency. Mrs Baker had wandered by the office one afternoon to thank the lady for what she had done for Marilyn. Years later Snively recalled the encounter, remembering Mrs Baker as an attractive woman, prim and proper, wearing a small hat and white gloves. 'She introduced herself as [Marilyn's] mother. Her reason for coming, she said, was simply to thank me for what I was doing for her daughter.' The overall impression however was one of pity, since the woman essentially seemed a pathetic sort of person – emotionally depleted and down on her luck. Shortly thereafter, Mrs Baker was readmitted to a California State hospital where she remained until she was transferred to a private sanitarium in Verdugo, California following the dead mother scandal which was leaked in 1952 when Marilyn was making *Clash By Night* at RKO.

6
Used Cars,
Fast Foods and Big Mac

The Doughertys set up housekeeping at a studio apartment in Sherman Oaks, a bible–belt suburb of Los Angeles. Two things Monroe remembers about the place were the pulldown bed and a pet collie named Muggsie. Accounts of the Dougherty's life indicate that it was routine to the point of monotony, with Sunday spent attending services at the Sherman Oaks Christian Science Church. Both Doughertys were abstemious, and later when Marilyn did drink, she confined herself to wine. Designer Travilla recounts occasional dates when they would go dancing, noting how Marilyn would sip a little bit of her drink and leave the rest. 'She drank to be sociable,' he says. While acknowledging that she was a flirt, the conspicuous display of a wedding band discouraged anyone from mistaking conviviality as an invitation for sex.

The genuine feeling for people and things which Marilyn projected in both still and animated photography reflected the core of what she was as a person. The spiritual centre which had been there almost from the time she could breathe was revealed to Dougherty after the most minimal period of marital adjustment. Her ability to experience transcendent quietude and profound fulfilment comes through in Dougherty's account of some of their evenings together. 'Our living room window overlooked the bay, and on moonlit nights we would sit on the window and watch the soft light on the water and sing to each other. I played the guitar, whilst Marilyn sang.'

When Dougherty was switched to the night shift Marilyn never forgot to stick a sexy note into his lunch pail which read: 'Dearest Daddy, when you read this, I will be asleep and dreaming of you. Love and kisses, Your Baby.' 'She was very, very sensitive,' he says, remembering one night 'when we went to bed after having an argument about something and she kept crying and crying. Finally I moved into the living room and went to sleep on the couch. When I awoke a couple of hours later [Marilyn] was asleep by my side. If I didn't kiss her good-bye every time I left the house, she thought something was wrong.'

Nonetheless the Christian ideal of marriage was distasteful to Marilyn, and although she was at the time an ardent churchgoer, she took exception to what she felt was the disparity of sex roles in relation to housework, money and conjugal rights. David Conover, the army photographer whose cover photos for men's magazines brought Marilyn to Howard Hughes' attention, was privy to some of her most candid thoughts about the marriage institution in the days when she was contemplating a divorce. 'Poor Jim,' she told Conover, 'I know I disappointed him. But I wanted more out of life than dishes, ironing and scrubbing.'

Later on Marilyn often spoke disparagingly of marriage. There is little doubt that she felt the sex option favoured the male, and while there is no suggestion that she was ever mistreated by Dougherty she did complain to Rupert Allan about being mistreated by Miller during *Misfits*. Recounts Allan: 'I went up to see Marilyn during the film. She was very upset. She had May Reis, her

secretary, and Ralph Roberts, her masseur and other
people around. She was crying – emotionally upset.
Coach Lee [Strasberg] was there. Paula [his wife] was
there. She had friends there. And that upset her enormously. It was a psychological thing.' (Monroe made it
a point to surround herself on the set with friends – she
often got them jobs in the film or crewing. And yet she
was always unhappy, never feeling that she got from
them the support she needed.)

It is significant that biographers consider it worth
mentioning that Dougherty's Lockheed foreman was
not invited to the wedding, and that shortly thereafter
Dougherty was transferred to the night shift. In any
case, the routine appears to have disrupted whatever
sexual rapport had developed between the couple and
within months of their first wedding anniversary the
union was on the decline. The latter three years of the
marriage were spent largely apart, except for Dougherty's occasional leaves home, as by then he had enlisted
in the Merchant Marines to assist America in the war
effort. Whatever sex they had was probably hasty and
unsatisfactory, since Dougherty was either in a rush to
get to sleep or go to work. By admission, Marilyn grew
agitated, filling her time with frivolous visits to friends
and the like, which only increased her irritability.

Perhaps the marriage could have survived if Dougherty had secured a day job. More probably not, since it
is apparent that at sixteen Marilyn was already too bitten
by her dream of becoming a filmstar. Overhearing her
mother (a cutter) and Aunt Grace (a film studio librarian)
talk shop day and night must have had its effect. She
was always a step ahead, forever denying herself any
satisfaction in the here and now.

As things transpired Dougherty departed Lockheed
for a job with the Merchant Marines as a physical training
coach before being shipped overseas to the Far East.
Although several accounts describe her hysteria over his

impending departure, there are other biographers whose assessment of her attitude confirms that Monroe was solidly behind the war effort, wondering aloud in letters to Dougherty why other men of his age had not enlisted. One wonders what her feelings were about Arthur Miller having been declared 4–F.)

Marilyn, meanwhile, could have been a character in a Miller play, and an incident at the Radio Plane munitions factory was almost identical to one that Miller used in *All My Sons*, although it was written before he met her. Having taken a job at the factory owned by the English-born actor Reginald Denny, Marilyn got into trouble when one of the parachutes she had vetted failed to open and the pilot died. For days Marilyn was in shock, recalls a friend, and while it later came out that the fault was not hers it took days for her to come round.

It was this taut, tense, working-class atmosphere which she drew on years later when cast in Fritz Lang's *Clash By Night* as a cannery worker hard pressed by the exigencies of poverty, class and sex. 'I never forgot what it felt like to be one of those women,' says Marilyn, who admitted to having taken the factory job because she felt the money was good, only to discover the reality of long hours, little money and a brief lunch break. Food was also cold, stored as it was in black tin lunch pails brought from home and consumed quickly side by side with her mother-in-law.

The austerity of life in wartime America, with its rationing and long work hours for small wages was enlivened when photographer David Conover, a US army private based at Fort Roach (the Hal Roach Studio converted into barracks) came along at the request of his Commanding Officer, Ronald Reagan, to take pictures of the distaff's contribution to the war effort. Having shot a couple of rolls of Marilyn, and finding her agree-able, he suggested that she moonlight over the weekend by coming along on a photographic shoot. (Conover freelanced for men's magazines.)

Years later Conover recalls his utter obsession with the girl who was to become Monroe. '"To be a great actress is more than a dream or a career," she told me. "It's my whole mission in life."' A sentiment expressed with a solemnity vaguely humorous, particularly since the kind of work she was doing was anything but classically dramatic. But what she was learning to do when posing for photos with grandiose natural landscapes was to use her body as an extension of the landscape – to speak through movement and suggestion (rather than mannerism and articulation). There was never anything theatrical or stagy about Monroe, and it is often attributed to her beginnings as a still model. There was also the effect of the ridicule heaped upon her by theatre performers and other Hollywood actors who despised her for doing stills and art photography which they considered to be degrading. Much of her work was cheesecake, more of it was erotic, but in neither case was it ever Marilyn's fault that publicity intruded upon the time spent in rehearsal or on the set. It was the studio which (long after she became a big star) continued to exploit her good nature by booking her into photo sessions, press interviews and gallery shoots long after work hours until she was forced, in order to survive, to walk out.

Conover's account of working with Monroe is full of powerful insights, particularly about the degree of patience and fortitude she exhibited when forced to perform in the most austere weather conditions: 'July 10. Second day in Death Valley. Shooting in the sand dunes. Very hot and tiring. Norma Jeane is very patient, stands for shot after shot in the blazing sun. She is learning fast that a model must keep her cool. We swim a lot in the pool. [Marilyn] can do about five strokes now before she starts to flounder . . .'

In those early years Marilyn's curiosity about the stars was insatiable. (This curiosity proved a fundamental link later on in her friendship with Robert Slatzer whose job acquainted him with a lot of the Hollywood old-timers.) Conover was also a buff. 'Like [Marilyn] I was hooked on the movies,' he recounts in *Finding Marilyn*. '. . . I knew a lot of movie stars personally – Gable, Alan Ladd, George Montgomery, Van Heflin, Joseph Cotten, Kent Smith, Ronald Reagan . . . Every detail of Hollywood fascinated [Marilyn], and she kept asking me what each actor I knew was *really* like . . . Ladd, I told her, was a kind man, bothered by his shortness. Van Heflin, intense, rugged and short-tempered; very much his own man. Joseph Cotten, I reported, I'd found hard to figure; very quiet, he kept much to himself and looked worried most of the time. He wasn't the friendliest person but he was always polite and spoke in a soft voice.'

Of the actors mentioned Monroe would work with both Cotten and Gable (both of whom adored her) whilst totally enchanting George Montgomery: the only male brave enough to dance with her at a Hollywood gala given by Rupert Allan for Gina Lollobrigida in the late fifties dressed as she was in one of her famous 'skin and beads' ball gowns. 'Where do I put my hand?' George kiddingly asked Allan, since Marilyn's dress was completely backless.

It was an advance of money from David Conover that allowed Marilyn to embark upon a modelling career which later led to films. Conover recommended that she make an appointment to see Emmeline Snively whose Blue Book Modelling Agency was headquartered at the Ambassador Hotel in downtown Los Angeles, site of the posh Coconut Grove nightclub. Accounts reveal that Snively projected the prejudices which a few years later characterized America during the McCarthy era. Her models appear to have been chosen on the basis of class and race. When she agreed to sign Monroe as a client (first having enrolled her in an evening charm course) it was with the provisions that she first bleach and then straighten her hair which was brown and kinky. Her face was also a problem; Snively noted that Eastern editors refused to run photos of Monroe as they objected to the unkempt look suggested by a piece of cartilage which planed the tip of her nose. Snively also attempted to get her to improve her smile (to reveal fewer teeth), to alter her walk and to effect better posture (she was slouch-shouldered). Consequently it is not surprising that the majority of placements were for men's magazines or industrial shows, which Monroe seemed to enjoy, as she was fussed over by lots of people who appeared to like the job she was doing.

Dougherty's reaction to Marilyn's career was little different from that displayed by DiMaggio and Miller years later: he didn't think that she was serious in her pursuit of acting, posing as she did for cheesecake. Recoiling at the abandonment of her own name for the pseudonyms Jean Norman and Carol Lind (which sounded blonde), Dougherty was furious to discover that Marilyn had both bleached and straightened her hair. The idea of his young wife embarking upon photo assignments, unchaperoned, couldn't have pleased him very much either. Writing about their marriage in *The Secret Happiness of Marilyn Monroe*, Dougherty says: 'It wasn't so much that I feared there would be other photographers pursuing her around the desert or their studios, even though that was at the back of my mind. I thought I'd given her modelling career a fair trial, well over a year, and she was letting our home life slide more and more. So I just told her that she would have to choose between a modelling career and maybe the movies or a home life with me . . . Then she got very emotional. She said I was gone too much. How could I expect her to be a housewife when I was at sea more than half the time? . . . If I had said, "Baby, I'll leave the Maritime

Service just as soon as they'll release me," she might have thrown her arms around me and told Snively and the rest "thank you and good-bye".'

It was during Dougherty's second trip away that Monroe began freelancing for other photographers, doing beer commercials for Tom Kelley and location shoots for Andre De Dienes, a Hungarian photographer who had immigrated to the USA and become a naturalized citizen. (It was for Kelley that Marilyn, after having been dropped by about four major studios, would do the nude calendar which was so spectacular that it sold over 8 million copies and graced the inaugural issue of *Playboy* magazine.)

De Dienes's account of working with Monroe is fabulous, since it identifies what it was about her that was appealing not just to Andre and to other photographers but to thousands of fans. Monroe was America itself – white clay unmarked by war, famine or plague: vital, young, energized and promising.

Were they lovers? Some say yes; that Monroe was cold-bloodedly exploiting her charms. Just as likely, she might simply have been flirting. Columnist James Bacon told me that she had the singular ability to make any man feel as if he was the most important person in the world. It was to De Dienes that she inscribed a photograph with the words 'Things worth having are things worth waiting for', perhaps hinting for posterity at the precise nature of the friendship.

De Dienes is one of the few people able to make comparisons between the Monroe Before and After. His first impressions are recounted in the photo album *Marilyn Mon Amour*. 'At first sight she did not look anything like what I was after: much too naïve, too awkward . . . She wore a wedding ring which seemed absurd: she was nineteen but looked much younger . . . The two-piece [bathing suit] she took out of her hat box did not do her justice. It did not matter, it revealed what

I had already surmised: firm, well-rounded breasts, a trim waist set off by the perfect curve of her hips, long, lithe legs. And now I could see the quality of her skin: smooth, polished, the type which reflects light instead of absorbing . . .'

Actually, it was this very assignment that brought Dougherty's seething anger to the surface, and for the first time there was an open confrontation between them. That she defied him hints at the depth of her emotional commitment: the days of their marriage were numbered. 'I had wired her from Texas that I was coming across the country from the east and would be home at a certain time,' relates Dougherty. 'She wasn't there when I got to the apartment. I waited more than an hour, and she finally drove up in the old Ford which looked as though it had been driven through the Mississippi mud. She gave no excuse and I didn't ask for any . . . I knew she was modelling in bikini bathing suits and pleaded with her not to do it. "Why not?" she said, "They pay me for it."'

Legend has it that Monroe was spendthrift, but her salary was far less than stars of lesser stature for years and would probably have remained so had she not gone on suspension at Fox. What Marilyn did discover whilst trying to live on a merchant seaman's allowance was that if she wanted to live in parity with the living standard, it took not only what he earned but what she earned and more too. This was accomplished, according to Dougherty, not only by taking freelance modelling assignments but by hocking the family silver (a wedding gift) along with everything else of value, including the radio. 'She loved to wear fine lingerie,' recounts Dougherty (a characteristic exploited by director Roy Baker when he cast her as the waif-like babysitter with fine tastes in *Don't Bother to Knock*. The irony was that the role lacked credibility since the audience, believing Fox PR about Monroe, could not conceive of her as being working–class and therefore financially hard up). Continues Dougherty: 'I recall having sent her $100 to buy a coat for her Christmas gift. She took $200 out of the bank for the coat. Another time she took every cent out of the account to go to West Virginia to visit the Goddards. I was not surprised,' says Dougherty, 'when I read years later that Marilyn would run up huge bills at the Waldorf and other places and not really know where the money was coming from to pay them.'

The praises heaped upon Monroe by the photographers for whom she freelanced did much to obliterate the doubts Marilyn had about the extent of her beauty and talent. Dougherty recalls sensing gradual personality changes. 'One time when I was home I found a script for a screen test and asked her if she was gunning for a movie career. She denied it and said someone had given her the script as a curiosity.' It has often been noted about Monroe, generally by detractors, that if the day had sixty-four hours, she would still be late for appointments, finding endless things to fuss about. During Jim's absences, however, she made time pay; her most significant achievement being landing a Fox screen test.

Several variations of how Marilyn got the screen test prevail, the first being that Howard Hughes having glimpsed some of Conover's covers of Monroe on *Laff*, *Peek* and *See* whilst convalescing in hospital, arranged a screen test for the model. Since it was well-known that Hughes often signed pretty girls to fabulous, long-term contracts without ever using them and since Marilyn was interested in being showcased as an actress (however meagre the salary) Emmeline Snively arranged a Fox test on the basis of Hughes' interest through the team of Harry Lipton and Helen Ainsworth – joint owners of a small Hollywood agency (now extinct) called NCAC (National Concert Artists Corporation). Another version is that for months Marilyn had been promised a screen test by Ben Lyon, Fox's Head of Casting, and that he only gave her one as a way of ridding himself of her.

Ironically it was Dougherty, home on leave, who drove Marilyn over to Fox for the screen test, whilst protesting: '"I don't like the idea. There are a thousand and one girls walking the streets of Hollywood who can sing and dance and act. And you want to be a movie star" . . . Anyway, I sat out in the car and waited for her. Pretty soon she came out, all in a huff. "You're right," she said, "They're just a bunch of fresh guys."'

Nevertheless, it was obvious that Marilyn's ego was not diminished by the experience, and that Dougherty knew he had lost not to another man but to an American ideal: fame. 'I knew I was losing the fight to keep us together,' he recalls. 'She knew what she wanted and I couldn't offer her anything except promises . . . I thought she was deluding herself about her chances for coping successfully on her own in such a tough business as the movies. I said: "You know this thing isn't all peaches and cream. You're going to be working long hours. You are going to be around people who are wound up tight. People who are going to shove and push. People who are going to be jealous of you, envious. You're going to be under tremendous emotional strain, physical strain. You won't have a chance to relax a minute while you're working. And then when you get home, you'll have to go back to work again and figure out what your lines are going to be for the next day." She just looked at me in silence. She was a very determined young lady . . . I saw there was no hope.'

Apropos of Dougherty's account, an interviewer once asked Monroe what she would have done if one thousand people had told her that she had no chance of becoming a star. To this she replied: 'If everyone without exception had told me the same thing, I should not have listened!'

The famous Fox screen test was shot by Leon Shamroy and directed by Walter Lang on the sound stage where

Betty Grable was shooting the Technicolor film *Mother Wore Tights*. Perhaps Lang never forgot being 'forced' into making the test, for long after Monroe had validated the support of her protectors by becoming Fox's number one box office star, the director continued to treat her disparagingly. When she was bullied by the studio into playing a brief part in *There's No Business Like Show Business*, which was directed by Lang, she was socially ostracized by him during filming.

Monroe's personal makeup man, Whitey Snyder, assigned to her by Darryl Zanuck (along with a personal hairdresser) about the time her career started to peak after her appearance in *Niagara*, recalls preparing Marilyn for that very first screen test. 'I was doing Betty Grable in those days and didn't have much time for Marilyn. I don't know how I got into doing the test, but I did. What was unusual about Marilyn is that she had a particular idea of what she wanted to look like and how she wanted to achieve that. In the makeup room she said: "Why not do this? Why not do that?" We got on to the stage and Shamroy looks at her under the lights and said: "Whitey, who the hell made her up?" I said, "I did." And she spoke right up. She said: "No, he didn't. I did." He said, "Go back to the makeup department. Have Whitey wash her face and do it right."'

Cinematographer Shamroy's remarks about Monroe following the test are worth noting: 'Marilyn is not good looking. She has a bad nose, bad posture and her face is too obvious. She has a bad profile. Hers is a phony sex. To be sexy you don't have to shake your behind. Sex is not a physical thing. It is something inside you.' (Years later in her final *Life* magazine interview, Monroe would echo the same sentiments about sexuality coming from the inside.)

Incidentally, Ben Lyon never confirmed the rumour that Marilyn and he had been lovers, which is unusual, since most of the men in Monroe's life were generally vocal about it. Lyon's version of the screen test runs like this: 'Before I actually tell you how [Marilyn] entered my life I must describe my office to you because it has a direct bearing on the story. That office was, without a doubt, one of the most beautiful rooms I have ever been in. The walls were dark leaf green, the settee was Chinese red, the lamps chartreuse, and the curtains Scots plaid. It sounds awful when you describe it cold like that but when you saw it altogether it really was something. One morning my secretary buzzed on the intercom: "There's a very lovely young lady out here to see you, Mr Lyon, but she hasn't an appointment" . . . The girl who walked through that door took my breath away . . . That dark green wall, the striving colours of that office of mine, made the perfect setting for her golden hair, peaches-and-cream complexion and the simple little flowered cotton dress she was wearing – an inexpensive dress but nicely cut and very nicely filled. The girl's entrance to my office was a picture I shall never forget. Maybe if my office had been in any other colour or if Marilyn had worn black the effect would have been different and the whole story never have happened.'

Her peaches-and-cream complexion must have dazzled Lyon sufficiently for him to have demanded a colour test, since Fox had a policy against shooting tests in colour and it could have cost him his job. 'I chanced it and it came out great. Zanuck saw it and we signed her to $125 per week.' The move proved prophetic since it was with the extended use of Technicolor (which was then being refined) that Monroe was catapulted to superstardom. Her contract stated that all her films had to be made in colour. Marilyn tested at 6 p.m., but Lyon had risked signing her earlier in the day to a standard seven-year contract at $125 per week with six-month options. It was a standard contract with a standard 'morals clause' – that loathed provision which gave the studio absolute right over a player's dominion by granting them the power to drop an option if their conduct was at any time deemed contrary to accepted moral standards. Marilyn's legal guardian, Grace God-dard, who had by then returned from West Virginia, was asked to countersign the contract, since Monroe was still legally under age. Whether Lyon changed her name then and there or waited until after having seen footage of her test, it is safe to surmise that his impression of Marilyn Monroe was solid enough for him to concep-tualize an identity for her. When Marilyn was given the good news by Lyon, she wept convulsively shaking her head in disbelief.

During one of Marilyn's several forays on to the Fox lot, while attempting to get an appointment with Ben Lyon, Marilyn met Robert Slatzer, a young, friendly mid-westerner about the same age as she working for the Scripps-Howard newspaper chain as their Hollywood-based reporter. Slatzer remembers Marilyn as being a bundle of nerves and recalls that in her excite-ment at the prospect of an interview she dropped the portfolio of covers she had been carrying, having tripped on something and broken the heel of her shoe (Slatzer recounts that Monroe always wore stiletto heels). 'I felt sorry for her,' he says, 'and wondered whether she knew what she was letting herself in for. In those days a girl age seventeen or eighteen was signed to a long-term contract which was a rip-off, since if they did go the distance they were finished by age twenty-nine or thirty. In other words, when they should have been making big bucks (at the acme of their appeal) the studio had them under contract and was paying them peanuts. You see,' he observes, 'the studios felt that this was their entitlement for having taken virtual nobodies and groomed them: giving them dental work, teaching them to eat, arranging dates with big stars, enrolling them in acting classes before launching them on a big promotion. To the public it seemed as if these girls had walked off

the street with the polish and glamour they projected
in films. What they failed to realize was that behind
every debutante was a working-class girl being exploited to bits just for the promise of a chance to make
good.'

Slatzer goes on to comment upon the things which in
those days were implied, but which couldn't be explicitly
stated in contracts. The studios couldn't, in effect, forbid
a girl to marry but they could suggest that the expense
being lavished by the studio to create a marketable
personality would be undermined if the girl became
matrimonially involved. They could point out that any
decision she took in that regard would affect whether
her option was picked up. They couldn't tell her not to
bear children, nor could they directly compel her to
abort. But it is common knowledge that studio phys-
icians often performed abortions. Furthermore they
couldn't coerce someone to have plastic surgery but they
could equivocate about picking up someone's option or
using them in films after they were signed until they
made the necessary improvements. More than one studio
had a resident dentist, electrolytic cosmetician (to re-
move facial fuzz common to stars such as Marilyn
Monroe) and a hair stylist (responsible not only for
dyeing and perming but also for altering the contour of
one's hairline).

It is apparent that Monroe was hypersensitive to
suggestion, for within days of signing the Fox contract
she had left for Las Vegas where she intended to establish
residency and file for divorce with monies advanced by
De Dienes. A note scribbled to Emmeline Snively was
typically starstruck. Dated 25 May 1946 it reads:
'. . . Las Vegas is really a colourful town with the
Helldorado celebration and all . . . Roy Rogers was in
town making a picture. I met him and rode his horse
"Trigger" (cross my heart I did) . . . Please give my
best regards to Mrs Snively and Miss Smith, also to

Dick Miller if you see him. I hope [he] has been able to sell some of those pictures, he is so nice. Is John Randolph or Paul Parry back in town yet? How's Mr Bloom? I wonder if Eccleston Agency is ever going to pay me? . . . Love, Norma Jeane.'

It is this story, embroidered by Miller, that Monroe relived fifteen years later when filming *Misfits*, but relived with the fury which the gods must have been saving up. Although it purports to be a woman's story, *Misfits* is coldly misogynist, little of the film's viewpoint decidedly female. If anything, Roslyn's sexual velocity is provocation for the men to behave belligerently toward one another. The only possible way one could construe the story as feminist is to dismiss Monroe's sexuality as sexist and to postulate a unisex woman as the ideal, representing as she does neither threat nor provocation to men.

Divorce papers were duly despatched overseas to Dougherty, whose reaction to receiving a 'Dear John' letter is recounted with considerable anguish. 'I felt as though I'd been hit on the head with a steam shovel. I had all sorts of thoughts in those first few minutes after opening the envelope. I asked the ship's officers what chance I had to telephone or send a cable to my wife . . . As the day wore on, I got madder and madder, and before nightfall I'd cancelled her allotment.' It is probably at this juncture that Marilyn pawned her wedding band. When Dougherty accused her of avarice, she rebutted with the accusation: 'You stopped sending money. I had to eat!'

Making a last stab at saving the marriage, Dougherty got some leave time to return home, and after prizing from Aunt Ana the phone number of the place where Marilyn had established residency, he rang up Las Vegas. 'The voice at the other end of the phone sounded strange,' he recounts. '"What the devil happened to your voice?" I asked her. "They want me to keep it low.

It sounds better," she said.' ('They' being the movie moguls.)

No match for the studio (a lesson DiMaggio would also painfully learn) Dougherty listened patiently while Marilyn explained how 'they' had also told her she must be divorced in order to have a contract. 'She said she'd made up her mind that the career was what she wanted, but that she'd never love anyone but me. She wanted me to sign the divorce papers and thanked me for not making any trouble about all this,' he remembers.

While the popular account of the divorce implies that Doughtery capitulated readily, the reality is that he put up a fierce struggle to save the marriage. 'We talked most of the next afternoon. I had calmed down overnight . . . I asked her to consider carefully the step she was taking.'

The last encounter between Jim and Marilyn was a very moving one. Dougherty stopped by to sign the divorce papers. He left her with both furnishings and car, but he took the phonograph, which is interesting since it is the first thing (in tandem with a new car) that Monroe bought when she began earning a bit of money. 'I recall she was very gay that day, full of high spirits. And it wasn't because I'd signed the papers but because the studio, Fox, had finally given her a new name, Marilyn Monroe. She said she'd taken the Marilyn from a grandmother on one side and the Monroe from one of her grandmother Della's husbands. 'What do you think of it?' she asked me. 'It's beautiful,' I said, and she beamed.

A postscript to the first marriage to James Dougherty is recalled in a visit he made several months later with a girlfriend. Monroe's response: 'You're not supposed to be going out with girls like that.' Warm, loving and protective, Marilyn never really let go of those she loved.

7
Fox – The First Time Around

When Monroe was interviewed by the late Edward R. Murrow on his *Person to Person* CBS television programme in 1955, she complained at having been cut out of all the films she made at Fox during her first run with the studio following the contract signed on 26 August 1946. (The contract lasted for twelve months, after which her option was dropped. Monroe then returned to Fox in 1950 on a week's contract when she was cast for a showstopping walk-on in *All About Eve*. Following her success in the role she was signed to a standard seven-year deal.)

At the time, however, Monroe believed that she would be given a chance to show what she could do, and she worked harder almost than any other actor to improve herself. 'She was the most conscientious youngster signed by the company,' said Lyon years later. 'She devoted all her time to study, training, and exercising so that when an opportunity came she would be prepared.'

Whilst the studio tutored you in voice, acting, movement and dance there were large gaps left in your education, Monroe discovering for herself the truth behind the axiom that the more you know the more you don't know. What finally emerged as the classic Monroe was the result of fifteen years commitment to the disciplines of drama, voice, movement, dance and mime. It was not uncommon for her to study with two or three acting coaches simultaneously; or, for that matter, to work out not only with the studio dance masters but privately to study mime technique. Fox production chief Darryl Zanuck was never enthusiastic about Monroe, finding her deportment lacking in 'class'. Right up to the time when she emerged in *Niagara* as a major film star he maintained that her appearance in films was 'decidedly wooden'.

For all its publicized glamour, life as a film starlet was not much fun. Monroe hocked everything of value to pay both for acting lessons and a room at the Hollywood Studio Club (a posh sounding women's residence but in reality an upmarket YWCA located in the heart of Hollywood a good distance from the Fox Studios which were situated in Century City). Only after years of struggle could Marilyn finally afford a flat nearby the Fox lot. A friend recalls: 'She'd eat junk food, often skipping meals entirely. She had few clothes, often borrowing ball gowns from the studio costume department (since starlets were obliged to show up at premières) which wasn't strictly "on" but since they liked her no one offered any objection. Producers often complained that Marilyn dressed poorly for interviews. One time she became so angry that she told a reporter: "Starlets should not be expected to dress grandly on what we earn." Zanuck or somebody saw the interview, and the next day a memo was circulated, calling attention to the confidence breach.'

Monroe, however, was determined to succeed. 'I spent my entire salary on dramatic lessons, dancing lessons and singing lessons,' she recounted. 'I bought books to read. I sneaked scripts off the set and sat up alone in my room reading them aloud in front of the mirror.' Whilst providing her with an in-house coach, Fox also underwrote for a period of two months the classes she enrolled in at the famous Actors Lab – the Hollywood home of the Group Theater, thought by the American Right to be a breeding ground for communists, radicals and free-thinkers – where for $10 per lesson Monroe got to observe some of America's finest actors such as John Garfield, Luther Adler, Morris Carnovsky, and Lee Cobb. It is here she struck up a friendship with another starlet, Shelley Winters, under contract at the time to Columbia Pictures. Capturing something of the schizoid approach to movie acting, Winters observes: 'The "acting" I saw there had nothing to do with the "acting" I was being paid to learn at Columbia Pictures.' A sentiment which Monroe might well have shared.

The very first film roles depicted by Monroe are omitted from her filmography altogether, and yet she did in fact have walk-ons in both *The Shocking Miss Pilgrim*, George Seaton's 1946 film starring Betty Grable where she portrayed a switchboard operator, and *You Were Meant for Me*, a Jeanne Crain film in which she was cast as a dance extra in a bandstand sequence. Walter Lang recalls having watched Marilyn in conference with the Fox coach discussing the way to play a two-minute walk-on in George Seaton's *The Shocking Miss Pilgrim*. 'Monroe had a bit part as a switchboard operator. Visiting the set one day, [I] heard a woman's voice repeating the word 'Hullo' over and over in various inflections. It was Marilyn, aided by her voice coach, practising for her big moment. But when it came she'd completely forgotten what to say.'

If Marilyn had known at the time when she entered films that everybody in Hollywood was partially 'bionic', she might perhaps have stayed away. Instead she was victim of the most outrageous innocence. She believed that by playing the game fairly its rewards would be hers. Having virtually exhausted all her time and money – hocking everything she owned of value –

it came as quite a shock when she was told by Fox that her option was not being renewed. A friend recalls: 'She cried and cried when someone (one of Zanuck's flunkies) told her plainly: "Your type of looks is definitely against you!"'

What turned Zanuck off? 'He had Betty Grable. Why did he need another blonde?' is Rupert Allan's assessment of the situation. Also, she was pigeonholed as a pinup – someone whose appeal was limited to truckers and workers willing to buy the newspaper or magazine which carried her photo, but unwilling to invest a couple of dollars at a film show. Or so they thought!

Fox PR man Flack Jones recalls having worked with Monroe during her first round at Fox and supports Ben Lyon's view. 'She was very co-operative. Everyone in the studio PR department at Fox worked on her – the picture division, the magazine division, the fan magazine division, and the planters who plant the columns. We did our best with her but she just hadn't grown up enough. She was great as far as looks went but she didn't know how to make the most of her looks or what to do with them. That came with practice.'

The art shots were similar to the camera work she had done with Conover, De Dienes and Kelley – shooting either at the Fox gallery or on location in colour or black and white at the beach, mountains, or fields, water skiing, picnicking, or walking – 'anything where we could use a beautiful girl with a great body,' says Jones.

'There was in addition a lot of art shot on the lot in the gallery: Marilyn was often called upon to hike from the publicity department to the gallery across a quarter mile of open studio space,' he says. One of the most memorable photo sessions was the one which had been arranged for the week when she was brought back to Fox to film the walk-on in *All About Eve*. Whilst she should have been allowed to spend the time conceptualizing the role and running through her lines, the PR people had booked her into a gallery shoot allowing her but the briefest warm-up time on the set. Then and now, if Mankiewicz had any complaint about the appropriation of an actor's time in any other capacity than that for which he was hired, the objection should have been lodged with the front office. The reality is that the studio never in any way sought to explain that the unreliability attributed to Monroe was actually caused by their own desire to utilize every precious moment she spent on the lot in photo sessions, art layouts, and press interviews.

That particular shoot was well remembered by Jones because it was one where Marilyn was scantily clad in a flesh-coloured négligé. 'She liked it so much she wouldn't take it off. Afterwards she had to walk a quarter mile back to the wardrobe department to get her clothes. A strong wind had arisen as she strolled up the company street past the administration building. Word of what was happening passed around like lightning. It was like the Lindbergh home-coming. People were leaning out of every window and there was Marilyn, naive and completely unperturbed, smiling and waving up at everybody she knew, didn't know or hoped to know.'

Curiously the one executive who missed the display was Zanuck, and it was not long thereafter that, still not having met Monroe, and being unaware of her charms, he failed to renew her contract. Having stormed into his office hoping to precipitate an encounter so as to discover *why* her option had been dropped, she was simply told by one of the great man's secretaries that he was in Sun Valley, skiing, and wouldn't be back until the following week.

The quality of absolute and total abstraction, peculiar to Monroe, was exploited knowingly by the lady some years later in complicity with director Billy Wilder in *The Seven Year Itch*, by which time she was well aware of what is referred to in theatre chat as one's instrument and how best it can be used. Which is rather sweet, since it proves that however wilful the studio had been in its campaign of sexploitation it had not been so severe as to handicap the lady altogether, since Monroe proved herself able to adapt what she had learned as a stills model and to use it in a manner that approached the mime work of the great silent film stars.

Designer Travilla having dressed Monroe in most of her films, ponders the question of 'why' she was such a superb stills model. 'Marilyn "knew" how to be a star (she had the way). The first thing was to get the public's attention. She would come on the lot almost daily. The cameramen were sitting there with nothing to do and they loved to shoot pictures of Marilyn. Before she became a star she probably was in every magazine there was. She had this thing with the camera. And she knew how to use herself. It was a remarkable combination. Remember this girl has never, ever been able to be copied. There may be look-alikes but no near-alikes. I think that the emotionalism was unconscious. It was just there. And that is why people cannot copy her. The Mamie Van Dorens and others come up with the sex, but they do not have the innocence.' In truth, Marilyn was nothing if not innocent – she believed in the Dream. She wasn't trying to fool anyone. But she was intelligent enough (more so as she aged) to be able to distil that essential quality in herself, the quality that was Monroe, and communicate it to the public. According to Travilla ever since she was a child she wanted it: 'She told me once: "Since I was a child, I had nothing to do. I was poor. I used to look at movie magazines and cut the pictures out of Jean Harlow and Clark Gable. That's what I wanted to be some day – a Jean Harlow and to act with Clark Gable." As you know she became far bigger than Jean Harlow. And her last film was with Clark Gable.'

Whilst designers Orry-Kelly (*Some Like it Hot*) and

Jean Louis (*Misfits*) dressed what shall historically be remembered as the Later Marilyn, it was Travilla whose flamboyant, theatrical fashions donned the Earlier Incarnation. And it is these fashions worn by her in *Gentlemen Prefer Blondes* and *The Seven Year Itch* with which she is most closely identified. His first meeting with Monroe was accidental, and yet the friendship lasted for years. 'I worked in what was called the gallery where two or three contract designers had our offices and fitting rooms,' says Travilla. 'One day there were no fitting rooms available and Marilyn asked if she could use mine. I said: "Fine, wonderful", and I helped her to find some things to put on. We did this many times to the point where Marilyn would never go in for a camera sitting unless I would be with her. If I happened to be on hiatus, I would have to be called in and paid by the studio because she wouldn't shoot without me.

'One of the fun experiences is that we had *nothing* left that she hadn't been photographed in that was current in styling, and she was in hot demand by the press. We had ten feet of white fox – a boa, which I gave her to put on. "You can wrap it around your shoulders," I said. "It will just look cuddly and wonderful. You won't even need a dress with your body."

'What happened next depends on your knowing the description of the gallery. It was a long, narrow section divided by sliding doors. One side was my office where I would draw my pictures which had a couch, radio and a plant; and the other room was strictly fitted with opening doors and at the far end was a bank with mirrors.

'I heard a rapping on the sliding doors – she popped her head in. She had this white fox boa draped around those beautiful shoulders, cuddled at the middle covering the front of her. "Is this what you mean, Mr Travilla?" She didn't realize, or did realize, that that was the first glimpse I got of her beautiful bottom.'

Coach Lytess once implied that Monroe had a problem getting along with women. Monroe properly took exception to the remark, reading into it as she did some invidious sexual inference. But it is true that whilst encountering both designers Helen Rose and Edith Head during the days she spent as a starlet, it was Travilla she chose for gallery shoots and feature films. Actress Jan Sterling, observing Marilyn in the early days remarks: 'She was conscious of the image she wanted to present and called Sidney Skolsky asking him about this and that and clothes and men and such. Which is okay, but to the wardrobe designer at the studio she would have been a bitch.'

'The press never tired of Marilyn,' explains Travilla. 'They couldn't get enough of her. One time I was up in Fox publicity and they were talking with *Photoplay* magazine. Fox wanted them to do a story about Susan Hayward. And they said: "We'll do a story about Hayward (which we find dull) if we can have a cover on Marilyn Monroe,"' says Travilla. She had already been on the cover for the previous two months. 'This is the time when I had to improvize to create something new. I took the turquoise satin and draped it on her naked body and gave her the jewellery at the throat and it made a wonderful cover. It looked as if she was wearing a glorious gown.'

Travilla, who knew her well over the years, says Monroe was a woman of extremes. 'She liked to shock – she could look both magnificent or hideous – like a dirty little bum or a sex queen. I recall getting a call from Marilyn one day to have lunch. She was wearing her typical rehearsal outfit – a great big turtleneck sweater – the big bulky kind with spots on it; and a skin-tight pair of Capri pants. Lanolin was smeared all over her face and hair. But she still looked pretty, 'cause underneath all that was a light eyeliner, lipliner, rouge on her nose, and chin. Everything was a pretence. I said: "You have got makeup on." She replied: "Sssssh. Don't tell any-one."'

There were plenty of times when Monroe would enter the Fox commissary in the grandest manner, causing, in Travilla's words, something approaching a riot. 'Marilyn would "never" go into lunch alone. When she was shooting a picture she would unfailingly make an entrance and she always did so on the arm of an attractive male escort.'

Screenwriter Henry Ephron, whose credits (in tandem with wife, Phoebe) include *There's No Business Like Show Business* which co-starred Monroe, refers to her inimitably as a 'Head Twister'. Says Henry, 'That was a term we bestowed on only two people: Cary Grant and Marilyn Monroe. His beauty and her beauty made them something special. Cary had the most winning personality of all time: smiles and everything – he shook your hand if he saw your picture and said how much he loved it; and Marilyn – irresistible. She had the most beautiful bosom in the world and the most "fuckable" mouth!'

On these occasions, when she was shooting a picture, she'd come to lunch in full makeup, wearing a wrap-around jersey robe that Travilla had made for her with ostrich on the sleeves. 'She wore nothing under it. Just that beautiful body,' he says.

'We'd sit at the far end of the commissary in a section known as the Café de Paris where all the stars had separate tables. I'd just watch as she slithered through – a cloud of ostrich feathers and jersey. Remember this was the lunch hour and the Fox commissary is very busy at noon and noisy with people banging plates and utensils and the waitresses serving. But when Marilyn entered the room, everything stopped. There was a silence. Big Fox stars like Bette Davis, Rita Hayworth, Betty Grable and Lauren Bacall, Gene Tierney were all eating and chatting; but when Marilyn passed by, everyone stopped. Bette Davis's spoon remained near the side of her mouth while she just watched Marilyn walk. They couldn't take their eyes off her. How did she dare to be that beautiful!'

Flack Jones also recounts the effect of Marilyn's appearance at a press reception in the days when she was confined primarily to cheesecake art. 'We took her to all the cocktail parties we thought were important. When *Picture* magazine had its reception we told Marilyn we thought she should show so that we could introduce her to various editors, columnists and radio/TV people. She waited until everyone had arrived and then she came in wearing a red gown in a size or two too small which had what [publicist] Joe Hyams called "breakaway straps". Everyone stopped what they were doing and their eyes went: "Boing! Boing!" She got sixteen simultaneous covers the same month from that single appearance alone.'

Yet however popular she appeared to be, she found herself unable to get anything more than a walk-on in a bona fide Fox feature. Her appearance in *Scudda Hoo, Scudda Hay* as girlfriend of leading lady, June Haver, was no doubt occasioned by the fortuitously accidental meeting with Fox's founder, Joseph Schenck, then an ageing mogul in his seventies whose visage Marilyn once described as 'resembling a lobster'. In the best B-movie tradition Monroe was stopped on the Fox lot by Schenck driving along in his chauffeured Rolls-Royce. He handed her his card on which he had scribbled his telephone number and invited her to come around for Sunday buffet. 'Ring me,' he bellowed. 'Come for supper. It's open house. Eat all you want. You'll enjoy it.' Schenck was famous for his Sunday buffets, which he loved to give amid the splendour of his glorious Holmby Hills mansion nestled in the rolling hills of Beverly north of Sunset Boulevard – a hamlet inhabited by millionaire superstars, businessmen and bankers.

Marilyn had always denied that there was any intimacy between them, describing Schenck instead as an ageing patriarch whose love of people and films was what, in its heyday, made the industry vibrate with possibility. 'The first few times I went [to his parties] was because he was the studio head, and then (later on) because I liked him. I enjoyed sitting around the fireplace hearing him talk about love and sex. It annoyed me to be referred to as "Joe Schenck's girl". He never laid a finger on my wrist. He was interested in me because I was a good table ornament and because I was what he called "an offbeat personality".'

Earl Wilson, a noted purveyor of scandal, confirms the possibility of a platonic relationship, offering up in support of the lady's character the testimony of stud, George Jessel. Quotes Wilson: 'George said that he held out to [Marilyn] the lure of fine clothes and good contacts if she would – and she wouldn't.'

Sheilah Graham, however, claims that Marilyn was more harlot than starlet. 'Her most important role was to serve drinks, cigarettes and cigars to Darryl Zanuck, Joe Schenck and their friends while they played gin rummy in a private room at the studio. There were other starlets besides her waiting on their masters. They were known as The Gin Rummy Girls and most of them were let go after six months or a year for a new batch of starlets who would perform the same duties. This one, because of her protector, Joe Schenck, remained for [eighteen] months.'

Equally cynical about the way in which Monroe manoeuvred a featured role for herself in *Scudda Hoo*, Graham suggests that Ben Lyon had used the prospective offer to get Monroe the Fox contract and that when it came time to deliver he prevailed upon his friend – a casting director for Sol Wurtzel, to find a small part for Monroe in *Scudda Hoo*, the Wurtzel film then being cast.

The circumstances surrounding Monroe's abbreviated

appearance in the film are fascinating, since they emphasize the kind of battle which raged over Monroe at Fox and ultimately resulted in her dismissal. But first, let us return to Schenck and the bond of affection between them that lasted years after Marilyn had become an international star and Schenck was *de facto* out of the business. Press agent Rupert Allen accompanied Marilyn on a trip to Schenck's house in the late fifties. 'She asked me one day if I would go to see Schenck at his house. He was dying,' says Allan. 'Marilyn said: "I don't want to go alone. Will you go with me?" She felt an obligation. Although there was never any romance, Schenck had been awfully good to her when she was living at the Studio Club. She'd go there for Sunday night buffet. He'd say: "Eat up. Have all you want!" The men would play poker (it was not an all-evening orgy).

'The nurse came running down the steps and said: "Of course Mr Schenck is waiting for you right now, Miss Monroe. Please go right up." From the room I heard peals of laughter – his, hers, telling old jokes. His brother says: "I don't understand it. I have been here ten days. Some days he won't even see me. It is the first time I have heard my brother laugh in years. It is the best thing in the world. It is the best treatment anyone can give. Please come back."

'About three weeks later Marilyn was at a dinner party given by David Selznick and Jennifer Jones: next-door neighbours of mine,' says Allan. 'Everyone was seated around a long dining room table. About three or four people up from Marilyn was Greg Bautzer (a Hollywood lawyer). He yelled at Marilyn in front of everyone that she really should be ashamed of herself – "You haven't even been to see Joseph Schenck and he was of so much help to you. You are nothing. You care just about yourself."

'This is the first time I know of Marilyn fighting back for herself. She said: "That is not true. I have been to see Joe Schenck. He is one of my dearest friends and I owe a lot to him. You are right. I had a long visit with him just last week." But,' adds Allan, 'usually Marilyn would burst into tears about things like that!' (It is worth noting that Monroe's life, although brief, was full of public humiliations.)

Curiously, for all her sweetness, generosity and warmth there was something about Monroe which turned off some men (very surprising) and women (less surprising). Whilst Shelley Winters and she got along, sneaking off to Hollywood premières, where together they'd star gaze, most of the other girls at the studio avoided Monroe. When asked about the friends she had made whilst living at the Studio Club, she named one: Eleanor Parker. 'We met at a big party. A few moments after I had been introduced to her, I went into the powder room where I heard some girls discussing me. They tore me apart – my clothes, my manners, everything. I stood listening, sick at heart. Then a third voice spoke up and said: "You say those things about Marilyn, but you don't know her. If you actually knew her, you'd realize that most of the things said about her are false." This gave me the courage to go into the room. Eleanor looked up and greeted me like an old friend: "Hello, Marilyn," she said. "How lovely you look tonight." I thanked her, trying to hold back the tears. When the others left hurriedly with mumbled excuses, I turned to her and said: "I don't know how to thank you." Her answer: "Let's be friends. That will be thanks enough for me."'

Despite the four or five films which had preceded *Scudda Hoo*, it is this film which is credited by Monroe as being her first, presumably because in conception it was a run-on role which only in the editing room was pared down to a walk-on. By the time she was cast in *Scudda Hoo* Monroe had been at Fox for nearly a year, long enough to have prepared herself for a proper supporting role. As originally envisaged the role of 'Betty', friend of the film's star, actress June Haver, was to be ongoing. But as it transpired, much of the footage was left on the cutting room floor. In effect, Monroe appeared in only two brief scenes: one, where she greets Haver as they leave church one Sunday morning; and the other, when she is in a rowboat with co-star Colleen Townsend. The reasons are two-fold: firstly, the studio felt it was too confusing with two blondes in the same picture. (Ironically, when Marilyn pulled rank at Fox arguing about hair colour on *Something's Got to Give* she was accused of being paranoid.) Secondly, it was Zanuck's decision that she was 'too trampy-looking'.

The Fox boss's myopia about Monroe, even taking into account her pathetic incarnation the first time around, has been a source of censure both at the time and for years to come. 'I think one of the few [Zanuck] missed among the beginners was Marilyn Monroe,' writes Sheilah Graham. 'In the first place he disliked her. And in the second she was having an affair with his boss, Joe Schenck.' Rupert Allan concurs: 'Zanuck wasn't perfect, you know. He did make a film called *Woodrow Wilson* which only he and his mother saw. He had a big star in Betty Grable, and he didn't need a second big star. He just needed someone to keep Betty Grable in line. He never believed in Marilyn.'

In reality, however, it was not Zanuck but Spyros Skouras (head of Fox's New York office) whose distaste for Monroe was the real reason behind her option being dropped. Biographers of Skouras insist that he liked distinguished, elegant ladies and was cold in consequence to both Marilyn Monroe and Jayne Mansfield.

Writes Zanuck's biographer Leo Guild, 'When Zanuck originally saw some film on Monroe in *Scudda Hoo*, he asked Skouras to look at it, saying: "I think we've got something here." "You're in charge of the stars," Skouras said. "I'm too busy with money to be bothered about bit players." Zanuck heralded: "She's no bit player. She's going to be a star." His answer was: "God-dammit, leave me alone," and he walked away. In the end Zanuck insisted Skouras look at some film on Monroe . . . His only comment was: "She has nice breasts. Do what you want."' (Years later when Monroe was a superstar contemplating marriage to Arthur Miller, it was Skouras who asked her if she'd like to be married at his home.)

In August 1947 Fox declined to renew Monroe's option and Ben Lyon was given the role of the bearer of bad tidings. Lyon vividly recounted the events of that ill-fated morning in an interview years later: 'My inter-com buzzed. It was Darryl Zanuck. He was brief and to the point: "Marilyn Monroe. Her option is coming up," he said. "That's right," I replied. "Drop her. We're not exercising the option," said Zanuck. I could hardly believe my ears. I managed to stammer: "You don't mean that?" down the phone. Zanuck said: "Yes" and rang off.

'When I recovered I rushed to Lew Schreiber, general manager of the studios and one of the most competent general managers in the business. "Is it true? I've got to call Marilyn and tell her she's fired?" I asked Lew. "That's right," he said.' (Incidentally Henry Ephron, in my interview with him, characterizes Schreiber as being in contention with Monroe. 'He didn't treat her well. I understand at one point that she went to him to borrow some money 'cause she had found a small house and they turned her down. There was no reason to turn her down. Marilyn had no other source of income except Fox. And they turned her down.' Why? 'Maybe she didn't play ball with the boys in the front office or maybe she did and they double-crossed her.')

Lyon continues: 'I phoned and asked her to come over. "Marilyn," I said, "I'm afraid the studio is not exercising its option on you." She broke down and cried. For the first time, I really saw the amount of emotion she was capable of. She wasn't acting. But it gave me some idea of her range, and made me feel more than ever that the studio was making a big mistake in letting her go.

'"I'm sure that, in spite of this setback, you'll be a very great star one day," I said. And they weren't just sympathetic words. I meant them.'

It is at this juncture that Monroe went storming into Zanuck's office only to discover that he was on a skiing holiday in Sun Valley. She questioned why Joseph Schenck couldn't have had her reinstated and that he didn't, couldn't or wouldn't put her into a mood from which it took weeks to recover. 'I hated myself for having been such a fool and had illusions about how attractive I was. I got out of bed and looked in the mirror. Something horrible had happened. I wasn't attractive. I saw a coarse, crude-looking blonde. I was looking at myself with Mr Zanuck's eyes. And I saw what he had seen – a girl whose looks were too big a handicap for a career in the movies.'

So what was the story? Why was Monroe fired? She was insignificant, a bit player, whose film presence didn't affect grosses – yet! But people with less talent had been retained and, besides, she pulled her own weight, fulfilling publicity demands above and beyond the call of duty. Why not keep her on payroll for another couple of months? Better still, why not use her in a part of substance?

A sceptic might infer that she had been had by Zanuck, Schenck and Skouras; and that having had her, there was no reason to keep her around, threatening her with the blacklist (which prevailed in those days) if she talked. Columnist James Bacon admits to being baffled. The circumstances seem to have been in contradiction. Zanuck was a ladies' man. 'Darryl – he loved women. Sex for Darryl was definitely a yes–yes!' says Bacon. And Monroe was a lady. 'Boy, if you think she was good-looking in the fifties, you should have seen her in 1947. She was gorgeous!' he sighs.

Was Zanuck on the make? 'Zanuck probably screwed almost every actress on the lot,' said a gossip. 'It was never a condition of any kind. It was just one of those things.'

Zanuck denies it: 'It was too big a gamble and a pay off meant a contract or exercising an option,' he told his biographer. 'I never touched a soul. There was a great rumour about a certain big star and me. A great great rumour. I swear I never even knew if she was a man or a woman off the screen. And Linda Darnell. I never knew Linda Darnell from Adam . . . not even Marilyn Monroe. I hated her. I wouldn't have slept with her if she paid me . . .'

8
The Columbia Débâcle

While Joseph Schenck did not, could not or would not pull rank to see to it that Marilyn was reinstated by Fox, he did wait for an opportune moment to see whether a contract could be negotiated for her at Columbia. Monroe remembers the incident in her autobiography compiled by business partner Milton Greene, vice-president of Marilyn Monroe Productions. '. . . Mr Schenck's secretary invited me to dinner . . . when we were sitting in the living room Mr Schenck said to me, "How are things going at the studio?" I smiled at him because I was glad he hadn't had a hand in my being fired. "I lost my job there last week," I said. Mr Schenck looked at me and I saw a thousand stories in his face – stories of all the girls he had known who had lost jobs . . . The history of Hollywood looked out of his tired eyes and he said, "Keep going . . . Try X Studio . . ."'

The three-month interlude set Monroe back a few paces, not just financially but emotionally too. Whilst a Fox starlet she could afford to live at the Studio Club and attend acting classes by supplementing her weekly salary with whatever she could earn as a freelance model. Having lost her job, she was once again living hand to mouth, and was forced to yield her Studio Club accommodation for something more economical in the way of a furnished room. Surely if she were Joseph

Schenck's mistress, she would have been maintained in a far grander style?

Marilyn's relationship with columnist Sidney Skolsky dates back to when she was Norma Jeane, living in Sherman Oaks and married to James Dougherty. In between photo sessions for men's magazines, she'd pop by Schwab's Drugstore where Skolsky kept an office. In the forties and fifties Schwab's was a coffee shop (now defunct) on the Sunset Strip which was then frequented by all the big stars talking deals with their agents or producers. It was a great little breakfast place, not dissimilar from what Nate and Al's or the Polo Lounge is today. In the days before she hocked her Ford, Marilyn used to drive Skolsky around town (he didn't drive) shuttling him from one interview appointment to another.

It was at Schwab's that Monroe was introduced to John Carroll: a musical comedy performer, currently freelance, and generally referred to as a road-show Clark Gable because of his uncanny (and unfortunately diminishing) resemblance to the famous actor. He was then married to MGM talent scout, Lucille Ryman. One of them must have come from money (most probably Ryman) as they lived in a big, plush apartment on the corner of Fountain and Crescent in West Hollywood not far from Schwab's. In addition, they had a ranch in Encino (a San Fernando Valley suburb) where director John Huston stabled his horses.

At the time, Marilyn was living in a furnished room where only recently she had been mugged by an off-duty policeman from whom she had asked directions, and it was in the spirit of comraderie that the Carrolls suggested that she use a spare room in their spacious West Hollywood flat. The offer of accommodation was only part of the deal, since what the team really had in mind was signing Marilyn to a personal management contract. This they did on 4 December 1947, and it lasted three

months until Columbia picked up her option. In return
for whatever percentage was agreed upon, the Carrolls
advanced monies for clothes, makeup and hair dressing
(the question each week was: what colour blonde?), plus
acting lessons. The nicest thing about the arrangement
was being coached by Carroll, a singer, which prepared
her for an unexpected singing role in the Columbia
musical *Ladies of the Chorus*. (The original plan had been
to dub Monroe, though this proved unnecessary when
she showed herself able to sing every note. Marilyn
would never use a double, which meant protracted and
often laborious sound takes, sometimes as many as fifty
or sixty.) For a superstar to do their own vocals in
the old days of Hollywood was both incredible and
unnecessary. That Marilyn struggled to be an authentic
performer elicited the praise of at least one columnist,
Dorothy Kilgallen, whose commendations were pro-
fuse.

During the day, appointments would be arranged for
Marilyn with producers and directors whom Ryman
knew were casting for players. Apparently Marilyn became something of a nuisance often bothering Ryman
four and five times a day with questions about hair
colour; clothes; readings, etc. When she could not get
hold of Ryman, she would call Carroll. Ryman told her
outright not to ring Carroll on the set when he was
filming. But what fundamentally precipitated the breach
was not Monroe's insecurity but her presumption that
Carroll was in love with her, since by Monroe's reckon-
ing, no man could be that good to her if he wasn't in
love with her. Ryman is reputed to have replied that
Carroll could have a divorce if he wanted one. Which
of course he didn't, leaving Monroe in the situation of
having lost Carroll, the management contract and the
prospect of going to the ranch the couple were building
in the San Fernando Valley.

It is worth noting that this is the first time (and there

would be others) that Marilyn found herself in a situation where she got, in Billy Wilder's inimitable words 'the fuzzy end of the lollipop'. Did she fantasize about Carroll – mistaking patronage for affection? Or did he lead her along – allowing her to believe that he loved her, wanted to marry her and would leave his wife?

The only other person privy to the circumstances of the affair, hitherto unreported, is Robert Slatzer. He told me of a conversation he had with Carroll about Marilyn years later: '"Sure we had an affair. But what can you expect when two people are alone together? What would you have done?" he asked me, adding defensively, "Lucille found out and I feared I would be sued, divorced or locked up."' (Evidently Lucille's hold was too strong.) Another version recounted by a friend insists that Marilyn and Carroll had a celibate relationship, as Monroe believed in the harmony of love and marriage. 'Carroll was trying to sound "macho". Actually he was a very gentlemanly, old-fashioned guy. He respected Marilyn and I doubt that he laid a hand on her.' The happy ending, of course, is that Ryman (who perhaps felt guilty about John's philandering) got Marilyn the coveted role of Angela, Louis Calhern's mistress in John Huston's *Asphalt Jungle*. A very meaty role, which had been promised to Lola Albright, it gave Monroe a real chance to show what she could do; and, in consequence of her superb performance, she was, at last, taken with greater seriousness by the film industry.

At last when Schenck made his move he did so not through crony Harry Cohn, founder of Columbia Pictures, but by purloining a favour from Jonie Taps, a Columbia Pictures producer who was then preparing a low-budget or 'B' musical called *Ladies of the Chorus* slated to topline Adele Jurgens, a contract actress whose grace designer Jean Louis (then under contract to Columbia) compared to cement. 'She didn't know how to move or to sit,' carps Jean Louis. Taps agreed to co-star

Monroe with Jurgens as a favour to Schenck. The contract, signed on 9 March 1948, was for a period of six months, and terminated on 8 September 1948. Although it was believed that her voice would be dubbed, it was agreed that Marilyn would nevertheless be coached by Columbia's vocal tutor, Fred Karger, as a standard part of studio training.

For all the horrid things which have been said about Cohn in relation to Monroe, it must be remembered firstly that he knew, liked and respected her mother whose paycheck he kept coming long after she was hospitalized for mental illness. Secondly, he liked Schenck and approved the Columbia contract even though he knew that the lady had been dropped by one major film studio. Thirdly, he made no bones about allowing Marilyn to co-star with one of his most important stars in a major film (which also featured in a bit part one of their finest contract players: Shelley Winters).

It is true, however, that Cohn prefaced the debut by making a few structural changes in his newest property, despatching Monroe for hair, skin and dental work. Naturally curly, baby soft and hard to manage, Monroe's hairline was drawn for her at Columbia and excess fuzz removed, first with hot wax, later by electrolysis. 'Marilyn's new wide brow transformed her from being merely attractive into a beauty,' writes Sheilah Graham. 'But she always had a problem with her hair. She had resisted dyeing it blonde (and when she had) her hair broke under the continual assaults of peroxide . . . There was fine, downy, blonde hair all over her face (later removed by electrolysis) . . . She would spend hours experimenting with makeup . . . She was never really sure she was beautiful and she thought her nose was unattractive, a piece too long (agent Johnny Hyde later arranged for her to undergo plastic surgery) . . . Her eyelashes, upper and lower, half an inch long, were completely white and had to be dyed constantly . . .

Like Cary Grant, she had a bad chin (also reconstructed). Stars of old were conscious of their defects,' concludes Graham. In addition, it was recommended that Marilyn undergo dental reconstruction to alter a protruding overbite which was rectified by Columbia's resident orthodontist.

Preparation for her role in *Ladies of the Chorus* placed Monroe in proximity with studio vocal coach, Fred Karger. Karger would later marry Jane Wyman, after her divorce from Ronald Reagan, but not before having a whirlwind affair with Marilyn Monroe which lasted until the Wyman marriage and culminated in Marilyn giving Karger a $500 inscribed watch which she paid for in instalments for two years.

When they first met, Karger was recently divorced and living *en famille* with his mother, Anne, daughter Terry, sister Mary and her children in circumstances not conspicuously different from those he enjoyed as a youth when his father, Max Karger, ruled MGM with paternalistic authority (he was a founding member) inviting players to enjoy the famous Karger open house at the old Hollywood hotel. Those were the days when it wasn't uncommon to bump into Jack Pickford, Valentino and Nazimova at the same party. Those who knew Karger (now deceased) say that he was a decent fellow. However, hailing as he did from one of the most influential families in town, he might easily have been spoiled by the availability of too many women. (A friend of mine was the grandson of one of Columbia's founders, and it took every ounce of character he could muster to pass up dates with starlets which the studio tried to arrange.) It is likely that Karger might have wrongly assumed of Marilyn that she, too, was fair game. Said to resemble Robert Wagner (some say better looking) Karger was young, handsome, athletic, talented, rich and eligible – the ideal catch for Marilyn. So what went wrong?

Columnist James Bacon volunteers an opinion: 'Yes. Freddie was a handsome guy and he had all sorts of girls after him all the time. Marilyn was always madly in love with Freddie. At the time she was like a fawning schoolgirl. I don't think Freddie reciprocated. But it was Freddie who she was crazy for all her life. He told her he wasn't going to marry her and that hurt her. She wanted to marry him very much.'

Marilyn's biggest booster, Bacon recalls first meeting her when she was under contract to Columbia. 'I first knew her when she was a brunette. I don't think she became a blonde until she did *Love Happy* with the Marx Brothers. If you think she was gorgeous in 1954 you should have seen her in 1947 . . . One day I got a call from a Columbia PR guy named Milt Stein who was the unit publicist on *Ladies of the Chorus*. Milt Stein was about four feet tall, bald-headed and odd-looking (he smoked big cigars) but he was always surrounded by beautiful women.

'Milt said, "Geez. There is someone you have got to meet." So I go up and met this girl. I can remember her so vividly. We met for lunch at a little restaurant on Gower Street [in Hollywood] up from Columbia Studios called Naples. It was the hangout for all the Columbia people. It wasn't Chasen's or the Bistro but a place where you could get a decent meal. It had leather booths and so on. And with Stein was Marilyn. She was very exciting. There was something about her. She exhibited that quality which she always had. She'd make a man feel like he was the only man alive. That was her great secret.'

Not intellectual, but intellectually omnivorous was how Bacon remembers Monroe. 'Having been a high school dropout Marilyn had enrolled in a UCLA extension course on "Backgrounds of Literature" and we compared notes since when I was at Notre Dame I had taken the "Great Books" course having read Aristotle,

Thomas Aquinas, Thomas Wolfe, and others. I gave her the list and by golly she had already read four or five of the books on the list.'

Recounts Bacon, 'I remember that I came back to the office and that I wrote a story about her for Associated Press, and at the time my boss said: "Write about Gable or someone but don't write about an unknown like this." So I sat on the story and when he went on vacation I put the story on the wire. That was the first big story ever written about Marilyn Monroe and it went around the world in 8,000 newspapers. For that reason we became very good friends.'

Perhaps it was the silly, nutty, sweet things she would do for friends that dissipated her finances, but, whatever it was, Marilyn was short of money and often skipped meals to save on food costs. It was then that Karger suggested she move in with him and his family. The proposal, while being of tremendous financial help, proved emotionally disastrous; Marilyn falling victim to a one-sided love affair.

Columnist Sidney Skolsky agrees that Karger was a mistake. 'Marilyn's first big Hollywood romance was with Karger. He was the only man, I believe, that Marilyn ever truly loved. But it was a one-sided romance. Fred took Marilyn bowling and to the Hollywood Bowl. He took her home to meet his mother and they became friends and remained friends from then on. Anything he wanted to do, Marilyn would do and it would be fun.'

Where did the romance go sour? 'Fred Karger . . . had a six-year-old [child] and didn't think Marilyn was the mother type. He terminated the affair and for some time afterwards Marilyn was very despondent.'

Monroe's own account of the affair, which she told photographer David Conover, runs similar to Skolsky's version. 'He was very shy and reserved and almost as unsure of himself as I was. Shortly after our first dinner

date, I discovered I was in love with him. I wanted to
marry him . . . I did everything to persuade him. But
the more I begged him to, the more he withdrew from
me. Still, we remained friends. He taught me how to
sing, and for that I'll always be grateful.'

In her autobiography, *My Life*, Marilyn goes on at
length about the intensity of their passion and the intimacy which developed when she moved into his house.
'When he came into my room and took me in his arms
all my troubles were forgotten. I even forgot Norma
Jeane . . . I even forgot about not being photogenic . . .
All the fame and colour and genius I had dreamed
of were in me. When he said "I love you" to me,
it was better than a thousand critics calling me a great
star.'

She was, however, terrifyingly aware that the relationship was ill-fated admitting '. . . His love didn't seem
anything like mine. Most of his talk was a form of
criticism. He criticized my mind. I'd say: "I've never felt
like this before." And he'd answer: "You will again . . .
You mustn't take a few sensations so seriously . . .
That's because your mind isn't developed. Compared to
your breasts it's embryonic . . .'

And yet her account of him is enduring testimony
to what became the foundation of Monroe's lavishly
romantic and wildly passionate spirit, revealed later on
with greater frequency as her sexual appetite increased.
'The first thing I saw when I entered any place to meet
him . . . was his face. It would jump up at me . . . I
stumbled when I went to sit down. My mouth hung
open. My heart ached so much I wanted to cry all the
time. If his hand touched mine by accident my knees
buckled . . .'

Conversations with Robert Slatzer about Karger
suggest that he was the worst sort of class snob; an
outrageous practitioner of the Double Standard within
the confines of his mother's house. It must have been

demoralizing for Marilyn to have been loved by a man whose afterplay consisted of *bon mots* about not being the sort of woman he'd want for a wife and mother. Slatzer describes Karger as profoundly and arrogantly middle-class. 'He would be embarrassed by her clothes, and would try to get Marilyn to change. Which made her mad.' (Slatzer describes Marilyn's wardrobe as classic Fredericks of Hollywood: a shop noted for unders.) 'Karger wanted her to pull herself together – to effect an image that was more chic.' (An idea which even if she fancied Marilyn could not afford and when she could afford to dress well she still preferred to be comfortable.) Adds Slatzer: 'I played golf with Karger before he died a few years ago. We talked about Marilyn. His attitude hadn't changed. He was a stopping point. She became serious. He felt sorry for her. He never pursued her that much. He wasn't like DiMaggio whom she met in March 1952 on a blind date and who proposed to her the same night, and every night thereafter until she accepted.'

Perhaps it was religious diversity which kept them apart, since when Karger remarried he wed Jane Wyman who came from a prominent mid-western churchgoing family. (The Kargers, Eastern European Jews, were Catholic converts – a popular persuasion amongst high-ranking film people in the Hollywood of the thirties and forties.) Ironically, the $500 gold watch that Marilyn bought Karger became a kind of perverse wedding present, since the last payment was made just before his marriage to Wyman. Writes Sidney Skolsky: 'The only bitchy thing I ever saw Marilyn do occurred one night at Chasen's. As we approached the checkroom there was an event taking place in the large private party room . . . [We] were told that the Fred Karger and Jane Wyman wedding party was in the room. I think it was the second time around for Fred and Jane . . . [Marilyn] boldly crashed the reception and congratulated Fred . . . The tension in the atmosphere would have been as easy to cut as the wedding cake.'

During the time she lived with the Kargers, it was suggested that Marilyn attend services at St Victor's Catholic Church. It was here she met Joan Crawford, then an ageing film star whose friendship with Monroe was sparked by her desire to smarten up the girl's appearance, which to her seemed unnecessarily sloppy. Writes biographer Fred Guiles: 'Marilyn was thrilled to be taken up by one of her early idols and began dropping by Crawford's home frequently . . . [Crawford] began to give her advice on how to dress and even offered her part of her own wardrobe, but since Crawford was petite and Marilyn was nearly five foot six, nothing would fit . . . At another brunch, and with the hostess slightly drunk, Crawford made a sexual pass at Marilyn and the friendship abruptly ended. Marilyn, who saw nothing wrong with lesbianism, recoiled more from shock than offence.' After this episode, Crawford nursed a grudge against Marilyn which she vented at the 1953 *Photoplay* Gold Medal Awards where she publicly proclaimed Monroe, winner of the Best New Star Award, a disgrace to the motion picture industry.

After Columbia dropped her option six months after having hired her, on 8 September 1948, Monroe left the Karger residence hoping that the separation would prod Karger into popping the question. Her second rejection by a major studio was terrifying to a girl whose entire livelihood – whose very life, depended upon making good (after all, Monroe had discarded the one secure possibility of livelihood when she divorced Dougherty in 1946).

When Harry Cohn first looked at the rushes on *Ladies of the Chorus* he was not enthused about Monroe's quality of 'flesh impact'. Quite the opposite! Norman Zierold writes: '[Cohn] asked: "Why'd you put that fat cow in the picture? You fucking her?" (he asked producer Jonie

Taps). "No. I think she's got something." "I bet you a buck she never gets anywhere.'"

Ladies of the Chorus, being a Columbia musical, was never going to be anything other than second-rate, since, like Warners, Columbia's forte was drama and it was Metro and Fox which excelled in the genre. A modern, musicalized adaptation of the Anna Christie story, Monroe and star Adele Jurgens are two hoofers (young and old) whose trials and tribulations are the basis for a sleazy screenplay, the only respite from which are the songs Monroe warbles including 'Every Baby Needs a Da Da Daddy' and 'Anyone Can Tell I Love You'. While the film was not successful – who since has heard of Adele Jurgens? – the critics did manage to praise Monroe for having done all her own singing (although it was rumoured that she had been dubbed). Tibor Krekes wrote in *Motion Picture Herald*: 'One of the bright spots is Miss Monroe's singing. She is pretty and with her pleasing voice and style, she shows promise.'

So why was she dumped at Columbia? The apocryphal story is that she wouldn't sleep with Harry Cohn. 'Believe it or not, it's true,' says columnist Bacon. 'Marilyn told me herself. Cohn invited her to spend a weekend aboard his yacht. She asked: "Is Mrs Cohn going to be with us?" That did it. You do not attack the families of the patriarchs of the movies. They are like the Mafia. Cohn got very mad at her, called her a horrible four-letter word, and ordered her out of the office. She never worked for Columbia again.'

Screenwriter Henry Ephron, however, takes a more jaundiced view of things: 'Cohn laid her too. She was too insecure and too willing to give herself away. I have heard some awfully vulgar stories about Harry Cohn.' If so, why didn't he pick up her contract? 'Perhaps *Ladies of the Chorus* lost money. Perhaps he just double-crossed her.'

It was during the time she moved away from Karger

that Marilyn struck up an acquaintance with Columbia drama coach Natasha Lytess. (For a while Marilyn rented a room from her.) Next to Paula Strasberg, and along with Michael Chekhov and Lotte Goslar, Lytess was to have the most profound effect on Monroe's development as a performer. She sought to guide Marilyn away from a popularized conception of herself into someone of greater depth. 'My whole work with Marilyn is to overcome this negative misconception of her, and inch by inch I am winning the struggle,' Lytess said at the time. Of Lytess Monroe has said: 'She was a woman of deep culture. She told me what to read. I read Tolstoy and Turgenev. And I would go around dreaming of all the characters I'd read and hearing them talk to each other.'

Thin, dark, bony and intense, Natasha Lytess was born in Russia, but immigrated to Germany when she was a child where she remained until the war, when she and her husband, novelist Bruno Frank, came to Hollywood. Having met Monroe when she was coaching at Columbia, Lytess was so captivated by her that she quit her salaried post to devote herself full-time to Monroe's education. (Since Marilyn was dating Howard Hughes at roughly the same time, it is conceivable that the billionaire underwrote Monroe's acting lessons.) The relationship's duration, along with the amount of time they spent together when working made Lytess privy to a great many of Marilyn's secrets. She witnessed the courtships with both DiMaggio and Miller from their earliest stages, and also observed Marilyn's flirtations with other important people in the wake of the Karger affair. But, as Lytess was given to remark in her memoirs, Marilyn remained possessively secretive about her private life, discouraging idle gossip about the most pedestrian matters.

Lytess's first encounter with Monroe came when she was under contract to Columbia, acting classes being an integral part of the studio regimen. 'She wiggled nervously into my Hollywood office,' writes Lytess recounting her first impressions many years later, 'dressed in a red frock of knitted wool that hugged her thighs. It was cut very, very low. Clearly, she was not wearing a bra . . . She perched hesitantly on the brink of a chair, clutching an untidy brown paper parcel. Her face was as wooden as a ventriloquist's dummy. I saw that her nose had a lump on its tip, which she had tried to disguise with heavy make-up. When she spoke her voice was like a knife clattering on a cafeteria plate . . . a girl with dyed, pale yellow hair, a petulant mouth which moved nervously, and a body . . . a *gauche*, vacuous-faced girl dressed like a trollop.'

So what made Lytess change her mind? And what (you may ask) made her conversion to Monroe-ism so fanatical that she quit Columbia (when Marilyn's option was dropped) to devote herself exclusively to grooming the player? Love? Sex? Columnist Sidney Skolsky thinks so, for when the DiMaggio débâcle hit the fan, Marilyn was rumoured to be having an affair with another woman; Skolsky volunteered his choice of correspondent: Lytess.

This is doubtful, since according to Lytess herself, the singularly decisive factor in changing her impression of Monroe from waif to champion came with the appearance in her life of RKO billionaire Howard Hughes. Earl Wilson validates Hughes's pursuit of Monroe: 'Marilyn Monroe . . . always excited and enchanted men of great power and great wealth . . . Marilyn's . . . stud list included . . . Hughes. She once explained that her cheeks were red because . . . Hughes hadn't shaved for several days.'

Lytess is too chic to admit openly that Hughes bought Marilyn's way into her heart, but her memoirs, reading between the lines, say as much. Writes Lytess: 'It has for years been one of Marilyn Monroe's most closely kept secrets that this powerful man once carried her off on a tempestuous escapade . . . His way of wooing a girl was like something from the Arabian Nights . . . With Marilyn it began with a dozen yellow roses for her and a dozen for me. Then he phoned: "I'd like you both to come for a walk with me," he said. But a "walk" with Howard Hughes meant "a walk in the skies" – in his private plane . . . It had a superb drawing room, couch, bedroom, bathroom and cocktail bar. And when he asked Marilyn: "Where'd you like to go?" . . . the only place she could think of was Palm Springs . . . "Why, fine . . . I believe I've got some sort of little house out there where we can change and have a swim . . ." This "little house" turned out to be a sumptuous mansion, fully staffed with servants, with its own private airfield, swimming pool, and two bathrooms . . . After this he called Marilyn constantly . . . Often he'd phone and ask: "Will you be my guest tonight?" A limousine would take us to dinner, cabaret and then home. At about 3 a.m. Howard himself would turn up in one of his Chevrolets. He must have had 100 of them. I would make him a meal and then I would leave them alone together on the couch while I went to bed.'

While Lytess claimed that 'she took over a wiggle and made it into a star', there is the conflicting theory advanced by several of Monroe's friends which contends that her temperamental, theatrical ways hindered Monroe in realizing her professional aspirations. Roy Baker, who directed Marilyn in *Don't Bother to Knock*, describes Lytess's presence as disruptive. Baker's real objection was not with the way they conceived a scene (he could override them in the editing room) but the more pedestrian aspects of coaching. 'Lytess worked by getting Marilyn to mimic her, which meant that there were times when I couldn't understand a word she said speaking as she did it in Natasha's thick German accent.'

Whitey Snyder regards Lytess' methods as antiquated

and stylized vestiges of Middle European theatre and argues: 'If they teach you to do something like you are supposed to do it instead of all those phony things it would have been all right. But Natasha would stop her dialogue unless she had a certain movement on a certain word. When she wasn't around, and Marilyn knew she wasn't around, she was much better. She was a natural comedienne. She ran around. She sang. She acted well. But when she was around, she was a crutch. She had to rely on her.' (It is significant that when Monroe left Lytess and took up with the Strasbergs, she chose practitioners of the Method, an acting technique which depends for its success on the improvisational sense-memory of the subject.)

Yet it was Lytess' conviction in Marilyn's abilities which helped her survive the Columbia disappointment, her second rejection by a major Hollywood studio. Encountered one day by Natasha in the studio canteen moaning about having been fired, Marilyn wept: 'My life is over. My career in pictures is finished. I'm washed up.' Lytess looked at her and replied: 'No Marilyn. You are only just beginning.'

9
Hand to Mouth

Following her Columbia dismissal in September 1948, Monroe was dogged in her attempts to secure freelance parts and her persistence paid off when she was given a part in a Marx Brothers comedy called *Love Happy* at United Artists. There is one scene where Groucho burlesques a private eye named Grunion which calls for him to interview a client whose complaint is that she is being pursued by evil men. It is only a 30-second walk-on, but the producers wanted to cast a girl whose entrance would summon up the sound of cymbals. One of her mentors, perhaps Joe Schenck, had introduced Marilyn to agent Louis Shurr, who sent her to producer Lester Cowan to audition for *Love Happy*. Like Hyde, Shurr was a short man (4ft 8in), described by his then client Jan Sterling as 'looking like King Kong – only worse. But he was so kind and so nice – very gentlemanly and very important.' In any event Groucho was present when Monroe was being interviewed.

Ever candid, Marx told his biographer Richard Anobile: 'Boy, did I want to fuck her. She wore this dress with bare tits. The scene I did with her took only about four days to shoot. I think she may only have gotten a couple of hundred dollars for the part. She was goddamn beautiful. I couldn't keep my eyes off of her. I may have tried to lay her once but I didn't get anywhere with her.

I don't think any of the boys did . . . She was the most beautiful girl I ever saw in my life. And she later turned out to be a great comedian in some picture Billy Wilder directed.'

According to one story, the actual audition was very funny and involved Groucho sashaying across the stage in imitation of the kind of movement he wanted, with Marilyn (and the other girls) following along behind him. Groucho's own recollection differs a bit: 'Lester Cowan called me to say that he was going to see some girls the next morning in order to cast the role she eventually got . . . So anyway I went over to his office that morning and he had three girls sitting there . . . He had the first girl walk up and down . . . Then the second girl walked up and down and finally the last girl, who was Marilyn Monroe. After they left Cowan asked: "Well, what do you think? Which one of the three would you pick?" I said: "You're kidding, aren't you? How the hell could you pick anybody but that last girl?"'

It was around this time that DiMaggio was trying to get an introduction to Monroe. Groucho heard about his interest through the grapevine: '. . . When [they were] married they used to sit home every night watching television. She was a beautiful girl and he was a washed up ball player. She didn't find watching TV very interesting so she finally decided that she would take a trip somewhere, maybe it was a round-the-world trip . . . Finally she returned and was eager to tell him about all the people she had met . . . She said, "Joe, you never heard such applause." And he turned around and said, "Oh, yes, I have." Of course he was referring to when he was the star player for the New York Yankees.'

There is another story which Groucho recalls about Monroe that tends to point up the honesty of her approach to things. After having been laid off by Columbia she wasn't eating regularly and when they were shooting *Love Happy* Groucho remembers often seeing her in the company of a fan (a wealthy businessman) in a restaurant across the street from the studio. Every night Groucho would watch Marilyn stuffing herself full of (he thinks it was Italian) food, promptly asking to be taken home upon finishing since she had an early morning call.

A pleasant diversion following her brief appearance in *Love Happy* was the six-city road show promotion of the film, which started off in New York before hitting Detroit, Cleveland, Chicago, Milwaukee and Rockford. Booked into New York's posh Sherry-Netherland Hotel on a warm, summer's day, it was intended that Monroe should send temperatures soaring by posing for photographers in a swim suit which the United Artists PR department had furnished. On this particular junket, however, Monroe sent temperatures plummeting, being what is called by the trade, 'a lousy interview'. Columnist Earl Wilson recalls his session with Monroe as having been a gigantic bore. 'I had no real desire to see her,' he says. 'She was an unknown. The press agents for the Shorehaven Beach Club in the Bronx had been trying to persuade the papers to print pictures of her in a bathing suit. When she came . . . to town as a starlet trying to promote a doubtful movie, I agreed to do the interview . . . I can't swear that I was the first New York reporter to interview her. It was either Sidney Fields, then of the *New York Mirror* or me . . . Neither of our interviews about Marilyn Monroe excited anybody very much . . .'

Unimpressed by what he considered to be the lady's 'wooden face' and 'stiff, almost graceless body', Wilson's views changed over the years, but at the time he was negative and it was left to producer Cowan to persuade him of her attributes. 'I remember Lester Cowan telling me that I was not to judge her by that wooden look,' recounts Wilson. '"This little dame . . . could really be a big star. The minute most guys see her they want to jump her."' In the end Wilson's angle on Monroe, entitled 'Mmmmmmmmm Girl', juxtaposed this breath of fresh air against the fetid, humid New York summer: a motif which years later Billy Wilder used when conceiving *The Seven Year Itch*, when he cast Monroe as the pneumatic Upstairs Girl whose undulating listlessness sparks the dormant fantasies of the lecherous Summer Bachelor in the downstairs flat.

The Wilson interview, while pandering to the burlesque in sensibility, is buoyed by a few classic Monroe-isms. 'Why do they call you the "Mmmmmmmmm Girl"?' 'It seems some people couldn't whistle, so they went Mmmmmmmmm.' When Wilson asked about her favourite performers, she mentioned Montgomery Clift. 'He's got tremendous talent,' she said. 'And,' she added, 'of course, Mmmmmm.' (Years later Monroe would become an intimate of Clift's during her courtship with Arthur Miller in New York City. She would, years later, according to housekeeper Lena Pepitone, attempt to seduce him; and whether or not she did, their relationship on *Misfits* during her breakup with Miller was intense to the point of being devotional.)

While the *Love Happy* walk-on was attention-getting, there was no contract offer forthcoming from United Artists; nor did she find that other producers were suddenly banging down the door. The cameo was written off as that of a mechanized bunny being chased by the Marx Brothers in a film where the 'girl' is used and forgotten. Monroe's success in getting freelance work was limited; producers failed to be suitably impressed by the girl whose hair was mousy brown and whose clothes were bargain basement chic. Aside from a bit part as a dancing girl in *A Ticket to Tomahawk* – an assignment which involved a five-week location shoot – Marilyn's existence was probably more precarious than ever it had been. (*Tomahawk* toplined Dan Dailey, her co-star years later in *There's No Business Like Show Business*.)

She also failed to get the part of the protagonist in a de Maupassant story entitled *The Necklace* (a role eventually landed by Eva Gabor) which Stanley Rubin was producing for TV. At this point Rubin found Marilyn too inexperienced, but a few short years later he specifically requested her for the role of the saloon singer in a film he was producing at Fox with Robert Mitchum called *River of No Return*.

How did they meet? 'Well,' drawls Rubin, puffing on his pipe (Rubin, like Conover, was a private whose CO during the war was Ronald Reagan), 'I had an assistant film editor who is still a very successful editor and associate producer named Danny Cahn. In the course of working on the script and preparing to shoot various episodes Danny emerged from the cutting room one day and sought me out in my office. "I have a girlfriend – a gal I date, who is very pretty. I think she can act. I think she has some talent. She's really kind of desperate. She needs a job. Do you think you could give her a bit in one of these half-hour films?" I must have said something like, "I'll be happy to meet your friend. But I see a problem. Because of our limited budget we concentrate on telling the story through three or four principals. (We eliminate all bit parts.) But let me know when she can come in."

'A day or two later he arranges an appointment and in comes this very pretty, sweet young lady. We talk and I realize she's not very experienced and wasn't right for a lead in one of these things. I knew that I was trapped – that I wouldn't be able to use her. I felt badly for Danny Cahn who was a very good assistant editor and a very nice young man to whom I had taken a liking.

'When she left Danny called me from the cutting room. "Well, did you see her?" I said that I had seen her. "Well, what did you think?" I said that she certainly was all he had said she was. Very pretty, very sweet. I said I'd like to offer her something but that I didn't want to encourage him to hope too much because I did not think it was going to work, primarily because the stories (period pieces set in Germany and England) did not lend themselves to her kind of part. She was a very contemporary young lady. I repeated that it didn't look likely and sure enough, nothing ever came up in which I could use her.'

The role went to Eva Gabor, whose talent barely causes a ripple, leaving film historians to write her off as a minor player. Where she excelled over Marilyn was in deportment and command. A wealthy Hungarian refugee from the Nazis, Eva had the advantage of being well-groomed and well-spoken. It would be Eva's sister, Zsa Zsa, whose husband George Sanders would fall passionately in love with Monroe when they played together in *All About Eve* (1950) and who would make life difficult by insisting that Sanders forebear lunching with her and confine his communication to good-morning and good-night.

I asked Rubin how bad was Monroe that first time around? What turned him off? 'When I first saw Marilyn she had done one thing, *Love Happy* and it was small. She was kicking around town and had been dropped by a studio. She was honey-blonde (before becoming platinum). She was slightly heavy, but not in any way too heavy. She looked sloppy, but not sluttish. And there is a difference.'

Says Rubin: 'I thought she improved in looks year by year. She was good-looking when she came in late 1948. But she was much more beautiful in 1951. She looked the same, only better. She never had confidence. She had determination.'

It was not perhaps what she did but how she did it: Rubin recalled how she'd come to rehearsals for *River of No Return* wearing a ragged T-shirt, from which the shoulders had been cut, and Capri pants, with lanolin smeared all over her face and hair. 'I asked her one day: "Marilyn, what have you got on your face?" "Sex hormones!" she quipped.'

The sloppy way she came to rehearsals annoyed the studio bosses, who let loose with a nasty memo when she appeared at recording sessions similarly attired. Editor Eve Newman, who cut sound on *Some Like It Hot*, perhaps Monroe's best film, recalls that a memo was issued by the front office asking Miss Monroe please to attire herself suitably when recording in tandem with an orchestra of twenty or thirty musicians.

'She had a hate on against the front office,' says Rubin, recounting one horrible conversation he had with Monroe where she told him: 'I'll show those bastards some day who I am, what I am and what I can do.' The picture Rubin conjures up of Monroe is contrary to the lady whose cookie box sexuality would crumble under the slightest affront. Instead the lady he describes is a tough cookie – a rebel. Is this fundamentally how Monroe impressed him? 'There was,' he concedes, 'something about Marilyn that made you want to break her – the anger, the ego, the defiance. It just got people's backs up!'

Many times over the four or five years she had been doing beer commercials for Tom Kelley, he had asked her to model nude for him. She had always declined, believing that the pose, if discovered, would cause irreparable damage to her career. Now, however, she was having to chase people for money and she was threatened with removal from the Studio Club, having fallen a few weeks behind in her rent. (Those were the days when landlords could evict tenants without prior notice.) Worse, the Finance Corporation had threatened to repossess both the 1941 Pontiac she was buying on credit and a phonograph which she considered a real treasure helping her as it did to unwind after a long hard day. So Marilyn reluctantly agreed, Kelley having assured her that one: his wife would be present and two: she would be virtually unrecognizable since he intended to light her in such a way as to obscure her features.

The fabled event took place on 27 May 1949. The exact location of the premises is on Seward Place, just south of the famous Hollywood and Vine thoroughfare and nearby to the Consolidated Film Industry laboratory where Monroe's mother had been employed as a negative cutter. It took quite a lot of coaxing to get Monroe actually to go through with it, Kelley's wife acting as a surrogate therapist. Mood music helped to alleviate nervousness: Artie Shaw's 'Begin the Beguine' playing in repeated succession on the phonograph turntable. Residual qualms were quelled by use of strobe lights which obscured her awareness of anyone else in the same room.

The photographs for which she was paid a paltry $50 and whose rights Kelley sold to a Chicago manufacturer for $500 (the man printed 8 million calendars), has become a classic. It graced the inaugural *Playboy* issue, although the standard of eroticism was never thereafter equalled in Hefner's publication. Using a rapid-fire exposure technique, Kelley shot quite a few variations but the two which excel are full face and profile: the latter, called 'Golden Dreams', being the one that gained international acclaim. Having placed her *in situ* on a background of red velvet, Kelley perched himself above her shooting down to establish a vantage point of photographic distance. Something about the shot in its evocation of quietude and undisturbed isolation – very much allied to the feeling of a hunter stalking prey in the forest – separates this nude from the hundreds of thousands of others which, by comparison, seem pornographic.

Even in the asexual eighties the incarnate female sexuality of that print is appreciated by aesthetes and Monroe-ians fixated upon, as one writer describes it – '. . . the athletic stretch of the 1949 Lo, pointing north by northeast, lying on her side, as lean as a steak, her

stomach hard, her breast and haunch like buds on a twig
. . . It could be called Ecstasy or Texture, like the picture
her character has posed for in *The Seven Year Itch*.'

Monroe used the $50 to pay the back rent at the Studio
Club and treat herself to a quiet dinner alone 'enjoying',
as she recounted later, 'every single bite'. If she regretted
having done the nude, it was not so much for its intrinsic
lasciviousness, for even she must have been able to see
that it was lovely, but for fear of the stigma attached and
what the studio would do if she were found out. In those
days there was something called 'a morality clause' and
it was not uncommon for studios to blackmail actors in
contract negotiations in view of whatever damaging
evidence had come to light during the months prior.

10
Hyde, the Flesh Pedlar

It was not long thereafter that her luck changed, when Marilyn met the man whose absolute faith in her potential to become a superstar of international calibre fundamentally altered the course of her life. That man was Johnny Hyde, at the time the number two man at the William Morris Agency – the most powerful theatrical agency in Hollywood both then and now. Hyde represented the brightest and the best – John Huston, Nunnally Johnson, Bob Hope, Rita Hayworth, Al Jolson and Betty Hutton. He was also credited with discovering Lana Turner whom he made into a big star.

Hyde came from a family of Russian circus performers and immigrated to the United States in the era of mass migration by Russian Jews whose talents and energies created the origins of the Hollywood motion picture industry. In tandem with Anglicizing the original family name of Haidabura, Hyde became a Catholic convert and, upon getting American citizenship, an agency man. Incredibly short and wiry, his face simian in character, Hyde nonetheless had the reputation of being a man of great magnanimity. Actress Jan Sterling says: 'He was very gentlemanly and very important. He really cared for Marilyn. He was the best friend she ever had – mother, father, lover, agent, friend all rolled into one.' Director Elia Kazan, who considers Hyde to have been 'one of the "best-loved" and "best-respected" agents in town', describes him thus: 'Short but nothing soft or small about him, nothing wasted in his body, and he had *good* manners. He was one of the few important men in Hollywood who had class.'

It was during a weekend in Palm Springs as the guest of Joseph Schenck that Marilyn met the man whose tenacity on her behalf would change her life. Hyde looked at her dispassionately, suggesting ways for her to improve an image that was now pretty but which could be made beautiful. And it was under Hyde's instruction that Monroe emerged as what the industry refers to as a 'Blonde' – a transformation which involved not only a change in hair colour but various improvements to both nose and chin. It is also rumoured that Hyde advised that she undergo surgery on her Fallopian tubes so as not to become pregnant – a condition which purportedly affected her capacity to have children in later years.

Producer Milton Sperling recalls seeing Monroe in Palm Springs at the Racquet Club after she became a 'Blonde'. 'I was talking to Johnny,' he recalls, 'and Marilyn was seated not far away on the swimming pool's diving board. Her back was to us, I remember. Johnny knew I knew her, and said – "Milton, guess who is here with me? – Marilyn!" He snapped his fingers and said – "Turn around, honey" and I caught a glimpse of this fabulously beautiful girl. My heart stopped. She was so appealing and lovely. She had done something to herself. Maybe it was the hair colour change. I had met her once as a brunette – she wasn't so hot looking as a brunette. But as a blonde, she was dynamite. She said: "We met when I was doing something at Columbia. But my hair was different." I murmured something, but I didn't really remember. Now I wouldn't forget. She was breathtaking!'

But it was not what she was, but what she could

become that attracted Hyde. Having seen her brief
walk-on in *Love Happy*, and being mightily impressed
with what he saw, Hyde followed up the Palm Springs
encounter with lunch in town and thus started a relationship which would extend beyond professional perimeters into the personal arena, culminating in the
autumn of 1949 with an appearance for Marilyn in *Asphalt Jungle* as replacement for Lola Albright.

In a word, Hyde went bananas over Monroe, leaving
his wife and children to set up a bachelor residence in a
mansion on North Palm Drive (an exquisite section of
Beverly Hills referred to as the flats, in proximity of
houses owned by Lucille Ball, Gregory Peck, Kirk
Douglas and James Stewart). Accounts of the relationship place Hyde in the active suitor role (not dissimilar
from DiMaggio), unrelenting in his pleas for Monroe to
marry him. That she declined suggests that she continued
to seek true love (she was still carrying a torch for
Karger) and career independence (being a 'star' meant
more to her than either men or marriage). It has been
suggested to me by Roger Kahn, author of *Joe and
Marilyn*, that the reason Monroe would not marry Hyde
is that she could not make it with him in bed. I find this
doubtful for any number of reasons; a more logical but
less lurid explanation simply being that she didn't love
him and as she didn't love him, why should she have
married him? What she did in bed with him is academic.

A friend admits that Hyde was perverse in regard to
Monroe, neglecting to change his will when his heart
condition was a continuing cause of alarm. (He died in
1950 just after having negotiated Marilyn's seven-year
Fox contract.) For someone so keenly aware of life's
vicissitudes the oversight indicates some measure of
ambivalence. Recounts a friend: 'I remember when he
talked about leaving Marilyn the house, but then he
wondered what she would do with it once she got it.
He was a funny fellow.' When in fact he did die, Marilyn

was shown little sympathy by the family, who not only forbade her to attend the funeral, but packed her lock, stock and barrel out of the Palm Drive mansion the moment Hyde was buried six feet underground.

The difference that Hyde made in Marilyn's life was fundamental. 'I didn't run around the studios job-hunting any more. Johnny did that. I stayed home and took dramatic lessons and read books,' she boasted. It was with him that she made her Hollywood debut. He escorted her to all the best parties in the most expensive ball gowns, furs and jewellery, so that she would make what he considered to be the right impression. (Since, following his death, most of the clothes were repossessed, one suspects that they were either rented or purchased on credit, the bills left unpaid.)

Characterized in her starlet days as being extremely shy, she was quite relieved to allow Hyde to do the talking. Columnist Radie Harris first met Marilyn at a dinner dance hosted by Sylvia and Danny Kaye, honouring Vivien Leigh and Laurence Olivier (whom she eventually contracted to co-star in and direct *The Prince and the Showgirl*, a film her own company, Marilyn Monroe Productions, would film in England six years later. Another of Hyde's clients, Olivier must have got the shock of his life when the quiet mouse emerged as an opinionated superstar whose ideas about production were as rigid as his).

Harris was to interview Marilyn several times in the course of her career and her first impression of Monroe is recounted thus: 'Norman Krasna . . . Groucho Marx, Eddie Cantor and Johnny Hyde . . . were at our table . . . Johnny's date [was] a very beautiful blonde [who] didn't open her mouth the entire evening. This was quite understandable. Unlike Eddie, Groucho and Norman this poor bewildered child could hardly expect to contribute much to a conversation full of inside gags and funny asides.' It was Krasna's RKO production colleague

Jerry Wald (when interviewing Marilyn for the role of the cannery worker in *Clash by Night*) whose description of Monroe captures much of the early primitivism which then characterized her demeanour: 'When she stands, she's like an antelope and when she moves, she's like a cobra uncoiling!' he praised. (It would be Krasna years later whose screenplay for *Let's Make Love*, calling as it did for an urbane European lead, cast Monroe opposite actor Yves Montand igniting a love match whose intensity cost Monroe her marriage to Arthur Miller.) Norman's wife, Erle Jolson Krasna, remembers Marilyn in the days when she lived on borrowed furs, jewels and so on. 'They passed her around like a box of candy. Everybody paid for her lessons and clothes. But,' cautions Krasna emphatically, 'she was not a promiscuous girl. She had one man at a time. And she was cute and sweet and never made the wives jealous. And let me tell you there were lots of girls who made us very nervous! Marilyn was adorable, though. We'd be dancing and she'd pull Norman's coat-tails. What a tease she was!'

Screenwriter Nunnally Johnson, who scripted a few of Monroe's films, including *We're Not Married, Gentlemen Prefer Blondes* and *Something's Got to Give* was not particularly impressed with her the first few times he met her. 'I'd see her sometimes at lunch with Johnny. She never said anything. I can't remember her saying a word. And I wasn't bowled over by her beauty either.'

While Sheilah Graham also characterized her as lacking in definition in those formative years, recounting a first impression she writes: '. . . she was with Johnny Hyde and a group at the La Rue Restaurant on the [Sunset] Strip. The talk was about acting and whether acting lessons were valuable. Marilyn sat through dinner without saying a word. Johnny, trying to bring her into the conversation, said: "Marilyn, what do *you* think?" She looked startled and said: "Well, I . . . I . . . I think . . . Stanislavsky . . .' Everyone was waiting for the rest of the sentence, but that was it.' (A couple of years later Monroe would astonish feature writer Pete Martin with a stupefying dissertation about the Stanislavsky Method.)

There is no doubt that it was Hyde who transformed 'a badly-dressed, mousy, kinky-haired, plump, no chin, bad hairline, less-than-ordinary-looking girl' into a beauty of the screen. A great deal has been written about the transformation both by biographer Fred Guiles and columnist Earl Wilson, who claims that Monroe's face was done by a prominent New York plastic surgeon. Whether the operation was sited in New York or Los Angeles, Monroe did recuperate at Hyde's mansion, taking a jocular view of the whole thing. She is remembered by friends as strutting around town with the bandages not yet off and making pilgrimages to Palm Springs before she was completely well.

Monroe's Second Coming incarnated as she was beneath a surgically perfect façade was what changed Darryl Zanuck's mind when faced with the proposition of signing her long-term in 1951. What counted to him was neither ambition nor sincerity – that Monroe would have sacrificed herself completely to make good as a star in 1946 meant nothing to him. What impressed him – what inspired and drove him to sign her – was the quality of perfectability which she emitted – a perfectability that the studio used in various psychological ways as a role model to educate people about sexual mores, fashions, religion, marriage, politics, divorce, etc.

Having waited for just the right moment to launch Monroe in a part with star potential, Hyde seized upon an opportunity to corner director John Huston (a client) into casting Monroe in *Asphalt Jungle* in the role (originally promised to Lola Albright) of Angela, secretary-mistress to Louis Calhern (the ultimate sugar daddy), a shady lawyer devising a plan to engineer a million-dollar jewel heist by corraling a group of underworld characters, each a master at his craft. (The censorious Hays

Office dictated that an illicit relationship between a man and a woman could not be credenced which is why Angela's role was changed to that of a secretary.)

Assembling a cast of authentic theatre performers including Louis Calhern, Sam Jaffe, and Sterling Hayden, Huston etches a life-and-death struggle of people who, for one reason or another, live on life's periphery. In the finale, his crime having been detected, Calhern shoots himself – an action that makes the viewer want to jump up and to tear apart the screen in defiance. Monroe is his perfect match: as completely sensual and defenceless as he is. When she herself breaks down in the betrayal scene – where, bullied by the police into making a confession, she incriminates her lover – she brings tears to our eyes.

The deal was struck as the result of a trick played upon Huston by Hyde, in tandem with Lucille Ryman, who was casting director at MGM where the film was shot. Ryman you may recall had at one point signed Marilyn to a short-term personal management contract, which fell apart because of friction between the two women over John Carroll. Whether or not Lucille felt any obligation to make it up to Monroe, or whether after having screened some footage of Monroe's Fox screen test she felt that the lady was right for the role, she told Marilyn to have her agent (Johnny Hyde) contact Huston. In effect, Lucille virtually blackmailed Huston into using Monroe, since he had stabled his horses at the Carroll ranch in Encino (part of the sprawling San Fernando Valley) without charge for years, and wanted to continue to do so. In harness with Hyde and Natasha Lytess (who coached her for the audition) Marilyn went along for the reading.

Marilyn's first impression of director John Huston is worth noting, since her appreciation of his own eccentricity suggests reasons for them having got along. 'Mr Huston was an exciting looking man. He was tall,

long-faced and his hair was mussed. He interrupted
everybody with outbursts of laughter as if he was drunk.
But he wasn't drunk. He was just happy for some
mysterious reason, and he was also a genius – the first I
had ever met.'

Of the actual audition, Monroe has recounted: 'I felt
desperate . . . "We're waiting, Miss Monroe," [Huston]
said . . . "Would you mind if I read the part lying on
the floor?" . . . "Not at all" . . . I stretched myself out
on the floor . . . I felt much better. I had rehearsed the
part lying on the couch, as the directions indicated. (This
is where she has to kiss Calhern resembling in this
instance a wet walrus.) "Oh, let me do it again." . . .
"If you want to . . . but there's no need. You were in
after the first reading."'

Forever seeming to court disaster, however unwittingly, it was during the audition that Marilyn's dress
ripped, revealing an expanse of naked skin. Generally
self-conscious, she was utterly traumatized in the presence of Huston, producer Arthur Hornblow and a gaffer
named Bill whose job it was to cue her. Having messed
up it took every bit of composure she could muster to
collect herself so that the audition could be concluded.

Columnist James Bacon vividly recalls accounts of
that disastrous audition. The ripped dress was one of
many things which went wrong. 'Johnny [Hyde] had
sent her over to MGM for an interview with John
Huston who was shooting *Asphalt Jungle*. To give you
an idea of how insecure Marilyn was I happened to meet
her going into the Thalberg Building to see John Huston
and Arthur Hornblow [the producer]. She had stuffed
her dress with cotton. Here is a girl with a 40in bust and
a fabulous figure. She looked like a dresser with the top
drawer pulled out. I knew her very well, and I said:
"Marilyn, you look awful. Geez, take those falsies out."
She said, "No, Johnny said they want a sexpot." The
next day I ran into Hornblow and asked: "What did you

do about Marilyn's falsies?" He said: "John reached in and said: "You've got the part, Marilyn."'

Perfectly cast as Angela, it was the role which for all time shattered the image Marilyn had until then of a floozie, setting her upon the path of serious screen acting subverted only by agent Hyde's untimely death. Looking lovely in designer Helen Rose's silk crepe lounging pyjamas, her hair coiffed in a simple pageboy style, Marilyn received both superb press notices and public approbation. Unaccountably, however, she was not offered a contract by MGM Studios.

The feeling when they were filming, was that a contract was inevitable, not just at Metro but at any studio in town. Marilyn recalled of Hyde: 'He was as excited as I was . . . He kept telling me: "This is it, honey. You're in. Everybody is crazy about your work."

'When the picture was previewed all the studio heads went to see it. It was a fine picture. I was thrilled by it . . . The audience whistled at me . . . I sat in the theatre with Johnny Hyde. He held my hand. We didn't say anything on the way home. He sat in my room beaming at me. It was as if he had made good on the screen, not me . . .

'A week later Johnny said to me: ". . . We've had a temporary setback . . . I've been talking to Dore Schary . . . He likes your work . . . But . . . he says . . . you haven't got the sort of looks that make a movie star."'

The observation seems utterly and cruelly absurd, considering the reality of Monroe's transformation in terms of looks, talent and professional poise, and Schary admitted years later to his biographer that he was guilty of an egregious error. 'Despite Marilyn Monroe's small and yet startling role I did not recognize her star potential . . . Darryl Zanuck signed Miss Monroe, she became an extraordinary figure in movie history and for years I blushed with embarrassment every time her name was mentioned.'

Columnist James Bacon sheds some insight upon the reasoning behind the rejection: 'I'll tell you what the problem was at MGM in those days. Bogie [Bogart] and I used to talk about it all the time. They had ten girls over there all of whom looked alike and they all were called "Debbie" – Janie Powell, Ann Miller, Debbie Reynolds, and others. Marilyn would have stuck out like a sore thumb. She was too sexy!'

It was after having landed Johnny Hyde as an agent that Marilyn took a studio apartment on Olympic Boulevard (nearby to the Fox lot) in the Beverly Carlton Hotel, which she used when she wasn't staying over at Hyde's or bunking up with Lytess rehearsing a film role. It was here that Rupert Allan, then a *Look* magazine West Coast staff writer, first interviewed Monroe following *Asphalt Jungle* for what was to be her first cover story, beginning a friendship which lasted until her death, with Allan handling all the star's personal press relations in the meanwhile. The extent to which typecasting affected her credibility is recounted by Allan in that preliminary meeting. The brittle, brassy floozie she often portrayed on the screen (coming as it did from weak and ineffectual technique, coupled with second-rate parts) was nowhere in evidence personally, and Allan departed the session believing there was more to Marilyn than met the eye. 'I found [Marilyn] another person entirely and I wrote the piece the way I saw it, which the New York editors wanted to change to be more in keeping with her screen image.'

He pauses: 'There was never any change in Marilyn. When I first met her she was reading Dostoyevski and she had pictures on her wall which she had got from a fine art magazine and had put up with Scotch tape . . . She hadn't enough money to put frames on them all . . . She had catholic tastes . . . [was] highly intelligent and self-educated. She had two photographs – one was a cutting which she framed of Duse (above her bed). The other was a small photograph of three men, and when I asked who they were she told me: Arthur Miller, Elia Kazan, and I forget the third. It amuses me that when she did *The Prince and the Showgirl* they said the "new" Monroe. But it was never new . . . There was never any change in Marilyn.'

It was often cruelly implied – occasionally even stated – that it was Marilyn who killed Johnny Hyde. My reading of the romance tells me that the sexual thrill in that relationship came from abstention. If Hyde was overtaxed it was because he drove himself into the ground by trying to make her a star against the most enormous odds. The attitude of the industry, almost unilaterally, was anti-Monroe. It took every ounce of drive to overcome this resistance, which he finally did by landing Monroe a seven-year Fox contract. This contract was prepared by Hyde in December 1950, just weeks before he died on 17 December (although whether it had at that stage been signed is doubtful). The seven-year contract was conditional upon Monroe's return to Fox on a one-week option for a walk-on role as 'a sweet young thing' (named Miss Caswell) in a film adapted and directed by Joseph Mankiewicz about backstage theatrical life called *All About Eve*. The film, a pot-pourri of show business clichés, toplined Bette Davis (replacing an accident-ridden Claudette Colbert) as an ageing thespian, Celeste Holm as playwright (Hugh Marlowe's) supportive wife, Anne Baxter as the scheming ingenue, and George Sanders as Miss Caswell's protector, ascerbic theatre critic Addison De Witt.

For all the personality conflicts (and there were plenty) the film is an acknowledged classic, masterful in its portrayal of backstage bitchiness. It won six Oscars in the 1950 Academy Awards, two of which went to Mankiewicz for adaptation and direction.

Exteriors were filmed in and around New York prior to production, at the John Golden Theatre, the 21 Club,

Eve's Park Avenue apartment, the Schubert Theatre and
the Taft Hotel, with additional footage being shot in
both New Haven and the Canadian border. The use of
the backstage premises of an actual New York theatre
(the Curran) rather than a Hollywood sound stage gave
the film its sense of authenticity. Having finished a day
and a half behind schedule, Mankiewicz returned to the
studio to work with the principals in scenes between
two and three people.

Assembling an all-star cast was a miracle of invention,
Bette Davis subbing for Claudette Colbert at virtually a
moment's notice. Miss Colbert had ruptured a disc as a
result of playing a scene in Fox's *Three Came Home*
(1950). Fitted with a steel brace, then put in traction,
there was no way she would recover to begin production
on *Eve* in five weeks. According to Mankiewicz, Ger-
trude Lawrence had been the second choice, but was
disqualified when her lawyer insisted that the scene
where Margo gets drunk at Bill's party be eliminated.
Darryl Zanuck approached Bette Davis directly (she had
been under contract to Zanuck when he was Warner
Brothers' production chief), sending her along a copy of
the shooting script which she read and agreed to do. The
key to Margo's character, Mankiewicz told her, is that
'she is a woman who treats a mink coat like a poncho'.

Mankiewicz insisted on having Celeste Holm at three
times the salary: Darryl Zanuck had broken her contract
when after winning an Oscar for *Gentleman's Agreement*,
a Fox film about anti-Semitism directed by Elia Kazan,
she held out for more money. 'He called the head of
every other studio and said he had fired me because I
was too difficult to work with,' recounts Holm, adding,
'but he got even on *Eve* by having my dressing room
put in the alley outside the sound stage. The others were
inside.' George Sanders was located in France and signed
for the role of the cynical critic; and for the role of
Miss Caswell ('a graduate of the Copacabana School

Reputed to be Marylin Monroe's father, Edward Mortensen, shortly before he died aged 85. He never acknowledged paternity.

Marilyn, born Norma Jeane, with her mother, Gladys Baker, a Hollywood negative film editor who has spent the majority of her life in mental hospitals.

Marilyn's marriage to James Dougherty, the boy-next-door, which Monroe later referred to as 'room-mates with sex privileges'.

Darryl Zanuck, Twentieth Century Fox founder and production chief. A ruthless man, who never believed in Monroe's abilities, he confounded her at every career stage.

Monroe with
Groucho Marx
in a scene from
Love Happy, the
film where she
went blonde.
On the screen
for only a matter
of minutes, her
performance
raised both
eyebrows and
temperatures.

Marilyn, with
director John
Huston
discussing a
scene from *The
Asphalt Jungle.*
Her role as
Louis Calhern's
mistress,
Angela, was a
career
breakthrough.

Monroe as the sexually frustrated housewife married to a mentally disturbed ex-serviceman (Joseph Cotton) in Henry Hathaway's *Niagara*. This is the film where Monroe wears the dress you have to make plans for when you are sixteen.

Newspaperman/screenwriter Robert Slatzer in 1986 holding picture taken at the time of his 'weekend marriage' to Marilyn about the time she finished making *Niagara*.

Monroe with designer
William ('Billy')
Travilla, who created
the Oscar-winning
gowns for *Gentlemen
Prefer Blondes*, *How to
Marry a Millionaire* and
The Seven Year Itch.

Marilyn's make-up
man for almost twenty
years, Whitey Snyder,
even did Monroe's
screen test, where they
argued about the
manner of application.

'Joltin Joe' famous Yankee outfielder. A national hero and sports legend, DiMaggio's courtship was great, but the marriage failed when he tried to boss Monroe around. He wanted a wife, she wanted a career.

A scene with Don Murray from *Bus Stop*, Monroe's first independent production for her own company formed in partnership with stills photographer Milton Greene.

Monroe entertaining the troops in Korea. Her performance started a riot, causing the US military high command to reprimand the American Armed Forces for an outrageous display of indecency.

DiMaggio with Monroe and New York columnist Walter Winchell to whom DiMaggio confessed the real story behind their marriage break up.

Sir Laurence Olivier and Monroe at the time of the press conference at New York's Plaza Hotel for *The Prince and the Showgirl*, Monroe's second independent production.

The London press launch for *The Prince and the Showgirl*. Marilyn got a bigger turn-out of photographers and reporters than either Dulles or Truman.

of Dramatic Arts') Mankiewicz recommended Marilyn Monroe who was signed for $500 a week with a one-week guarantee. 'There was a breathlessness and sort of glued-in innocence about her that I found appealing – and she had done a good job for John Huston in *Asphalt Jungle*,' said Mankiewicz, adding that fundamentally it was the persistence of agent Johnny Hyde which really got her the role.

Kenneth L. Geist in his biography of Joseph Mankiewicz relates just how much in-fighting there was among the players. Holm wasn't speaking to Bette Davis, having been mocked by the star for manners which Davis considered cloyingly high-tone (especially first thing in the morning). George Sanders (having earned the Academy Award for Best Supporting Actor) required seven or eight takes to get it right, driving others up the wall with his necessity of repetition. He spoke to no one, except Marilyn Monroe, to whom he had taken a fancy, having met her at a party given by photographer Tony Beauchamp and his wife, Sarah Churchill, where he promptly proposed marriage to the lady he described as deliciously pneumatic. His wife Zsa Zsa Gabor scolded Beauchamp for inviting 'that kind of a girl to the party' and months later, when she and Sanders worked together, a call came through from Gabor that they were not to lunch together in the commissary, and that Sanders was instructed to confine his communications with Monroe to salutations: good-morning and good-night.

That Marilyn was late for the two brief scenes in which she appeared was to become a precedent for Monroe: this group of professionals making no excuses for the fact that the studio might have been diverting her time elsewhere. Gregory Ratoff, cast as the producer, proclaimed in his Russian brogue: 'That girl is going to be a big star.' 'Why?' huffed Holm. 'Because she has kept us all waiting an hour?' Their antipathy made

Marilyn nervous, and when she became nervous she
blew her lines, and when she blew her lines, they'd
become more antipathetic, which increased her nervousness. And so on; it reportedly took as many as twenty-
five takes on the party scene alone. Ratoff, in particular,
seems to have taken perverse pleasure in picking on
Marilyn. He even tormented her about that lovely Edith
Head ball gown, arguing pedantically that it was not a
ball and therefore she looked ridiculous. Head's costumes won Oscars that year for her work both in colour
and black and white, the latter for her *All About Eve*
designs.

Twenty-five years later both Mankiewicz and Holm's
opinions remain the same, Holm confirming: 'I never
thought of Marilyn as being an actress. Even in the films
she did later on. I mean – even a puppy dog will act cute
and silly, if you give it enough encouragement.' Her
reaction at the time: 'I confess I saw nothing special
about her Betty Boop quality. I thought she was quite
sweet and terribly dumb and my natural reaction was:
"Whose girl is that." . . . She was scared to death,
because she was playing in a pretty big league . . . but
Joe relaxed her into it.'

So what was Monroe's opinion of Mankiewicz? Like
Huston he figured at the top of a list she compiled
following her walkout from Fox of directors she considered suitable collaborators, although it is quite obvious that he terrified her. 'Mr Mankiewicz was a different
sort of director than Mr Huston. He wasn't as exciting,
and he was more talkative. But he was intelligent and
sensitive,' she said.

In addition, Mankiewicz teased her about pseudo-
intellectual diversions. Having noticed that she was reading *The Autobiography of Lincoln Steffens*, Monroe
recounts that he took her aside and said: '"I wouldn't
go around reading Lincoln Steffens . . . People will
begin to think that you are a radical." "A radical what?"

I asked. "A political radical," Mr Mankiewicz said. "Don't tell me you haven't heard of Communists."'

The abrupt demise of Johnny Hyde on 17 December 1950 was the most colossal disaster to have befallen Marilyn since Grace Goddard departed for West Virginia, leaving her in the conjugal custody of James Dougherty. Having been brought back to Fox on a one-week contract Monroe had no idea of what the future held and without the guidance of Johnny Hyde to direct her career, she was in limbo. There was nothing phony about Monroe's hysteria at Johnny Hyde's funeral, where, despite being barred by the family, she threw herself screaming across the casket at the Forest Lawn cemetery.

Travilla remembers her return to the studio that afternoon, her face covered in heavy grease, wearing a black veil and a black dress. 'She was very dramatic – very theatrical, crying and all. It was overdramatized if you know what I mean. She was so histrionic that even the wardrobe ladies were laughing – thinking it was funny that she was making such an emotional display.'

So what is the consensus about Hyde? Did she love him? Or was she using him?

Coach Lytess has always maintained that Marilyn was using Hyde – having wrapped him securely around her little finger. 'She'd ring him from my house and say silly things: "Whisper something sexy to me so that I can fall asleep thinking of you" – that kind of thing.' Columnist Bacon agrees: 'Marilyn was using Hyde – he was the number two man at the William Morris Agency. This was no love match.' The dissenting voice is that of screenwriter Henry Ephron: 'Hyde was father, mother and agent. When he died that was a period of downhill for Marilyn. The Morris Agency didn't want to be bothered.'

True enough, since it wasn't until after the New Year (1951) that Monroe learned that Fox had ratified the seven-year option prepared by Hyde. And even then, it was incredible that the options were exercised, since no one at the Morris Agency other than Hyde had any interest in guiding her career with any degree of commitment and, in consequence, the film roles in which she was cast were all vapid dumb blondes. In short, *persona non grata* at the Morris Agency (she claimed they were only interested in Betty Hutton) Monroe had to sort things out for herself. That her career, following Hyde's death, not only survived but accelerated to superstardom says a lot for the acumen of a lady we like to think of as a cream puff.

11
RKO Loan-Out

The 1951 Fox contract showcased Monroe in a succession of cheesecake roles where she was alternately cast as a wife, a mother, a secretary and a girl-next-door, all of which ignored the dramatic flair she showed in *Asphalt Jungle*. Beneath that porcelain façade beat the heart of a rebel, and it is ironic that whilst she was cast as happy, domestic types, her personal life was concerned with independent and intellectual pursuits. Almost her entire weekly salary was spent on acting, singing and dancing lessons and she confined her other expenditure to a small bachelor pad at the Beverly Carlton Hotel and a charge account at Hunters bookshop in Beverly Hills (a landmark which recently has been expanded in size).

If Monroe emerged as greater than the sum of her parts, most notably in *The Seven Year Itch*, no one is more responsible than drama coach Michael Chekhov whose workshop she enrolled in at the beginning of the autumn in 1951. (Chekhov's widow, Xenia, was remembered in Monroe's will.) Nephew of the Russian playwright and student of Stanislavski (originator of the Method) Chekhov combined classical acting with modern technique, using Shakespearean classics as text. Monroe said of Chekhov that he was the most brilliant man she had ever known. Chekhov returned the compliment by raving about her talent, lamenting the way it was being misused by Fox Studios. 'Why won't they take you seriously? Why won't they allow you to do serious roles?!' he exclaimed, so taken was he with the emotion she was capable of bringing to a scene. Dramatic coach Lee Strasberg was to echo Chekhov's sentiments years later when he said that Brando and Monroe were the two greatest talents of their time.

Monroe proved an assiduous student and is remembered by others in the class for her human portrayal in *King Lear* of the daughter whose witness of her father's madness is as critical as the man's own lunacy. If sense-memory held the key to characterization, perhaps Marilyn fixated upon her own mother's mental instability. Either way, what transpired was a portrayal which was remarkable for the way it cut through the artifice of period and theatrical convention, liberating the character from within artificial constraints. It is this preparation, however brief, which compensated for years missed at RADA when the actress proved herself not only equal but superior to the technique of Sir Laurence Olivier, whose role in *The Prince and the Showgirl* suffers in comparison to the immediacy of Monroe's performance.

Whilst the Hollywood moguls derided Monroe's earthiness, believing that sex was something you did in a bawdy house, Chekhov's praise bolstered her confidence, encouraging her to relate sexually to the characters she portrayed. It is a kind of tribute to him that Monroe's comment about Grushenka, the heroine in Dostoyesvki's *The Brothers Karamazov*, prevails. As far as those in the movie profession were concerned, Grushenka was a dowdy, plain slag. Consequently when Monroe in an interview said that she wanted to play Grushenka ('She's sexy!') it became an international joke. But the interesting thing is that Monroe, in Chekhovian fashion, had *begun* to understand literature and character. Quick to detect her way of working, Chekhov had this to say after having played a scene with Marilyn: 'It's very strange, all through our playing of the scene I kept receiving sex vibrations from you. As if you were a woman in the grip of passion. I stopped because I thought you must be too sexually preoccupied to continue.'

It should have been natural for Monroe to have made the leap into the kinds of neo-realistic films which directors such as Elia Kazan were making. She would have been lovely in the Eva Marie Saint role opposite Brando in *On the Waterfront*, and why Kazan, whose friendship she esteemed, neglected to cast her in the role is attributed to one singularly important factor – Harry Cohn. It is worth noting that, even after she became a big star, Monroe never made a film at Columbia.

It was a story with a waterfront theme which led to Arthur Miller's introduction to Monroe in 1951. A Pulitzer prize winner for *Death of a Salesman*, Miller's play of *All My Sons* had been adapted for the screen by Chester Erskine three years earlier in 1948 and since Miller did not feel that the screenplay had enhanced the work in any conspicuous way, he elected to try to peddle an original idea. As late as 1986 at a screening of the film in New York City at the YMHA, Miller (still vigorous in his seventies) criticized the studio system which compartmentalizes playwrights and screenwriters. And while it is true that Erskine wasn't an exceptional screenwriter and that his adaptation excised some of the speeches which give the viewer insight into the characters, the screenwriter in Hollywood was, and is, sacrosanct. No matter how fine his skills, it was a leap Miller would not himself make until after his marriage to Monroe, when in addition to having sold an original story to John Huston (following his wife's commitment to play the leading role), he got the job of also writing the screenplay. That, however, was preceded by a bit of script 'doctoring' on Norman Krasna's screenplay *Let's*

Make Love, although it took every bit of his wife's clout, in tandem with his own Pulitzer credits, to gain Miller entry into that select fraternity of screenwriters. And even then Miller was treated shabbily, *Let's Make Love* producer Jerry Wald sporadically and rudely demanding: 'Arthur, where are those additional pages?'

It is difficult to imagine, since the starchy white image of Monroe is so indelibly etched in our minds, but she was, essentially, one of Hollywood's first hippies. Her heroes were intellectuals, Kazan and Miller both forming a part of her inner circle, their pictures occupying prominent places both on her bedroom wall and in her heart. She had known and dated Elia Kazan when she was being represented by Johnny Hyde (their relationship was non-exclusive). Their romance is a fundamental part of the Monroe Myth. At the time, Kazan was married to Molly Thatcher, story editor of New York's Group Theatre, a WPA spinoff of Roosevelt's New Deal. Kazan's marriage was flexible, however, and although he never divorced his wife (he only married Barbara Ferris after his first wife died) he was known around Hollywood as a ladies' man. For a while Kazan and Monroe were what is known as an 'item'. It was Kazan, one of the three founders of New York's Actors Studio who made the necessary introductions for Monroe at the playhouse where she learned her craft. Without Kazan, one can only speculate at the reception she would have received, since, even with his blessing, it took a while before the theatre people of New York regarded her with any measure of seriousness.

So how serious was Monroe? Screenwriter Henry Ephron offers the following observation: 'Marilyn was always being talked about – it was part of the game to talk about *who* was laying Marilyn at the moment. She was so easy to get to lay.'

What about Kazan? 'Kazan loved women. So one night Phoebe (my then wife) and I were having dinner in a Chinese restaurant on Rodeo Drive, where we see Kazan sitting with Monroe. He sees us and doesn't know we see him. So when they are ready to go he comes by our table and says: "Hello Phoebe. Hello Henry." Now Kazan is by stature a short man. But he walked out of that room ten feet tall with Marilyn Monroe on his arm. Marilyn was a showpiece. That is how men regarded Monroe. She was status.'

Arthur Miller was also very much married when he met Monroe, and it surprised friends of both Marilyn and Miller, such as actress Maureen Stapleton, when Miller finally divorced his wife, Mary in 1956. 'He was married, if you know what I mean,' says Stapleton. 'Very married.' Other friends noted the similarity between Monroe and Mary Miller; both women were described as 'sweet, quiet and shy'. If Kazan believed that Miller posed any sexual threat, he failed to protect himself, since the three were a joyful trio during Miller's Hollywood sojourns.

What was Monroe's first impression of the man who was to replace Fred Karger in her affections? Eleven years her senior, Miller at the age of thirty-six was 6ft tall, lean and lithe as a cat; a sex symbol in an offbeat way who was closer to her fantasy than Clark Gable or Robert Taylor. Beneath the brainy façade raged the soul of a bear and I was not surprised to read that as a youth Miller enjoyed both ice skating and skinny dipping. When once asked by a columnist what she saw in Miller, Monroe remarked: 'Have you *seen* him?' That sums it up! (Curiously I glimpsed Miller myself during the years he was married to Monroe. He must have been about forty-two or forty-three. I was then about eighteen. I confirm it: he was divine!)

Actress Jan Sterling, who lived across the street from the apartment building in New York where Monroe kept a flat which both she and Arthur used when they were married, first met Marilyn, then a starlet, in Hollywood at a dinner party she gave for Elia Kazan. Recalls Sterling: 'Paul Douglas (my then husband) and I were living in Hollywood, and had invited Gadge [Elia Kazan's nickname] to come for supper. I had been in plays which he directed and Paul had done *Panic in the Streets* with him. He asked: "Can I bring Arthur Miller?" We said: "Sure," and suddenly there was this lady [Marilyn Monroe].

'Paul had tested with Marilyn for a film role which in the end went to Linda Darnell. It was the same kind of a part she had played in *A Letter to Three Wives.* Paul remembered her because he spent all day there and said he wouldn't go back and put himself through that kind of abuse again. He wouldn't have done the picture if she had got the part. It was very difficult, apparently. Paul said to me: "She spends so much time getting her tits in line."

'So when she showed up with Kazan, I rushed upstairs to Paul and said, "Be nice. Be nice.' He didn't speak to her all evening. Paul would call them "coosburgers" – those ladies. He wouldn't deal with cheesecake types, which is one reason I loved him. He felt she was a cheesecake type, I think, but I don't know what he thought since it was not something he even dealt with. It's an attitude that is unfortunate, but the attitude is that she was just a little tootsie.' Continues Sterling: 'Hollywood has its own kind of snobbism. My foundation is that I was married and there was no room that I could not walk into where anybody could say: "I've had her." The smartest thing you could do was to refuse everybody.

'It is an ironic distinction that Miller met Monroe in our house,' says Sterling, adding that while later their public rows became vociferous, when they met Monroe was as quiet as a church mouse. 'Marilyn was silent the entire evening. I remember Arthur [Miller] teasing: "What does one say to this loquacious broad?" I think

Miller was tempted by her, and I know that from that night he occupied a place in her consciousness. When she and Paul worked together on *Clash by Night* all she talked about was "Arthur, Arthur, Arthur".'

It is Sterling whose long-range observations offer some explanation of where the marriage failed. 'He thought he was marrying the blonde goddess – the perfect daughter – and she perceived him to be Abraham Lincoln. She worshipped him.' When the glow wore off and each confronted the other, there was bound to be a certain amount of disillusionment. Apparently in their case it was insurmountable for, as Sterling recounts: 'Here is a woman who knows that she can get attention from any man in the world and here Miller is married to the lucky thing, so why isn't he responsive? I think he was a tremendous putdown to her ego!'

Columnist Sheilah Graham turns it the other way round: '[Marilyn] believed that Mr Miller, as Johnny Hyde had been before his death, was someone who wanted to take care of her, who understood her and who worshipped her.'

But it is coach Lytess who has the last word: 'Marilyn met Miller [again] at a party given by Charles Feldman. She came home thrilled, recounting how Miller had held her big toe or something. I knew then that she was in love.'

Sterling crossed paths with Monroe later that year at the 1950 Academy Awards ceremony held at the Hollywood Pantages Theatre – an old Victorian movie palace tarted up in the style of the Art Deco period with ornate plaster work, mirrors, chrome and leaded lights. It is here that as a youngster Monroe had been despatched on Saturday afternoons with the price of admission and a box of popcorn, and where she would fantasize about Gable, Taylor, Rogers, Colbert, and others, some of whom she would later work with.

Presenting the Oscar for Best Costume in Black and

White Picture to Edith Head for *All About Eve*, Sterling exchanged a few words with Head (who also won the Oscar for Best Costume in a Colour Picture). Head said: 'I never thought I did good work for DeMille (she won for director C. B. DeMille's *Samson and Delilah*). I always had to do what that conceited old goat wanted, whether it was correct or not.'

Having appeared that year in both *Asphalt Jungle* and *All About Eve*, Monroe was asked to present the Oscar for Best Sound Achievement, won by *All About Eve*'s sound man (the film was nominated for fourteen Oscars). It is no coincidence that this was the *only* Oscar ceremony at which Monroe was a presenter, the event later becoming just one among many legendary public humiliations. Sterling recalls the derisive attitude of her boss, Fox chief Darryl Zanuck when referring to Monroe: 'Wait until you see our girl,' he roared; 'she can barely speak.'

To complicate matters, Monroe had the first of what was to become a tradition of crises at important moments. Preparing herself for her debut at the Awards show, she noticed her dress was torn. An account of the incident is recorded in *Inside Oscar* by Wiley and Bona. Apparently she burst into tears and said she couldn't go on. 'Debra Paget, Jane Greer and Gloria de Haven consoled her while a fashion attendant did some quick mending. Monroe pulled herself together when it was time to make the presentation but had become so flustered she barely looked up from the podium when she was on stage.'

There are several accounts as to how Marilyn landed the supporting role of Peggy in Fritz Lang's *Clash by Night*, most are agreed, however, that she is superb. Her performance earned her plaudits not only from the critics, but also the group of actors with whom she played. And whether it was Fox in negotiating the loan-out or the actors themselves who supported it,

Monroe was given star billing alongside Barbara Stanwyck, Paul Douglas and Robert Ryan. (This is the first time Monroe had actually got star billing, although for years the theatre owners had been putting her name above the title on their marquees.)

Without Hyde's guidance, Monroe depended upon her own abilities to ferret out the choice parts, and it could well have been that she got wind of this role from Elia Kazan, a friend of Clifford Odets whose play *Clash by Night* was the basis of the screenplay. Perhaps, too, Monroe imposed upon the good will of Howard Hughes to put in a word for her at RKO, the studio he owned.

Columnist Sidney Skolsky takes credit, however, for arranging the interview with RKO assistant production chief, Jerry Wald (second in command to Norman Krasna). 'I was working for Jerry Wald on a script, and he was casting the film *Clash by Night* . . . and he needed "a young sexpot" to play opposite Keith Andes. I suggested Marilyn Monroe. Wald was against it. "She made a picture at MGM, *Asphalt Jungle* . . . They didn't pick up her option. She did a bit in a picture for Fox, *All About Eve* . . . They let her go. Something must be wrong. What makes you think she's so good?"'

Having convinced him that Marilyn's rejections had as much to do with Betty Grable (Fox's star) and Lana Turner (MGM's star) as Monroe herself, Wald agreed to see Marilyn. 'I advised Marilyn on what to wear when she met with Wald. I was acquainted with her limited wardrobe,' says Skolsky. 'I suggested she wear a pair of black and white checkered pedal pushers and a white silk shirtwaist blouse. The top three buttons of the blouse were unbuttoned and a rose protruded from her cleavage. The pedal pushers clung to her so tightly they looked as though they were painted on.'

Zanuck's biographer Leo Guild confirms Skolsky's pivotal role in the power play. 'Skolsky insisted she was another Jean Harlow . . . She was twenty-five but looked younger and was right for the part. He thought she was sexy.'

Wald, who compared Monroe to both a cobra and an antelope, was hooked. Writes Guild: 'He called Lew Schreiber, one of the executives at Fox, and asked for six weeks of Marilyn Monroe's time . . . What almost ruined the deal was that Schreiber asked for $3,000 for six weeks and it sounded like so little Wald thought she couldn't be very good . . .'

That Wald was confident of Monroe's abilities is revealed in an account by Jan Sterling, originally cast in the Barbara Stanwyck role of the wife. 'I was supposed to play opposite Paul Douglas in the film, and my agent was negotiating the deal. But then they said: "Well, no. We have got Marilyn for the other part and you two are too much alike. (I was under contract to Paramount, and they said they'd loan me out.)'

A fatalistic story of inequity and struggle set against the background of the San Francisco fishing community of Monterey cannery workers, *Clash by Night* was directed by that genius of *film noir* Fritz Lang. A refugee from the Nazis, Lang had his own reasons for making the movie and embellished playwright Clifford Odets' tale of Depression workers with bits and pieces from his own experiences. He ran foul of the Un-American Activities Committee for promoting anti-fascist working-class views, and also had problems adapting the play to the screen in accordance with rules set down by the censorious Hays Office, which dictated Hollywood's moral codes until the mid-sixties. '. . . the play was set against a social background of unemployment and so on, with a murder at the end: husband kills lover.' The film adopts a more discretionary posture, developing the story of marital infidelity and reconciliation and casting the lover in the role of invader, loner or odd man out. 'I did a lot of research . . . about the faithfulness of wives,' says Lang in conversation with filmmaker Peter Bogdanovich. 'And I found . . . that 75 per cent of married women betray their husbands with extra-marital relationships. This became the problem in the film.' (Barbara Stanwyck plays the wife, Paul Douglas the husband, Robert Ryan the lover, whilst Marilyn Monroe is cast as the girlfriend of the woman's kid brother, Keith Andes.)

Essentially told from the woman's viewpoint, the pivotal character is the wife, Barbara Stanwyck, a middle-aged woman who has returned to her home town of Monterey after a long absence with nothing to show – neither fortune nor husband. Fearing that life has passed her by, she sacrifices grand illusions and accepts a proposal of marriage from a simple cannery worker (Paul Douglas), with whom she has a child. Sexually unfulfilled, she has an extra-marital affair with Robert Ryan, a fisherman. Douglas discovers their infidelity, but agrees to take her back if she renounces the lover. This Stanwyck does, but not before, in a concession to the Hays Code, she has upbraided Ryan for not really caring what happens to her.

The impossible ending aside, Lang intended to make a neo-realistic film. He shot it on location in Monterey, requesting (and getting) ample rehearsal time for the actors to feel comfortable in the community. For all her dramatic ineptitude, Monroe sincerely tried to do the right thing. And in order to prepare herself for the role, she rode all night on a bus to Monterey some 300 miles from Hollywood to absorb the realism. When she arrived, she spent all day talking to boat owners and cannery workers about their experiences.

The conflicts engendered by having Monroe on the film were monumental. Firstly, Wald had agreed with Fox to give her star billing, which enraged Paul Douglas. 'I will never give my permission, never! Who is she? A newcomer! She will never make it to the top grade.' Douglas, it may be remembered, had tested with

Monroe for a role in a film he was making at Fox, and had threatened to quit if she were cast. Jan Sterling recalls Douglas' version of working with Monroe on *Clash by Night*. 'In the film Marilyn did most of her scenes with Keith Andes, so Paul really didn't have to deal with her. He did most of his scenes with Stanwyck. But when she was there it made everything fifty times longer. She couldn't get the lines right and when she did, she fell or something which messed up the shot.'

Then there were the gossip hens and columnists catering for Monroe to the complete exclusion of the other actors, which antagonized any relationship she had begun to develop with them. 'It wasn't Marilyn's fault,' says Lang, 'but it was a blow to the other actors. It was especially hard on [Barbara] because . . . [she] was the star. But the reporters said: "We don't wanna talk to Barbara. We wanna talk to the girl with the big tits." Another woman would have been furious. Barbara never. She knew exactly what was going on.'

Press agent John Springer, who in tandem with Arthur Jacobs represented Monroe in later years, first met the actress when he was doing magazine publicity for RKO during the time that Monroe was filming *Clash by Night*. He confirms that Monroe got the lion's share of attention, but is quick to point out the good will shown towards her. 'Paul Douglas might have resented Marilyn. Stanwyck didn't. She was wonderful. I don't know any actor who didn't like working with Stanwyck. "Missy" (her nickname) would go out of her way to help young actors who were beginning. And Bob Ryan thought she was marvellous. "This sexy blonde really has something. She's something else." Up to that time she had played mostly dizzy blondes, and that is what she played in *Clash by Night* but it was a stronger role.'

Although Springer attributes the casting of Monroe to Fritz Lang, the problems the director had in coping with her suggest that it was Wald whose interference on her behalf landed Monroe the role. 'It was not easy to work with Marilyn Monroe,' Lang told Peter Bogdano-vich. '. . . She was a very peculiar mixture of shyness and uncertainty and – I wouldn't say "star allure" – but, let me say, she knew exactly her impact on men . . . Now, just at that time, the famous calendar story came up. I don't mind – what a woman does with herself is nobody's business – but the thing was, because of her shyness, she was scared as hell to come in the studio – she was always late, I don't know why she couldn't remember her lines . . . but she was very responsive.'

Columnist James Bacon, who visited the location when they were filming, offers his observations of Lang and Monroe. 'Lang was a Teutonic director, a tough German who came out of Ufa Film Studios. I can re-member vividly that they had one scene on a boat where everyone had lines and all Marilyn had to do was to walk down the steps and to say one line. They did twenty-four takes. They even gave her a cue card which outside of John Barrymore was unheard of in those days.'

Another scene required Stanwyck to hang up clothes and speak her lines at the same time. 'Marilyn had one or two lines in the scene which she fluffed constantly,' said Lang. 'I never heard one bad word from Barbara. She was terribly sweet to her.' Screenwriter Henry Ephron suggests that Monroe's difficulty in playing with Stanwyck was because she was scared to death of her. 'She had trouble with a lot of big stars and was terrified of working with them.'

Screenwriter Daniel Taradash who scripted Monroe's *Don't Bother to Knock* recounts his discussion of Monroe with Lang. 'He said directing Monroe was like training a dog. The implication was that she didn't have much ability as an actress. Personally, I think she was probably scared to death of him. He would terrify Rex Harrison. So you can imagine what this little girl thought of a man who wore a monocle, no less. Lang was a very Prussian and dramatic man. We became good friends, and I liked him very much. But he was imposing.'

Lang's belief that Monroe worked best when the Pavlovian theory was applied couldn't be less right, since it was just that kind of dictatorial approach that increased her nervousness. Reports writer Anthony Thompson: 'Director Fritz Lang frightened her, so she was late for performances . . . the more strained she became before Fritz Lang's stares the more she kept [the other actors] waiting. The others resented it. They thought it was an act. No one knew that Marilyn was practising every gesture and every motion over and over.'

What Lang couldn't or wouldn't understand was that Marilyn had a viewpoint. The conflict erupted one day when Lang ordered her coach Lytess off the set. Lang recalls: '. . . [Marilyn] asked me would I mind if her female coach was there during shooting . . . I said, "No, under one condition, that you don't let her coach you at home, because when an actress has learned her lines and thinks she has caught the feeling of the part, got under the skin of a character, it's very hard to change it." At the beginning I had trouble – until I found out that behind the camera, unseen by me, this female coach was standing and gesturing with her hands. I said to Marilyn, "Look – either/or . . ." and told her the coach could not come on the set any more.'

The calendar exposé actually broke when Marilyn was filming *Don't Bother to Knock* at her home studio, although it also coincided with the release preparations on *Clash by Night*. Marilyn had posed nude for photographer Tom Kelley for $50 in May 1949 when she was broke, hungry and without any promise of film assignments. Kelley later sold the photographs to a Chicago manufacturer who mass produced the print on calendars, placemats, T-shirts and coasters. Apprehensive at the time she did it, Monroe knew that discovery could mean dismissal from a studio on the basis of the highly sensitive 'morals clause' which was included in all contracts and gave studios the right of immediate dismissal of anyone whose behaviour was contrary to accepted social norms. That she agreed to pose nude merely underscores the vulnerable position in which she had been placed by an industry willing to cast her aside after the briefest period of indenture.

The official account of how the calendar first came to Wald's attention is that a copy of the print was sent to him at RKO and that Wald then arranged for Marilyn to be interviewed by UPI's Hollywood columnist Aline Mosby, hoping to avert a scandal by letting Mosby tell the story from Marilyn's point of view. But columnist James Bacon refutes this and suggests that Mosby published the story in the first instance after being sent a copy of the calendar by someone wishing to discredit Monroe. Says Bacon: 'I knew about [the calendar] about a year or more before the story broke. I never ran the story. All the men columnists protected Marilyn . . . I was glad I didn't do it, but the story got a big play. Why did Mosby do it? You'll have to ask her. The last I heard she was either in Paris or Moscow for UPI. One time they fired Aline Mosby, but they couldn't keep her fired because her father owns most of the newspapers, TV and radio stations in Montana.

'Marilyn called me up and said that she was going to have a meeting with Zanuck and asked me what she should say. I counselled: "Whatever you do, Marilyn, say something funny." The next day the story came out that he had asked her what she had on when she posed nude, and she said: "I had on the radio." Which is a very funny line and her own line. For that reason it worked in her favour and she didn't get sacked.'

Always frightened of the front office, it was at times like these that Marilyn's terror amounted to what would be called in the rock idiom 'a whiter shade of pale'. Roy

Baker, director of *Don't Bother to Knock*, recalls Monroe's utter panic at the prospect of being found out. Says Baker: 'I couldn't understand what the fuss was about. A photograph of a naked lady seemed perfectly harmless. But everyone was shocked to the core. The people in charge of the studios affected to take an extremely high moral tone. I think they were terrified that the Women's Association or the Mothers of the Revolution would get up on their hind legs and say: "This is disgraceful and this must not go on."

'Those lobbies in the twenties and thirties were extremely effective. It's the old story. There was no censorship originally in movies until 1922 and I think Fox was one of the culprits. He made a picture called *Dante's Inferno* and it was largely made because he could have hundreds of scantily clad ladies waving about meant to be devils in hell or something. This was one of the things which caused such a fuss. Along came a body of people and they set up the Hays Office, led by ex-Postmaster General William Hays. And it was there forevermore. They brought it on themselves in the first place. It became a terrifying weapon against them and they were frightened out of their wits of people being accused of immoral acts and all this kind of stuff.'

He pauses: 'Marilyn never had the luck. She had nothing but bad luck . . . I could never quite understand why she was tied to the studio system, and terrified of being sacked. Although she was sacked from about five studios before I had her. She would have been better without that. In those days we thought you had to have a studio contract. Otherwise you are dead. We didn't know any better.'

Five years later, of course, having walked out on Fox, Marilyn had absolute mastery over her own career. But at the time the prospect of ruination was devastating and conjured up a lurking maternal image of someone whose career was eclipsed in their prime.

Designer Travilla recalls the moment when the nude calendar broke. 'Marilyn was in my office. She had no makeup on. A call came through for her to get up to Zanuck's office right away. She was a nervous wreck. She said: "They've just found out that I have done a nude photo. They want me up there. What am I going to do, Billy?" I said, "At least put on lipstick. Go up there looking good. Don't go up looking like a slob." She was so nervous. She used to use four or five colours on her mouth to paint the contours. From his office the telephone kept ringing. "Where is Monroe? Where is Monroe?" She was shaking and crying. I said, "Honey, go on up." And she did.'

Columnist Sidney Skolsky's version of the story has Monroe personally confessing the scandal to Mosby, although the reason for doing so isn't quite clear. Did Mosby know about it prior to the Monroe interview? Was she intending to publish the story anyway? Or was Skolsky having a bit of fun at Monroe's expense by encouraging her to make a confession which could (and did) get her into a lot of trouble? Most likely Skolsky got wind of Mosby's discovery and counselled Marilyn to give Mosby a routine interview, culminating with the calendar disclosure (but in the greatest confidentiality). Marilyn followed his advice to discover that Mosby, an ace reporter, dismissed the trivia, pitching the piece around the calendar exposé.

The upshot, of course, was pandemonium. Recounts Skolsky: 'After the story broke, Harry Brand, Fox's publicity director, told Marilyn that the studio was considering not releasing *Don't Bother to Knock* and cancelling her contract on the basis of the morals clause. In a panic, Marilyn phoned me.

'"Oh, Sidney, what shall I do?" she said. "I've been advised to deny the whole thing – to say it isn't me. I've also been advised to think up a good excuse for having done it. Do you know one?"

'Her own good instincts and her honesty turned what could have been ruination for her into a triumph. She won the public's interest and sympathy at the time, and they began to love her. She was never troubled by the calendar incident again. It brought her publicity she couldn't have obtained with a dozen press agents.'

Another version places Zanuck in the driver's seat. Biographer Leo Guild quotes: 'There were long meetings with the publicity department. The first reaction was to have Marilyn deny she ever posed for the picture. Zanuck was against it. The orders were now that Marilyn was to tell the truth: that she posed for it, that she needed the money, that she was broke and there was a payment due on her car.'

There is yet another version which points the finger at RKO production chief Jerry Wald, an old publicity pro. Confronted with a blackmail demand of $10,000 Wald decided to release the exposé himself, figuring that any harm it did Monroe would only affect her reputation at Fox since she was merely on loan to RKO, which had everything to gain from the publicity.

The Mosby UPI exclusive, which appeared on 13 March 1952 in the *Los Angeles Herald Express*, while hurling Monroe into a hornet's nest of moral taboos, was not entirely unsympathetic. Mosby actually captures that quality of Monroe whimsy which for the actress was something of a safety valve and quotes Monroe as follows: 'I was a week behind in my rent . . . I had to have the money. A photographer, Tom Kelley, had asked me before to pose but I'd never do it. This time I called him and said I would as soon as possible, to get it over with.

'Tom didn't think anyone would recognize me . . . My hair was long then. But when the picture came out, everybody knew me. I'd never have done it if I'd known things would happen in Hollywood so fast for me.

'I was told I should deny I'd posed . . . but I'd rather be honest about it . . .'

The reaction at Fox? According to Mosby, 'Marilyn's bosses at plushy Fox Studios reached for the ulcer tablets when the calendar blossomed out in January.'

Norman Mailer reports the following dialogue between Monroe and a studio executive after the discovery that she had posed for Tom Kelley's nude calendar picture:

'"Did you spread your legs?"

"No."

"Is your asshole showing?"

"Certainly not."

"Any animals in it with you?"

"I'm alone. I'm just a nude."''

Ironically it is the nude's essential modesty (a seeming contradiction) which sanitizes it for mass consumption. 'The myth of Monroe is fulsome: no pornographic displays, no sodomy, no perversions,' says writer Anthony Thompson, explaining the reasons Monroe was able to survive a scandal which assuredly would have devastated anyone else.

In her autobiography Monroe sets down for posterity the surprise she experienced over the paradoxical turn of events attending the calendar exposé. 'A few weeks after the story became known I realized that far from hurting me, in any way it had helped me. The public was not only touched by this proof of my honest poverty a short time ago, but people also liked the calendar – by the millions.'

Having barely recovered her composure from the nude calendar débâcle, Monroe was to flounder in the mayhem of another political scandal before 1952 was over. While still shooting *Don't Bother to Knock* at her home studio, Marilyn was called into Darryl Zanuck's office and asked if it was true that her mother was in a mental hospital? When she confirmed it, Zanuck looked at her beseechingly and said: 'Please, Marilyn, if you have anything else to tell me, tell me now.'

Columnist Bacon recounts: 'Erskine Johnson broke the story about her mother being in a mental hospital. I think she was in a county institution. (Later Marilyn had her transferred to private accommodation.) It was tough, but Marilyn weathered everything.'

The Johnson story which appeared in the *Los Angeles Daily News* on 3 May 1952 ran as follows: 'Hollywood's confessin' glamour doll who made recent headlines with the admission that she was a nude calendar cutie — confessed again today.

'Highly publicized by Hollywood press agents as an orphan waif who never knew her parents, Marilyn admitted that she's the daughter of a one-time RKO studio film cutter, Gladys Baker, and that "I am helping her and want to continue to help her when she needs me."

'Recovering from an appendectomy in a Los Angeles hospital, Marilyn gave me an exclusive statement through the 20th Century-Fox Studio: ". . . My close friends know that my mother is alive. Unbeknown to me as a child, my mother spent many years as an invalid in a State hospital. I was raised in a series of foster homes arranged by a guardian through the County of Los Angeles . . . I haven't known my mother intimately . . . I am helping her and want to continue to help her when she needs me."'

Concludes Erskine: 'The news that Marilyn's mother is alive and in Hollywood came as an eyebrow-lifting surprise because of extensive studio publicity that Marilyn had never known her mother or father.'

Wald's success in riding the wind of the nude calendar gaffe had encouraged Zanuck to take a more lenient view of Monroe, casting her in his own version of *film noir* as a psychotic babysitter in *Don't Bother to Knock*, a film directed by a youngster called Roy Baker who he imported from England. *Don't Bother to Knock* was a precursor of *Niagara*, the film which firmly established Monroe as a star.

12
The English Connection at Fox

The film which Roy Baker had been hired to direct
Monroe in concerns a poor and lonely girl Nell (Marilyn
Monroe) whose outlook on life is voyeuristic. The film
picks up with her when she is babysitting for the child
of wealthy parents in a plush downtown Los Angeles
hotel. Alone, she fantasizes about what it would be like
to be rich, preoccupying herself with trying on the
woman's nélige and scent until she is woken from her
reverie by the stare of a strange man (Richard Widmark)
in the room across the courtyard. He reminds her of
a man she had once loved and who died in the war.
She invites him over for a drink. The man, an airline
pilot, has had a row with his girlfriend (Anne Marno,
later Bancroft) who works in the bar downstairs and
he is looking for a little action. Anything which might
transpire between them, however, is forestalled
when the child becomes hysterical; Monroe threatening
to push it out the window. The parents return just in
time.

The limits of plausibility were strained even in the
morally pedantic fifties both by casting Monroe as a
psychotic and creating a storyline which censored not
only the act itself but any expression of sex interest by
either partner in a normal way bereft of psychosis.
Presumably to cater for the Hays Office, screenwriter

Daniel Taradash made Widmark a pilot (to explain his dallying in some strange lady's bedroom) and invented a dead lover for Monroe (who could imagine anyone walking out on her?). Even in Hollywood of the fifties sex symbols were allowed to be lusted after if the lust was contained within moral perimeters. To have cast Monroe in a role which by virtue of the murder attempt on the child defined her as unbalanced and therefore beyond the pale was so ridiculous that Baker received hoots and boos which after thirty-five years have only just begun to subside.

Whilst Marilyn's name above the title added another couple of zeros to receipts on *Clash by Night*, the appearance she made in *Don't Bother to Knock* was responsible for earning a million dollars profit in the first three months. That Zanuck had to import a British director to work with Monroe on the film, however, says something about her reputation on the lot and why directors for whom she worked once would not work with her again.

'Everyone was bored with her. There was a distinct lack of enthusiasm for Marilyn,' recalls director Baker. 'They all knew about her background of instability, illegitimacy – her mother in the loony bin. All that. I didn't know any of that.

'Designer Billy Travilla was totally sympathetic to what we wanted to do – to transform this glamour girl into a waif. Don't forget it was contrary to anything they knew of her – that she was illegitimate or that her mother was in a mental home. That she posed for a nude calendar. I didn't know, and it didn't occur to me to ask.

'When Fox colleagues heard that I had been asked to do a picture with Marilyn Monroe, they said: "No, not that one again. Wrong. Mad." All this kind of stuff. I later discovered that she had been in about ten pictures with small parts of one sort or another. So she was not

unknown, not by any means. It was just that no one
wanted to work with her.

'Marilyn was never on the set before 11.30 a.m. in the
morning. And there's Richard Widmark pacing up and
down screaming: "Where is that goddamn lady?" and
all that.' But he admits that she was probably at the
studio before that and implies that she was preoccupied
fixing her makeup, choosing a costume, or rehearsing
her lines. In reality, her time was being dissipated in
photo sessions and newspaper interviews which the studio insisted she did. Yet again she was accused of lateness
when it was not her fault.

'But,' cautions Baker, lest he be perceived as too
unfair, 'when she was there Marilyn was a very hard
worker indeed. You meet a lot of people who say: "I
want to be a star." But rather like the other man used
to say: "Do you really want to be successful?" The
surprising fact about most people is that they don't.
Marilyn did!'

Although the film both made a lot of money, and
assisted Monroe in her quest for roles of greater dramatic
scope it was not an artistically successful venture, needing someone with director Otto Preminger's psychological insights to make the character relationships work.
Scripted by Daniel Taradash just prior to the Oscar-
winning *From Here to Eternity* it was kept on ice by Fox
for a year until Zanuck decided he wanted to capitalize
on Monroe's success in Fritz Lang's *Clash by Night* by
starring her in *film noir* at his own studio. Shot at Fox's
Western Avenue lot in the mockup of a Hollywood hotel
(a tempting replica of the Knickerbocker hotel where
DiMaggio was living when he met Monroe), the movie
is significant for having been shot in 'actual time' – which
means it begins when the film starts at about 7.30 p.m.
(when the couple leave the child with the sitter) and
concludes at 9 p.m. when they return. There were no
dissolves, no time lapses of any kind. Every single

change of scene was a 'straight cut' filmed on two floors of this mock-up hotel: the ground floor and the upstairs floor.

Screenwriter Taradash firmly believes that the film could have worked better with a director who knew how to handle material which at best was oblique. 'Roy Baker is a nice man, but a bad choice to direct this picture. He didn't bring anything to it. He shot the script but someone who was more attuned to working with a young girl – and a young girl who was insecure, could probably have got a much better performance. She had a much bigger part here than in *Clash by Night*. She "was" the picture. But she needed a director who could put her in harness. I think that Baker had a schedule problem. This picture was shot inexpensively. There were no exteriors (maybe a stock shot). I think that one of his problems was bringing in the film on time and on budget which he did. If they had spent more money and had got a better director, they might have had something. As it stands now, it is an oddity – a cult film.'

Of Taradash, Baker is more generous. 'It was a unique story and an almost unique picture. Because it observed the unities. The screenwriter was a very good man indeed. He cut the dialogue right down and all that. It was very good and it was beautifully put together.'

Baker had wanted Jane Wyman for the role of Nell. Zanuck, however, insisted on Monroe, confirms Baker. 'But I thought Jane Wyman would have been wonderful in the role. It was a melodramatic story and when you are searching for the willing suspension of disbelief you have to have really sincere powerful actors who can carry us into a fantasy. They will believe it. They will accept it, from someone like Jane Wyman. But if you put into the role Marilyn Monroe who has nothing going for her but a very trivial image of showgirl, chorus girl – a rather tarty sort of thing, there is nothing going for her at all in the first place. You either have to have Marilyn Monroe looking like Marilyn Monroe for most of the picture which you can do – she is wearing the other woman's clothes and makeup. But she looked too beautiful and it was impossible to make her look *un*beautiful for the beginning. And so it knocked the bottom out from the whole story. The story would never have happened to a girl who looked like Marilyn Monroe whether she was nuts or not. We made her a waif and dressed her in a plain cotton dress. She stuck out in all the right places. And she looked wonderful. There is nothing you could do with her to make her look a slag.

'One of the reasons I feel very exercised about all this aspect of it is that I made a very bad picture and every critic slammed it. They took it to bits and me with it. It was a turning point in my career. And the *New York Times* critic said that you could expect anything of a man who would cast Marilyn Monroe as "a psychotic babysitter". I wrote to the *New York Times* and said: "I didn't cast her. You have got it wrong. I was fighting like a mad steer *not* to have her. Once I had got her I did my level best to make it work – convincing and credible."'

As a working partner, however, Marilyn was anything but a sweet, pretty, vapid doll. Baker admits that he 'never knew anyone who came along when Marilyn was present who didn't want to touch her – the continuity girl, the cameraman Lucien Ballard, the gaffer. It was extraordinary. She had scrupulous manners and was intensely polite.' Like Joshua Logan (Monroe's *Bus Stop* director) and drama coach Lee Strasberg he believes she had genius – the kind that stuck out all over.

This impression was further confirmed when she arrived in England at Pinewood Studios to film *The Prince and the Showgirl*. 'She was a genius – an eccentric oddball different from everyone else in the world,' says Baker.

'Once Marilyn had got the experience of having done about ten pictures it was more than instinct. She had learned to place herself extremely well. If you look at clips of her films, there is an expressiveness with which she tilted her head or angled her eyes or whatever, which is remarkable. You know the famous still from *The Seven Year Itch* of the girl standing over the hot air grate whose skirts blow in the breeze. If you look at that you wouldn't get a ballerina to do it better. It's an attitude – the toes, the tilt of the head, the hands. The thing I find interesting about Marilyn Monroe's later pictures is the sheer quality and sheer standard of her style. Some of the things she did in those later pictures are on a very high level. It tells me that there was a lot more going on inside her than even she knew about. We have an expression when discussing an actor. Can she do it? Oh, yes, she can do it, means she is acceptable. I would put Marilyn in that class. She could do it all right. It has to be exactly the right thing. It has to be perfectly done. You cannot worry about budgets and schedules.'

Budgets and schedules were precisely what Baker worried about on *Don't Bother to Knock* since he had a shooting schedule of twenty-eight days, which was hardly enough time when working with Monroe who was an actress renowned for improvisational techniques. She always had to warm up to a role. She was never a one-shot performer, getting it on the first take. 'Marilyn was erratic,' recounts Baker. 'She never played a single line the same way twice. It is not absolutely essential. It is a great help since it affects continuity. If you are going to smoke a cigarette during a scene, you have to puff the same way. Otherwise you can't cut it. One minute she would pick up a scent bottle with her right hand and the next minute she would do it with her left hand. I can get round those things with nursing and a certain amount of fudging. It just makes life difficult.'

The real contention was over coach Lytess whom

Baker fired from the set on Christmas Eve 1951 (the previous Christmas had also been unhappy for Monroe, since following Johnny Hyde's death, she did not know whether Fox had signed the seven-year contract he had prepared). Recounts Baker: 'Marilyn was on the telephone from that moment on conferring with Lytess. We had a telephone on the set in those days.'

Says Baker: 'I have never had the slightest brief for coaches, dialogue directors – any of those people,' observing that Lytess' presence only seemed to contribute to Monroe's confusion. 'She had another woman there, too. There were two of them. It got to the point where I couldn't bear it. Natasha spoke with a German accent and we had Marilyn speaking one or two lines in the picture reading it as if she was a Kraut. I couldn't stand it. I thought: "This is ridiculous."

'Marilyn wanted me to give her "motivation" for this and that – for twitching her finger, for scratching her ear. I refused. I didn't want to compete with Lytess. Too much motivation is senseless. But Marilyn urged me for my input. She could never get too much subtext.'

How did she fare with the other players? 'She never had a scene with Bancroft. Richard Widmark was as accommodating as he could possibly be. But the problem in a scene is if the other actor is waffling about all over the place it is liable to ruin your performance. No question about it: Richard found this extremely distracting and hard work indeed. He never let on. He never shouted or anything. He used to say: "Come on, Marilyn. For crissakes: come on, baby." That sort of thing. Trying to jolly her along. He would pull her leg a bit. It got nowhere with her. She was very strange. You never knew quite whether the information was going in or being totally rejected with her. You could rehearse it and rehearse it, and then suddenly during the take she does a click and something goes on in her mind. You're off in another direction altogether. So you have to stop and start – argue it all out – bring her back to square one.'

Like Monroe, Widmark was a Fox contract player. He had established a reputation for playing psychotic villains, so for him, too, the film was a change of pace. 'Richard was a skilful actor and knew what he was doing. But he wanted to do the film for another reason. He had a long history of playing hysterical villains. Now this was a chance for him to play an absolutely straight leading man who finds he has a nut case on his hands.' The press wasn't convincing. *Variety* observed that Widmark 'doesn't appear too happy with his role as a man confronted by a tragic situation when he realizes the girl is a potential killer'. Whilst *Film Bulletin* remained sceptical of his co-star Marilyn Monroe's 'homicidal tendencies'.

The film also cast in the supporting role of Widmark's girlfriend a newcomer calling herself Anne Marno (later Bancroft). 'She had the discipline of an actress,' says Baker. 'She knew what she was doing. Here was a fully-fledged actress in the straightforward theatre sense of a fully qualified actress at the age of nineteen. She was terrific. And you had the contrast of Marilyn Monroe who was totally instinctive.'

Although they don't have a major scene together in the film, there is an occasion where they confront one another as Monroe is brought down to the lobby to be held for the police. 'I was just somebody in the lobby,' recalls Bancroft, 'and I was to walk over to her and react, that's all; and there was to be a closeup of her and a closeup of me – you know, to show my reaction. Well, I moved towards her and I saw that girl – of course, she wasn't the big sex symbol she later became, and she wasn't famous, so there was nothing I had to forget or shake off. There was just the scene of one woman seeing another woman who was helpless and in pain, and she *was* helpless and in pain. It was so real, I responded. I

really reacted to her. She moved me so that tears came
into my eyes. Believe me, such moments happened
rarely, if ever again, in the early things I was doing out
there.'

Apparently Marilyn was somewhat paranoid about
being photographed badly. 'I told her not to worry
about the camera and stuff and showed her how to
handle herself on the screen in the scene (which she
cottoned on to quickly). We photographed her very
well,' says Roy Baker. (Cameraman Lucien Ballard invented the 'Obie' or baby spot for his wife Merle Oberon
which obscures physical imperfections such as fuzzy
facial hair, beauty marks, moles, etc.) 'She could also be
a devil about clearing a take, and if she felt that she was
off (even a bit) – never mind the others – she'd stamp
her feet, look at the floor and mutter until I'd do it over.
I tried to cover for her inconsistencies,' says Baker. 'I
would say – "I'm going to cover in a closeup, darling,
anyway. So don't worry!"'

Designer Travilla's account of the *Don't Bother to
Knock* shoot differs slightly from Baker's. 'It was difficult
for Marilyn to remember her lines and the more that
was demanded of her, the harder it was for her. That
was the time of Natasha [Lytess]. Marilyn depended
upon her coach to the complete hatred of the directors.
The directors were big important guys and she would
look right past them to the woman. Natasha would nod
and Marilyn would go into a tantrum if she couldn't
have the scene done again.'

Not intense, but tense is how Travilla describes
Monroe, noting how everything in her life seemed to
create (rather than reduce) tension. 'Say she's at work
today and she goes home at the end of the day tired.
She probably eats something light and rehearses with
Natasha for tomorrow's shooting and works herself into
a frenzy. She had to take sleeping pills to get to bed and
go to sleep to awaken in the morning at 5 a.m. Then

the next day she tries to please Natasha and the director, so there would be hassles. She would be in a constant turmoil. She was totally destroyed by it half the time.'

How did she get on with her leading men? Poorly, it seems. For all the superficial cheesecake charm Monroe liked to lead. 'She had no trust in anyone other than her coach and hardly ever listened to the actors next to her,' says Travilla. 'It made people resent her – her leading men. Because she was out to take care of Monroe as a big star. Her busy head was so busy planning and doing these things that people often thought that she was rude. "Please" or "I forgot" or "Good morning" were not in her head. She had a lousy memory. I've got to remember my lines. I must walk three steps to do that and to turn and look. And if the director tried to change any of the staging, since she had worked all night, that would throw her completely and cause an awful fight.'

Makeup man, Whitey Snyder, defends Monroe. 'She was not a bitch, although she might have seemed bitchy at times.' Nerves were apparently her problem. 'She was conscientious about the time she arrived at the studio. She'd be afraid she wouldn't get up in time. So she'd go to bed at 7.30 p.m. to awaken by 5 a.m. She wouldn't be able to fall asleep so she'd take a pill. The next morning she'd be crabby. I used to tell her: "Go home. Play around until 10 p.m. and then go to sleep." She'd go home by herself, study her lines and then try to get to sleep. She was uptight!'

It was during *Don't Bother to Knock* that she met Joe DiMaggio, her future husband. Twelve years Monroe's senior, the American sports legend was earning $100,000 a year from the New York Yankees when Monroe was getting 5¢ a month for washing dishes at the orphanage. Yet when they met DiMaggio was a retired baseball player doing sports commentary for the television networks and Monroe was an actress whose star was in the ascent.

An oddity in the sports world, DiMaggio was a conservative who eschewed flashy clothes, cars and cabarets, preferring the quieter life. Owner of a seafront San Francisco eatery, DiMaggio spent most of his time in the city where he was born, except when he was based in New York doing television sports commentary. A five-year marriage in the forties to Dorothy Arnold, an actress of minor acclaim, had produced one son Joe Jr (then aged twelve).

Although DiMaggio seemed to be a simple sort of fellow, appealing to Monroe in a shy, quiet, retiring, even old-fashioned sort of way, his behaviour once they became intimate was decidedly bizarre. In particular, there was the incident, described by Robert Slatzer, which Anthony Summers refers to as 'the DiMaggio disaster'.

Recounts Slatzer: 'DiMaggio was jealous if she even looked at another man. He couldn't bear show people. And he couldn't bear it that she was divorcing him . . . She started seeing a psychiatrist after she married DiMaggio. Before that she was a nice, normal girl with no mental problems.'

DiMaggio's notorious darker side was eclipsed when they first met by the more old-fashioned paternalistic side of him, and it was not unusual to find Monroe's flat filled with bouquets of flowers he had sent. She also received daily marriage proposals from the Yankee Slugger. The jealous possessiveness which Anthony Summers refers to at length was not in evidence in the initial stages of their relationship. For all her protestation about men coming on too strong, Monroe needed fervent reassurance that she was loved and needed and wanted.

Things went sour between them when DiMaggio tried to usurp the studio role as ultimate authority over Monroe's destiny, setting himself against Darryl Zanuck in a power play which got quite ugly. Prior to that, however, he had run-ins with her coach Lytess, her business partner Milton Greene, and with Marilyn herself, when he attempted to involve her in business dealings and parade her as showpiece at his San Francisco eatery.

According to Roger Kahn, author of *Joe and Marilyn*, Monroe was being used by DiMaggio to satisfy his sex needs, after which he would retire and watch television leaving her devoid of pleasure. I suspect, however, that DiMaggio had too big an ego to have allowed himself to behave with sexual indecency, and it seems more logical to suppose that any frigidity between them was the result of Monroe succumbing to demands at the studio at the expense of marital obligations. Anyway, Travilla turns it round the other way, recounting stories DiMaggio told him about Monroe's narcissism which, given the starlet mentality, seems closer to the truth.

But when they first met in March 1952 the pair were inseparable. Columnist James Bacon was privy to the affair almost from inception. 'I met Marilyn after their first date. I said, "You know who he is, don't you?" She said, "Yes, I know. He's a 'famous' baseball player. But we didn't talk about baseball."' Continues Bacon: 'DiMaggio is a strange kind of guy. He loves sports, hates show business, and only had one show business friend (Frank Sinatra) and that was because of the Italian relationship. They had nothing in common. He was very jealous of her show business thing. He would not go to any function with her. But there was a strong physical attraction – at least at the beginning. DiMaggio is a well-known coxsman [stud].'

Cogently terse, Henry Ephron offers his own views about where the romance failed. 'Joe was incredibly dull, but an amazing physical specimen. In his prime he was 6ft 1in, 195lb. He was not good-looking, but nice-looking. What did they have in common? Maybe she laid him and she loved him. I think Joe loved women,

but he liked his mates, too, and that meant poker, pool
and going to the races. Maybe Marilyn wanted him to
spend more time at home.' Would Ephron rate him as
a stud? 'He never had much personality. He was no
Mickey Mantle. But even as a ballplayer he was a model
of efficiency.'

Accounts differ about *who* actually arranged that
famous tryst and where it took place. Columnist Bacon
names actor Vince Edwards as matchmaker, but the
standard version is that the date was arranged by business
manager David March. It is also possible that DiMaggio
asked a number of people to fix him up with Monroe,
because for months, maybe years, DiMaggio was eager
to get an introduction to the actress fast becoming America's hottest movie ticket. While studio bosses were slow
to exploit the Monroe personality, theatre owners across
the United States had begun to put her name up on the
marquees over professionals such as Ginger Rogers,
Cary Grant, Claudette Colbert, David Wayne and Bette
Davis, knowing full well that hers was the name that
brought in the customers. It is conceivable that DiMaggio, an avid reader of the racing sheets, was impressed
by what he perceived to be the unlimited potential of
Marilyn Monroe. That, combined with the loveliness of
her personality, may have prompted him to try to meet
her.

The celebrated introduction took place at the Villa
Nova, an Italian restaurant where weeks earlier DiMag-
gio had run into David March, a business manager
seeking to represent Monroe in financial dealings. Re-
counts March: 'I was standing at the bar of the Villa
Nova restaurant when DiMaggio walked up to me:
"What's new?" he asked. "I'm trying like hell to get
Marilyn Monroe as a client." "Gee, do you know her?
Can you get me a date?"

'So, I called Marilyn and I asked her: "How would
you like to meet a nice guy?" She was in a depressed

mood. She was a depressed little kid lots of times. "Are there any?" she asked wistfully. (Fred Karger and Arthur Miller were then both married.) I told her it was Joe and she agreed.'

Monroe's own version of events differs slightly. She insisted that she turned down the blind date. '. . . One night a friend at the studio [asked me to come for a meal with] Joe DiMaggio. "I've heard of him," I said . . . "He's a football or baseball player," I said. "Wonderful," my friend laughed. "It's time you were coming out of your Marilyn Monroe tunnel. DiMaggio is one of the greatest names that was ever in baseball. He's still the idol of millions of fans." "I don't care to meet him," I said. Asked why, I said that I didn't like the way sportsmen and athletes dressed, for one thing. "I don't like men in loud clothes . . . with checked suits and big muscles and pink ties. I get nervous." But I went to join a small party with whom DiMaggio was having dinner at [Villa Nova] restaurant.'

The afternoon of the date she tried to call it off and an account of the evening has Monroe being a couple of hours late. Having arrived home from the studio exhausted, she had neither the inclination nor the energy to socialize. She did, however, show up (March apparently rang and said they were waiting dinner). According to March, 'She looked like a million dollars and Joe just stared. But shortly after they were introduced, actor Mickey Rooney (he had co-starred with Monroe in *Fireball*) came over to the table and started yacking with Joe about baseball. Marilyn got tired and said she had an early call at the studio the next morning and had to go home. DiMaggio got right up, asked me if I'd take care of everything, and asked Marilyn if she'd drive him back to the hotel.'

Quite why Mickey Rooney should have intruded himself into the group, involving DiMaggio in a conversation which excluded Monroe, is unclear. Possibly he intended to warn DiMaggio about Monroe's insular reputation around town, as if they got on making *Fireball* it wasn't apparent.

And yet it ended happily with the couple smooching in the back seat of Marilyn's 1950 Pontiac (she had sold the Dougherty Ford). Whether or not he actually scored (DiMaggio claims he did) the couple saw each other every night until he left for New York, where he was responsible a couple of nights per month for covering the Yankee-Giant games for a major television network.

Another contender for Marilyn's hand at the time was Robert Slatzer. In retrospect it seems bizarre that someone as good-looking and sexually vital as Monroe should have been hard-up for dates; not only that, but that one man (Fred Karger) should have passed her up for Jane Wyman and that another (John Carroll) should have led her down the garden path. The reality, however, was that she had only two serious suitors: DiMaggio and Robert Slatzer.

Slatzer confirms that Monroe received an average of five thousand letters per week from Arab sultans, English lords and Texas millionaires. (Prince Rainier had also fancied her as his mistress prior to his marriage to Grace Kelly.) According to Slatzer, however, 'Marilyn was not interested in money; but even if she had been, I was no pauper. I was earning $700 a week as a writer for Monogram Films, which in those days wasn't peanuts and was twice what Marilyn was earning.'

Slatzer's primary attribute was his solidity. There were many occasions during Monroe's checkered film career when she was without rent money and since at the time California landlords could chuck you out without prior notice it was to Slatzer she came until she could sort herself out financially. What is more, Slatzer's career was more stable than Monroe's. Hardly ever out of work, he lived in a spacious home high up in the Hollywood Hills which had once belonged to the playwright

Clifford Odets. It was a favourite place of Monroe's, who believed that it was haunted by the ghost of the plays which had been written there.

Then, too, Slatzer was congenial. He was fun and, unlike DiMaggio, he was non-competitive. One time Marilyn had confused things having made a date with both men for the same night. Recounts Slatzer: 'Marilyn was like she was on the screen – disorientated. She made a date with me for 7.30 p.m. to go to a show but had forgotten that she had agreed to go out with DiMaggio. We both arrived at about the same time. Marilyn was flustered. "I am tired. I think both of you should leave," she said. "I am staying," bellowed DiMaggio. (Now DiMaggio was big and brawny. I had no intention of fighting him.) Marilyn said: "No. If Bob leaves, you leave too." And Marilyn meant it. DiMaggio was burning.'''

When Zanuck saw the *Don't Bother to Knock* rushes, he was not enthusiastic. 'She's an amateur. Her voice is too small and her body is too stiff. You've got to work harder on training. You've got to make an actress of her. She's a tremendous personality. But that's it.' Skouras, however, who was generally negative in his comments about Monroe, dismissed Zanuck's criticism, noting that her name on the marquee increased grosses by $500,000. The word went out: Cast her. Use her. Exploit her. Now!

Two significant films Monroe made prior to the star buildup in *Niagara* were *Monkey Business* (where she is cast as a secretary who cannot type) which was directed by Howard Hawks and served as a sort of primer for Monroe's kooky golddigger portrayal in *Gentlemen Prefer Blondes*, and *O. Henry's Full House* (where she plays a streetwalker in an adaptation of the W.S. Porter short story *The Cop and the Anthem*) which was directed by Henry Koster. The latter role gave Marilyn the chance to work with the consummate British stage actor, Charles

Laughton (whose workshops she had been attending along with some of the finest actors in theatre and film), and to prove herself capable of doing period pieces. (Her success no doubt embarrassed producer Stanley Rubin, who failed to cast her as the heroine in *The Necklace* a few years earlier.)

Monkey Business, a silly comedy by I.A.L. Diamond and Charles Lederer, concerns America's fixation with youth. Cary Grant is cast as a chemist who has invented a formula for age regression: Ginger Rogers plays his wife; Monroe the secretary who can't type and object of the male's adolescent lust.

The pairing of Monroe with Cary Grant was offbeat and it is not surprising they never played together again; for in much the same way that her seductiveness overshadowed Donald O'Connor in *There's No Business Like Show Business* she also succeeded in diminishing Grant's considerable appeal. (This, incidentally, is something which even Mae West was unable to do!)

Marilyn, it is rumoured, did not get on terribly well with Grant. Travilla (whose designs Marilyn wears in the film) when asked if there was any antipathy between them says: 'Insofar as Marilyn got a lion's share of the PR, yes! Marilyn was out to take care of herself as a big star, which some of her leading men resented. When *Monkey Business* came out, the billboards sent around by the studio said *Monkey Business* with Cary Grant and Ginger Rogers and down below it said Charles Coburn and Marilyn Monroe on the left in smaller type. But since she already had made it with the public, and not with the studio, the theatre owners in the marquees with the lights put: "*Monkey Business* with Marilyn Monroe." There was no mention of Cary Grant or Ginger Rogers. The theatres said: "This is our star. This is our draw."'

But according to makeup man Snyder, who was assigned personally to Monroe at about this time, there was nothing remotely pushy about Marilyn and the tensions which were created when theatre owners elected to showcase her name instead of those of major stars handicapped her ability to perform.

Says Snyder: 'They were having trouble with her, so I got her on and off the stage. She was afraid to show up on the set. She'd stay in the makeup room and wouldn't come out to face the public [cast and crew]. She had the greatest inferiority complex of any person I ever knew.' He pauses: 'For some reason she trusted me. I had known her for a long time. I could push her along and get her out of there.'

Probably more comfortable with Howard Hawks than with any other director, Monroe responded to his direction. In a sense they shared a lunatic view of things, Monroe in every sense the perfect screwball comedienne. The working relationship was also eased by the friendship which had developed between them at Joe Schenck's Palm Springs home where Marilyn would often sing and dance for friends, many of whom, like Hawks, were important industry people.

Although it was not until the comedies of Wilder that Monroe really came into her own, she does excel in *Monkey Business*. Whereas with Wilder the characters adjust to the lunacy of life by making themselves believe that black is white (and vice versa) – the prime example being the tag line to *Some Like It Hot* where Joe E. Brown rationalizes his marriage proposal to Jack Lemmon with the response 'Nobody's perfect!' – Hawks creates havoc which catapults his characters to and fro: their singular response being one of extreme bewilderment.

Hawks' comments about Marilyn to John Kobal are worth noting: '. . . I made the thing with Monroe for a very simple reason: Zanuck . . . I put Monroe in with Cary Grant and she did a damn fine job . . . not much to do . . . So the studio got terribly interested. And they made pictures with her that lost their shirts. And . . . Zanuck called me and said, "Howard, we ought to have a great big star here and we're losing money. What the hell is happening?" I said "Darryl, you're making realism with a very unreal girl. She's a completely storybook character. And you're trying to make real movies."'

It was around the time of the Fox buildup, and just prior to being cast in *Niagara* in a role previously earmarked for actress Jean Peters that Monroe vacated the Beverly Carlton flat and took a short let on a spacious Hollywood Hills home with actress Shelley Winters. According to Henry Ephron, Monroe asked studio boss Lew Schreiber for a $1,000 advance and was turned down. However, since Winters' account of the story established that Monroe paid her share, it must be assumed either that Fox did advance her the money after all or she borrowed it from a friend.

Doubtless, the most productive aspect of her friendship with Shelley Winters was the introduction to Charles Laughton, whose acting seminars had gained popularity as workshops for some of Hollywood's finest professionals. The group was small; selection was competitive. And although Monroe was only an observer, Winters had been accepted as a student.

Winters' account of a typical workshop shows just how hard they worked. 'Sitting with Mr Laughton around a luncheon table were Peter Ustinov; his then wife, Suzanne Cloutier, a beautiful French Canadian actress; Paulette Goddard; the Robert Ryans; and Charles Chaplin . . . For the next four hours Mr Laughton talked about the priceless gift Shakespeare had given to all posterity. He explained to the whole class, and that included Chaplin and Paulette Goddard, that if we did the workshop, we would have to work every night since we all had daytime jobs, and for this kind of intense ensemble work we needed uninterrupted continuity.'

Apparently having won over Laughton, Monroe was granted an auditor role similar to that which she had at the Actors Studio. In her autobiography, Winters recalls

Marilyn's appearance at one of the sessions. 'I took Marilyn with me a couple of times to Laughton's group, which I was attending religiously. Her whispery voice would become completely inaudible, and she seemed to shrivel up. After the second time I realized it was such agony for her that I resolved not to invite her again unless she asked me and I really felt she could handle it.'

When Laughton was asked to co-star with Monroe in a dramatization of the W. S. Porter short story 'The Cop and the Anthem', which was part of a five-story package Fox produced under the banner *O. Henry's Full House*, he agreed without hesitation, commenting later on how well Marilyn played the role, without artifice or preconception.

13
Niagara and Monroe Falls for Slatzer

The turning point for Monroe was undoubtedly *Niagara*. It was the first time she got her name above the title; it was shot in Technicolor with lots of glossy closeups; and special pains were taken to make her look good. By this time she had her own makeup man and hairdresser, which probably did much to allay her shyness about her looks. Certainly she felt that she was not naturally beautiful, and Whitey Snyder admits that she always wore 'too much makeup' conscious as she was about the fuzzy facial hair which grew back rapaciously.

The most significant thing about *Niagara*, however, was that it was a starring role which was formulated for the image of her that had crystallized in the public's mind as a result both of the PR engendered by Fox and the scandalous things about her which had been leaked to the press. Essentially, Monroe was a merging of Myth and Anti-myth, referred to in film language as 'the good–bad girl'. The good–bad girl is a Parker Tylerism: the film historian noted for a structural approach to cinema. Tyler defines this prototype as someone who does – but with class. Using a natural landscape, the world's seventh wonder, psychologically reinforces in the public's mind an association of the lady with amoral sexuality: which, as a cinematic icon, was courageous and broke ground in American cinema. (All of Marilyn's films had natural backgrounds but for two duds: *Let's Make Love* and *Something's Got to Give*, both directed by George Cukor.)

Originally written for Jean Peters, a Fox contract player noted for her serious, refined persona, the part as conceived would have made the film a weepy saga about the shattering psychological effects of warfare, with the returning Army hero (played by Joseph Cotten) the focus of controversy. Instead it is Monroe as the frustrated wife whose character dominates the film and whose taunting of her husband's impotency triggers his enmity, whereupon he kills her in a jealous rage.

The plot, briefly, deals with an invalided Army officer (Joseph Cotten) and his wife Rose (Monroe) honeymooning in rented holiday accommodation at Niagara Falls, honeymoon capital of the world. Psychologically disturbed, Cotten is unable to provide his wife with any sexual gratification and as a result she takes a lover (Richard Allan). Discovery of the affair disorientates Cotten, whose stalking and murder of Monroe in that famous bell pealing scene is one of the classically memorable film sequences of all time.

Unless you were aware of the battles for artistic control which raged between the actress, the director and the front office, you might write off *Niagara* as an uneven bit of filming, since it continually struggles between being campy and melodramatic. Director Henry Hathaway was concerned with making an 'action' film pitting Man against Nature (a world in which if they had any place women occupied a sexist role as nonentities without morals or egos). The front office was terrified of the American censors and was concerned that the sex be sanitized and that women be constrained in any expression of a sex drive. There are times, however, when the sensuality and luminosity of Monroe's performance

suggest a young Jeanne Moreau, except that Moreau
was able to work in an atmosphere devoid of the stric-
tures placed upon American actresses in the fifties. The
scenes with her lover (filmed in long shot) of their
rendezvous in the bowels of the falls – those amazingly
torrential downpourings as backdrops – are some of the
most erotic scenes ever filmed. The 'kiss' scene where
Cotten intercepts Monroe *en route* to an assignation is
one of the most realistic scenes of sex frustration *ever*
captured on celluloid. Monroe shatters the distilled sex
images which had for so long passed for sexuality,
replacing them with a pulsating, vibrant, vital sexuality.
It is in *Niagara* that Monroe really discovered where she
was going and how to get there. It was sweet, shy, simple
Marilyn Monroe whose battles forged new frontiers for
women in films. (Eventually leading to her walk-out on
the studio and the studio system, and the formation of
her own independent production company, a precursor
of what was to become the norm in Hollywood.)

Sexism *vs*. Feminism? These forces in contention
produced a situation both fraught and comical, and while
it may be argued that Zanuck was scared to death by
the Daughters of the American Revolution and their
campaign to preserve sex purity, he noted at the same
time that Monroe's instincts about changing American
mores and morals were remarkably accurate.

In the end *Niagara* made back five times more than
what it cost, although objections raised by women's
groups against the film's unmitigated sexuality seriously
imperilled its release in various USA cities.

By all accounts *Niagara* was the steamiest film to
come out of Hollywood since the C.B. DeMille sagas
produced before the existence of the Hays Office which
because of their Biblical themes were full of scantily-clad
dancing girls and sequences of orgiastic revelry. The
scene in *Niagara* that seems to have been most offensive
is the one where Monroe warbles the title tune, 'Kiss',

sinuously stretching her body (which is clad in a skin-tight red satin dress jokingly referred to by Jean Peters as 'the kind you have to start making plans to wear when you are age sixteen') within inches of Casey Adams. (Adams and Peters play honeymooners holidaying at the falls.)

In terms of getting people's backs up the 'Kiss' scene is closely followed by the famous tracking shot (150 feet) of Monroe's walk. In a skin-tight red satin dress, on platforms five inches too high, Marilyn slithers up a cobblestone path (her bottom to the camera). Had she been another actress, I daresay the DAR's complaints would have been justified, but being Monroe she manages to effect the walk with a certain dancer's grace. Steaming with flesh impact, notoriously provocative, there is something in the way she moves that maintains artistic distance, thereby preserving moral and artistic sanctity.

The Hollywood *Daily Sketch* had this to say about the controversy: 'A film called "Niagara" in which Miss Monroe croons a song called "Kiss" had proved the last straw for the matrons. And they have made it clear to Miss Monroe's boss, Darryl Zanuck, that Hollywood is in for another purity campaign unless something is done to curb the present spate of suggestiveness in films and publicity. Do their words carry any weight? The film company have postponed the release of a "Kiss" record by Miss Monroe.'

Time magazine confirms the above, while adding: 'To top it off, moviemakers were worried about a United Press poll of editors which revealed that they were tiring of the sort of news Marilyn and other starlets have been making lately. At week's end, the word was out to Hollywood's press agents: go easier on the sex angle.'

Henry Hathaway was not the ideal choice to direct this kind of a film. The film he set out to make (which concurs in a strange way with Monroe's) was one about a sexually neurotic wife locked into a relationship of mutual torment with her psychotic husband. A man with genuine pretensions to the Spanish throne, Hathaway was a headstrong and opinionated director whose films reflected his obsessions with Man, Nature and the battle that raged between them. His westerns, location films and dramas are masterpieces of economy in evolution and execution, comparable to the very best of John Ford. On the other hand, and unlike Ford, Hathaway manoeuvres his women around with characteristic male arrogance and in his films they are little better than male appendages. It defies the imagination to consider exactly how Hathaway perceived Monroe, and the subconscious war which she would have to have waged to penetrate his entrenched ideas about women and sex.

Robert Slatzer, who was on location with the *Niagara* company for most of the shooting schedule, describes Hathaway as a brilliant fellow but a bully. 'He could make it so tough that if you fluffed a line, you'd never be able to regain your composure.' Apparently the only person Hathaway could not fluster was John Wayne. While he did not go out of his way to pick on Monroe, there was tension between them. Director Roy Baker, who knew Hathaway during his Hollywood years comments: 'He had no patience with actors at all. He was an "action" director primarily. Mostly with men, and very good. Excellent. But not the director for Marilyn of all people.' Whitey Snyder also observed friction, which was compounded by the masses of press interviews which wearied Monroe, and about which she was publicly vocal. 'Hathaway was a hard guy in those days to get along with, because he liked professionals,' says Whitey. 'He disliked Marilyn's coach Lytess, forbidding her to come on to the set. But that was okay since he told us to stay in the General Brock hotel until he was ready to roll, which gave Marilyn time to prepare herself to face the public.'

Like Billy Wilder (whom Bogart took to task for his authoritarianism on *Sabrina*) Hathaway was intractable regarding interpretation and dialogue. A line had to be delivered exactly as written or he'd make an actor do it over and over and over until he got it word perfect. He held no brief for improvisation, and bridled when lines were embellished or ad-libbed. He didn't like coaches much, believing them to be parasites, and he thought that Lytess kept her job by making Monroe dependent upon her. Hathaway told John Kobal: '[Marilyn] had a voice teacher, she had this goddamned Russian woman called Natasha with her all the time. She took walking lessons and all the rest, trying to do something with herself.'

He continues: 'To most men she was, I won't say a bum, but something that they were a little bit ashamed of . . . even Joe DiMaggio. I don't think anyone ever treated her on her own level.' He is critical of 'those bastards in the front office' who, he says, continued to rip her off years after she had become a star. 'When I did *Niagara* I said: "Look I want you to wear your own clothes" . . . She said she hadn't got anything. I didn't believe her, so she said to come over to the apartment and look. It was one goddamn room and a bath and a little stove thing above it. She opened up the closet . . . and in the back was one black suit (which she wears in the famous bell pealing scene when she is murdered) . . . She said she'd bought it when Johnny Hyde died for the funeral. [This confirms my suspicion that the gifts which Hyde had given her were repossessed.] "That's why I have to borrow clothes from the studio when I have to go out. I don't have any of my own," she told me.'

Following the completion of *Niagara*, Monroe's Fox option was due for renewal, and it was in a state of perpetual (and characteristic) trepidation that she awaited their decision. Location shooting had finished on 4 July 1952, and the following Monday interiors started shooting back on the Fox lot. It was at this time that Monroe did something rather inexplicable: she married for the second time, not Joe DiMaggio, but Robert Slatzer.

Monroe's relationship with Slatzer dated back to their first meeting at Fox when she tumbled into Ben Lyon's office, having broken a stiletto shoe heel. A deeply caring and considerate friend, Slatzer was always the one to whom she turned when her high-flying friends deserted her (which often they did) and on several occasions she bunked up with Slatzer following both emotional and economic crises. They both throve on old Hollywood myths, often visiting the stately homes of comedian Harold Lloyd; comedy director Mack Sennett; or matinée idol John Barrymore, which while appearing beautiful on the outside was actually a shrine to everything that went wrong with the man.

It was on the weekend of Friday, 3 October 1952 that the couple decided to elope. Slatzer insists that marriage had been something they had considered for some time. When I met Slatzer, I was amazed at his physical resemblance to James Dougherty. Like Dougherty, Slatzer is big, brawny, quiet and, I suspect, romantic. I wouldn't presume to ask anyone about their sex life; however, Slatzer volunteers that while Monroe was responsive she was often peevish – rolling over and going to sleep if she wasn't in the mood. While Slatzer lacked both the puritanism and emotionalism Monroe liked in her men (Miller and DiMaggio were both jealous and paternalistic) he was reliable. And whilst the marriage may have lacked the highs and lows of grand passion, it had a steadfastness which, had it survived, would probably have enabled Monroe to have escaped the emotional problems that plagued her life.

For the weekend marriage in Tijuana (documentation of which exists in the *Los Angeles Herald Examiner* files), Monroe wore a ponytail, no makeup, sunglasses and slacks. Slatzer, one assumes, was also casually attired.

Having arrived in Tijuana late Saturday night, they paid a cabbie to find a storefront registrar capable of conducting the marriage.

Recounts Slatzer: 'The door to the narrow office was open for customers even at that late hour. The bare wood floor was grimy, and the roll-top desk in the office was piled high with documents and books that presumably had to do with the law. On impulse Marilyn removed her shoes, left them outside and walked in like a child entering a church for her first communion, though she was hardly dressed for the part.' (It later transpired that the registrar was a crook, for when they returned to Mexico after Zanuck had convinced them of the need to annul the marriage, they learned that the man had pocketed the $10 without having registered their certificate.)

The showdown with Zanuck had a dreadful effect upon Marilyn, says Slatzer. 'There were tears on both sides,' he recalls. 'We sat in a quiet area and talked things over. Months later, we considered if we had done right. It was something we regretted and that I still regret.'

Yet at the time Monroe was not a big enough star to have stood up to Zanuck. 'Marilyn rang me on the Monday or Tuesday following that weekend and said that Zanuck wanted to see us both in his office at 7 p.m. that night,' says Slatzer. 'I said: "We'll have to face the music." Marilyn was timid: shaking and crying and stuff. But Zanuck was nice. He knew me, 'cause I had dated his daughter Susan. Roaring with laughter, he asked: "Is it true that you two have married?" I said: "Yes." He said: "We have spent $½ million promoting Marilyn's image as the Ideal Girl waiting for Mr Right to have kids. If it gets out that she is married and no longer accessible, her fan mail will drop." He stopped laughing. His voice grew very serious. "We are contemplating whether to renew her option. I do not want the marriage to last."' Concludes Slatzer: 'We went back to

Mexico and had the marriage annulled.' Had she come to
Hollywood from Broadway or another studio, Marilyn
would have had bargaining power. Had it been one year
later she could have told them to go to hell, as by then
the star system was over. No doubt the episode made
her eventual triumph all the sweeter.

Thus it was that *Niagara* became Monroe's nemesis.
The film won her international stardom but lost the
very thing that might have enabled her to enjoy it: a
committed relationship. The marriages which were to
follow (and which were unopposed by Zanuck) led only
to heartbreak and betrayal.

14
Hawks Again

An indication of Zanuck's perversity about Monroe is the fact that he cast her in a musical after she shone brilliantly as the housewife in the melodramatic *Niagara*. Following *Gentlemen Prefer Blondes*, however, her loan-out price escalated to $½ million.

Fox had purchased the film rights to Anita Loos' musicalized stage version of her play and novel, *Gentlemen Prefer Blondes* for $500,000 as a vehicle for Betty Grable. The 1925 novel had been adapted for the screen in 1928 before being turned into a stage triumph with music and lyrics by Jule Styne, Leo Robin, Hoagy Carmichael and Harold Adamson. Grable was envisaged for the Monroe role of golddigger Lorelei Lee, with Monroe (whose hair Fox had intended to dye brown) being cast in the Jane Russell part of the wisecracking Dorothy Shaw, best friend of the heroine. However, since Grable's popularity had begun to wane in the postwar years, it was decided to remove her altogether from the project. There would be one more film she would do at Fox before being forced to quit (even though her contract had five more years to run).

Marilyn, after years of waiting, got the plush white dressing room previously occupied by Grable. As a starlet, Monroe had only warranted a cubicle in the studio changing room. It was the stars who got the dressing rooms, and Grable's was the nicest on the lot: soft beige walls and thick white shag carpeting. Usurpation of Grable's dressing room had more to do with power than convenience, and the studio let Grable know in no uncertain terms that Monroe had taken over as Fox's primary Blonde. 'They tried to take me into her dressing room as if I were taking over,' said Marilyn at the time. 'I couldn't do that . . . Grable got typed . . . How do we know what she might have done if she had had the chance? I'll never tie myself to a studio . . . I would rather retire.'

Quite a coveted film role at the time, Anita Loos' Lorelei was simultaneously being burlesqued on the Broadway stage by Carol Channing. Although different from Loos' 1928 film version, Channing's interpretation expanded on the original concept which depicted the dumb blonde golddigger as having not only a heart of gold but a will of steel! The way Channing played her, she emerged as an emasculating shrew – in the nicest possible way. Anita Loos has said that she based the Lorelei character on a girlfriend of Hollywood columnist Wilson (or Addison) Mizner (possibly Mae Marsh), the implication being, of course, that it is these icons of feminine submission who are the most lethal suffragettes of all.

The musical differs from anything which had prefaced it at Fox since it tends to parody all the traditions we have come to associate with the Fox musical. In this respect, it allowed the director Howard Hawks the latitude to turn a straight piece into his own unique brand of screwball comedy. In short, he reversed the clichés – the leading ladies are man-eaters. The men are myopic idiots. The child is precocious. Romance is tantamount to seduction (worse, entrapment), and marriage is the be-all and end-all when everyone gets his just desserts.

Hawks admits: 'It was a travesty on sex. It didn't have normal sex. Jane Russell was supposed to represent sanity, and Marilyn played a girl who was solely concerned with marrying for money. She had her own little odd code and lived by it. The child was the most mature one on board the ship and I think he was a lot of fun. We purposely made the picture as loud and bright as we could and completely vulgar in costumes and everything. No attempt at reality. We were doing a musical comedy pure and simple.'

It probably would not have worked in the thirties and forties, but in the fifties, when people proved willing to accept parodies of their most cherished traditions, it did (even when those parodies were as bleak as the 'drag act' impersonation that Jane Russell does of Monroe in the French law courts scene). It is testimony to her wit and style that Monroe transcends a role which Hawks undoubtedly meant to be cloying, rendering up a performance, which for all its clichés, is impressively sympathetic. It was not a prototype which would outlast the fifties, however. By the sixties and seventies we find films which pervert the cliché as a means of coping with the arrival of unisex. The status quo has not radically changed, but a woman's place within it has been drastically altered and it is almost tantamount to sexual suicide for women to use any of their traditional wiles in interactions with men.

Monroe was the last of the sugar blondes, and it is both to her credit and to the credit of the film that the dizzy way she had of interacting with people – allowing herself to be totally and completely vulnerable – ultimately validates both her character and the nature of her marriage to a myopic millionaire.

The most curious part about the project is the way Hawks sought to undermine the sex images of Monroe and Russell. At the time both ladies were monumental sex symbols: huge box-office draws. In terms of physiques alone, Monroe's bottom was acknowledged to be the best in Hollywood, whilst Jane Russell's bosoms were the inspiration for a brassiere designed by Howard Hughes. And yet Hawks, in an utterly insane manoeuvre (which works!), proves that black is white by casting the stars as sexless sex objects.

'I never thought of either of them as having any sex,' he recounts to John Kobal. 'Nobody would ever take Marilyn out . . . nobody paid any attention to her. She sat with no clothes on the set and everybody just walked right by her. And some pretty little extra'd go by and everybody'd whistle. And she couldn't get anybody to take her out. And Jane Russell had never known anything but one man from . . . the beginning of high school and she married him and lived there. She was like an old shoe . . .'

Whether or not Hawks actually chose to do a film that derided the two biggest sex symbols in Hollywood is unclear. It is possible he got roped into doing it as a favour to Zanuck; most probably because he was both one of the few directors who was willing to go a second round with Monroe and a genius of a man who saw a way to do the film that would translate Anita Loos' theories about man-eaters on to the screen.

Whilst I don't think Hawks would agree with director Walter Lang that Monroe was impossible to direct, he does recount to Kobal some of the difficulties involved in communicating with her. 'It wasn't [too] difficult because I had Jane there . . . I'd hear them talking; Monroe would whisper: "What did he tell me?" Jane wouldn't say, "He's told you six times already," she'd just tell her again.'

Zanuck, surprisingly, was unaware of Monroe's musical accomplishments, although she did all of her own voice tracking for the title song 'Kiss' on the film *Niagara*, and so it remained for Hawks to play the role of agent. '"She can't sing" [said Zanuck]. "The hell she can't" [replied Hawks]. "How do you know?" "See she used to come to parties down in Palm Springs and she'd come

over and say, 'Mr Hawks, would you take me home?'
And she's so goddamn dumb that one time I said to her,
"Look, if you can't talk . . . the radio's playing . . .
sing." And she sang . . . She sings good.'

If the film was intentionally ironic, the circumstances
surrounding the casting of Jane Russell opposite Monroe
at twenty times the salary is even more ironic. Russell
at the time was no longer the moneymaker she had been
when Howard Hughes had cast her as the lady with the
big bosoms in *The Outlaw*. Whilst one might conceiv-
ably understand the reason why she was under contract
to Hughes for the astronomical sum of $10,000 a week
for twenty years (whether or not she worked) it is
slightly more difficult to understand why Darryl Zanuck
agreed to pay out that kind of money in a loan-out when
his own star, who had eclipsed Russell's popularity and
was responsible for adding $500,000 to the box office
receipts of every film in which she appeared, was earning
a paltry $500 a week even after her option was renewed
in 1951.

'The fact is,' says Travilla, who did the costumes
for the picture, 'people immediately identify Marilyn
Monroe with *Gentlemen Prefer Blondes*. You hardly ever
hear someone mention Jane Russell.' It is also worth
noting that the followup film *Gentlemen Marry Brunettes*
co-starring Russell with Jeanne Crain didn't make nearly
the money in its initial run, and has nowhere near the
cult following of *Gentlemen Prefer Blondes* in terms of
reissue.

Russell's financial superiority gave her the edge, however; and whereas it might have seemed to Monroe (and
indeed to the viewing public) that it should have been
she who was deferred to, the reality was that whilst
Marilyn walked around on tip-toe, it was Russell whose
whims were catered for, since it was she whom Zanuck
and Hawks had earmarked as their breadwinner.

Choreographer Jack Cole, who was responsible for

the dance sequences on the film, recounted his impressions of the Russell build-up to John Kobal. 'It was a big deal to get Jane Russell . . . for this film . . . [and in consequence a lot of concessions were made to keep her happy] . . . They were all rather evil to [Marilyn] . . . But she was never bitchy [in return] . . . She wasn't amused with women particularly but she wasn't a woman-hater . . . The cameraman [was] Jane Russell's cameraman [Harry J. Wild] . . . Jane got a whole new wardrobe because, next to Monroe, [she] looked like . . . an iceman in drag . . .'

The fact that Monroe managed to keep a sense of humour amid the star-baiting is a tribute to her own good nature, since she was always being criticized for upstaging Russell in some way or another. Exceedingly polite, she is reputed to have gone into Zanuck's office to complain about the salary disparity protesting meekly: 'But I'm the blonde!' Cole recounts: 'As soon as the camera would go on, Marilyn would [cross in front of Russell]. I said to her: "Darling, Jane Russell is Jane Russell, so don't walk in front of her." She just unconsciously would cross in front of her.'

Travilla remembers the circumstances of the film very well indeed – since to him it typified the appalling treatment meted out to Marilyn at the height of her career. 'As far as I am concerned they kept Monroe from being a star for as long as they could, until they were stuck with her. Why? Because she wouldn't play ball, I guess.' He pauses: 'When Marilyn was there during those years, most people said terrible things about her acting. People didn't appreciate her. They laughed at her. They thought she was gorgeous and sexy but didn't know beans about acting. What about Grable? No one laughed at Betty Grable. These are the unanswerable things.'

Travilla continues: 'Jane was the "star" in *Gentlemen Prefer Blondes*. When they signed her, I was in the office. Hawks said: "Thank goodness we've just signed a

$200,000 deal to get Jane Russell. Now we have secure box-office to support Marilyn in the role." No one really remembers Jane Russell, only Marilyn.'

Even now, Russell makes no apology for the way her needs were catered for to the exclusion of Monroe's. But suggests she was unaware of any tension: 'Marilyn had Whitey for her makeup man and she got her first big dressing room next to mine. We got along great together. Marilyn was very shy and very sweet and far more intelligent than people gave her credit for.'

What was her impression of Monroe? Physically unkempt ('no makeup, tangled hair and blue jeans'), workaholic ('She'd stay an hour or two after me rehearsing the dance routines with Jack Cole') and terrified of appearing on the set. 'I talked to Whitey,' recounts Russell, 'and he told me she came in long before I did, and was really ready, but she'd stay in her dressing room and putter. "I think she's afraid to go out," he said. So from then on I'd stand in her doorway and say, "Come on Blondie, let's go," and she'd say, "Oh, okay," in her whispery voice, and we'd go on together.'

Cole says that Marilyn's timidity and lethargy were often caused by not getting enough of the right kind of 'sleep'. 'What made her not show up [on the set] was that she couldn't sleep, she had a great deal of problems with that. (Her furnished Beverly Carlton bed-sit was equipped with a cot.) She'd come to the studio with the line that she was sick, because the one thing she counted on was the way she looked. If she had a line in her face, she would not be photographed. But she'd get into makeup and always comb her hair "just one more time", because she was frightened of coming out.' He pauses: 'It was very funny, her look on screen was very different from in person. She was a most attractive lady and she never wore makeup. On the screen she did, but off screen she looked like the most attractive sex-maniac girl-next-door.'

In much the same way as she approached vocals, Monroe was determined to become if not a fine dancer at least someone who moved well. However, whilst she had a natural rhythm which revealed itself in the way she used her body, it appears that she was decidedly clumsy when it came actually to performing dance steps. Russell recalls: 'We started dance rehearsals with Jack Cole and Gwen Verdon (his assistant) . . . Jack worked dancers to death, but with Marilyn and me he was patience itself. He knew we didn't know our left foot from the right, but he stayed tirelessly with us. I worked until I got fuzzy headed . . . Marilyn would stay for an hour or two after I left and he'd stay with her.'

Travilla confirms this and says: 'Jack adored her. I remember him telling me: "This girl is a doll. She has three left feet. But I am going to make her look good, if she is willing to work." And she worked hard and you never felt that she wasn't a good dancer.'

Whatever the reasons for Natasha Lytess' commitment to Monroe at the beginning, by the time they worked together on *Gentlemen Prefer Blondes*, the coach was 150 per cent sure that Marilyn had the makings of a huge talent, and her views were made clear to photographer David Conover when he visited the set. Conover made some remark about them being lucky to have so important a star as Monroe in the film. Russell added: 'And so beautiful!' While Lytess' response was: 'And so *talented*.'

Lytess did not allow herself to be taken in by either the superficialities or the exploitation of Monroe's surface charm. For this reason she was an invaluable asset and it is regretful that directors such as Hawks were unwilling to allow the lady any latitude. Her presence was also crucial to Monroe's concentration. At some point in the course of production, however, Hawks fired Lytess; but before that there was a tense accord; Travilla observing: 'I think Hawks liked Marilyn. He had to like her. But I think he resented her looking over to Natasha for the "okay". What director wouldn't? It was an insult to the director. I don't ever remember walking into Marilyn's dressing room and finding her without Natasha.'

The Lytess/Hawks discord became a clash of titans; Marilyn caught in the middle of the sword play which, according to Russell, played havoc with her emotions. 'She was torn between the front office who was calling her a cheap, dumb blonde and Natasha Lytess, her drama coach who worked with her every night. It started going wrong when Natasha began directing her on the set. Marilyn's eyes would turn immediately to her when a scene was finished. Howard Hawks, who was trying to direct the picture, wasn't pleased at all . . . Finally Hawks threw Natasha off the set, but things continued to be strained.'

'It was difficult for her to remember her lines, and the more that was demanded of her the harder it was for her,' says Travilla. 'Marilyn depended upon her coach. The directors were big important guys, [but] she would look right past them to the woman. Natasha would nod and do this and Marilyn would go into a tantrum if she couldn't have the scene done again.'

During filming, Russell, an evangelical Christian (as is her mother, although the family name is Jacobi: her great-great-grandfather having been a Prussian-born court painter and friend of William I) tried to convert Monroe. Writes Russell: 'It was suggested that we start meetings in our homes for people in show business who felt it was difficult going to a strange church. We had different ministers to speak. Dale Evans and Roy Rogers, Donald O'Connor, Hugh O'Brian, Beryl Davis, Peter Potter and lots of others met with us once a month. It was called the Hollywood Christian Group. I even talked Marilyn Monroe into coming to a meeting at Connie Haines' house when we were doing *Gentlemen Prefer Blondes*, but she didn't think it was for her.'

Whatever went on at these gatherings – whether participants gave Christian witness, or became involved in rituals of one sort or another – Monroe was considerably put off. Columnist Sidney Skolsky quotes her as having said: 'She and her mother took me to one of those religious meetings they have in the valley where she lives. It was wild. I'd never go again. I want no part of it. But at least Jane invited me . . .' But it is her afterthought that is most revealing. 'Jane, who is deeply religious, tried to convert me to her religion and I tried to introduce her to Freud. Neither of us won.' Jane got the message: 'It's funny,' she observed to David Conover. 'Diamonds are the last thing on [Marilyn's] mind. That girl would rather have several good books.'

Oscar-nominated for his costumes for both *Gentlemen Prefer Blondes* and *How to Marry a Millionaire*, Travilla's celebrated 'Diamonds Are a Girl's Best Friend' ball gown was actually second choice. The original creation was discarded following the notorious 1953 *Photoplay* scandal at the Gold Medal awards (Monroe was cited as Best Newcomer) at which Joan Crawford publicly denounced Monroe for the tarty image she cast upon the film industry by dressing in a vulgar and lewd way. Recalls Travilla: 'I was designing the costumes for "Diamonds Are a Girl's Best Friend" and the original costume which cost $5,000 (a fortune in those days) was a pair of fishnet hose that were built on to a leotard that came up to a barebreasted top. Actually nude fabric. A necklace of diamonds covered her breasts, a brooch here. A necklace adorned her hips with a huge brooch of diamonds in front pulled across the back into a ponytail of black velvet and diamonds falling to the floor. That costume was almost finished when Zanuck said "Whatever you've got Monroe in. We have to clean her up because of the Crawford *Photoplay* attack. Throw the costume out and cover her body."

'Instead (as you know) she wore shocking pink taffeta

lined with a layer of felt – the kind that you cover beer tables with – wrapped on her body to the back and belted to the middle. No fit lines. An easily constructed wraparound strapless gown. The word was: "Cover her body. Do not let the world see her naked. Clean her up or we'll get the picture thrown out by the censors." It wouldn't have been released.'

According to Jack Cole, Marilyn almost had to go into hospital when she learned they were not going to do the number the way they had rehearsed it. 'I had done the most extraordinary beautiful pastel for "Diamonds Are a Girl's Best Friend" . . . with Empire bed, pale pink chiffon sheets, black satin cover with the Napoleonic emblems, a big blackamoor maid with an 18th-century turban, a great mahogany tub. She was in bed, this lady with diamonds, just brushing them, it was beautiful. Anyway, we didn't shoot the number until last. By that time there had been a lot of trouble with public relations because the studio was getting letters from women's clubs who were asking members not to see Monroe's pictures because she was too flagrantly sexual. So Zanuck called me up and said: "No way, baby. You can't do that test for real." And it was so beautiful because she was to be wearing nothing but diamonds with a little horse's tail coming out of her ass with a little diamond horsefly on the tail.'

Fox PR chief Harry Brand (now old and sick) said it all in the late sixties after the abolition of the Hays Office when he said: 'Today a goddamn star could fuck an ape and it might create a vogue.'

In the fifties, however, the vogue was conspicuously different. Referring to censorship problems encountered by Fox in preparing *Gentlemen Prefer Blondes*, Doug McClelland in *The Unkindest Cuts* cites the omission of the Napoleon sequence as the result of some high-level pressure. Stills from the much-publicized musical number had already had a great deal of play by the media in television and billboard advertising and had featured Monroe and Russell in 'exaggerated Napoleonic head-gear . . . climbing a ladder to a quarter-moon in the shadow of the Eiffel Tower'. Another production number with Freudian overtones was also excised: 'When the Wild Wild Women Go Swimmin' Down in the Swimmin' Hole'.

At this juncture, realizing that he had a big star in Monroe, Zanuck made some attempt at repairing the breach between them by suggesting that Monroe move out of her furnished room and into a $750-a-month suite at the Beverly Hills hotel until her unfurnished flat on posh Doheny Drive was ready for occupancy. Having broke up the Slatzer romance, it is typical of Zanuck's perversity that he is also said to have said to colleagues: 'What [Marilyn] needs is a love affair. Someone that cares for her and who she cares for.' Confirms a friend: 'The salary perk enabled her to live better; Zanuck recommended a suite at the Beverly Hills hotel as a temporary refuge. She said she was lonely. Zanuck tried to find her men and women who would spend time with her.'

Ever the ardent suitor, DiMaggio was unabating in his attempts to win over Monroe. Following the Slatzer marriage and annulment, he inundated her hotel room with flowers; David Conover observing on one occasion: 'The door chime rang and another huge basket of flowers arrived, long-stemmed velvety roses. Marilyn put them on a table and quickly read the accompanying card. The message did not seem to please her. "Oh, no," she groaned, "not again" . . . "It's always the same message: 'I love you, I love you.' It comes every day. Day in and day out. As if I didn't know it."' Asked by Conover about her feelings for DiMaggio, Monroe equivocated: '"I don't know. He's very sweet and kind. And very much a gentleman. But sometimes he's so boring. I could scream. All he knows and talks about is baseball . . ."'

It was around this time that she started going out with Billy Travilla. Having been subjected to lots of the same kinds of things as Slatzer, Travilla gives us some insight into Monroe's *modus operandi*. 'I had a date with Marilyn one night and went to pick her up at the Beverly Hills hotel. While I was waiting a young actor at the studio came in and knocked and she said: "Just a moment!" I said: "What are you doing here?" He said: "I have a date with Marilyn." And I said: "I have a date with Marilyn." Then came the bell boy with a huge bouquet of red roses. She told the young actor that he had misunderstood and she had a date with Bill Travilla. She took the flowers and excused herself.' Adds Travilla: 'She was always a thoroughly disorganized and chaotic person. When I first arrived and had knocked on the door, I heard papers being shoved under things being pushed here and there. Under the couch were the papers where she had been shopping and some magazines. She tried to clean it up a little like a kid would. It was part of her cuteness. When she got the bouquet of flowers she didn't know what to do with them. 'Cause we were late leaving. So she put them in the toilet to keep them wet. She was adorable.'

Just prior to filming *How to Marry a Millionaire*, Marilyn moved into the ritzy new flat she had leased on Doheny Drive – then and now a very fashionable area for starlets and business managers close to Beverly Hills. This flat, like the others that surrounded it, was part of a commune of four in a snow-white Spanish stucco building with a wrought-iron entrance gate leading into a courtyard with separate doors to each flat. One of the things that attracted Monroe to it was the Italianate decor, timber beams and carved fireplace. However, when she leased the flat in 1961 on her return to the West Coast prior to moving into the Brentwood residence, she found the place to be oppressively ornamental. But at the time, she liked it and the added space of two and one-half rooms gave her the extra option of a separate bedroom; along with a sitting room and kitchen. This was one of the reasons DiMaggio became a part-time roommate, although the affair was something about which (perhaps for paternity reasons or maybe simply puritanism) he wished to keep a low profile. The romance generally was conducted quietly, the couple dining at out-of-the-way places, eschewing the celebrity spots of Ciro's and Mocambo.

Although it sounds terribly romantic, according to director Henry Hathaway the way DiMaggio conducted the affair had as much to do with his embarrassment over being seen publicly with Monroe as it did with his desire to be alone with her. 'Men thought of her as a little bum . . . I'm not saying DiMaggio did. But he was embarrassed by her,' says Hathaway. Socially, DiMaggio was a washout as he would not escort Marilyn to premières, so she ended up going either with columnist Skolsky or an old married couple, or alone. It was at the *Gentlemen Prefer Blondes* première that she struck up an acquaintance with Frank Sinatra, then married to Ava Gardner. Sinatra was utterly bedazzled by Monroe's performance (I don't think he ever separated Lorelei from Monroe) and was determined to try to work with her. In demand himself after his triumph in *From Here to Eternity*, Sinatra proposed co-starring with Monroe in *Heller in Pink Tights*, which she rejected on account of the disparity in salaries. He was earning about $100,000 per film while she was only making $500–$750 per week.

But it was at the 1953 *Photoplay* awards where Monroe was awarded the plaque for 'Fastest Rising Star of 1952' that she could really have done with some public support. Involved in preproduction on *How to Marry a Millionaire* at the time of the *Photoplay* awards, Travilla vividly recalls the episode since it involved a fracas with Marilyn over whether she could wear the gold lamé film costume to the awards. (It was not until after *The Seven*

Year Itch when her contract was renegotiated that Monroe was able to afford to buy her own ball gowns.)

Says Travilla: 'Marilyn came to me and said: "I'm going to the *Photoplay* awards tonight. I want to wear the gold lamé gown." I said: "You cannot. It is a costume." (It was a pleated lamé with a paper thin lining and was of such delicate cloth that it couldn't hold a zipper. It had to be hand stitched on her. It was a movie costume, not for what I do for my collection evening wear.) I said: "That's a costume, honey. You can't go that way." She said: "What do you mean, I can't?" She said: "I'm going to the boss." I said: "If you give me an order from the front office, you can go looking like an idiot." I got a call: "Give Marilyn whatever she wants." She came back laughing. "I've got the dress, tee hee." And I said: "Tee hee, you're going to have to do some answering to me. Firstly, you are too fat." She said: "I'll take colonics." (She went on two high colonics to rid her system to be thin for the night.) I said: "Don't wear jewellery – simple earrings, simple hair. And my God, Marilyn, walk like a lady." She said: "I promise." The stage had a table which was on the dais, and Marilyn had to come up from the audience – come up to the stage and around the table, to get the award. And as she went around the table the hip moved with all this biased lamé. Jerry Lewis makes a huge joke of the whole thing and jumps up on the table and starts to hoot. Joan Crawford who is publicity-mad is the first to report about Marilyn's vulgarity. Marilyn is crying about it. She was so ashamed. It didn't hurt her press. But she was hurt. She said: "I walked like a lady. And they all jumped on me. Why?"'

Wanting as she did to be accepted by industry people, it was extremely humiliating for Marilyn. Actress Jan Sterling who was present on that infamous occasion says: 'The room treated her like some sort of pornographic entertainer. She got up to accept her "Best Newcomer"

award and she had to walk up the aisle to the podium.
She had those knees that do those funny things. I think
it was Jerry Lewis that started it. He went "Whooooo"
and the whole room broke up in laughter with screams
and cat calls. She was so sexy that they treated her like
a *dirty joke*. It was a threat to all the ladies. It was a
come-on to all the fellas.'

What made it so unfair was that Monroe's private life
wasn't half as lascivious as that of most of the other
people in the room – Crawford herself had a more lurid
past – but it was Marilyn who was the target of it all.
Says Travilla: 'Crawford was a bitch. She was okay if
she liked you. If she didn't like you, watch out.' Sterling
agrees: 'She hadn't worked with Monroe or anything
and she just blasted her.' Adding insightfully: 'Here was
an established star slightly on the wane at the moment
who had a lot of trouble with young actresses. She was
wonderful to me because I was married and happily
married and therefore no threat. I did *Female on the Beach*
with her, and I wasn't going to try to flirt with the
leading man or do any of those things. So she couldn't
have been sweeter. The day that Paul [Douglas] died I
got this call from New York at about 2 p.m. She said,
"Jan, this is Joan. I'm so sorry. If you want I'll get on a
plane and come out and sit in your kitchen. You won't
even know I am there. I'll go out, and do errands." I
really started to laugh. It was the only funny thing that
ever happened to me.'

Mortified, Monroe mumbled something publicly
about being shocked by Crawford's diatribe since she
was well known for the kindness she has shown to those
little children she adopted. Privately however she was
terrified, and it is not surprising that in later years it took
considerable courage (and lots of Frank Sinatra music)
to get her to make an appearance at public gatherings.

Little sympathy was forthcoming in the wake of the
Crawford put-down. Zanuck assumed an obstinately

didactic posture which characterized Monroe as a moral reprobate. The columnists, too, were on the side of law and morals. *Time* magazine reported that 'The girl who likes "to feel blonde all over" accepted her plaque demurely and got a polite round of applause. Then she turned and started back in the hip-flicking "walkaway" that has contributed to her fame. It was suddenly too much for the audience. They cheered, leered, whistled and made wolf noises. But amid all the good-natured laughter and shouting, Marilyn's boss, Fox's Darryl Zanuck, sat with a stiff, straight face.'

Sheilah Graham's impression was much the same. Confirming the absolute riot engendered by Monroe's half-clad appearance in gold lamé, she writes: 'The crush of photographers and reporters has never been equalled before or after. Not even for Elizabeth Taylor. I realized then from the shoving and the hysteria that a new star had arisen in Hollywood and that she could make any demands and she would get them. One thing about Hollywood once they are sure you are a star, every door opens, everyone is rushing to kiss your rear end, and how Marilyn flaunted her rear end! In her public appearance gowns, you could see every crevasse. I hope I was not among the reporters who wrote "How shocking!" but I might have been, because I *was* shocked. I had never seen anything like it in public. She was the living end.'

15
Blonde All Over –
Monroe Trounces Grable

The big play-off pitting Monroe against Grable came in
How to Marry a Millionaire, Fox's second big Cinemascope opus. Also in the cast was Lauren Bacall and the
three of them played husband-hunting golddiggers based
in an east side penthouse apartment in New York City
(not far from the place Monroe leased in 1955 when she
moved to New York with the purpose of starting her
own production company). In deference to Grable's
longevity, she was given the marginally larger role of
Loco which entitled her to star billing, but by the time
the film was released (*Gentlemen Prefer Blondes* having
already earned about $10 million) Grable had handed in
her notice, terminating a contract which had five more
years to run, and Monroe received top billing above
her.

Although Monroe was not by nature a bitchy lady,
she must, nevertheless, have taken some degree of
pleasure in her victory over Betty Grable. After all, it
was a Grable film that they were shooting the day she
crept on to the set in 1946 to prepare for her first screen
test. It was Grable's makeup man who crabbed about
being despatched from his services to the star to make
up this interloper. It was Grable whose plush white

dressing room she coveted, relegated as she was for years to a small cubicle in the studio changing room.

For thirteen solid years Grable held her position, having replaced Alice Faye as Fox's number one pinup in 1940. She was every soldier boy's fantasy – a symbol of what men were fighting for. (Corny but true!) She had a bottom which seemed buoyed by helium. In contrast, Monroe seemed in some respects pedestrian. Evaluating her physique, Travilla admits: 'Marilyn had an ass which was a trifle low and she had a tendency towards plumpness. But Marilyn had all those things that men love to watch.'

By the time she retired, Grable was earning $5 million a year for Fox compared to the $250 million Monroe had grossed by the time she died. She was the number one box-office star during the war; in 1947–8 she was the highest-paid woman in the country earning $208,000 a year. Monroe in comparison generated product which grossed $1 million in three months and yet she was earning $500 per week, $26,000 a year.

Whilst the two ladies were very much aware of each other, their encounters were confined to snubbing each other in the Fox dining hall or silently passing each other in the corridors of the main administration building. It was therefore necessary for formal introductions to be made the first day of shooting. Travilla recalls that: 'Grable was all made up and ready to do the scene. The scene was of all three girls (Lauren Bacall, Betty Grable and Marilyn Monroe) for a nine o'clock shooting. Ten a.m. rolled around. Marilyn hadn't appeared yet and Lauren Bacall was making snide remarks: "Who does she think she is?" That kind of an intolerant attitude. Betty Grable said: "Honey, give it to her. Let's listen to records until she gets here. It's her time now. Let her have fun." And they became good friends. There was no jealousy on Betty's part. But Bacall had no tolerance. Maybe Marilyn was fussing with her makeup and with

her hair to be really pretty to walk out in front of such
big stars as Betty Grable and Lauren Bacall. She had
fear, as a child would. She was coming out of her
comfortable station and it was frightening to go on that
set. People didn't understand it. They got angry, and
they didn't like her for it.'

In his Betty Grable biography, Douglas Warren confirms Travilla's account of the tension on the set that
first day of shooting. 'The crew was again charged with
anticipation when Grable and Monroe had their first
eyeball encounter on the sound stage. Betty, fully prepared for this, chose a moment when the stage was
silent, so everyone would hear her words clearly.
"Honey," said Betty warmly, "I've had mine – go get
yours!"'

Grable's humour was wry and offbeat and Monroe
did not always get the joke. Warren recalls that 'Betty
loved to make subtle jokes at Marilyn's expense, probably because Marilyn was so exceedingly serious about
everything. For example, when Marilyn would make a
telephone call to Betty, the unmistakable whispery voice
would say, "Hello, Betty. This is Marilyn." "Marilyn
who?" Betty would always ask. Marilyn never caught
on that she was being kidded.'

A side of Monroe that revealed itself in her relationship
with Grable and which burgeoned during her marriage
to Miller when she *de facto* adopted his children by his
first marriage, was the solicitude she expressed for other
people's families. She could be abrupt when confronted
by children who proved tedious; for example when
Lauren Bacall's son Stevie made a general nuisance of
himself on the set, Monroe asked him his age. When he
replied: four, Monroe retorted: Oh, I thought you were
younger! On the other hand, she couldn't do enough for
Grable when her daughter Jessica took a fall riding.
Recounts Warren: 'Betty left the set in a rush to be at
her daughter's side. Jessica survived with only minor

injuries, but Betty never forgot that it was Marilyn who called that evening to find out if her daughter was all right – and she was the *only* person to call.'

Publicist John Springer confirms Marilyn's affection for children. 'She was so thoughtful and sweet,' he recalls. 'Marilyn would call me and June (my wife) would answer and she would say: "June, this is Marilyn" (as if it could be anyone else with that voice). "Is John there? I hear that Gary is sick. How is he? Are you taking care?" She wasn't just saying it either. She sincerely cared whether my little boy was recovering from his bad cold. She was that kind of person who when she put her trust in someone who cared, cared deeply for those people.'

The buoyancy of their relationship didn't for a moment change the reality of things – Grable was out and Monroe was in. Turning down the role in a Columbia picture loan-out resulted in Grable's third suspension in two years. On 1 July 1953 she entered Zanuck's office, proceeded to tear up a contract which had five more years to run, said: 'Merry Christmas or Happy Chanukah' and walked out.

Bacall's memories of working with Monroe confirm the impression Travilla had that their relationship was tense. Bacall found it difficult to play with someone who had rehearsed every manoeuvre with her coach. '[Marilyn] wasn't easy to act with because she never looked at you. She didn't react to what you'd say. She'd rehearse, she had a coach, she'd gone through the scene with the coach and the coach had told her how to do it and screw what anyone else did, which was great for her because she had a magic on film, but it wasn't terrific for the rest of us poor slobs . . . she was really very selfish but she was so sad you couldn't dislike her. You just had to feel sorry for her, her whole life was a fuck-up . . .'

Precisely why Zanuck chose this film as his second

Cinemascope venture is a moot point. It was a drawing-
room comedy, but for the brief location shots of the
Canadian rockies where Grable is 'kidnapped' by a lecherous lover, with an American background set in the
fifties. The majority of scenes are within the confines of
a de luxe east side New York penthouse apartment or
posh nightclub, neither of which lend themselves to a
medium designed to showcase a small figure against a
panoramic background (and getting them both within
the pan of the same frame).

Columnist Doris Lilly's story about three husband-
hunters, loosely based on her own experiences as a
society writer and world traveller being wined and dined
by multimillionaires such as Onassis and Rockefeller,
was adapted for the screen by Nunnally Johnson. The
three parts were Loco – a wisecracking lady played by
Grable; Pola – a nearsighted female – played by Monroe;
and Schatze – a serious sourpuss – played by Bacall.
Totally unreal and thorough clichés, they were nonetheless conceived as representative and therefore played
'straight'.

Screenwriter Nunnally Johnson claims he modelled
the characters on what he perceived to be the personalities of his three leading ladies. 'I based the Betty Bacall
character . . . on Betty Bacall,' says Johnson, in conversation with writer William Froug. 'That was Betty.
That's the way she acts and in this particular case I didn't
have any great obligation for reality. We were putting
on a charade. Betty Grable is not going to be anything
but Betty Grable. There's no need of asking her to do
something else. You know so you try to keep it within
her baby-blue eyes kind of comedy thing. As for Marilyn
Monroe, God only knows what she would turn out. I
didn't think she was a very good comedienne, but I
managed to do one thing which I think made her liked
more in the picture than any other. I made her near-
sighted. I put her in glasses and she was very self-

conscious about this . . . It was the first time that Marilyn
was not self-consciously the sex symbol. The character
had a measure of modesty. She didn't think she was the
end. In other words, you also base your character on
what the hell the material is around you.'

If Lilly's characters in the novel were difficult to define,
they were no more plausible in the filmscript. Johnson
may have thought that a near-sighted, frigid lady with
an empty stomach was easy to play, but Monroe found
the character of Pola completely lacking in texture. Director Jean Negulesco recalls the conversations he had
with Marilyn about accepting the role:

'. . . Marilyn's voice quiet, childlike, out of breath:
"Mr Feldman (her agent) asked me to see you" . . . "Mr
Feldman said you'll explain to me" . . . "My part" . . .
"Who *are* we?" "Miss Monroe, you are three beautiful
girls, Loco, Schatze, and Pola, wishing to marry millionaires. And the kind of girls you are, the contents of your
icebox explains: hot dogs, orchids and champagne. Does
that answer your question?" . . . "What is the motivation of my character?" Now it was all clear. Her Russian
coach, Natasha Lytess, had put her up to this . . . "The
motivation, Miss Monroe? You're as blind as a bat
without glasses. That is your motivation."'

The near-sighted metaphor may well have been accurate for someone unable to see the way their life is going,
but in other respects the character of Pola was totally
alien to Monroe. Perhaps because she never traded off sex
for money she was unable to understand the mentality of
women who love to be cosseted and catered for. In
Gentlemen Prefer Blondes there was the myopic Mr Es-
mond (Tommy Noonan) whom she mothered (never
mind that he was filthy rich!). But in *How to Marry a
Millionaire* she is a mindless cartoon pursued by loonies
who merely happen to have money. Nonetheless, due
greatly to the assistance of both coach Lytess and mime
teacher Lotte Goslar, Monroe pulls off the role and

succeeds in giving it a kind of wordless grace – exhibiting the timing, the rhythm, the deadpan movements and grimaces of a silent film clown. Director Negulesco for one appreciated what she accomplished with a very difficult role. '[Marilyn] had such a right sense of knowing the character she was playing – the way to enter a scene, to hold singular attention as the scene developed, the way to end a scene – so that no other actor existed around her.'

Not surprisingly even in this bubblegum comedy Monroe played the nude scene as written, luxuriating naked on the rich, shiny silk sheets summoning up the sense-memory of her subsconscious. Recalls Negulesco: 'Her alluring face shone with divine anticipation. Of men, love, fame, the charming prince? No, the script. She was dreaming of a colossal, juicy Cinemascope-size *hot dog*.'

Yet as appreciative as he was of results, Negulesco wasn't always sympathetic to the means used to achieve goals. David Conover describes how Negulesco, like Mankiewicz, mocked Monroe's literary pretensions. 'Jean Negulesco had asked her what she was reading and she told him Tolstoy in glowing words. He said that she shouldn't be seen reading such stuff, that it might get her into trouble. That really confused Marilyn and she asked Negulesco why. He said that people would think she was a radical – red. She wrote that he seemed upset that she didn't know what a communist was, and she asked me if they weren't a Russian ball club.'

It was in such circumstances that Lytess proved her worth, projecting back at Marilyn the image she wished to see of herself. Douglas Warren confirms Monroe's dependency on Lytess. 'Lytess . . . didn't want Marilyn to follow in Betty Grable's footsteps. "I want Marilyn to do dramatic roles from now on," she said . . . but Lytess was only one of Marilyn's advisers. Marilyn had a retinue of "wise men" ranging from Los Angeles to

New York . . . Everyone but Marilyn herself seemed to know what was best for her.'

Conover also observed Lytess' influence. A nod from Lytess would determine whether or not a scene was to be re-shot. 'On one occasion,' he writes, 'she had a brief but difficult scene to shoot, and time after time she fluffed her lines or forgot them. After the twenty-sixth take, her director tried a different approach. He walked over to Marilyn and took her hand. "Relax, honey. We'll try it again tomorrow. Just don't worry." Marilyn's big blue eyes looked up, puzzled. "Why? Is anything wrong?"'

Adds Conover: 'This infuriated both Negulesco and Johnson. Retakes were wearying and time-consuming, causing the picture to go far over budget. Johnson ordered Natasha off the set. Marilyn retaliated with her only weapon: she didn't report for work the next day . . . Without its star, the studio quickly capitulated and reinstated Natasha.'

Directed by Billy Wilder, the film could have become a surrealist American classic along the lines of *The Seven Year Itch*. As it stands, it is a non-entity, created purely to market the new medium of Cinemascope. The camera is static. The cutting is invisible. And the characters are plastic. Carped one critic: 'Miss Monroe looks silly, impossibly big and drawn out – a figure of nylon and helium for the Macy Thanksgiving Day parade in New York.'

If she emerges as an overgrown mama doll, however, it is intentional, unlike Dolly Parton for whom the role is reality. Much of this was accomplished through the work she did at Lotte Goslar's where Monroe studied dance mime, movement and acting from 1953. Goslar ran a small rep theatre in Hollywood called the Turnabout. Monroe was enrolled in a class with ten pupils. Recalls Goslar: 'She wore no makeup except for a little lipstick. At first she was shy in performing before the

others, but soon she didn't mind being observed and
criticized once I set up a project for them to become
infants and work out a destructive character and behaviour for that baby, then progress to childhood, youth,
maturity and finally old age with the same character in
mind. Marilyn was terribly good at it and everyone was
much impressed.'

The Hollywood première of *How to Marry a Millionaire*, held on 4 November 1953, received the following
notice in *The Hollywood Reporter*: 'Nothing like it [Mari-
lyn Monroe's entrance] since Gloria Swanson at her most
glittering . . . Lauren Bacall was there, too. Pics third
star, Betty Grable, wasn't . . .' Typically, DiMaggio
(who was living with Monroe at the time) refused to
attend, preferring instead to watch television (there was
even a TV set in the bedroom). Monroe rang Harry
Brand, head of Fox publicity, and asked him what to
do. Brand rang Nunnally Johnson and asked him to
include Marilyn in his party.

Columnist Edward P. Hoyt chronicled the elaborate
preparations to ready Monroe for the event. 'Marilyn
had a permanent to straighten her hair. She had platinum
polish put on her fingernails. Two women from the
wardrobe department came in with her slippers, gloves
and evening dress. Diamond earrings were delivered.
She had her own white fox stole and muff . . . Marilyn
remained in the makeup room all afternoon. She was
literally sewn into the dress, which was a white lace
body lined with fresh crêpe de Chine and embroidered
with Marilyn's favourite sequins. It had a train, which
she had to carry as she walked slowly.'

Director Negulesco had the last laugh. Budgeted at
$2.5 million (huge at the time) the film grossed $12
million within a few short months.

But never mind. The will of coach Lytess prevailed:
Marilyn's next project was to be a drama set amid the
grandeur of the Canadian rockies. Her co-star was to be

Robert Mitchum, an old pal from when she had been married to Jim Dougherty and Mitchum was a mate at Lockheed's aircraft factory.

16
Up the Creek with Preminger

The director of Monroe's next film was Otto Preminger,
a pompous Teutonic man with a reputation for being
domineering and rude on the set. He was the worst
possible choice to work with Monroe, but Zanuck had
Preminger under contract. He was obliged to make six
or seven consecutive films using the newly-developed
Cinemascope process. And he had on tap a fine action
story set in the Canadian rockies which Fox producer
Stanley Rubin wanted to develop starring Robert Mitchum. *River of No Return* was therefore a natural for
Preminger and Monroe: the biggest female star on the
Fox lot.

The mixture, as any fool should have seen, was akin
to putting oil with water; Monroe was terrified of Preminger's menacing exactitude – and Preminger was infuriated by her ethereal approach to acting. He resented
the trance-like state she summoned up before performing
and accused her of being unprofessional. He also
suggested she return to her former occupation (i.e. pros-
titution). What he really couldn't stand, however, was
the divine posture she assumed in contrast to that of
other actresses generally gritty about their work.

Jokingly referred to as 'the Prince von Preminger', he
was in fact an Austrian Jew whose talent was so highly
regarded by the Nazis that they offered him a high-

ranking cultural position providing he agreed to convert to Catholicism. Preminger instead emigrated to America where he kept his faith and where for over forty years he made personalized films which distinguished the American film industry. Vigorous politically and socially, he was not easily intimidated, standing up to censorship as determinedly as he defied Hitler. *The Moon is Blue*, filmed a year before *River of No Return*, was released without the Production Code Seal of Approval, Preminger electing to retain such previously unmentionable words as 'virgin' and 'pregnant' in its dialogue track. Anyone who has seen the film will, I am sure, confirm the decided lack of prurience. A glimpse at *Angel Face* made by Preminger in tandem with *The Moon is Blue* and just prior to *River of No Return* will further confirm the director's courage in coping with both actors and eroticism.

All of which suggests that Preminger was not a pedantic and small-minded man, but one who allowed both actors and sex a great deal of scope. Precisely why he failed to get along with Monroe is anybody's guess; producer Stanley Rubin observes that 'Otto was always very careful to be diplomatic with people that he had to get along with, but would rip apart the people who were working under him – the costumer, the makeup man, the property master. He was an autocrat on the set. Most people he would yell and scream at, but he was pretty careful with the stars. In spite of that he treated Marilyn shabbily. Marilyn hadn't got along with Preminger very well.'

Looking back, Rubin acknowledges that the film didn't come off (perhaps owing to the mismatch of Preminger and Monroe), pointing out that he had not originally wanted Preminger for the job. 'Preminger was a talented man. But he was the wrong director for that picture. And I knew it. Preminger was good at gritty, hard melodrama; *Laura, Man With the Golden Arm*

– sophisticated hard melodrama or even urbane comedy: *The Moon is Blue*.

So why not Hathaway, who worked well with Monroe on *Niagara* and was noted for his action films? 'Hathaway could have done it, but he was a difficult man to work with. He was a terror on the set. Those same words could be used to describe Preminger except that he was graceful, sophisticated and urbane.

'I thought that *River of No Return* could be a lovely piece of Americana and I said to Zanuck: the guy who should direct this picture is "Wild" Bill Wellman or Raoul Walsh. Because they were familiar with these ingredients and they knew what they are doing. Zanuck said: "Give me time and I'll think about it." Within a week I got a call from his office and he said: "We're going to go with Otto Preminger." I said: "Why?" "Because we have a pay–or–play commitment with him for $65,000 and we're going to use him. He'll do fine. You watch him. He's a good director.'

Set amid the Gold Rush of 1875, the film is a curious tale about a man called Matt Calder (Robert Mitchum) who is released from prison after serving a sentence for shooting a man in the back. Matt Calder plans to develop his land bordering the River of No Return as a homestead for himself and his son (Tommy Rettig). A horse and a gun are all he's got to survive, and when he's robbed by a gambling man, he tracks him down in Council City where there is a showdown. To save his dad's life, the boy shoots the guy in the back. Monroe plays the gambler's wife, a saloon singer named Kay who takes up with the cowboy when she's dumped by her husband.

The idea, according to Rubin, was to make an American version of De Sica's *The Bicycle Thief* set in the American West about a man who needs his horse and gun and will kill (if necessary) to keep them. 'I wanted to explore what would happen if in *The Bicycle Thief* the man's bicycle was stolen and he had to pursue that bicycle or die. So in our story the guy's horse and gun are stolen and he has to pursue the horse and gun through whatever, 'cause if he can't get them back, he and the kid will die.'

Shot on location at Lake Banff and Lake Louise in British Columbia on the United States border, at a cost of $3 million (in deference to Cinemascope), *River of No Return* was for Monroe what would later become known as a 'disaster' picture, since not only was she publicly humiliated by Preminger, she also had to do her own stunts (which resulted in injury, laying her up for ten days and putting the film twenty-eight days behind schedule).

Shelley Winters, who visited them on location, offers the following observations about Monroe and Preminger in her autobiography: '. . . Otto Preminger, never having been known for his patience . . . was terrorizing Marilyn into total immobility . . . She was terrified of not knowing her lines the next day, and she was convinced that Preminger hadn't wanted her in the picture . . . and that he was secretly planning to do away with her while she was going over some rapids in a raft, then claiming it was an accident. These difficult stunts were usually done at the end of the picture by stunt people, but for some strange reason Preminger was doing them at the beginning and *not* with the stunt people.'

Apparently the more Preminger needled Monroe, both about not knowing her lines and returning to her former profession, the worse she became and the more confused, muddled and unco-ordinated. Consequently when Monroe went out to get the raft, she slipped on a rock spraining an ankle which put her out of commission for ten days. It was the second accident the same week, but this time it was crucial enough to warrant medical attention. 'The chauffeur turned as white as Marilyn's hair,' says Winters, 'and ran to the studio's office in the hotel. Two big crew members came out, made a seat with their hands, and carried Marilyn to her suite . . . Tears were rolling down her face . . .'

Makeup man Whitey Snyder, one of those who fished her out of the water, recalls: 'I carried her out of the river. She had slipped. She went out to get the raft, stood on a rock and slipped. There was a sprain. The doctor put a cast on it. I carried her on my shoulders for the next week or two.' Blaming Preminger for the disaster, Snyder says: 'He was a Nazi. He didn't like people to say anything to him or argue with him or anything else. There was a point of view and it was his. He badgered Marilyn. He made her nervous and uptight, and unsure of herself.' Confirming what Travilla has said about the prevailing antipathy towards Monroe long after she became a star, Snyder observes: 'A big star would usually stand around with a director and they would discuss how to do the scene. But they would never do that with Marilyn. They never respected her for having any brains, power or talent. While Stanwyck, Grable and Gable were catered for, Monroe was always treated as an outsider.'

Despite Marilyn's protests, Zanuck insisted on sending a studio doctor, an orthopaedic specialist and X-ray equipment by private plane. Although no sign of a break could be detected from the X-rays, Monroe insisted upon being fitted with a proper cast on her left leg from the arch of her foot to her knee, with a steel heel so she could walk on it, just in case. Why? A local doctor had told her she had a torn ligament and advised her to stay off the leg for a couple of weeks or otherwise there would be permanent damage. Unfortunately the accident terminated plans Monroe had made with DiMaggio (decked out in fisherman's gear) to take weekend cruises in the lake district to view the fabulous scenery of the Pacific northwest.

In more subtle ways, too, Preminger's approach suc-

ceeded in stifling Monroe's creative flow. But for the
love scenes with Mitchum (always hot as a pistol) her
performance is static, and it isn't until *Bus Stop* that she
shows what she can do with the same kind of character
role.

Having previously worked with Mitchum (opposite
Jane Russell) in *Macao* producer Rubin was enthusiastic
about pairing him with Monroe. 'I wanted Marilyn
Monroe – the girl one and one-half years before I had
turned down for a bit part in the television series. I
now went up to Zanuck, wheedled, pleaded and finally
succeeded in getting her. But,' says Rubin, 'when I
looked at rushes, I remember being very disappointed
and having a terrible fight with Preminger, because I
thought he left out key elements in scenes and motivation
allowing her to make certain changes in her feelings
about Mitchum and the kid. Because she liked the kid
from the beginning. You were not able in the development of a couple of key scenes to see Monroe begin to
understand what Mitchum was all about – why Mitchum
was the way he was, and to see how that affected her
and her visions.

'I didn't feel that Preminger was getting under the
surface of Marilyn in the handling of the scenes, that's
what we fought about. I thought in *Bus Stop* somebody
did get with her and get under and expose a multi-
faceted, three-dimension personality.'

Preminger's own remarks about the film clarify precisely *why* he did the picture: 'This is one of the films I
owed Zanuck under my contract. I liked the script and
I was interested in using the new lenses called Cinemascope. It is actually more difficult to compose in this size
. . . Somehow it embraces more, we see more widely
and it fits into long takes better. On the wide screen,
abrupt cuts disturb audiences. I don't believe in cutting
too much or doing too many reaction shots.'

The reason the film survives is due almost entirely to

Mitchum. The pair were old friends from when Marilyn's first husband Dougherty worked with Mitchum at the Lockheed aircraft factory. Jollying her along, Mitchum would swat Monroe on the bottom and say: 'Now stop that nonsense, madam! Let's play it like human beings. Come on!' Producer Rubin agrees: 'They were lovely together – unreal and sensual. I think there is an especial quality to Monroe (lyrical and so on) when she did that picture. I can't say I saw that quality before she did the picture. I just thought that she was perfect casting for the girl.'

Mitchum's style, uncannily like Widmark's, was credited by critics as causing Monroe to forget her mannerisms and revert to a spontaneous, natural flow of talent. Although the scenes played Mitchum's way are good, I would argue that having been thrown off balance (in more ways than one) Monroe's performance lacks both clarity and purpose. She was an actress who needed both character subtext and guidance on the set, neither of which she received.

The scenes, however, worked in spite of themselves, the heat engendered by Mitchum capable of melting an iceberg. Mitchum recalls doing the love scene in the barn where he takes Monroe in his arms. 'She began to move slightly as she tilted back her head and opened her lips tremulously. I looked at Preminger – "How the hell can I take aim when she's undulating like that?"'

A lot of the hostility directed against Monroe came from Preminger's antipathy towards coach Lytess, whom he fired when they returned to the studio to film interiors and process shots. But even on location the relationship was strained, Preminger complaining that Lytess had insisted Monroe drop 'the soft, slurred voice' which he liked in favour of 'such grave ar-tic-yew-lay-shun that her violent lip movements and facial contortions made it impossible to photograph her'.

Monroe combatively referred to Preminger as 'a

pompous ass', complaining at the way he had barred
Natasha from the set, and vowing revenge. 'That bastard
thinks he's God almighty,' she told David Conover. 'So
I'm screwing up the picture so badly he'll never get
another job at Fox.'

The dispute was resolved when Zanuck persuaded
Preminger to reinstate Lytess in exchange for a favour
he promised him next time around. Even so, producer
Rubin concedes that the problems prevailed. 'Any director, especially a well-known one like Preminger, would
have been highly aggravated by having one of the two
stars of his picture having a coach standing behind her
telling whether the scene was good or not good. It is an
aggravating situation. Preminger was easily aggravated,
but I can understand the aggravation.'

If Monroe hadn't got on with Preminger on location,
she got on less well with him when they returned to the
studio to do the closeups which Preminger planned to
intercut into the long shots he had filmed on location of
Monroe, Mitchum and the boy on the rapids in the raft.
Whilst Rubin believes that Monroe delayed doing the
shots both because she was getting even with Preminger
and because she feared being compromised by the messi-
ness of the routine, my own thinking is that she feared
for her safety.

Producer Rubin observes: 'Preminger was an autocrat
on the set but Marilyn got her own back. She would
delay and delay and delay. Firstly, she hated the shots
because they were exhausting and unpleasant. Then, it
was a way to get back at Preminger to stall him until
there was no time left and he would run over. I remember
one day when she wouldn't come out of her dressing
room on that tank stage. Preminger couldn't get her out.
The assistant director couldn't get her out. I finally got
her out after 45 minutes of talking to her through the
locked door and then inside the dressing room. Firstly,
she didn't want to do the shots because they were

unpleasant (she was nervous about how she would look – like a drowned rat) and then, my secret feeling is that she was getting back at Preminger.'

Mitchum's account of the circumstances surrounding completion of the process shots confirms my suspicions and suggests that the actors were placed in considerable peril. Apparently the set was mocked-up with a big tank doubling as the river, inside of which was a raft. Huge shoots would pour the water down into the tank to shake everything and go roaring past the raft for tight shots of Marilyn, Mitchum and Tommy Rettig. Mitchum recalls: 'In one of the few scenes shot at the studio, I stood on an oak raft in front of a process shot of the raging river while special effects experts shot steel-headed arrows all around me and between my feet. The force of the projectors drove the arrows so deeply into the oak that heavy tongs were required to pull them out. This action was repeated five or six times before Preminger was satisfied he had obtained what he wanted.'

If Monroe was going to survive without the side effects of an ulcer (which intermittently erupted) or any other related nervous ailments, she knew she needed some measure of control over both the kinds of roles she was being offered and the directors with whom she worked. The way out came in a pint-sized package of a thirtyish New York stills photographer: Milton Greene. Not enough credit has been given to Greene for his achievement – which was to establish a precedent, in an era when the studios dominated stars with an iron fist, for what later became known as the star hyphenate. The term, relating to independent film production, refers to a secondary function assumed by a star (such as director, producer or writer) for purposes of control in the film in which they agree to appear. The bank puts up the money for the movie on the basis of the box office value of their name and whereas in the past the studio assumed risk and reward, the burden now is assumed by the star alone.

Greene was a trendsetter. He had the presumption to ask Marilyn Monroe to quit the studio and go into business with him, despite not having been either a low-budget American or prime European producer. He had the insight and intelligence to make it all work out and to recognize the legal loopholes in her Fox contract.

Years before the advent of the independent producer this is no minor bit of power politics. Aside from United Artists (the Pickford, Fairbanks, Chaplin consortium) and Four Star television, Marilyn Monroe Productions was the very *first* independent production company of its kind. Today, of course, the independent producer is quite common. Studios no longer hire and develop stars, writers, producers and directors. Any number of stars produce (write or direct) their own films, including Goldie Hawn, Ellen Burstyn, Paul Newman and James Caan. Unfortunately Greene, whose black silk shirts were reminiscent of George Raft, died in his late fifties, but I met him in the late sixties when he was about forty-seven.

The initial meeting was set up by Monroe's publicist Rupert Allan. Allan, now in his seventies, has both the looks and charm of Gary Cooper, and the business sense of Rockefeller. He has the knack of sensing a sound proposal and seems to know precisely when something is right. (He was also responsible for introducing Prince Rainier to Grace Kelly.)

Monroe, recounts Allan, was thrilled at the prospect of going independent: 'I asked [Marilyn] if I could bring another photographer around. She said, "Yes." She always said: "Yes." She always had time for another photographer. When I introduced her to Greene, she said: "But you're just a boy." And he said: "Well, you're a girl." That was the kind of humour she loved. She roared with laughter.' She told David Conover about

meeting Greene and their plans to liberate her film career.
'In October [Marilyn told me] she met the New York
fashion photographer Milton Greene, who would have
a profound effect on her screen career,' says Conover.
'Soon after they were introduced, they met again at a
party given by Gene Kelly, where they retreated together
from the noisy play of charades to a quiet corner and
they struck an immediate rapport . . . [She said] he was
very sensitive and creative, with a boyish manner that
had a very worldly outlook. She was very excited about
his ideas . . . It was, she said, as if Greene could read
her mind. He seemed to know instinctively the type of
film [she] should do. She appreciated that he had guts,
too – he wanted to liberate her from 20th Century-Fox
and form their own film company, to be called Marilyn
Monroe Productions. She was delighted by his enthusiasm and just knew he was going to [make things work
out].'

17
Slugging It Out With Joe – Monroe Weds DiMaggio

After completing *River of No Return*, Fox announced that Monroe's next film was to be *Heller in Pink Tights*, an updated re-make of the 1943 Betty Grable film *Coney Island*. Her co-star was to be Frank Sinatra, considered hot after his Oscar-winning performance in *From Here to Eternity*. Monroe bridled. Firstly, because Sinatra was to receive $5,000 per week as against her $500–700. And then, more importantly, because she wasn't shown a copy of the script. 'I was informed that Mr Zanuck didn't consider it necessary for me to see the script in advance. I would be given my part to memorize at the proper time,' recounts Monroe in her autobiography.

Marilyn never quite convinced herself that Zanuck wasn't in some way purposefully trying to foul up her career and she expressed great concern over the script's working title. She believed, probably quite correctly, that the studio would try to cash in by crudely exhibiting her in pink tights, when what she was trying to become was a serious actress.

Having notified Fox that she couldn't agree to accept the role until *after* she had read the script, Monroe left for San Francisco where she remained with Joe DiMaggio as a guest of his family. She was promptly

put on six-month suspension, but this was resolved
two and one-half months later as a conciliatory gesture
following her marriage to DiMaggio when she agreed
to report back to work to star in the Irving Berlin musical
There's No Business Like Show Business.

There is no reason to assume that the couple had any
intention of marrying when they left for San Francisco.
DiMaggio, according to Hathaway, did not perceive
Monroe to be the wifely type, whilst Monroe, according
to Slatzer, doesn't seem to have been sure of his intentions: 'She told me that one morning DiMaggio whisked
her off to the City Hall and said: "Let's get married!"'
says Slatzer. 'She thought he was joking. But he was
serious. Dressed in a pair of slacks, a head scarf and a fur
jacket, she couldn't have been more unsuitably dressed.
Taken off balance, she agreed.'

In fact, they delayed the marriage until the following
day (DiMaggio was superstitious and didn't want to
wed on Friday the 13th). The couple appeared before
municipal judge Charles S. Peery on 14 January 1954 at
1.47 p.m. in San Francisco City Hall, to take their vows;
Monroe promising to love, honour but not to *obey*
DiMaggio. It was a serious step for DiMaggio since,
being Catholic, he risked ex-communication by re-
marrying.

Accounts of the ceremony reveal that DiMaggio wore
a simple pin-striped suit, whilst Marilyn wore an outfit
she had purloined from her designer friend Ceil Chapman. Comfy rather than chic, Monroe was attired in a
dark brown broadcloth suit with a dark ermine collar.
Joe placed a diamond solitaire ring on her finger, and
presented her with a full-length mink coat as a wedding
gift. The whole thing lasted three minutes.

The DiMaggio interlude was the first break that
Monroe had in her seven-year Fox indenture. The
columnists were quick to pick up on it, Louella Parsons
writing: 'This is the first time that Marilyn has ever

kicked up her heels. She has been the most co-operative girl on the lot. Apparently she feels that money is a girl's best friend. She has had two terrifically successful pictures, *Gentlemen Prefer Blondes* and *How to Marry a Millionaire* and she is Fox's biggest moneymaker.'

Columnist Hedda Hopper agreed. She wrote: 'The blonde actress who is vacationing in San Francisco was due to report to the studio to begin work on the film *Heller in Pink Tights* but did not show up. She might have been having too much fun with Joe DiMaggio. Marilyn and DiMaggio were reported being seen yesterday in San Francisco. A report from there said they were planning to motor to Las Vegas to get married.'

Actually the couple spent the honeymoon night at the Clifton Motel in Paso Robles, a small, sleepy beachfront village on the Pacific Ocean, where they dined by candlelight on steak in a secluded corner of the dining room, before heading on to Monterey (where Monroe filmed *Clash by Night*) where the Bing Crosby Golf Tournament was in progress. DiMaggio was what we would today call a 'jock', whereas Monroe engaged in no formal athletics. She wasn't even a particularly good social dancer, depending a great deal upon the skill of a partner to get her around the dance floor.

Anyone looking for signs of discord might have noticed that the marriage got off to a bad start when Monroe arrived at the airport bound for an extended honeymoon in Japan with her thumb in a splint – hidden most of the time under her mink coat. 'I just bumped it,' she told reporters.

The ostensible reason for the trip was to accompany 'Lefty' O'Doul, manager of the San Diego Padres, a Pacific Coast League, on a trip to Tokyo to open the Japanese professional baseball season. However, upon arrival in Tokyo, it was obvious Monroe's presence upstaged the Yankee Slugger to such an extent that his appearance was barely noticed. Four thousand people

chanting 'Mon-chan' (love chant) stampeded past guards
and rushed forward when Monroe stepped from the
airliner, and another thousand tried to storm through
the front door of Tokyo's Imperial Hotel. In their efforts
to glimpse Japan's number one foreign draw, fans threw
each other in fish ponds, jammed themselves into revolv-
ing doors and broke plate glass in the halls and filters of
rock gardens; 200 police were needed to restrain them.
DiMaggio and Monroe cancelled a series of press interviews planned for her during their appearance in Tokyo,
which upset the Japanese. A press report describes him
as 'her dour, glowering husband'.

There were further battles as to whether she should
appear before the Korean troops, but, in the end, she
fulfilled her promise to entertain the 45th Division
(100,000 men) and gave them a show that went down
in history as the most shocking and provocative performance ever seen on an Army base. In sub-zero temperatures Monroe stood alone on a bare stage wearing
open-toe sandals and a flimsy Dior skin-tight beaded
purple dress warbling famous Monroe tunes such as
'Diamonds Are a Girl's Best Friend', 'Do It Again' and
'Bye Bye Baby'. (Predictably she suffered pneumonia
and was hospitalized for a week prior to her USA return.)
Junketing from one base to another as part of a four-day
tour, Monroe was asked on one occasion to sing 'Do It
Again' less sexily. Monroe's retort: 'How do you sing
it less sexy?' was something she would one day also ask
Sir Laurence Olivier.

Although there had been other pin-ups who had enter-
tained troops it was Monroe whose effect stimulated
men's desires for participation rather than voyeurism. It
was reported that soldiers actually stampeded the stage
where she was performing, causing one casualty who
had to be removed by ambulance. The distinction wasn't
missed by the US military which used the display to
occasion a diatribe about the decreasing level of Army

morale. If Monroe's performance was shocking, however, it was shocking not because of its obscenity, but
because of its intrinsic honesty. The Pentagon was livid.
Congress was furious. Senator Joseph McCarthy gave
an interview to the *New York Times* military expert in
which he criticized Monroe's 'disgraceful performance'
in Korea and urged the Army high command to correct
it and to correct weaknesses in service morality. He
compared the behaviour of the riotous troops to bobby
soxers in Times Square instead of soldiers proud of their
uniforms.

Monroe's reaction was simplistic: she loved both the
limelight and the attention, boasting to DiMaggio: 'You
ought to have been there, Joe; 100,000 fans cheering
and screaming. You've never seen anything like it!'
DiMaggio's rejoinder: 'Oh, yes I have!'

When Monroe and DiMaggio returned from Tokyo,
they set up housekeeping with Joe's sister in the North
Beach section of San Francisco not far from Fisherman's
Wharf where they had a seafood restaurant. Monroe's
star was in the ascent, whilst Joe had passed his prime
many years before. A tense, uptight man with a super-
sensitive ego, it must have offended him greatly to take
second place to his wife and to see the financial effect of
his marriage. His fee for a television appearance was
reported to have increased considerably; one newspaper
quoted it as having risen from $250 to $2,500.

And yet, it was not beneath DiMaggio to try to exploit
the commodity he had married for personal gain. 'He's
using me!' Monroe complained to Robert Slatzer when
Joe suggested that she might drop in at their restaurant
a little more often, since people liked seeing her there.
But it was when he began putting together his own
company on the basis of her name value that she bolted
headlong back to the calculable exploitation of Fox,
Zanuck and Charles Feldman.

The two and one-half month separation had worked

wonders and Zanuck agreed to Charles Feldman's demands for a raise of $100,000 a year, together with a separate recording deal with RCA. Having sung four tunes in *River of No Return* – 'Down in the Meadow', 'I'm Gonna File My Claim', 'One Silver Dollar' and the title tune – which sold 75,000 copies in the first three weeks of issue, Feldman was able to negotiate the album rights on Monroe's next project separate and apart from the film soundtrack. That is why actress Dolores Gray sang vocals on the LP of *There's No Business Like Show Business* while Monroe's numbers were released independently on the RCA label.

One often forgets how really superb a singer Monroe was. She had no formal training at all, but was extremely enthusiastic and it is not surprising that the *River of No Return* score sold well, since, as producer Stanley Rubin recalls, 'She was interested in costuming, hair and in the dance routines. Jack Cole was the choreographer, and I had Lionel Newman to conduct the preproduction scoring. She was far more interested in the character as a singer, dancer and saloon entertainer than she was in the rest of the story about the girl. She said: "I'll tell you the truth, Stanley. I'm doing this picture because I want to do these songs, and I want to do the dances in the saloon." But when she did the picture and enacted the role of this girl, I think she did it beautifully.'

It is worth noting that in the months prior to her year-long dispute with Fox Monroe finally attained 'status' in the community where for years she had been an outsider. The new contract allowed her to live better, and prompted Monroe to lease an $800 per month house on North Palm Drive in the heart of Beverly Hills, only a few houses down from the Johnny Hyde mansion and around the corner from director Billy Wilder, actor James Stewart and comedienne Lucille Ball. It was (and is) a neighbourhood to which one arrives!

Much grander than the Brentwood residence Monroe

purchased towards the end of her life, this rambling Elizabethan dwelling with its obligatory swimming pool and ornate blue mirrored walls was a showplace. The upstairs private rooms were transformed by Monroe into both study and master bedroom for which Monroe purchased a luxurious king-size bed. (She disliked both the idea of separate bedrooms and sleeping apart.) DiMaggio's contribution was, predictably, a portable television set.

The lease was taken by Monroe who, according to Slatzer, also paid the rent. When they divorced, Monroe's lawyer Jerry Geisler was quoted as having asked DiMaggio, who continued to live on the premises *after* his wife had filed, if he intended to remain until the lease ran out. (A reference, one suspects, to his alleged parsimony.) Later, Arthur Miller would also, according to Slatzer, continue to use the New York City flat she had leased when he was in town even though they might not have spoken to each other for weeks.

The DiMaggio disaster has been scrutinized ad nauseam. I shall briefly quote Whitey Snyder on his view of where it went wrong: 'They had lived together for a while before they got married and had a good time. When they got married Joe was different. He started to boss her around. He didn't like this and didn't like that. She couldn't do this and she couldn't do that. She rebelled.'

Whether Monroe believed she would change Joe after they were married or if she misread things to begin with, the fact is that the relationship evolved into one which hurt her emotional equilibrium, her ability to concentrate, and her professional reputation. Where DiMaggio erred in particular was in failing to realize how he contributed to his wife's frailty by opposing Zanuck. Whilst filming *There's No Business Like Show Business*, Monroe had three fainting spells and it is at this stage that neighbours began to notice her walking the streets alone bundled up in her mink coat at 2 or 3 a.m., crying because DiMaggio obstinately ignored her. When she came home at the end of a hard day, ready to unwind, DiMaggio was either playing cards, watching TV, or chatting with friends. One lady friend recalls glimpsing a naked Monroe and having teased: 'I think she's trying to tell you something.' DiMaggio looked dour. Perhaps he thought she was trying to tell *her* something. Isolation was clearly DiMaggio's way of getting even.

So did the marriage fail because of rivalry? Yes, but also, and more importantly, because of DiMaggio's dislike of role reversal. A middle-class, traditional, conservative male, DiMaggio found it impossible to relate in a manner free of role stereotyping. He wanted a wife. No doubt he perceived Monroe's abrupt, preoccupied behaviour as an indication of bad manners. The idea that a woman could comport herself in the same determined, idiosyncratic manner as a male would have discomforted him.

Totally feminine, Monroe wished to please; and when she wasn't wiped out by exhaustion she made the effort to be a good wife – buying a double bed, bringing Joe supper on a tray in front of the television. Mostly, she was too tired to bother. DiMaggio didn't understand. Neither did Miller, as is demonstrated in James Goode's account of an incident that occurred during the filming of *Misfits*. Monroe, who had had a hard day on the set, encountered Miller in their suite talking with a reporter. He made no effort to cater for his wife's needs, and rambled on. At last Monroe interrupted. 'Glad you've finally brought someone home, dear!' she said, hinting for the man to get lost. Miller was dumbfounded. It didn't occur to him to consider her feelings although he was hypersensitive about her intruding upon his privacy when he was writing. But while Miller got his own back by taking up with another woman, DiMaggio proceeded to lash out at Monroe by implying that she had deviant sexual tendencies. These accusations, totally false and totally unexpected, catapulted Monroe into therapy for an average five times per week, but this didn't stop Monroe from believing, contrary to reality, that maybe DiMaggio was right. Over the years, the rumour intensified and more and more people began to believe it was true.

18
No Biz, Show Biz and Joe's Biz

When Monroe returned to the studio in spring 1954, agreeing to co-star in the Irving Berlin musical bonanza *There's No Business Like Show Business* for which Zanuck needed a top banana, she took it on the understanding that her next project would be the comedy lead in George Axelrod's successful Broadway play *The Seven Year Itch* which Fox had purchased for $500,000 with the intention of having it directed by Billy Wilder.

Opting to return to films, Monroe found herself besieged by all. DiMaggio was annoyed because he thought by marrying her he had landed 'Marilyn Monroe' as the perfect housewife. The studio was unamused by the power play, and got their own back by once again scheduling interviews and press sessions long after the working day, sometimes as many as five or six hour-long ones each night. It is not coincidental that it was on this film (where Monroe had comparatively little to do) that she *collapsed* three times in the course of filming, although many assumed it was because she was pregnant. The following story was carried by a local reporter. 'When the news got round that . . . Marilyn Monroe had collapsed for the third time in Hollywood yesterday, her studio's switchboard was jammed with calls . . . "Is she going to have a baby?" "No, definitely not, though my husband and I do want a family." Marilyn married to ex-baseball star Joe DiMaggio is making her latest film *There's No Business Like Show Business*. She had been ordered to rest.'

In this regard DiMaggio's fury at the studio system and eventual combat with Zanuck are understandable. However, even Monroe's closest friends weren't completely supportive of her clash with the studio, although they agreed that she was being perilously exploited in financial terms.

Travilla recounts: 'Marilyn was no different from any other actress who comes along. They put them under seven-year contracts – groom them, build them, and then at the end of seven years they all get mad. They're by then big stars and want the money. They forget that they wouldn't be where they were if it wasn't for Fox. Give them credit. You owe it to them. They were willing to stake you.'

How much was Monroe really earning at the time? 'I think when she was hassling she was making $600 a week and they were saying she was making $4,000. Marilyn told me that I was probably making more than she was, and that what the newspapers reported she was earning was a lie. By this time she was a big, big star (having made $25 million for Fox by 1952).'

There's No Business Like Show Business was misconceived from the beginning. In the thirties, RKO had used Berlin's music for such films as *Top Hat*, *Follow the Fleet* and *Carefree*, all of which were made with tremendous wit and style by Dwight Taylor and other vintage pros. The Fox production, however, was to be an effort teaming Walter Lang (director), Leon Shamroy (cameraman) and Lamar Trotti (screenwriter) – a triumvirate of vulgarians if ever there was one, responsible for the big, brassy Betty Grable musicals which did so much to ruin her talent while furthering her career. (Incidentally Lang and Shamroy you may recall executed Monroe's screen test.) When Trotti died of a heart attack in the middle of writing the script, he was replaced by Fox contract writers Henry and Phoebe Ephron. Top-flight contract writers, the Ephrons have turned out some sophisticated Hollywood comedies, including *Desk Set* and *Daddy Long Legs*. It is unfortunate that they couldn't have done something to save this film, but by the time they got at it, it was beyond resuscitation. The project was conceived as a showcase for some lovely Irving Berlin tunes (surefire box-office success), but it also evolved as a way of using the talents of several actors whom Zanuck had under contract for another picture. Toplining Ethel Merman, Dan Dailey, Donald O'Connor, Mitzi Gaynor and Johnnie Ray in a nostalgic story of a vaudeville family's ups and downs, Monroe is cast as an interloping chorus girl who falls for their son (O'Connor) and after a series of false starts (where she is accused of stealing their material and upstaging the act), she finally joins their team.

There's No Business Like Show Business is *not* Henry Ephron's favourite film. '. . . I think it was the hardest job we ever had. From the nature of the story, all the scenes were clichés. Our problem was to try to write non-cliché dialogue. We can a couple of Hope–Crosby pictures to get the rhythm and feeling of a big picture. Whether we succeeded or not, we don't know. We were only two days ahead of the scenic designer. They kept taking pages out of our typewriter.'

Monroe's performance on the other hand is one of the best things he's seen her do. 'You know how she got into the picture, don't you? – Irving Berlin saw the nude calendar on Joe Schenck's piano and said: "She's gotta be in the picture,"' said Ephron. 'She came into the picture against five big musical comedy stars – O'Connor, Ray, Merman, Dailey and Gaynor. The best number in the picture was "Heat Wave". Merman wasn't as good. Nor was O'Connor as good.'

Having committed to the film without seeing a shooting script, Marilyn begged the Ephrons (after she heard the story) *not* to make her Donald O'Connor's girl. Ephron recalls the meeting: 'That afternoon we met with Marilyn. She was spending her days in one of the musician's bungalows which were popularly known around the studio as "the little motels". They were furnished with a piano and a couch. When we came in, Marilyn was sipping wine from a glass. So was Mickey, the piano player. The place looked like a cubicle in a whore house. Marilyn's sweater was pinned, a few buttons were missing. Her shirt could have stood a trip to the cleaners, her hair a trip to the beauty parlor. She didn't even bother with "Hello". She just said – "Don't make me Donald O'Connor's girl. I could eat him for breakfast."'

The star system, then and now, rises or falls on the back of one person – the star! No matter what the studio head, writer, producer or director says, it is incumbent upon the star to make decisions which will affect his professional standing. The critical panning of *There's No Business Like Show Business* went down hard with Monroe, who raged against the studio conspirators who had talked her into doing the project. To New York housekeeper, Lena Pepitone, she ranted that the film '. . . was supposed to be a big hit. But when it wasn't, who do you blame? Me! I was "obscene". I was a "menace" to kids. Can you believe it? . . . I was wearing this open skirt – I think they call it flamenco – with this black bra and panties underneath. The dance people kept making me flash the skirt wide open and jump around like I had a fever. They called it a native dance . . . They said it was good for me, good for the picture. Shit! Good for them, that's all.'

During the filming, Monroe had once again been tireless in her pursuit of perfection. Vocal coach Hal Schaefer recounts how she'd arrive every morning at 9 a.m. at the bungalow in the big new convertible she received from Jack Benny as a gift for having appeared on his television programme for 'scale' (the minimum rate). 'I tried at first to get her to relax. She's tense when she starts, because she is determined to become a really good singer. The sessions went like this. "Think of your stomach," I advised her. "Breathe from there. Not from your chest." As she practised Marilyn roamed from sofa to overstuffed chair and back to the piano again. Singing into an amplifier I took her to the top of her range (B-flat), coaxed her even higher until she just barely touched a bottom D-flat in a husky whisper.'

It was with Hal Schaefer or Mickey (her rehearsal pianist) that she'd grab a bite after work, too tired to prepare something for herself when she got home and unwilling to interrupt DiMaggio's poker game or TV addiction to suggest they dine out. Schaefer was later linked with the 'Wrong Door Raid' (he was the escort or front or third party). Some say they were lovers. (He says so.) But when columnists reported them together they describe Marilyn as looking decidedly 'grim'. David Conover recalls receiving a note about Monroe from his brother Austin, a Hollywood reporter. 'I have seen Marilyn on two occasions, both at night on the Sunset Strip, each time squired by a different man. Both times she looked unusually pale and bored; but last night at La Scala, with Hal Schaefer, she looked positively grim.'

Director Lang wasn't impressed by the amount of time and effort Marilyn put into rehearsals. He was beastly to her, which affected the quality of her work. 'Lang hated her,' says Henry Ephron. 'He had heard the stories. You fucked yourself into stardom. He ostracized Monroe. He would invite Gable, Stanwyck, and other big stars around to his place, but never Marilyn. She was *non grata*.'

When asked about working with Monroe, Lang charitably admits that while, yes, she did her own singing, the amount of patience required to get the tracks was demanding. 'It was very difficult to get that soundtrack. She ended up doing most of it herself, but only little bits at a time.

'She didn't seem to fit in with that group. She was worried about herself. All the time. It just didn't work out as far as we were concerned. I guess her limited ability worried her for one thing, because these were all professionals and also good . . . She never seemed to work by the clock: if you wanted her at nine o'clock you might get her at ten-thirty, no matter what the set-up. She did that without any regard for the cost . . .

'Apart from that the picture was a great joy, and because it was a show business story the studio just wanted to load it with names – because, as I said, Ethel Merman wasn't the star they expected her to be; she didn't make enough money. So even with all those other people in it, that didn't seem to be enough without having Monroe's name in it too. She was the hottest thing in the business then, so they put her in it. She fitted the part all right, and did several good numbers in it but just didn't seem to be able to work with the rest of us.'

The truth is that Monroe was an easy scapegoat for everything that went wrong. When 200 extras were dismissed from one of the numbers, for example, Monroe having walked off the set in disgust, it was alleged it was *she* who had them fired. In reality she had nothing to do with it.

The film's most grievous fault is neither script, direction nor Monroe's torso-twisting, but the static camera-work which photographed the whole thing as if it was a stage play set for the screen. It was one of the first Cinemascope pictures and they still didn't know how to handle the new camera. So they used to shoot two or three pages of script without a cut unsure about the cutting.

Travilla, who designed the costumes, says it was

Monroe's toughest shoot, because of the clash of personalities. 'I remember one Friday evening we were on the
third page of dialogue doing a scene which had the whole
cast. Marilyn had one line. It had built up in her to wait
through all the dialogue until she could say her one line.
I was on the set. They said: "We've got to get this shot
in the can tonight or we'll have to come back on Monday
when we should be on stage 15." They shot it again and
Marilyn blew it again. (She was wearing the little French
maid's costume.) She ran to her dressing room and was
crying. The makeup was smearing down her face over
the ruffle in her costume in front. I said: "Now look.
There is not time. We are already on overtime." She
was hysterical. I said: "At least go out and apologize to
the crew." Like a little girl with sobs she went out to
the company and apologized to the cast that she was so
sorry she couldn't get the scene. That evening Marilyn
and I went over to the coffee shop on the lot. I stayed
with her until 10.30 p.m. that night. She said: "You
know, Billy, every day I lose another piece of my mind."
I said, "Marilyn, you are crazy to talk that way. But
crazy you are not. Get a hold of yourself."

'It was working with all those big actors and maybe
she didn't remember the line. 'Cause it was so long to
wait through three pages of dialogue to come up to say
it. If you think to yourself: there's a word that I'm going
to fluff, and if you fluff it, oops! She probably built up
that she was going to fluff it and she did. She was
minimized in her own eyes and everybody else's. And
like a child she had to apologize. It was enough to make
you weep.

'But they were all getting short-tempered. It was
Friday night. "Let's go home." "I'm going to Palm
Springs." "It's 6.30 p.m. I'm going to Hawaii." "We
should have wrapped a half-hour ago."'

Marital difficulties could not help but add to her
problems, presenting Monroe with the age-old dilemma

of marriage versus career. I have always found it intriguing why DiMaggio tried to make her remain at home. It must have been that, like Dougherty, he simply refused to see her for the superstar she was, and chose to disregard the grosses her films earned which ran into millions of dollars.

DiMaggio's negative impression of Monroe's career was apparent to Lena Pepitone, who in her memoirs wrote: 'When she signed for *There's No Business Like Show Business* Marilyn thought she would be making a movie Joe could be proud of . . . But even before the première of the film, Joe told Marilyn that it was nothing more than a cheap Hollywood exploitation of the New York stage . . . When studio executives asked him to pose for publicity photos on the lot with Marilyn, Joe flatly refused. But the next day, he was more than happy to pose with Ethel Merman and Irving Berlin . . . 'He told me they were real pros. They deserved to be stars because they had real talent and had worked hard to earn their reputations' [Monroe told Pepitone] 'He thought that being a star just because you were pretty or sexy, well, that was cheating. "Look at you and look at Ethel," he yelled at me. "What could you do on a Broadway stage?"'

DiMaggio's implication that she was a no-talent cutie who got where she was because of sex or looks or both was insulting. But more than that his lack of faith in her ability to mould herself into a star through tireless study, rehearsal and experience was terrifying indeed. 'He didn't believe I had any talent to fall back on,' Monroe told Pepitone. 'That scared me to death. I wanted a career, and even though I couldn't act then, I sure wanted to learn.'

The marriage progressed in the way that worlds do before they collide – two separate planets each in their own orbit. DiMaggio would have nothing to do with show business (surrounding himself at their Palm Drive mansion with hard-nosed sports types) and refused to mingle socially, which proved a handicap considering that they lived in the movie capital of the world where it was necessary professionally to see and be seen. Complained Monroe to Pepitone: '. . . for Joe there are only two places [that exist] – San Francisco and New York . . . He [hates] Los Angeles . . . I wasn't so crazy about San Francisco . . . I got bored just hanging around the restaurant or going out on Joe's boat. And that fog! I could be plenty romantic without that fog. I just kept catching colds and then I didn't feel romantic at all.'

Columnist James Bacon confirms DiMaggio's jealousy of Monroe's career and the emotional problems caused by his refusal to accommodate the smallest demands she made in regard to its professional longevity. 'Marilyn called me one day and said: "Come over for dinner, because you know show business and you know sports. I think you and Joe would get along." We made a dinner date for Tuesday of the next week and Monday is the day she walked out of the house.' He pauses: 'They had nothing in common. Joe was very jealous of her show business thing. He would not go to any function with her. I can remember several occasions when Sidney Skolsky took Marilyn to the *Photoplay* awards. I remember that I walked out with Sidney and Marilyn and Joe was waiting outside – where they park the cars at the Beverly Hills hotel. He wouldn't go in.'

A friend observes: 'She tried to sympathize with his discomfort at being part of what she called "a three-ring circus". She really was very sweet about it. But he was seriously offended by the privacy invasion and wouldn't play along.' In consequence DiMaggio barred reporters from the house to the extent that one magazine offered $6,000 to anyone able to get a home photograph of the couple together.

Whether or not DiMaggio was purposefully obstructive, his invisibility at public functions hurt Monroe's image. Says Pepitone: 'Joe did nothing to encourage Marilyn's career. In fact, he did everything he could to slow it down. He refused to escort Marilyn to Hollywood parties, so necessary to a star's public image.'

Henry Ephron recounts a conversation Marilyn had with Phoebe about the state of their marriage. 'Whenever she comes home at six o'clock, there are about thirty guys in the house with Joe, looking at television, playing gin rummy, calling the bookie. "What does Joe do?" I asked. "He puts down his cards, kisses her, then picks up his cards again." "Did you have any advice for her?" . . . "I told her to sit on Joe's lap while she's yelling . . . I told her to unzip his fly first . . ."'

Sex, however, was only part of the problem, the overwhelming issue was domination – I will not consort with you unless you do things my way. Pepitone concurs: '[Marilyn told me that] Joe wanted [her] to forget about acting altogether. He loved her for herself and wanted her to be his wife, full-time. He was a rich man and she didn't need a career to support herself. He thought [she] was the best woman there was.'

Slatzer recalls how DiMaggio tried to order Marilyn's life around his own routine: 'She was nervous and tense – couldn't eat or sleep. Her ulcer flared up again. She was exhausted – looked awful; tried to sleep and was late. Zanuck stepped in, ordering DiMaggio not only out of the studio but out of Monroe's life; hiring the best criminal lawyer in the country to extricate the star from her matrimonial involvement. True to form, as Zanuck predicted, DiMaggio did play dirty to keep Monroe from filing but Zanuck beat him in the end.'

Prior to the infamous 'Wrong Door Raid' where he sought to compromise Monroe in bed with a woman, DiMaggio cast aspersions on anybody and everybody posing a threat to her time and affection. He suspected everyone of having some hold on her; Monroe complained to Slatzer that Joe's accusations were so unmerciful at times that she often declined to go home, bunking up at the studio or with Lytess after a 15- or 16-hour work day merely to avoid a quarrel. 'He's the moodiest man I ever knew. He goes for days and days without even speaking to me. His idea of a good time is to stay home night after night watching TV.'

Lytess, in particular, was a bone of contention between them and DiMaggio made no attempt to hide his dislike of the woman – 'Either she goes or I do!' he shouted to Monroe one night as the two women made their way up to Monroe's compartment to rehearse her lines for the next day. When Monroe departed for New York set locations on *The Seven Year Itch*, however, it was DiMaggio, not Lytess, who stayed behind.

The problem, according to one psychiatrist was competition! 'When a woman becomes a big star, then she has found a sure way of self-destruction . . . To have a workable marriage, an actress must find herself a very weak or a very eminent husband. Marilyn's trouble was that she found a husband who *used* to be eminent.'

If DiMaggio resented Lytess because she was a necessary adjunct of Monroe's desire to become a serious actress, Lytess was not beyond putting Joe in his place, and it was to Lytess whom Monroe turned when DiMaggio became physically and emotionally abusive. Coach Lytess was cynical: 'This marriage was Marilyn's biggest mistake. I feel she has known this for some time. I don't think there is any chance of reconciliation. It is probably best this way . . . Marilyn has considerable intellect and hungers for the finer things in life like music, art and literature. She and Joe have little in common.'

Monroe's nine-month folly was over before it began. The response of Ben Lyon, Fox's Head of Talent (and Monroe discoverer), was typical: 'Marilyn needed all her strength of character to deal with her marriage to Joe

On honeymoon, Miller and Monroe relax in the garden of Lord Moore's country estate in Englefield Green, Surrey. The different regimens of their lives precipitated rumours of discord from the first.

Marilyn Monroe and Tony Curtis in the famous 'kissing' scene from *Some Like it Hot*. Although their relationship at the time was cordial, Curtis later compared kissing Monroe to kissing Hitler.

The 'Runnin' Wild' sequence from *Some Like it Hot*. Marilyn was coached for the part by Judy Garland.

Monroe with choreographer Jack Cole who accepted the *Let's Make Love* job only because Zanuck made it financially attractive.

Director George Cukor, directing Monroe in a pretentious bit of Fox fluff *Let's Make Love*. They got on like oil and water, Cukor communicating with Monroe using only third parties.

Marilyn's 'Jewish Mother', Paula Strasberg, who coached Marilyn through her last six films. Both Paula and her husband, Actors' Studio Director Lee Strasberg, believed that Monroe was a genius.

Marilyn, Arthur Miller and Louella Parsons, a powerful film columnist, but always a friend of Marilyn.

Proving that he still has the touch, co-star Clark Gable puckers up for Monroe, sending goose bumps up and down her spine. Playing with the King was the realization of a dream, no mean feat for Hollywood's illegitimate daughter.

Monroe cuddling co-star and Actors' Studio cohort Eli Wallach on the set of *The Misfits,* the last film she completed.

US President John Kennedy and his brother, US Attorney General Robert Kennedy. Jack Kennedy's mistress since the early '50s, Monroe is thought to have aborted their love child shortly before her death, believing the affair was over.

Top: Monroe leaves Columbia Presbyterian Medical Centre, on 5 March 1961, where she had been transferred for rest and relaxation afer being confined for three days under restraint at the Payne Whitney psychiatric hospital, accompanied by her publicist Patricia Newcomb.

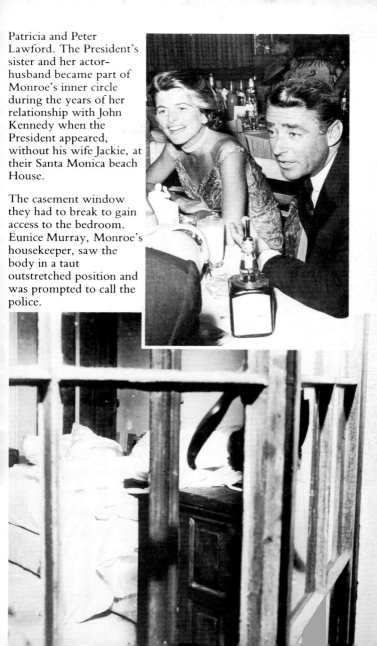

Patricia and Peter Lawford. The President's sister and her actor-husband became part of Monroe's inner circle during the years of her relationship with John Kennedy when the President appeared, without his wife Jackie, at their Santa Monica beach House.

The casement window they had to break to gain access to the bedroom. Eunice Murray, Monroe's housekeeper, saw the body in a taut outstretched position and was prompted to call the police.

The Brentwood residence where Monroe spent the last months of her life. Monroe really wanted a place overlooking the Pacific Ocean, but this was all she could afford.

The small group of mourners at the Westwood chapel where the Monroe's have been buried for generations excluded many who wanted to pay their respects.

DiMaggio. The truth is that they should never have married, and I'm afraid I wasn't surprised when they parted.'

19

Seven-Year Itch,
Nine-Month Hitch

Having taken a virtual cameo (or incidental role) in
There's No Business Like Show Business as a way of helping
Fox to fulfil its commitment to several musical stars
under contract, it was understood that the next project
Monroe would be given would be *The Seven Year Itch*,
a George Axelrod stage play which Fox had purchased
for $500,000. The director was to be Billy Wilder, an
Austrian refugee who lost family in the concentration
camps. Not unlike Fritz Lang and Otto Preminger,
Wilder's temperament was mercurial – something which
Monroe discovered not on this film, but on their next
movie together *Some Like It Hot*.

Having severed his long-term relationship with Paramount (one reason for the break was reputedly his run-
ins with stars of Bogart's magnitude, who jeered that he
was a Nazi), Wilder found himself at Fox in the precarious position of having to negotiate his role in a deal set
up by Irving ('Swifty') Lazar in tandem with Charles
Feldman (Monroe's agent who also would produce the
film) and navigate his way in a project, which because
of Monroe's contractual rights, had to be shot in colour
(which Wilder eschewed) and Cinemascope.

As history records, the film, which went $1.5 million

over budget (blamed on a three-week delay incurred by Monroe's hospitalization to abort an unwanted pregnancy), was nonetheless Fox's top grosser in 1955, earning $15 million in its initial run. Wilder proved himself adept at handling both colour (lovely as a pastel print on a warm summer's day) and Cinemascope. But his real skill was to use the medium to convey a message. He took a quasi-serious American comedy about stultified fifties' sex values and transformed it into parody. Wilder, in collaboration with playwright Axelrod, discarded the play script completely and started again from scratch. The resulting screen adaptation is dotted with wonderful witticisms sending up the text of the parody itself by lampooning such sacred objects as 'Marilyn Monroe' and 'Cinemascope' in the course of the dialogue.

The plot, simply, is a comedy of manners about a summer bachelor (played by Broadway leading man, Tom Ewell) and a toothpaste model (Marilyn Monroe) who live in the same block of flats and whose proximity causes the man to fantasize about the Upstairs Girl. Whereas in the play they actually do go to bed together, the film, bowing to the pressures of censorship, leaves it to our imagination. The conclusion, in tandem with the play, sees the man going back to the arms of his wife and son.

Taking the satire one step beyond Axelrod's intentions to the level of farce, Wilder lampoons not only fifties morality on a surface level but on a subliminal level too. Monroe is not only a single girl (and toothpaste model) with whom the married man has a fling, she is also a voyeuristic and self-conscious projection of the Dream mythology and consumerism which is daily being forced down our throats. She is, in the French sense, a surreal figment of the consumer mentality: both real and unreal.

More than a satire about the summer bachelor syndrome in American marriages, *The Seven Year Itch* is a satire about voyeurism – the most lethal psychological hangup of all. And for this Wilder needed a genius: someone who feels rather than thinks – someone with no preconceived moral ideas. Someone, dare I say it, positively and rabidly *amoral*. It is not accidental that *The Seven Year Itch* is perhaps Marilyn's finest film (although she herself preferred the films produced by Milton Greene, *Bus Stop* and *The Prince and the Showgirl*, to the Wilder comedies). Certainly if not her finest film, *The Seven Year Itch* is the first one to showcase Monroe as the accomplished mime performer she had become.

Of course, in an age of programmed amorality, where the amoral instinct has become acceptable anti-social behaviour, Monroe's tentative manoeuvres to discover things for herself probably appear naïve and comical. But at the time, and in revolt against the oppression of fifties moral taboos (personified by the repressive DiMaggio), Monroe's struggle to experience sensuality and social definition struck a blow for American woman-hood.

Whilst Paula Strasberg has got a lion's share of the credit for Monroe's growth as an actress, not enough acclaim has been given to Lytess for having taken the wiggle and turned it into a star. It was Lytess who liberated a repressed, conditioned and programmed zombie into someone whose body became an instrument of self-expression. Describing the struggle she endured in putting Monroe in touch with her emotions, Lytess recounts: '[She asked me] "Natasha, what is sensual?" I tried to explain, "Well, dear, being able to enjoy things with your body. Like if you eat a luscious fruit, your tongue enjoys it sensually. Not just to undergo a physical sensation, but to revel in it – like being made love to by a wonderful man is sensual . . ."'

If one looks closely at the film (and I have seen it at least a dozen times) you notice that Monroe's complete approach to the role is neo-Freudian. There is barely one

line she utters devoid of some phallic association. She
keeps her undies on ice. She uses a blower to dry her
hair. She trips over an oar. She uncorks a champagne
bottle. She hovers over a subway grate to feel the breeze.
This bit of technique, an integral part of the evolution
of Monroe's persona, was nurtured by Lytess, who in
the course of this film was dumped by Monroe after
seven long years together, causing one gossip to refer to
Natasha's dismissal as 'the seven-year ditch'!

Whereas Lytess seems to have emphasized the adaptation of lovemaking principles to accommodate dramatic techniques (recommending for Monroe all sorts
of erotic literature), it was Paula Strasberg whose neo-
Freudian approach ran a lot closer to things with which
Monroe could identify. Strasberg helped her to break
down motivation into small bits of sense-memory by
fixating upon all kinds of tactile images. 'You are a
soggy soda cracker . . . You are enjoying a bubble bath
. . . You are sipping Coca-Cola . . . You are listening
to Frank Sinatra . . .' By the time Monroe posed for the
skirt blowing scene, she had become physically adept
at translating emotion into action. Observes director
Roy Baker: 'If you look at clips from her films, there
is an expressiveness with which she tilted her head or
angled her eyes or whatever that is remarkable. You
know the famous still from *The Seven Year Itch*. If
you look at that, you wouldn't get a ballerina to do it
better. It's an attitude – the toes, the tilt of the head, the
hands.'

Wilder's biographer, Tom Wood, chronicles the
breach with Lytess in *The Bright Side of Billy Wilder,
Primarily*: 'Another split that occurred during the filming
was that between Marilyn and her drama coach, Natasha
Lytess. At the start of shooting, Miss Lytess was with
her day and night. They discussed the meaning of each
scene, Miss Monroe's relationship to each character, and
her own interpretation. About midway through the

filming, however, Marilyn met Paula Strasberg, the wife of the head of the Actors Studio in New York. Soon Miss Lytess vanished from Marilyn's life.'

Although Lytess technically finished out the film, it appears, according to Wood, that Strasberg had replaced her on the set for much of the picture. 'The actress began to lean heavily on Mrs Strasberg, who hovered over her and made her go through a daily ritual of special hand exercises [actually Monroe was observed by director Roy Baker doing them on *Don't Bother to Knock* years before Strasberg came on the scene] presumably from Stanislavsky, which Billy compared to shaking her hands dry in a washroom with no towels.' Emphasizing the considerable moral support she received from the Strasbergs, Wood mentions how Paula kept reminding Monroe that there was no reason why a great actress should expect to be happy. 'Wilder, however, had a different opinion,' comments Wood. 'He sincerely believed that the day Marilyn stepped before a movie camera she was already a genius. "She can't improve on that," he said. "She can only overanalyze it out of existence."'

Principal photography began in New York on 15 September 1954. The famous Times Square subway grating sequence was filmed at Lexington Avenue and 51st Street (not far from the Waldorf Astoria – DiMaggio's favourite New York hotel) at 2.30 a.m., which meant closing one full city block to traffic for four hours. The site, usually deserted, attracted a mob of 1,000 spectators (held back by police barricades) who gathered to watch Monroe film the shot. Filmed above the grates of the Lexington BMT subway line, Wilder had previously got city permission to hook up a series of blowers underneath the grating (operated by a special effects man) so that at the right moment it would appear that a gust of subway wind had wooshed her skirts into the air. Except that it didn't work – they couldn't get enough air out of the power, causing Wilder to reconstruct and reshoot the scene on the Fox lot.

Surpassing himself in the costume he designed for the air grate sequence, Travilla threw together a thin, ivory-coloured, pleated Georgette crêpe sundress with a halter top and fitted with briefs so minimal that it appeared as if Monroe was knickerless. Probably the best known of all Travilla's creations, the idea for it came rather quickly – he roughed it out over a weekend so as to keep the holiday plans he had made in Mexico. 'I wanted to get the hell out and I worked and worked and did it in about three days. I did the drawings; then I fitted them and got off the show as fast as I could since I wanted to go on a vacation. I designed the whole show in a weekend.'

But wherever did he get the inspiration for the dress? 'The script. It said it was a hot, humid, sultry, ugly August day in New York where people smell of perspiration. You have a beautiful girl. How do you have her look delightful? The wind will blow on her and we want to have her look cool and pretty standing in a subway grate. The vision came to me: a halter dress! Yes, right. That dress is the most publicized dress in our history.'

Looking at it from DiMaggio's viewpoint (which I confess I have great difficulty in doing) it would appear that Monroe's antics were an insult to the sanctity of their marriage vows. His irritation at watching his wife film the historic scene was savage. '[Marilyn told me that] Joe would get furious when she did sexy shots for photographers,' recounts David Conover, 'almost like a wild bull. Often she'd get a naughty streak and pull her skirt up even farther just to irritate him. Joe was so old-fashioned and stodgy.'

Columnist Sidney Skolsky, side by side with Earl Wilson and Walter Winchell, recounts that DiMaggio (having flown in from the coast unannounced) watched in silent rage as Monroe did the stunt over and over beneath the piercing gaze of the crowd. Winchell's presence is noteworthy, since he is the *only* reporter DiMaggio admitted to the funeral, and it was to Winchell that DiMaggio confessed the 'real' reason for the divorce. Officially, DiMaggio claimed that his wife had been overworked; that she was highly nervous and was tired when she came home in the evening, never having any time to herself. It was to Winchell, however (weeping), that he broke the ugly story about Monroe having a female lover. Of course, Winchell never ran the item (how could he – there was no proof) but he did write that DiMaggio, sobbing, had told him the real reason for the split (which he couldn't print).

Why did DiMaggio behave so badly? It is possible that he got a lot of ribbing from pals about the quality of their sex life (which would have to have been Herculean to compare with what they saw on film). It is also possible that he, like the others, failed to distinguish between the actress and the woman, placing emotional demands upon her which it would have been impossible to fulfil. Monroe never said it about DiMaggio, but she complained to Henry Hathaway that Arthur Miller wanted her to be 'that thing on the screen'; a thing which Monroe herself characterized as a put-on.

The thing about gossip is that it hurts – words can indeed harm you. Whether or not they ran the story, reporters certainly would have been affected by DiMaggio's disclosure which in consequence would have altered their perception of Monroe. One odd thing, related to me by Maureen Stapleton, happened at the New York première of *The Seven Year Itch*, which was timed to coincide with Monroe's twenty-ninth birthday on 1 June 1955, and has bearing on what I have just said. Monroe arrived with DiMaggio – a sort of makeup date following the divorce petition which would become final in a year. In the course of merrymaking, DiMaggio's pal Jackie Gleason said something to Monroe that sent her into absolute and total shock. Whatever it was, it was enough to blow the truce with DiMaggio and sent Monroe storming out of the party *alone*.

It was the famous subway stunt, however, which while professionally appealing, obliterated any hope of saving the DiMaggio marriage. He was furious, recounts coach Lytess: 'I was standing alongside Joe. His face grew darker and angrier until – with a snarl that was also a sob – he suddenly shouldered his way through the onlookers and went home. When someone asked his views on the scene he replied angrily: "No comment."' The scene in New York's posh St Regis hotel early the next morning has been recounted as surpassing in intensity the Ali–Frazier fights. There were raised voices, loud noises, and things being dropped and banged about. Whitey Snyder, who came round the next morning, says: 'Joe was in bed and I felt uncomfortable. It wasn't a big suite like they should have had. I had to make her up in the morning and we had to do it in the bedroom. I didn't want to be this close to Joe, but there was no other place to make her up but right there.'

DiMaggio's displeasure was further aggravated when the fabulous subway grate sequence was crystallized for all time in the form of a gigantic 24ft cardboard blowup of Monroe, skirts ahoy, atop Loew's State Theater on Broadway's Great White Way for the duration of the New York run – one of several inventions used by Wilder to exploit voyeurism as an alternative to the censorship codes strangling the American film industry.

Playwright Axelrod wasn't entirely amused by the subversion of his serious play about fifties morals and manners into a voyeurist farce. It does appear, however, that he grasped the problems in conceiving a script which would pass muster of the Hays Office and the Legion of Decency commenting: 'Everything I know about writing films I learned during those five terrible months. Wilder is fond of paradoxes of character, and one of his favourite ploys is to exaggerate the compelling allure of vice and the dreary respectability of virtue.'

It is worth noting that when Axelrod was given *carte blanche* as both writer and director on *The Secret Life of an American Wife* his characters lacked the credibility of their English counterparts and there was not the compensation of Wilder's flair for creating farce.

Monroe's anti-existential approach to the character, developing herself as a fantasy creation, dovetailed with Wilder's conception and obviated certain censorial problems; yet when she suggested that she do the love scene nude they thought she had gone a bit too far. Recounts columnist Earl Wilson: 'When she was filming *The Seven Year Itch* . . . she [said] she wanted to do a nude scene, which in those years was unthinkable. "But it would be true to the story," she said to director Billy Wilder and producer Charles Feldman, who overruled her. Marilyn would have been far ahead of the pack if she'd shown herself in the flesh on screen. She was also ahead of the mob in her attitude about sexual freedom.'

The idea is mind boggling: Monroe stark naked in an era when even the slightest hint of bosom was enough to warrant an 'X' rating. And yet – given her supreme sense of style and impeccable taste (not to mention her incredible foresight) – it would have been sensational. How would she have played it? I imagine in absolute and utter contrast to the anal nudes we see today. Monroe, I suspect, would have been soft and supple – more innocent than erotic, realizing Wilder's vision of The Girl as a symbol of Vulnerability.

Creating sequences not in the play allowed Wilder to remain within code limitations. In one precious scene The Girl punctures the 'macho' myth in a sweet speech which in its simplicity is far more exciting than any bedroom manoeuvring. 'You think a girl goes to a party and there's some guy – a great big lunk in a fancy-striped vest,' she tells Ewell, 'strutting around like a tiger, giving you that "I'm so handsome you can't resist me" look and from this she's supposed to fall flat on her face . . . But there's another guy in the room . . . maybe he's kind of nervous and shy and perspiring a little . . . That's what's really exciting.'

The Times Square subway scene (not in the play) was designed to bring the action outside the apartment confines to allow for physical contact between the couple. In a moment of whimsy approaching Vigo or Renoir The Girl tells the man she fancies the scary creature from the black lagoon (a movie they've just seen) punctuating the remark with an affectionate smooch. This sequence precedes the bedroom scene climax of the play; the film action placing the man soundly on the living room couch whilst The Girl awakens the next morning alone in the bedroom. European distributors, free of the petty restraints handicapping Americans, asked whether it would be all right to excise the scene altogether so as to maintain the illusion that the couple had spent the night together.

Having seen both versions, I conclude that the American one is superior; an opinion shared by French film writer André Bazin who feels that fifties Hollywood voyeurism is as much a sex stimulant as a depressant. 'The famous scene . . . in which the air from the subway grating blows up her skirt . . . could only be born in the world of a cinema with a long, rich, Byzantine tradition of censorship. Inventiveness such as this presupposes an extraordinary refinement of the imagination, acquired in the struggle against the rigorous stupidity of a puritan code. Hollywood, in spite and because of the taboos that dominate it, remains the world capital of cinematic eroticism.'

The prevailing legend about Wilder and Monroe is savage; the director is reputed to have said that she was the meanest woman in Hollywood. Contrary to everything he said about Monroe after *Some Like It Hot*, however, his initial reaction was exceedingly kind – even blissful. 'At no time did I find her malicious, mean, capricious, or anything but conscientious. There are certain urges and drives in her which made her different, but as a director, I think it's worth putting up with those things and living with them in order to work with her.'

Kind, endlessly thoughtful and patient, Wilder sympathized with those emotional problems which interfered with her concentration and performance on *The Seven Year Itch*. 'He didn't ask her why she came late or why she forgot her lines,' writes David Conover. 'He allowed her to go at her own pace, and to do take after take. His air of nonchalance gave Marilyn comfort as well as confidence.'

Closer to the truth is that they were both perfectionists. If a scene was not filmed word for word, action for action the way Wilder had envisaged it, he would make an actor do it over. Marilyn, by the same account, was her own severest critic. 'She always reserved her best performances for the projection room . . . It was the moment of truth . . . She sat and squirmed, and did her entire scene all over again while it was on the screen,' recounts Wilder. Tom Wood recalls a typical working situation when they were shooting the scene where Marilyn, wearing a flimsy nightgown, slips downstairs to Ewell's flat carrying a hammer in one hand and a glass of water in the other. 'Feeling that she had done it to the best of her ability, she walked off the stage. Billy wanted to shoot another take. "Did I do all right?" she asked, in a manner of a child who wants to be told that she has pleased. "You were wonderful," Billy replied. "I never saw anyone sneak downstairs so prettily. But I think you can do it better. Shall we try it again?"'

One of the few to credit Monroe with having any brains *before* the walk-out when she went on suspension for a year setting up her own company in New York with Milton Greene, it was Wilder who supported Monroe in her bid to play serious roles such as Grushenka in *The Brothers Karamazov*. 'People who haven't read the book don't know that Grushenka is a sexpot . . . They think this is a long hair, very thick, very literary book . . . There is nothing long hair about Grushenka. Marilyn knows what she is doing, too. *She* would be a Grushenka to end all Grushenkas.'

Terse in her gratitude, Monroe was nonetheless euphoric over the performance Wilder 'clawed' out of her. 'It's due to Billy Wilder. He's a wonderful director. I want him to direct me again. But he's doing the Lindbergh story next. And he won't let me play Lindbergh,' she quipped when complimented on the part. (Next time 'round the same line wouldn't be so funny, since Wilder had lined up Shirley MacLaine for a role in *The Apartment* which would have been ideal for Monroe, reasoning that he was both too old and too rich to endure another round with Marilyn.)

Meanwhile, the Zanuck–DiMaggio battle was waged with a rancour which surpassed expectation. Neither would give an inch; Zanuck insisted that his stars were Fox properties whose obligations first and foremost were to the studio, whereas DiMaggio resented the studio's infringement upon his wife's private life (although it does seem, from the way he tried to frame her into giving up her career and remaining with him, that there was more than a little selfishness in the manoeuvre). Comments biographer Zolotow: '[Joe] had never liked the idea of her being a film idol at the expense of being a wife and had frequently told her: "You're married to the studio, not me." And she, for her part, had never been able to give herself up entirely to domestic chores . . . She resented the fact that Joe wanted to deny her fame . . .'

Having returned in October 1954 from principal location shooting in New York, two fundamental decisions were made by Monroe – decisions which affected both the status of her marriage and her popularity with the public, since she was shattering the image of an American folk hero.

Firstly, she decided not to have the baby she was carrying by DiMaggio and entered Cedars of Lebanon for a surgical termination of pregnancy. Attended by Dr Leon Krohn, her regular gynaecologist, Monroe was released after four days, ungroomed and haggard, refusing to speak to reporters. Secondly, and more importantly, she made the crucial decision to opt out of the DiMaggio marriage and on 3 October 1954 filed a divorce complaint against DiMaggio for mental cruelty. Coach Lytess wasn't surprised: 'They quarrelled a lot. One argument doesn't bring a big decision like this. They kept hoping for the best, but Mr DiMaggio never could consider her feelings.'

Monroe, on the other hand, was perversely contrite, sounding a bit like that silly 'Dear Joe' note supposedly found by her death bed, apologizing for not having been a better wife. While I don't believe she gave a hoot for domesticity, I do think she loved DiMaggio and must have been very disappointed when they couldn't resolve their difficulties. 'The trouble is I still love Joe,' said Monroe when they divorced. 'That's what makes it so hard. I feel terrible, I've treated him so beastly these last few weeks. Always working, never at home, too tired to cook and too busy studying my lines when I should have been giving him attention. I don't think he'll ever speak to me again.'

However, what he cooked up in retaliation was so bizarre and so shattering that it took Monroe years to cope with it; and, frankly, I doubt she ever did, since by the time she died the rumour which had been implanted had taken root.

Infamously known as the 'Wrong Door Raid', it was in an attempt to compromise his wife in bed with a woman that DiMaggio (together with Frank Sinatra, who was also having problems with wife Ava Gardner) visited the apartment building where Monroe was having a meal with a friend and bashed down the door to the flat they thought she occupied. Since, however, the lady had moved into a different flat, they broke down the wrong door. DiMaggio fled to Florida (to avoid becoming involved in litigation) whilst Sinatra placated the woman out of court in a settlement.

Biographer Gerry Romero describes the incident in *Sinatra's Women*. '. . . Marilyn told Bob Slatzer that DiMaggio had somehow got it into his head that she had lesbian tendencies (which was totally untrue) and that he wanted to get photographs he could use to blackmail her into giving up films . . . While Marilyn was having a quiet dinner in her friend's apartment (on Waring Avenue) the detectives (some claim DiMaggio and Sinatra too) burst into the wrong apartment and awakened the woman tenant with flash bulbs popping.'

Slatzer expands upon his impression of DiMaggio: 'He couldn't bear it that she was divorcing him. He simply couldn't bear it, and tried to frame her into staying with him. She was friendly with an actress who kept an apartment at the Villa Capri. DiMaggio suspected that they were lovers so he bashed the door down, hoping to catch the girl with Marilyn in a compromising position. Marilyn and the girl had had dinner and by the time Joe arrived she had already left via the back stairs. In any event the girl had recently changed apartments and so he had bashed down the wrong door.'

Monroe's friend, Sheila MacRae, told me that as a result of what happened Marilyn began seeing a psychiatrist and that whatever doubts had been implanted by DiMaggio were not easily dismissed by the analysts she consulted.

On 27 October 1954, dressed in black widow's weeds, heavy makeup failing to conceal the weariness in her face, Monroe won an interlocutory decree of divorce from judge Orlando Rhodes on the grounds of 'mental cruelty'. When asked how it affected her to live with a loveless husband, Monroe answered that she was presently under a doctor's care. She testified that her husband starved her desires for love, warmth and affection. She said that he would get into moods where he wouldn't speak to her for five to seven days at a time; sometimes ten days. 'I would ask him what was wrong. He wouldn't answer. He would say: "Stop nagging me." I was allowed to have no visitors: maybe three times in the nine months we were married. Once when I was sick he did allow someone to come and see me. The relationship was one of coldness and indifference.'

DiMaggio's fans were antagonistic towards Monroe and their behaviour contributed to her instability. The night before the divorce hearing had been unpleasant: 'I had to sneak over the back fence there were so many reporters and fans in the front yard,' says Whitey. 'I knocked on the back door at about 6 a.m. The door opens and it is Joe DiMaggio. I was surprised. I said: "I hear you are getting divorced." I told him I was there to make her up to go downtown with Jerry Geisler (the lawyer) to the courthouse in Santa Monica.

'Marilyn was upstairs in the bedroom. She was hysterical. I took a long time to get her ready because she didn't want to get ready.'

Travilla confirms how awful it was for her. 'In front of the house were DiMaggio fans who loved him and hated her, screaming and yelling and throwing things: "Come on out, Marilyn." I never knew this girl to drink. But she was drinking that day. A note was delivered to her front door. It was on toilet tissue and written on it in fecal matter was scrawled the word: "Whore". These were his fans. She was hysterical.'

The atmosphere was tense; DiMaggio made a theatrical exit by stalking out to his limo. 'I'm going home – to San Francisco. That is my home!' he muttered to fans.

About ten minutes later Monroe emerged, sobbing, on Geisler's arm. She was all broken up. Everybody was pushing and shoving. A lady reporter kicked a crime columnist for the *Los Angeles Mirror* in the shins.

The following day Monroe was back at work on *The Seven Year Itch* and within two weeks she was the life and soul of the 'wrap' celebration following completion of the film, which was three weeks late and $1.5 million over budget. Hosted by Billy Wilder and producer Charles Feldman (Monroe's agent), the party, held at Romanoff's swank nightclub (now extinct), was tantamount to Monroe's Coming Out Party. People who previously dismissed her as their social inferior were present – every big name in Hollywood was there.

Monroe was half an hour late for the party because the car had run out of gas – a situation reminiscent of an out-take from *All About Eve* where Margo is stuck in a car with the playwright's wife the night that Eve makes her Broadway debut. Marilyn was thrilled at finally being accepted by her peers. 'I feel like Cinderella. I didn't think they'd all show up,' she whispered to columnist Sidney Skolsky, who had agreed to be her 'date' for the occasion, although Saturday night was generally reserved for his wife, Estelle.

'They' refers to 'A' list Hollywood: the Clark Gables, the Sam Goldwyns, Gary Cooper, Clifton Webb, Doris Day, the Jimmy Stewarts, Jack Warner, the Darryl Zanucks, Claudette Colbert, the William Holdens, the Leland Haywards and Susan Hayward, among others. One columnist caught the importance of it all by writing: 'This party was a big deal for Marilyn because it signified in its peculiar Hollywood manner that the so-called Elite of the town had finally accepted her. Marilyn never felt that she belonged. She had gained her fame because of her popularity with the fans and always felt put down as far as the movie town's celebrities were concerned.'

Typically, the red chiffon gown Monroe wore be-

longed to the studio. She couldn't afford an evening
dress of her own until after the formation of her own
company and the new Fox deal, when she began to see
money accruing from *The Seven Year Itch*. Says co-star
Tom Ewell: 'When it came to dressing for her own
party, Marilyn didn't have any evening clothes. She
borrowed a dress and a fur coat from the wardrobe
department driving herself to Romanoffs. She even ran
out of gas. That's why she was late.

'She was told she could ask anyone she wished to the
party, but confided to me: "Golly, I don't know many
people. I wonder whom I could ask. I know Betty
Grable. We worked on a picture together. Maybe she'd
bring Harry James. And I know Lauren Bacall. She was
in *How to Marry a Millionaire* too. She and Humphrey
Bogart might come." . . . Yet, when she came into
that room filled with [dozens] of Hollywood's finest –
including the Jameses and the Bogarts – she outshone
everyone in it.'

Said Ewell at the time: 'Marilyn has that odd spark
that's more than beauty or brains. Although she is personally shy and reserved, she can turn on her personality
so that you forget anyone else is present.'

The party occasioned the first meeting between
Monroe and the hero of her dreams: the King – Clark
Gable. Five years later they would work together in
Misfits, a film which for both would be their last. 'Do
you think he'll ask me to dance with him?' Monroe
asked. Following a few polite words with Claudette
Colbert, with whom he starred in *It Happened One Night*
(and who toplined a film which featured Monroe entitled
Let's Make It Legal), Gable did indeed ask Marilyn if
she'd like to dance.

Some gossip recorded their conversation. Monroe,
sighing: 'I've always admired you and wanted to make
a picture with you.' Gable: 'I ran *Gentlemen Prefer Blondes*
a couple of months ago. You were magic and I'd like to

do a picture with you. Provided they could find a really good script.'

The film premièred in New York City at Loew's Theater on 1 June 1955 (coinciding with Monroe's twenty-ninth birthday), and was occasioned by a rare appearance with DiMaggio at a public function. Whilst the marriage to DiMaggio was over, there was no reason why they couldn't be friends. DiMaggio, Monroe said, was the only one she wanted to escort her to the New York première; and in a gesture of good will she asked him to do so. He, in turn, returned the compliment by hosting a birthday bash in her honour (reminiscent of George Raft's surprise party assassination in *Some Like It Hot*). Suddenly at the party something happened between Joe and Marilyn. Their looks turned cold. They exchanged some harsh words. They both left separately.

What transpired between them? One can only surmise about the series of events which took place. According to actress Maureen Stapleton, who was there, it was comic Jackie Gleason who said or did something which upset Marilyn; and yet it was DiMaggio with whom she had the tiff. 'I remember asking: "What is the matter?"' says Maureen. '"Why are you so upset?" She said he whispered something horrible to her. I said: "He's drunk. Forget it." But it lingered. She couldn't just forget it. It haunted her for days.'

It is perhaps a testament to the perversity of the film business that, following Monroe's colossal success in *The Seven Year Itch* (which grossed millions in its first few months of release), she was offered two pieces of junk: *The Girl in the Red Velvet Swing* (cast as Stanford White's mistress) and *The Revolt of Mamie Stover* (cast as the prostitute). The latter was eventually filmed with Jane Russell but it did little to enhance her career. The final piece of fluff Marilyn was asked to accept (and rejected) was Nunnally Johnson's script of *How to be Very, Very Popular* (eventually made with Sheree North and for which Betty Grable was brought back on a one-off basis). Johnson recounts that he had written the role of 'Curly' for Monroe, but she turned it down. 'She wanted out of her Fox contract, and she simply left the studio. She announced that she wanted to do more serious parts.' Monroe was right. The film was reviewed as a 'dreadful comedy'; Sheree North was described as 'amazingly untalented'.

It appeared that while Charles Feldman was successful in getting Monroe a bit more money he was unable to get her the kind of parts she wanted. Did he sell out to Fox — was he in league with the power bosses? Who knows? What is important is that Monroe, following her rejection of *How to be Very, Very Popular* dashed off to New York where, together with Milton Greene, she finalized plans to establish Marilyn Monroe Productions.

20
The Unholy Three:
Greene, Strasberg and Miller

Marilyn Monroe's 1955 Fox exit on 15 January was one of the most publicized walk-outs in movie history. Marilyn sought to create a vision of herself separate and apart from the images based upon masculist traditions and myths. In so doing, she struck an enormous blow for women's liberation. It is Monroe who best will be remembered for lifting the Dumb Blonde cliché to the level of brilliant, surrealist farce. For evolving the Blonde with a Brain; sacrificing trivial considerations of men, money and marriage for profound preoccupations: Freud, Marx and Method.

Whenever future generations pause to reflect upon the work of this fine comedienne, they will undoubtedly appreciate the work of Monroe's early period, but it is the films she made following the walk-out which establish her as an actress of Chaplinesque capabilities. A favourite of the French existentialist philosopher, Jean-Paul Sartre, it is in her roles as Sugar, Cherie and Elsie that Monroe epitomizes the loss of definition experienced by modern women; the type of woman who feminist writer de Beauvoir describes in *The Second Sex*. It is in the later period that we see the results of Monroe's struggle for knowledge, technique and stimulation.

The deal which Charles Feldman had negotiated prior to her appearance in *The Seven Year Itch* whilst giving Monroe more money was actually less generous than it seemed, since the $100,000 per year was dependent upon the studio's whim – they could cast her in two, three maybe four films per year. In any event, no concessions were made regarding script approval, which was Monroe's paramount concern, since she strongly believed that without creative control she had little chance, if any, of maintaining career longevity, and that appearances in such second-rate films as *The Revolt of Mamie Stover* and *How to be Very, Very Popular* would diminish credibility.

The formation of her own production company was envisaged by Monroe as a way of giving her a voice in the parts she played; something which Fox had declined to do on principle, claiming that it was something they were reluctant to give any star. However, it was a major issue and one that Monroe and Greene, with their lawyer, Frank Delaney, used as a bargaining weapon in contract negotiations with the studio, claiming that Fox had not held to its end of the deal by offering a star of Monroe's magnitude films of limited artistic merit. Delaney advised Monroe that the work she had done on *The Seven Year Itch* had been undertaken as a single-picture contract, and insisted that the 1951 Fox contract had been terminated by abandonment by both parties. The studio countered the claim by pointing out firstly that Monroe had been turned down by two other majors (Columbia and Metro) and that whilst at Fox she was given every consideration; surrounded by the finest creative talent available; cast in multi-million dollar productions; and given a careful and world-wide publicity campaign.

Fox buried the hatchet on 31 December 1955, when it capitulated to Monroe's terms and signed a non-exclusive, multi-picture deal with the actress for seven years, which gave her $100,000 per film with the option

of pursuing outside assignments. In addition, she was
given approvals of director, script, cameraman and
makeup man. (The one thing she failed to get was a
guarantee of writer approval, something she was to
regret later when confronted with the numerous script
changes on *Something's Got to Give*.) The icing on the
cake was the $500 a week she received as a contribution
towards the cost of having an analyst, secretary, acting
coach and maid. This was a hugely magnanimous gesture, since both publicist John Springer and Robert
Slatzer confirm lawyer Delaney's own assessment of the
situation – that in reality Monroe's legal position was
indefensible since she was technically under contract to
Fox. Had the studio wished to be obdurate, any visions
of independence on Monroe's part would have been
infinitely more difficult to fulfil.

When, however, Monroe's partnership with Greene
was announced in January, it was done in spite of her
legal commitments, since at the time there was no indication of any capitulation on the studio's part; Fox remained in their position that Monroe would not be cast
in serious roles. The clarion call was made at a press
reception and cocktail party that lawyer Delaney hosted
at his book-lined Manhattan home on East 64th Street.
Among the guests were Greene and his pert wife, Amy;
composer Richard Rodgers; dramatist Sidney Kingsley;
actresses Janet Leigh and Marlene Dietrich; and actor
Tony Curtis. Anybody expecting Monroe's metamorphosis into a brainy, bohemian type would have been
disappointed, since she arrived an hour late from the
hairdresser, looking every inch the *belle dame sans merci*,
clad in a strapless white satin sheath gown and an ankle-
length white ermine coat – her hair the identical shade
of platinum.

'I've severed my connections with Fox,' Monroe told
reporters, which was a joke since the company had a firm
contract with her until 1958 and had issued a statement of

their intention 'to use every legal means to see that she keeps up to it'. But the bigger laugh came with Monroe's announcement that she wanted to portray the Russian temptress, Grushenka in *The Brothers Karamazov*, Dostoyevsky's psychological study of sordid murder, involving a love triangle in nineteenth-century Russia. The role had become a symbol of the actress's crusade against sexist exploitation and whilst the studio argued that they were satisfied with both the artistic and financial results of Monroe's recent films, she herself insisted: 'I just don't like myself in some of my recent films.' Fox was intractable: 'We have no intention of granting Miss Monroe's request that she play in *The Brothers Karamazov*,' a position, incidentally, which they never changed, finding after a while that it became irrelevant since Marilyn Monroe Productions had undertaken to produce two projects, *Bus Stop* and *The Prince and the Showgirl*, neither of which had anything to do with Dostoyevsky.

The impact of Monroe's Dostoyevsky remark cannot be emphasized strongly enough, since its effect threatened the very foundations of a Myth which Hollywood had nurtured from inception. Giving Monroe control of her Myth was tantamount to placing the A-bomb in Hitler's hand and Fox, in an effort to dispel any pretensions the lady had towards oligarchical control of her career, ridiculed the endeavour. The item was parodied by burlesque comics, newscasters and gossips, all villainously deriding the notion of a pretty girl wishing to be smart. This duality, singularly American, stuck for many years and it wasn't until the advent of women's liberation leader Gloria Steinem that there was an acceptance by the mass media of the complete and integrated female personality. Even that year's Oscar ceremonies couldn't resist its send-up of Monroe: Bob Hope quipped: 'Is Marilyn Monroe here?' Thelma Ritter responded: 'Yes, she just walked in with *The Brothers Karamazov*.'

Recalling the absolute and utter hysteria engendered by that fateful announcement, publicist John Springer recalls: 'Do you remember the press reaction when Marilyn said she would like to play Grushenka in *The Brothers Karamazov*? Everybody howled! But what a perfect idea! She would have been the perfect Grushenka. I love Maria Schell (who played the part when a film was made of the novel). But Marilyn would have turned in a performance which was classic. People laughed at her. This idiot thinks she can play Dostoyevsky. She wasn't such an idiot. She knew! If anybody had paid attention to her, and cast her as Grushenka, that might have been one of the great movies of all time.'

Columnist Sheilah Graham agrees: '[Marilyn] would have been superb as Dostoyevsky's sensual, confused heroine. She was born for the part, and Maria Schell with her assured smile was completely wrong.'

Monroe's New York move was an enterprising manoeuvre for someone whose career as a sex goddess was already well established and it also showed foresight, as Springer recognized, in perceiving the short-term possibilities of Fox typecasting. 'In Hollywood Marilyn was treated as the "broad of broads". When she came East she was treated like a person – like a human being, not a thing. And she hated being treated like a thing! They might have thought she was a desirable property, but so was Rin Tin Tin and Lassie. She was gorgeous and had a body. And that was how people thought of her – as a windup toy. This year's Blonde. And Marilyn didn't want to be disposed of. She was not going to be used. They had used her for so long that she rebelled against it.' Adds Springer: 'She was used the same way any young gorgeous glamour girl was used as a starlet but long after Marilyn was already a starlet. She was a star, and they were still using her the same way. They treated her like Marilyn said – "a thing". Not as a great actress but as a pinup girl – a brainless, dizzy blonde long after she was an important star — a dizzy chorus girl.'

One might have expected Monroe's appearance at the press conference which launched the start of her own production company to have reflected something of the changing direction she envisaged for her career, but the actress made no attempt to modify the existential Marilyn — the Myth. Milton Greene had captured a unique facet of her persona in photographs where she is bundled head to toe in black, but for the stark intrusions of head and feet in contrasting white. Monroe, however, had no intention of tampering with her persona in any way to suggest that she had gone 'bohemian'! However downbeat or farcical were the film roles she essayed, it is safe to say that Monroe's Myth remained inviolate: the image purveyed for public consumption unerringly upbeat.

It is this ambiguity which, perhaps jealously, was challenged both by DiMaggio and Miller. They failed to see how a serious actress could also be a public clown. It is undoubtedly Monroe's ability to walk this narrow line which accounts for her phenomenal international success; she instinctively knew (the way Jane Fonda does with a good script) what the public Monroe could and could not do so as to safeguard the popularity she enjoyed. One only has to glance at the grosses her films have enjoyed over the years to observe the impossibility of successfully dominating Monroe. And whereas at the time columnists complained that she was being dominated by Greene, and was consequently less accessible to them, the reality was in fact the reverse. Marilyn exploited Greene so she could secure the independence she zealously coveted; when after only two productions she disbanded their neophyte company, she left him in an awful mess.

Opinions about Greene vary. Marilyn called him 'the most valuable friend I ever had.' Whilst at the other extreme a Fox official described him as 'a real Svengali, that guy. He's got Marilyn right under his thumb.' Natasha Lytess agreed: 'I think [Marilyn] is very confused and groping her way out of an inner disorder. I'm afraid she is surrounded by people who have in mind only what they can make out of her.'

The New York City offices of Marilyn Monroe Productions operated out of Milton Greene's Lexington Avenue photographic studio – a rambling cheaply furnished suite of rooms clustered with antiques, Tiffany lamps, an old piano; the walls teeming with portraits of stars photographed by Greene. Monroe, meanwhile, was ensconced at the Greene's Weston, Connecticut home – a red-painted barn they renovated with the idea of living *en famille* with Monroe when their business venture commenced. 'They' included 33-year-old Greene; his wife, Amy; and baby son Joshua. When asked by friends how she thought she'd cope with another of the triangle situations which in the past had caused problems, Monroe quipped that she had matured; adding, parenthetically, that a fondness for older men placed Greene safely out of the picture.

What became known as Monroe's period of seclusion was as much an attempt to recover from the trauma of the failed marriage to DiMaggio; lawyer Delaney explaining that the actress was enjoying a brief recuperative period after feeling tired, anaemic and overworked.

The interlude, however, appears not to have significantly buoyed Monroe's spirits. She is described in press accounts of the respite as being in high spirits – romping through the woods with the dogs, playing in the snow with the children, or caring for the Greene's baby Joshua. Yet she was harassed by a couple of neighbourhood hooligans. The press seized upon the opportunity to comment upon the incongruous casting of Monroe as the local babysitter, scoffing – 'Hollywood star Marilyn Monroe has been playing a new role – a babysitter

. . . She was staying at the home of Milton Greene, vice-president of her new film company, at Weston, Connecticut, when Greene and his wife were invited to dinner by neighbors . . . The Greenes have a baby boy, Joshua. Marilyn said – "Go and enjoy yourselves. I'll sit with Joshua." The Greenes had just finished dinner when Marilyn phoned: "Please come home," she said. "There are people looking at me through the window. I'm scared."'

It would be another couple of months before Monroe would bolt from the sanctuary offered by Greene and his wife; but already the seeds of discord were evident in the petty conflicts between Monroe and Greene's wife Amy. Although in the future Monroe would claim that Greene was trying to promote himself and his wife at the expense of her career, the original source of contention was pedestrian – Monroe objected to Amy Greene's attempts to interfere with various aspects of her life. Publicist Rupert Allan explains: 'Amy Greene may have influenced [Marilyn] regarding makeup and clothes, I think wrongly; until she got back into her own stride.' Robert Slatzer's description of the situation, however, is a lot tougher. He says that Marilyn told him that she found living with the Greenes 'unbearable . . . Marilyn found Amy to be not only refined and self-possessed, but to be a bossy lady who wasn't going to let anyone stand in her way including Marilyn. During the months she lived with them, she found herself constantly being coached by Amy about what to wear and so on.'

Former beauty and grooming editor of *McCalls* magazine, Amy Greene is the kind of woman whom Sylvia Plath might have described in *The Bell Jar* – she rigidly applied a set of manners and mores which in contrast to Monroe's foresight placed her twenty years behind the times. Amy Greene was, in short, 'an organization woman', antipathetic to the controversial role which Monroe envisaged for herself and which with Milton

Greene's help she would achieve. Like Monroe, Amy Greene was also a careerist; but unlike the actress, she proved capable of negotiating both wife and careerist roles with superb dexterity. Her thinking, basically, was conservative rather than revolutionary; and whilst she never significantly affected grosses, the orderliness of the way she did her job contributed towards keeping the magazine at a consistent level of success. My own dealings with Amy Greene found her to be one of the least imaginative editors, remaining very securely bound up within guidelines of social codes and precedents previously established. It is this essential conservatism, combined with an irritating didacticism, which could have contributed to the problems she and Marilyn had.

That Monroe was able to buck the system without so much as losing an iota of public esteem is testimony to the genius she displayed for public manipulation. And yet, as poet Norman Rosten confirms, Monroe was very much in contention with the Establishment: 'It is an *inside* story that Marilyn hassled it out with the studios and had as tough a time as those on the Blacklist – only the kind of harassment was different.'

According to Slatzer, the reasons behind Monroe's move back into the city had as much to do with the DiMaggio divorce as they did with life at the Greenes. 'When Marilyn left that situation it was hostile,' he says. 'She was street-smart. She knew they were using her; but what could she do? She had a contract which she had to see through.'

During the Greene interval DiMaggio tried to patch up their marriage (the divorce decree would not be finalized for a year) and the two spent long weekends together in the country at Joe's brother Dom's house in Wellesley, near Boston. A press report chronicled Monroe dining out with Joe, Dom and his wife Emily in a private room of a Boston restaurant. Recounting conversations with the couple about a reconciliation, the reporter wrote: 'DiMaggio turned to Monroe and said – "Is it honey?" Marilyn hesitated, then said – "Let's call it a visit."'

Persistent entreaties to get her back continued after the Greene upheaval when Monroe returned to New York City. Joe called upon her every morning before breakfast, frequently dining in her suite at the Waldorf Astoria hotel. Seen around town on several occasions, Monroe was again asked about a reconciliation. 'I can't talk about that,' she said. A telephone call to David Conover around this time says it all – '[Joe] just doesn't fit into my life.'

The manoeuvre which precipitated Monroe's move to the Waldorf occurred on 8 April 1955, when Monroe was interviewed on American television by correspondent Edward R. Murrow in tandem with Amy and Milton Greene. A teenager at the time, I keenly recall my discomfort at watching Monroe's performance. The situation was not designed in her favour. Firstly, she was being interviewed with a married couple, which placed her in the invidious position of appearing to be an interloper. Secondly, she showed herself to be at odds with her image – unconventional even for Monroe, whose publicity was wilfully conceived to promote a euphoric persona. Compared to Amy Greene, whose appearance was bright, confident, relaxed and most of all contented, Monroe seemed neurotic and dissatisfied. And whilst the interview was conducted on a high level – Edward Murrow being a first-class reporter – there is little doubt that Monroe lost more than she gained from the exposure, leaving us to accept the actress' own verdict of the undertaking as 'dismal'. Quite right, and it is just possible that this was the one medium Monroe couldn't have handled, since in my opinion the primary requirement to cope with television (reducing as it does everything to a level of absurdity) is: confidence. Any confusion or uncertainty on the part of the subject – any

minor hesitation – is perversely picked up by the viewer
as indicating that the person has negative characteristics.
This is why those whose talents succeed in this medium
are generally smaller-than-life personalities, aided and
abetted by vanity rather than ego.

Monroe was ill equipped to cope with the new medium and whilst I don't suspect that Amy Greene set
out to show her up, she was a natural for this kind of
exposure. 'Marilyn was shy!' recounts Robert Slatzer,
'which looks bad on live TV. Amy's confidence made
her look worse.'

There may be some truth in what Slatzer says, for
soon after the programme aired, Monroe set up housekeeping at the Waldorf Astoria hotel in New York City,
which may have been her way of getting even with the
Greenes. 'She turned her apartment into a beauty salon,'
Greene complained. 'She had her own personal hairdresser and he came three, four times a week. She had
manicurists, masseuses, specialists in this and that. And
I have her bills to prove it. And she'd use perfume like
water. Maybe $50 per week on perfume alone.'

Whilst she might have originally perceived the
Greenes as emotionally supportive of her quest for independence, actually living with them exacerbated a burgeoning identity complex. She saw her therapist, who
was recommended by Actors Studio Director Lee Strasberg, five times a week. Dr Marianne Kris was a Freudian
and, like Anna Freud, with whom she was closely associated, she was similarly renowned for her work with
gifted children. Marilyn spent some seven years in
psychotherapy, visiting her therapist an average of five
times per week. Mrs Greenson (the widow of Monroe's
Los Angeles psychiatrist) told me that a great many of
Monroe's problems evolved out of the instability she
had experienced as a child having lived in numerous
foster homes. But since I neither accept the suicide
theory nor the idea that her psychological profile was

self-destructive, I find no relevancy in presuming that twelve sets of foster parents contributed towards anything more than a variety of emotional experiences.

In fairness, I shall quote what one Freudian analyst had to say about Marilyn. 'She would seem to be a typical hysteroid personality. Lack of love and affection in her early youth has produced marked subconscious feelings of insecurity. Hysteroids are exhibitionists constantly in need of sympathy and attention. Being late, her illnesses, her phobias are in the main subconscious efforts to draw attention to herself. Treatment is designed to enable them to grow up, for in many ways they are still children. Hysteroids crave to be loved but unfortunately there is never enough love in the world to satisfy them.'

Director Billy Wilder was certainly right when he declared that Monroe was a genius from the first moment she stepped before a camera, and that tampering with that kind of genius would spoil it. But the genius which Monroe had in her starlet days was the natural and instinctive kind; and had she been used by Kazan, Huston and Mankiewicz with any amount of regularity, we might have seen the 'natural' evolution of that talent. Since, however, she was 'misused' so much during that initial period, Marilyn was forced to combat mismanagement through a battery of survival techniques (i.e. Method, analysis, etc) which in consequence produced a style that was brilliant, although, at the same time, slightly artificial.

Nonetheless, it was this manipulation of her talent through technique that resulted in much of Monroe's finest work; and the credit for this must be attributed to Lee Strasberg and his wife Paula who replaced Lytess as Monroe's coach on the films she made until her death.

Classically trained under prima Russian actress Ouspenskaya at the American Lab Theatre, Lee Strasberg had been a refugee of the Group Theatre before becoming Artistic Director in 1948 of the Actors Studio where, together with his wife Paula, an actress in the Yiddish theatre, he singularly transformed American theatrical presentation by emphasizing an inner technique as opposed to the plastic repetitive acting nurtured by Hollywood.

There has been a great deal of contention about Monroe's relationship with the Strasbergs. Some people feel that Lee was bedazzled by her and therefore lacked credible artistic distance. Others believe that the Strasbergs did not do enough for Monroe. Playwright Miller wasn't enamoured of them, and regarded them as freeloaders; but, then, he disliked anyone whose demands upon Monroe rivalled his own. Monroe herself vacillated between feeling beholden and antagonistic; at the end she wanted to cut them out of her will, as she felt she was being exploited by them.

It is worth noting that whilst Monroe never became an Actors Studio member, she was an auditor (which means that she was allowed, on occasion, to do a scene with a member). Whether the auditor role became tedious, or whether Marilyn resented having to fork out close to two thousand dollars per week to retain the coaching assistance of Paula Strasberg, it can only be lamented that the Strasberg saga ended with ill feeling on both sides. Paula has been quoted by her daughter, actress Susan Strasberg, as having expressed the opinion that Monroe could, on occasion, be both unprofessional and abusive. If she was abusive, she had a right to be, says a friend, who points out that Monroe failed to be accepted by the Actors Studio both times she auditioned. 'Those hateful New York snobs were giving it to her worse than they did in Hollywood. Twice she asked for auditions and twice she failed to make the grade.'

However, when they first met the Strasbergs were charmed, believing the star equal only to Brando in the level of genius she was capable of reaching. 'There is no law about what will happen, but Marilyn has a God-given talent and an extraordinary range. Nothing she does seems beyond her,' said Lee Strasberg.

Son John Strasberg recalls their first encounter: 'I remember when she first came to our house after Milton Greene called my father to ask him to help her, she tiptoed in and out.' Says daughter Susan: 'Marilyn was psychic and intuitive. She had feelings she couldn't prove. My father, loving talent and beauty in women, was neither frightened nor repulsed by her genius.'

Offering his usual ironic observation, Henry Ephron says that a lot of Monroe's sexual self-consciousness (and pain) in later years came from the sublimated aggression of New York intellectual men. 'I liked Paula more than I liked Lee,' he says. 'Lee was a cold fish. I'll tell you about Lee Strasberg. When his daughter Susan was in *The Diary of Anne Frank* people said how proud he must be. Lee replied: "*She* should be proud of me!" That was the kind of man he was.'

Rupert Allan disagrees: 'The Strasbergs made it possible for her to work. They believed in her. They were like the parents she never had.'

Whatever things went on beneath the surface, the superficial tenor of their relationship was cosy; Strasberg's patronage opening up all kinds of doors. 'For Marilyn, Actors Studio was a big family, with Strasberg the strict patriarch (and priest/psychiatrist as well). His wife, Paula, herself a drama coach, became her closest friend. Marilyn felt at ease and safe,' writes David Conover. 'The Strasbergs reinforced her belief in herself, helped her to improve her talent and saw in her the potential greatness of a serious actress.'

It was to Conover that Marilyn wrote long, cheery letters which show that the year in New York was one of the happiest of her life. She loved the city, could blend into the crowds unnoticed, and did not have to wear fancy clothes or makeup. 'Every day was her own to do as she wished,' he recalls. 'She slept late; she went shopping and to parties; she began seeing an analyst; she made friends in the legitimate theatre. She met . . . [director] Joshua Logan . . . [who] would direct her in *Bus Stop* and become one of her most ardent supporters . . .'

In his account of the Actors Studio in a book entitled *The Actors Studio on Stage and Film*, Foster Hirsch confirms my suspicion that Monroe went to the Actors Studio to learn what in fact she already knew, which was, in essence, to use herself – her past and her pain in terms of performance. 'Her vulnerability, her fear of inadequacy, her sense of not belonging – [were] channelled artfully into [her roles].'

Colleagues at the Actors Studio included Shelley Winters, Marlon Brando, Eli Wallach, Montgomery Clift; Anne Bancroft, Geraldine Page, Kim Stanley, Ellen Burstyn and Maureen Stapleton, but none of them surpassed Monroe in terms of being a box-office draw; and it was not overlooked by people in the business that America's number one superstar opted to improve herself when she could have been content to sit on her laurels. It is this effort that won the respect of publicist John Springer: 'Marilyn was a big star when she enrolled at the Actors Studio. She didn't have to elect to plug away at her craft; she chose to. [Marilyn] was very bright, very aware, very hip of who Marilyn Monroe is and was. When she felt like living up to her legend she did. And when she decided that she did not want to be Marilyn Monroe, she could walk down the street very anonymously. I remember one time when she was walking down the street with actor Eli Wallach (on their way to the Actors Studio), she was wearing a scarf around her head and she said, "I can walk down the street without people recognizing me." And then she said, "And I'll show you what it is to walk down the street and to be recognized."

She took off the head scarf. Marilyn knew how to do it. She knew how to turn it on and turn it off.'

Actress Maureen Stapleton recalls that it was during Monroe's New York period of residency that she and the star struck up a friendship. 'She was shy because of that whole Hollywood thing. I was in playwright Tennessee's [Williams] play *27 Wagons Full of Cotton*. She went to see it and she didn't come backstage. One day she said she saw the play and I said, "Why didn't you come back?" She said, "Oh, no. I didn't know you."'

Monroe found the coy mannerisms of her starlet days an invidious intrusion into her adult life and was mortified by people she thought had been seduced by the screen image. 'We went to a party once and there was this girl who was being coy and silly and sexy the way Marilyn is on screen. "My God. She's acting like the parts I play," said Marilyn.' In reality she was a *natural* flirt, which Clark Gable discovered when he described Monroe as someone wholly without feminine guile. Her responses, like Stanislavski's, were gut reactions. 'We got into a cab to go to the Studio,' recounts Stapleton. 'And the man who didn't speak English very well took us to the east side when it should have been the west. It went on and on and on. It was like a joke! Finally we got there. I don't know what it cost. I don't remember whether she paid or I did. But when we got out I said, "Look, buddy, you have got to learn east and west." And she said: "Don't ever lose your accent. It is so charming!" I said, "Don't tell him that, for crissakes. If he gets two businessmen, they'll kill this guy!" She could be daft. She'd say to a guy on the street wearing a peanut vendor's hat, "Are you really Mr Peanuts?"'

Arthur Miller's sister, actress Joan Copeland, is also an Actors Studio member, and recalls Monroe's auditor role, but was not really aware that she was seeing her brother. Copeland recalls the awe felt by the entire class

at having a famous Hollywood film star amongst them.
'Did we know who she was? Of course. How could you
not know? It would be like not knowing who won the
World Series.' She pauses: 'I do think that it was brave
of Marilyn to walk out on Hollywood. But it probably
was harder for her to stay on than to leave. She couldn't
deal with the situation. She was being misused as an
actress and a human being.'

Although most of her preparatory work was confined
to Lee's private classes, on a few occasions she was
permitted, as an auditor, to participate in front of the
class. On such occasions, her adolescent thrill at being
accepted by bona fide members of the Broadway stage,
no matter how lowly their rank, was obvious.

Nothing seemed to dampen her high spirits, and
David Conover vividly recalls the excitement she felt
at being able to blend in with the crowd. 'Here she was
student, not star, and she saw herself that way. When
she called another student about working on a scene
together, she introduced herself simply, and unselfcon-
sciously: "Hi – it's Marilyn – from class."' Strasberg
was a good influence on her, dispelling much of the stage
fright she experienced when she was performing before
the cameras. 'Even some of the nervousness which at
times made her stutter disappeared temporarily, Lee
Strasberg encouraging: "Nervousness, for an actress, is
not a handicap. It's a sign of sensitivity. All you have to
do is to channel this excess energy into your work,"'
recounts Conover.

Those who recall Monroe from the Actors Studio
describe her as a shy, quiet girl who sat in the back of
the class where she could not be seen, dressed in a baggy
sweater, jeans or slacks; no makeup, her platinum hair
covered by a head scarf.

After six months, on 16 February 1956, Monroe appeared before Studio members in what is referred to as
'a work in progress', where members render up cold

readings to demonstrate their ability to handle Method techniques. The sequence she performed was the twenty-minute saloon scene from Eugene O'Neill's *Anna Christie* where Anna comes looking for her father and chats to an older streetwalker. Monroe played Anna; whilst Maureen Stapleton partnered her as Marthy. Although it was to be a cold reading, Monroe prepared the piece with the exactitude of a pro; the rendition going down in Actors Studio lore as a memorable one-nighter.

Everybody in New York's theatre world wished to obtain a ticket, although few did. Publicist John Springer, one of the lucky ones, recalls that: 'The day that Marilyn did her scene with Maureen Stapleton at the Actors Studio you couldn't get close to it. Everyone was there. Most of the great stars of the Actors Studio were there to see Marilyn do *Anna Christie* with Maureen Stapleton. I was there, and it is a night I'll never forget.' How was she? 'She was marvellous. It was Marilyn's own thing – Marilyn playing this beat down old street-walker. She walks into this bar and chats to this older hooker. It was a joke that Marilyn was going to do a scene from *Anna Christie*. But it was no joke. It was really an extraordinary moment in the theatre. She would have been marvellous in the theatre.'

Actress Maureen Stapleton recalls the circumstances surrounding the performance. 'Lee Strasberg suggested that I do a scene with Marilyn. I don't know why he chose me. And he suggested that we do a scene from *Fallen Angels*. I bow to no man in my admiration for Noël Coward. I just adore him. But I could never do him. We rehearsed it for a while and I said to Marilyn: "I don't know about you. But I can't do this." I was nowhere. You can either do him or you can't.

'So I found *Anna Christie* – it was an okay part for me (Marthy) and an okay part for her (Anna). And the first time I read it, I knew she was okay. I said, "Do you feel any better?" She said: "I feel exactly the same." I said,

"Oh, shit. It seems a lot better to me or a lot easier. At least we have a fighting chance in this one. I don't think we have the chance of a snowball in hell in the other one.'"

During the period which prefaced their performance, Stapleton got to know Monroe pretty well, often spending the evenings rehearsing at her East 57th Street apartment. 'That was the time I knew her. She was very good indeed. She could have gone on to become a good theatre actress.'

Personally as well as professionally she found Marilyn enchanting. 'She was the consummate flirt. She brought out the mother in everybody. She was a very appealing woman and a very strong woman. A bright woman.'

What was she like to work with? Absent, late, difficult? 'The scene we did is an early one where Anna first comes into the South Street saloon looking for her father,' says Stapleton. 'Marthy, my character, and she just talk. There was always some section in the scene where she couldn't remember the words. A couple of nights before we were going to do it, I said: "A lot of people do this. You can leave the book on the table and when you go off you can look in the book. It is a work in progress. We are not opening tomorrow night." She said: "If I do that now, I will do it for the rest of my life." Right up to the night before we were to do it, she still would have places where she would go off. But the day when she did it I was more nervous than she was. She remembered every word.'

It was when they worked together that Stapleton glimpsed the superstar mentality that lay hidden beneath the easy-going, casual façade Monroe created for her New York theatre friends. 'To be a superstar and all the things that entails is an awful pressure,' says Stapleton. 'Eli [Wallach] once told me: "Hey, she's smart." And I said, "I know she's smart." She knew about capital gains. (Eli knows about all that stuff.) It turns out that she knew as much as he did, and more. He was stunned.'

She continues, 'The day we did the scene we got there early. [Marilyn] knew about lights. There is a little balcony or someplace where the lights were and there was a guy who handled lights. She knew exactly which light and where it should go – I had no idea she knew all that stuff.'

Columnist Pete Martin, who interviewed Monroe during the Actors Studio period on a radio broadcast, recalls his amazement at her comprehension of many things, not the least of which was the Stanislavski technique. 'She let go with a twelve-minute dissertation that set me back on my heels. She said she agreed with Stanislavski on certain points. She disagreed on others and she explained why. It came over on the radio a couple of nights later and people who heard it said, "Oh, yeah. Some press agent wrote that interview for her." The press agent said, "What press agent knows that much about Stanislavski?"'

If Monroe surprised friends by displaying an intelligence which equalled, if not surpassed, her native intuition, she stunned them further with the fierce temper she displayed when confronted by the ineptitude of a business associate. Maureen Stapleton recalls one such incident. 'She was always worried about projection. Projection. Her voice. And one night at her place there was a business call. I went into the bedroom. She was angry. I closed the door. I could still hear her. I put a pillow over my ears. I didn't want to hear all this shit. Later she came in. She was all sweet again. I said, "Marilyn, you don't have to worry about projection. They can hear you in England." Apparently she wanted to find out who did what to whom? And she didn't want any bullshit. And who she was talking to was trying to fob it off. And she wanted to know.'

Greene would later claim (and rightly) that Monroe's exalted lifestyle bankrupted the company before they even got into production. Following a brief interlude at the Waldorf hotel Monroe leased a flat overlooking the East River on New York's posh Sutton Place (57th Street). Described by one columnist as Monroe's 'brand-new and expensive Manhattan flat', the place had the peculiar distinction of being close to the building whose exterior was used for the penthouse flat occupied by the three girls in *How to Marry a Millionaire*. Spacious, airy and bright, the place was decorated in beige and white and was reminiscent of the Fox dressing room. The bedroom was limned in 'skin beige'; the living room had totally white furnishings, including, in pride of place, the white baby grand piano which had once been owned by Frederic March and which had also belonged to Monroe's mother.

Whereas in Hollywood Marilyn was perceived as glamour without brains, in New York, like other good-looking girls she was expected to pull her own weight; the prevailing belief amongst New York intellectuals being they were all latent man-haters seeking to compete with and dominate the opposite sex. In some ways, the response to Monroe was disturbingly asexual, which explains poet Norman Rosten's assertion that: 'The only man I ever heard of who wanted to marry Monroe in addition to Miller was Henry Rosenfeld, a businessman. He helped her when she came to New York by giving her dresses and things. Along with Milton Greene, he staked her.'

Monroe was enjoying the only real time off she had since the two-and-a-half month suspension a year previously. Her days were filled with both work and play. She often nipped into Saks Fifth Avenue or wandered round a local book shop. Weekends were spent in the company of a new circle of friends: either at the Greene's Weston, Connecticut home; with the Strasbergs at the Fire Island summer cottage; or in Port Jefferson, Long Island, with Norman and Hedda Rosten.

It was on just such an occasion that Monroe rekindled a friendship with playwright Arthur Miller, whom she had first met four years previously on the Fox lot through director Elia Kazan. 'One night Marilyn, dressed in a simple white dress, accompanied Eli Wallach and his wife, Anne Jackson, to a party,' recalls Earl Wilson. 'Shortly after she arrived at the party, a tall, gaunt man came over to Marilyn and said hello. It was Arthur Miller.' Biographer Zolotow, describing Miller at the time as 'living apart from his wife', says: '[Miller] saw Marilyn, looking serene in a simple white dress and went over to her. Immediately she found her heart bumping uncomfortably and warned herself that she would do well to be more careful this time about showing her feelings. They spoke in a casual way. He didn't take her home but friends recall that she looked "dreamy" and seemed absorbed in happy thoughts.'

Whilst it is convenient to blame Monroe for the trouble in Miller's marriage, the reality was somewhat different. Norman Rosten claims that 'it is absolutely not true that Marilyn broke up Arthur's marriage'. The playwright's fifteen-year marriage (he met and wed his wife Mary when they both were struggling students at the University of Michigan) was on the wane long before he met Monroe; both of them were pursuing independent social lives. Mary, incidentally, was said to bear a striking resemblance to Marilyn, and both of them were described as 'simple, unaffected and quite shy'.

Whereas the press chronicle their dates as secretive, implying that the social gatherings they attended with friends were but fronts for the extra-marital romance, the truth appears to be much less sensational; actress Maureen Stapleton describes the relationship as platonic (for months), and Miller as sort of a lone wolf ultimately returning to the marital fold after a bit of socializing with writer and artist pals.

A fine interpreter of the Miller mystique, having

portrayed roles in *The Crucible* and *A View from the Bridge*, Stapleton's friendship with the playwright goes back many years, and began when her husband Max was producer Kermit Bloomgarden's general manager (Bloomgarden having produced Miller's play *Death of a Salesman*). 'I knew [Arthur] through his marriage to Mary,' says Maureen. 'I never thought he would divorce. Because he was like "married". He wasn't looking. I was quite surprised.' She pauses: 'I think Mary was shocked by the divorce. There were their two children to consider: Bobby and Jane.'

Columnist Sidney Skolsky does blame Monroe for the breakup of Miller's marriage, commenting: 'If Marilyn's intention of marrying Miller was not an obsession it was certainly more than a notion. She didn't seem to regard Miller's wife as an obstacle to her plans either.' Confirms Stapleton: 'She set her cap for him and she got him.' Five years later, the role would be reversed; Monroe finding herself cast in Mary Miller's role when photographer Inge Morath, who appeared on the scene when their marriage was in trouble, replaced her in Miller's affections.

Miller's own reaction to the press probe was cynical. 'There is *no* romance. I met Marilyn in 1951 in Hollywood. I often see her at the homes of friends but we have never been alone and there is definitely no romance.' Monroe concurred: 'How can they say we are having a romance? He is married!' Years later when she says the same thing about Yves Montand people will laugh. This time, however, for the moment at least, she was speaking the truth.

Before long, the status of their friendship had changed – Monroe and Miller indisputably becoming a romantic item. Maureen Stapleton recalls that, 'It was all very hush-hush. When she was at her house or my house she would be on the telephone and talk for about an hour to Miller. I'd say, "I know it was Arthur. It is not such a big secret. The world knows it." She'd blush. It was very sweet at the time.'

According to Stapleton, Miller was totally and utterly besotted by Monroe – too enamoured to have any perspective about the match. He loved her idiosyncrasies; he romanticized her obsessions; he indulged her peculiarities. 'I remember we went to a dinner party at their flat. There were about ten people – Arthur, Marilyn, his father, his sister, his brother-in-law, myself, Nancy Walker, and Monty Clift . . . Marilyn was late. Her own house – her own apartment – and she was late. I said to Arthur: "What is this? It's her house. She can't be late here. (Two hours she kept us waiting while she was in the tub – in the bedroom.) We weren't late at rehearsals, or for the performance. And this was her family. Arthur just laughed and said, "You know how she is!"'

Omniscient Earl Wilson was among the first to observe that the romance had become serious, noting the romantic involvement much earlier than most. 'About two weeks after the party he obtained Marilyn's unlisted phone number from Paula Strasberg . . . and phoned her for a date. Over the next seven months they saw each other steadily. Their dates were a well-guarded secret because Miller had not yet broken openly with his wife, Mary. They met in secluded places on Long Island and in Connecticut, dined in small, obscure restaurants in New York . . .'

Whether or not she believed she would get him to marry her, Monroe was candid about the depth of her affection for Miller when she talked to friends. She told David Conover: 'It seems half my problems disappear when I'm in love . . . I have more time to think – and to give. I feel more eager to learn and enjoy. I get up early, yearning for Arthur to call. When he does, my heart races. I can barely utter a word. I am warm all over with happiness.'

In spite of the lurid exposure attending the romance, things progressed unabated; the couple were often glimpsed cycling in Brooklyn; driving in the country; attending a play. Often Marilyn would descend from her flat, pack two bicycles into the car and drive into Brooklyn. There she and Miller would pedal down to Coney Island where they'd wander unnoticed in the crowds, washing down frankfurters with root beer.

When, after seven months, Miller spirited her off to meet his parents, Mr and Mrs Isadore Miller, in their cramped living accommodation in the Flatbush Avenue section of Brooklyn (a neighbourhood best described as cheap and cheerful), Monroe knew she had got him. Within months Miller would fly to Reno, Nevada, where he would obtain his divorce from wife Mary. Zolotow describes Monroe's meeting with the Millers: 'Marilyn was simply dressed in a grey skirt and a high-collared blouse. She wore no makeup. "This is the girl I want to marry," Arthur told his mother . . . [Marilyn] told them . . . of her decision to enter the Jewish faith, which pleased them very much.'

A great many apocryphal stories have grown up around Monroe's friendship with Miller's parents; the most prevalent one concerns an occasion when Marilyn had to use the WC which, because of the shortage of space, was next to the kitchen. Since the family traditionally grouped themselves around the kitchen table, and since Monroe feared that they would hear any noises emitted from the chamber, she turned on the tap to obscure the sounds. It is reputed that when Mrs Miller heard the noise she commented in Yiddish to her son and husband: 'My God, that girl pees like a horse!'

The story, unfortunately, is mythical. When I asked Joan Copeland if it was true she said: 'It may have gone through my mother's mind but my mother simply would not have talked like that.' She continues: 'We have never been a religious family. I don't know why

[Marilyn] converted to the Jewish faith. She always felt the need to belong somewhere – either to the family or the community or, in this case, a religion. Our family was never religious so it was not something which came up as an ultimatum – either you become a Jewess or you don't marry.'

Did she keep a kosher household? 'No. She took Judaic instruction from Rabbi Robert Goldberg (the Roxbury, Connecticut clergyman who married them). I took piano lessons. That doesn't make me a concert pianist.

'She never had the Passover or observed the High Holy Days. But she wanted to be married as a true Jewish woman. It probably was her idea to have a religious ceremony, and she probably wanted to know all these things. When she gave herself over to something like this that was important to her, she did it completely. She went further in being a Jewish wife than I, who was born a Jew, ever went (not in formalized ways but in the spirit of the thing).'

While the press had a field day fantasizing about the 'owl and the pussycat' and 'beauty and the brain', news of their engagement was not altogether welcome. Several of Marilyn's friends objected. Director Joshua Logan did not feel that Miller was half good enough for Monroe. 'I was sick that she fell for Arthur Miller,' he says. 'I never felt that he was equal to her. I was very upset. He was an opportunist. He married her to become more and more famous. She fell for him because he was an intellectual. She was very naïve about that.'

Publicist Rupert Allan observes: 'Miller was the apple of her eye until she married him . . . She told me a year after they'd wed that she was used and the marriage was going downhill . . . But at the time she was delighted that a solid American Pulitzer prizewinning playwright would choose her – would want to marry her. She accepted but she was absolutely astonished.'

Publicist John Springer, whilst admitting that he only knew Miller through Marilyn, criticizes the playwright's send-up of the star following her death by representing her in *After the Fall* as a drunk, addicted nymphomaniac. 'He didn't write about the warmth, the sweetness and the generosity. Then he gave a statement saying: "I didn't mean it to be Marilyn Monroe." Bullshit!'

Director Roy Baker, who glimpsed the couple when they were in England filming *The Prince and the Showgirl*, also felt that the marriage was a mistake. 'The understanding (I assume) was that he would supply the genius and she would supply the presentation (the realization of the material). It was a marriage based on ambition rather than regard, not to say love.'

Meanwhile, the new Fox deal was proposed in August 1955, but wasn't signed until 31 December 1955. The terms of that deal were non-exclusive, Monroe committed to Fox for four films over a seven-year period at a sum of $100,000 per film, plus $500 weekly for maid services, and other expenses. In addition, and most importantly, Monroe got approvals of director, script, cameraman and makeup man. The studio also agreed to pay $60,000 back pay, which was a godsend since her own production company had been on the verge of bankruptcy.

It was agreed that Monroe's next project for Fox would be William Inge's hit play *Bus Stop* (which starred Kim Stanley and Albert Salmi on Broadway). The film she would do for her own production company, which Warner Bros. would distribute, was Sir Terence Rattigan's *The Sleeping Prince*: a Ruritanian romance written for the Coronation of Queen Elizabeth II about an encounter between a Prince and an American chorus girl who had come to London for the Coronation of George V in 1911. The play had already enjoyed a nice run in London's West End starring Sir Laurence Olivier and Vivien Leigh. Since Monroe envisaged few changes,

Rattigan was an acceptable screenwriter. The title was changed to *The Prince and the Showgirl* so as to exploit Monroe's presence in the film; everything else, however, was left alone. Monroe wished to change 'Gosh' to 'Golly' but when Rattigan objected she consoled herself by saying: 'I'll think "Golly" and say "Gosh".'

The work she did for her own production company is credited by Monroe with being amongst her finest; and whilst there were problems on both films (there are *always* problems), she felt that they reflected a lot of what she had learned about Method, creating classic moments filled with emotional nuance drawn from her own life. Since for years Monroe was derided by a large majority of America's intellectual community, I was delighted to read Foster Hirsch's appreciation of her work in his book about the Actors Studio. Writing about the two films she produced, he says in reference to *Bus Stop*: '. . . Two moments illustrate her mastery of the inner technique: the pause before "that loving stuff" ripples with affective memories and her "relationship" to Bo's jacket is sensory work of the sort that is holy writ at the Studio.' Likewise he finds Olivier's performance in *The Prince and the Showgirl* stultified by comparison to Monroe's impressionist rendition of a silly American luxuriating in the working-class vulgarity she makes no effort to conceal. 'Monroe hides behind nothing, exposing herself both physically and emotionally,' he says. And therein lies her strength. 'She wears a revealing white dress and talks the way she always does . . . Nevertheless Monroe's Method steals the picture . . . commenting on his remarks in the way she selects and eats her food.'

Bus Stop director Joshua Logan concurs: '. . . I think [Olivier] threw it away. He remained a caricature. He threw away the Reality.'

Monroe's success in landing the deal as a vehicle for herself, and getting Sir Laurence Olivier to co-star in and to direct the film proves unequivocally that the lady had something more upstairs than just a mass of golden curls. For all her fame and fortune, she was headstrong – working like a dog both in pursuit of artistic excellence and professional expertise; nailing down the kinds of projects which were right.

Upon hearing that Sir Terence Rattigan was on his way back to England and had a ten-hour stopover in New York, Monroe endeavoured to have him paged at Idlewild Airport (now Kennedy), offering to buy him a drink in town at the posh Barberry Room. Never having seen a Monroe film, the playwright had no idea what her credibility might be; however he was in the mood to make a deal, having had an uneventful time on the West Coast where he had hoped to sign a deal with William Wyler to direct a film version of *The Sleeping Prince*. The trip was not a total loss, however, since Rattigan used the occasion to nip down to Palm Springs where the Anglo-American Ryder Cup golf match was being played that weekend.

Obviously keeping an eye on developments, and discovering that no deal was struck, Monroe pulled what in the trade is known as a publicity stunt by kidnapping the playwright for a few hours, during which time she effectively sealed the deal with a sale of the play's film rights.

Rattigan later described Monroe as 'a shy exhibitionist', whose nasal congestion reminded him of Tallulah Bankhead. 'She walked into the Barberry Room an hour late – wearing dark glasses and greeted me with that deliciously shy self-confidence that has overwhelmed so many thousands of tough and potentially hostile newspapermen . . . Gazing into those beautiful and childishly knowing eyes – she had removed her dark glasses – what could I reply but yes? . . . Did I think there was a chance that Sir Larry would do it with her? . . . I was sure that "Sir Larry" would leap at the chance . . . I said I would leave no stone unturned to see that he did.'

The deal, envisaged as a joint production, was appealing because of Monroe's financial generosity, coupled with her artistic flexibility (which allowed Olivier both to direct and co-star in the film). Besides, Sir Laurence wanted to do it because he was (unlike Rattigan) a keen fan of the lady, having seen most of her films. The upshot was that in the most historic pairing since black and white Olivier agreed to work with Monroe.

Their working relationship has gone down in history as a disaster – Olivier contends even today that Monroe was rude, vulgar and unprofessional and that far from falling hopelessly in love, he found the lady decidedly lacking in allure. I suspect from the first that he imposed a mental block to check the emotions which could lead him astray. At the time Sir Laurence was precariously coping with an unstable marriage to Vivien Leigh, who was then aged forty-two and fearful of losing both her looks and the career for which she had worked hard and long. During the course of the film she also discovered she was pregnant.

The meeting of the 'Big Five' has passed into legend. A newspaper account of the Summit reads: 'At six sharp Sir Laurence, Terence Rattigan, Milton Greene, and Jay Kanter, her agent, assembled in [Monroe's] flat and began to wait for Marilyn. She was in the bedroom getting ready . . . It was not until seven o'clock that she finally appeared. She was wearing the simplest of dresses and apparently no makeup. But Larry was very gracious about it. He kissed her hand and said, "You can keep me waiting as long as you like but don't do it to the British press."'

The press conference to announce the famous pairing took place on 9 February 1956 at New York's Edwardian Plaza hotel overlooking Central Park. A typical Monroe freak show, over 200 reporters hung from chandeliers and over balconies for a glimpse of the lady who appeared in typical Monroe drag, wearing a banana-skin black velvet sheath with a V-neck that narrowed down to the waist, held up by two thin spaghetti straps.

The questions were provocative. Do you mind Miss Monroe playing your wife's role? Monroe interrupted, 'But it is *I* who own the film rights to the play!' Oh! How do you think Sir Laurence will like working with Monroe? Next! Would Miss Monroe meet her British counterpart, Miss Diana Dors? Hum, well. Next! It was a very odd press conference. Olivier said he didn't mind working for a woman; that he had been working with women all his life. And Monroe, when asked, replied that Olivier 'has always been my idol', and listed him before Marlon Brando and Charles Laughton as her favourite actor.

Sending up the event was the untimely snap of Monroe's spaghetti shoulder strap; film critic Judith Crist came to the rescue with a safety pin. (Oddly, when the same thing *had* to happen for the opening sequence in the film, it took two hours to break the strap successfully.) Monroe tried to remain unruffled while photographers were busy snapping photos. Olivier blushed, 'No more leg pictures, fellas! From now on she is too ethereal.'

It seems apparent that Olivier was alarmed by the extent to which Monroe went to publicize their working relationship. Described by the press as chain-smoking nervously, he gave the impression of being dreadfully uptight. His discomfort was surpassed only by that of Rattigan, who was also present, sitting alone in a corner, unrecognized. Perhaps Olivier had an inkling of what was about to ensue.

21
The Bus Stop Fiasco

Preproduction on *Bus Stop*, Monroe's first film under the new Fox contract, began in March 1956. Joshua Logan was earmarked by Monroe as its director, primarily because of his previous experience of having studied with the legendary Method guru, Stanislavski. In addition, he was terribly good at handling the wistfully tragicomic work of playwright William Inge, and had already directed the screen version of *Picnic*. Undecided about whether to take a job which involved working with an actress previously thought of as 'a honey-coloured girl who breathed heavily and wiggled her bottom', Logan's fate was sealed when Lee Strasberg credited Monroe with 'being a great, huge genius talent' – one of only two (Brando being the other) of the hundreds of actors with whom he had worked that he felt were capable of doing absolutely anything.

Choreographer Jack Cole recounts: 'Josh . . . was good for her . . . He'd get everybody on to the set, lock the doors, get everybody crazy and then start photographing.'

Playwright George Axelrod, who adapted his own play *The Seven Year Itch* for the screen, was assigned to write the screenplay. This he did superbly, opening up the script to include the natural landscape suggested but never stated in the stage play, where the action is confined within one room of a roadside café. The screen version inserts sequences set at a world championship rodeo; in a bus travelling across the country; in a roadside café in the picturesque countryside of the snow-capped Idaho mountains; and in a boarding house.

The story essentially is about love and losing the ability to love; the touring coach is used as a metaphor for our journey towards self-understanding. Cherie, a Hollywood-bound nightclub singer is travelling on the same coach with Bo, a young rancher. When they hole up for the night at a roadside café, waiting for the snow to abate, they confront one another's dreams and by the time the road clears (and they reboard the coach) they discover that their goals are not so far apart.

Monroe played the role depicted on stage by Kim Stanley and it was hoped that Albert Salmi, who played Bo, would repeat his stage part in the film. Fox, however, thought him unacceptable and began looking for a suitable leading man willing to work with Monroe. Rock Hudson agreed, but Universal (to whom he was under contract) wouldn't loan him out even when Monroe offered to do a film for them in return. 'They obviously didn't believe in her,' says publicist Rupert Allan. 'We had a devilish time casting the role of Bo,' says Logan (who spoke to me about Monroe in 1986, despite the fact that his health was failing and he was advised by his doctors *not* to give interviews). 'They kept refusing the part. Men were afraid that she'd steal the picture.' Travilla concurs: 'People didn't want to work with Marilyn, because they felt they wouldn't be seen; that she would wipe them out!'

The role eventually went to a newcomer, Fox contract player Don Murray, son of a theatrical dance director who had made a couple of appearances on Broadway. Monroe was devastated. If she was going to have a newcomer, she didn't see why it couldn't be Salmi. Despite Murray's Oscar bid, the truth is he was awful:

his stilted, unemotional performance ruining what could
have been an interesting film. Even the front office
complained (after having seen the rushes) about the
hysterical timbre of Murray's performance. (It is a pity
that actors like Salmi, De Niro and Pacino were in-
variably cast in 'character' parts in Hollywood's golden
days. When casting for the glamorous hero, Michael, in
The Godfather the studio was determined that the part
should go either to an established star such as Warren
Beatty, or a newcomer with Robert Taylor's kind of
good looks. It was quite a milestone when Al Pacino
got the role.)

For all the superb things Logan has said publicly both
about the quality of Monroe's work ('She is the most
extraordinary talent I ever have worked with') and the
film itself ('It is perhaps my own favourite of all the
films I have made') I find *Bus Stop* a definite oddity.
Monroe's performance jars with that of Murray, whose
sensibility seems more suited to soap operas). It also
suffers from the offbeat physical concept of the character,
de-glamourized by Milton Greene (straw blonde hair
and ghostly complexion) which Fox derided until the
bitter end; and the patchiness of Logan's direction, playing off the naturalism of the stage actors (Betty Field
and Arthur O'Connell) against Monroe's superbly visual
performance. There is always a danger of discord when
film actors are sandwiched together with stage actors,
and it is a problem with which Monroe had had difficulties with earlier when working with Bette Davis and
Anne Baxter on *All About Eve*.

Unlike Logan's *Picnic* which has a wonderful reson-
ance amongst its characters, *Bus Stop* has an irritating
cacophony almost as if, knowingly, Logan set out to give
Monroe enough rope to hang herself. Firstly, Monroe
burlesques the character which had she played it straight
might have been sympathetic. (She needed directional
restraint.) Secondly, she was working in a way that was

unique to herself, which had nothing to do with the ensemble spirit envisaged by Logan. On Broadway, Kim Stanley played Cherie as a woman whose dreams of glory crumble when, at the climax, she finds the all-consuming love of a male. Monroe's performance on the other hand, was so exaggerated that one can only infer that her intention was to parody men and marriage, sending up the myths of western paternalism with bizarre abandon. Navigating her way throughout the film in a manner befitting a surreal Earth Mother, Monroe transcends the trivial, earthly pursuits of the other characters by suggesting (in nuance and move-ment) unspoken fidelity to an inner voice. When Kim Stanley talks about wanting a man to protect her but not to browbeat her, you know what she is saying really is that she wants to be loved. Coming from Monroe, the words take on another tone altogether and you know that her goal is less love than sovereignty.

In some ways, *Bus Stop* is the psychodrama of the ménage with the Greenes, in which Monroe felt herself placed in the awkward role of the 'outsider'. It is the Hope Lange character (as the girl on the coach hurrying to meet her fiancé) with whom the viewer identifies, since she is everything that Monroe is not and should be: patient, sweet, understanding, and virginal. Monroe is cast as the anti-heroine: feminist, neurotic, demanding – the implication being that when and if she goes along with Bo, theirs will be a marriage which will culminate in divorce. It is an ironic perversity that once Monroe confronted the sex doll image which Hollywood had assigned her, she became a *non grata* icon. Not one of her films captures any of the pathos and longing for love and identity which were so much a part of Monroe's psyche without making some snide comment in either writing or direction.

In this instance, however, it wasn't the front office but Monroe's own team which evolved a concept that

was anti-romantic to the point of being ghoulish.
Although my view might be a minority one and unpopu-
lar, it is shared by Monroe's makeup man, Whitey
Snyder, who objects to the physical denigration of the
actress by Greene and Logan. 'I didn't like her look in
Bus Stop. I hated it, but their idea was to create the look
of a girl who never sees the daylight or the sun – and
that meant having *white* makeup. She looked like hell as
far as I was concerned next to Hope Lange. You can still
do pale nothing makeup but have a little colour into it
and still light over here when you shoot camera-wide
for balance and it would have looked a helluva lot better.'

Director Logan disagrees: 'I believe that the makeup
was right. Milton [Greene] came up with the idea (which
Marilyn liked) of having a very pale, pearly makeup. It
was not only beautiful, charming and sweet but also it
wasn't slick; it was sort of clownlike which gave her
performance a more pitiful look – just that little white
face. Marilyn was excited by it and the costumes.'

Travilla, who did the *Bus Stop* wardrobe of a theatrical
costume, a simple dress and a raincoat, recalls that 'They
[the front office] were fighting Marilyn on her makeup.
She wanted this pure white makeup ('cause the girl
hadn't been in the sun – this is a gal of the night time).
Marilyn insisted on that white look (she sleeps in the
day). She wanted "neo-realism" in Technicolor. They
said, "We're used to Betty Grable with pink cheeks."
No matter what part she is playing they wanted to see
"pretty" colour.'

True enough, but you don't want to patronize your
character either, and I think that by striving so hard to
avoid the pretty but dumb type, Marilyn fell into the
trap of creating a character beaten down by life (and
somehow wanting to be beaten down), which made her
unappealing. The costume she wore, whilst credited as
having been designed by Travilla, was actually a shabby
frock they pinched from the Fox stock room which they

built on to by adding bits of tulle and stuff since she wasn't allowed to show cleavage.

Recounts Logan: 'The costume designer came with sketches and Marilyn and I both felt they were too fancy, not right for the pitiful comic character she was playing. [We went] to the wardrobe department and found a threadbare, old, wrinkled green-gold lamé coat which was as sad as could be, put some terrible little rabbit fur around the edge of it, and that was her main costume in the film.'

The film was pleasantly received by the public, but it was its effect on her colleagues that was most significant, as they recognized her courage in mocking the very origins of her own star mythology. Publicist John Springer observes: '*Bus Stop* is such a classic because [Marilyn] came back after doing all these silly little parts and did *Bus Stop* which required something more than being a dumb blonde. She was playing a dumb blonde but she was playing it with all kinds of nuance. You could understand the poor sad woman who had to go out to do "That Old Black Magic". She had a role of some depth and God knows – she was marvellous.

'She was very happy working on *Bus Stop*. Josh [Logan] treated her like an actress instead of a thing. It was a good experience for her. It was a good movie and she was marvellous in it.'

It was Springer, whose office handled the film, who assigned Patricia Newcomb to the project as Monroe's personal press agent. About ten years Monroe's junior, Newcomb was an American bluestocking, the daughter of an Army judge advocate general who had been married once and divorced. Much of her life in society had been spent in Washington, DC before entering show business. It has been claimed that in the year before her death Monroe was reduced to a state of abject psychological dependency upon her press agent. At this juncture, however, Monroe's fury at Newcomb's intrusion into her personal life resulted in Pat's dismissal from the picture. Biographer Guiles recounts the famous *Bus Stop* incident: '. . . Monroe seemed to like [Newcomb] on sight . . . Then suddenly they became sexual rivals . . . Marilyn's love for Arthur Miller and her unofficial commitment to him did not prevent her from accepting dates with other men. While the *Bus Stop* company was still in Phoenix, an attractive man in his thirties got interested in Marilyn and was courageous enough to ask for a date. When he came up to Marilyn's suite to pick her up, Pat Newcomb was in the sitting room, not quite dressed – the two women often wandered between their suites with little on and the man was visibly shocked to see Marilyn's press agent when he expected to see Marilyn.'

Publicist Rupert Allan confirms: 'Marilyn told me the story – how in Arizona, Pat had done something which she thought was reprehensible – something about insinuating herself between Marilyn and a fan or a lover (a would-be lover). Whatever it was Marilyn was real off on Pat.'

Don Murray's relationship with Monroe during filming has been described as fraught. (That he fell wildly in love with Hope Lange couldn't have helped things.) He had to cope with mood shifts verging from disdainful superiority to downright rudeness and, on one occasion, is supposed to have stalked off the set refusing to work with Monroe again. During the sequence where Monroe warbles 'That Old Black Magic' she swished the tail of her nightclub costume in Murray's face, accidentally striking him. When asked to apologize she agreed, but later reneged, huffing: 'No, no. I won't. Not to you. No. No.'

Time has obviously softened his memory of Monroe, for when I interviewed him in 1986 he preferred to talk about her genius: 'The nightclub scene was an emotional scene – what they call "a problem scene". "You haven't got the brains of a monkey. Give me back my tail" was the line, or something like that. When she first did it, she pushed me so hard in the chest that I bounced on to the floor. I said to Josh [Logan], "I got totally out of character. Can we do it again?" It was all right for her, so she got mad and said, "Can't you *ad lib*?" The next time we did it she slashed the costume across my face and cut my eye. And the next time Monroe started talking about Freud and phallic symbols.' He pauses: 'At age thirty she was going through what we did at eighteen: reading Freud and so on. I remember that about her. She was Freudian-obsessed.'

Whether or not he fancied her, Murray's acting was as cold as ice, although in the famous bedroom scene she shattered his psychological wall of resistance in a funny, witty way. Director Logan recalls: '. . . There was a scene that George Axelrod had invented which was a terribly funny idea. Don comes to the boarding house to wake Cherie up. She's sleeping naked under a heavy, raw sheet. He pulls up the window blind and says: "Wake up, Cherie. It's nine o'clock." "Nine, I didn't get to bed 'til five." ". . . No wonder you're so pale and white." We shot it . . . I said, "Let's try it again.". . . So we did it. This time Don said, "C'mon. No wonder you're so pale and scaly." . . . Marilyn began talking in a hushed, excited voice. "Don, do you realize what you just did? You made a Freudian slip. You see you were in the proper mood because it's a sexual scene and you said 'scaly' which means that you were thinking of a snake. A snake is a phallic symbol. Do you know what a phallic symbol is?" Don was angry with her by that time. "Know what it is? I've got one."'

Murray remembers the shock of seeing Monroe not only naked but scaly, too. 'You see, if Marilyn got very nervous when she acted she broke out in a rash all over her body,' he explains, 'which they covered with makeup. My line was ". . . No wonder you are so white and pale." I made a mistake and said "scaly". Then she brought that up about Freud.'

Whilst there were problems between them, Murray recounts it was the humour and wit that Marilyn showed in the love scenes that got him through the ordeal of his first film.

'A love scene for film is mechanical. Don't create a shadow. Turn the chin this way. Don't cause a light. The most gorgeous woman you won't get excited by in the movies. Marilyn put a lot of emotion into her part. The crying scene at the bar, when we kiss, she opened her mouth and drooled. The censors objected.'

Logan concurs: 'The censors were terrible to her. They didn't like saliva running or nose snot. They wouldn't allow her to do anything sexy. When Don Murray first kisses her we couldn't have anything sexy . . . we couldn't even have them lie down on the hay-stack 'cause it was too sexual. I think that it was Marilyn who was supposed to have said "Well, they could have just as easily done it standing up."'

Typically, when Monroe discovered that some of the really earthy bits of her performance had been excised, she lashed out at Logan, accusing him of not understanding what went on between a man and a woman. Actually Monroe was being unfair, it was the film editor (William Reynolds) who took out the sexy bits. 'He wasn't *allowed* to do it,' objects Logan. 'He just did it. He was revolted by things like saliva coming from the mouth and tears streaming down her cheeks. So I put them right back. I was shocked to see them go.' Nonetheless, the final print of the film lost much of what was shot, in order to appease the censors.

Logan's account of working with Monroe is not much different from what others have said, except that in this instance one understands a bit more of the psychological manipulation that went on and how this nurtured Marilyn's feelings of insecurity. According to Logan, she spent hours in the makeup chair doing and re-doing her face, worrying about lines and other blemishes. She preferred being there, however, to sitting around for hours waiting for the director to set up a shot (which *can* take hours). They only once had a clash about tardiness, when Logan, fearing he'd lost the sunset, strode up to the hotel and dragged her from the suite where she was deliberating about whether or not she looked well enough to perform. 'I was determined to show real life Phoenix,' says Logan. 'And I waited and waited for Marilyn. I got more and more nervous. She was making up in the hotel . . . Suddenly I burst. I ran down the street. I was looking up at the sun. I ran up the hotel stairs – three flights up . . . I opened the door. I grabbed her by the arm and I ran her down the stairs. She was calling out, begging: "I was coming. I was coming." I said, "That's all right. Get there and roll 'em." And we got the shot just before the sun went down.'

Another legendary Monroeism was her inability to remember lines. Logan discovered that it was not inability, so much as spontaneity (a new way of seeing something) which prompted her to change the reading and in so doing to alter a word or gesture. Logan recounts: 'At first I was so startled by this happening that I thought . . . Maybe she doesn't have all the brain power. But I soon realized that it was just her personal critic looking at her performance who said "Marilyn, that's not good enough."' Logan solved the problem by declining to do re-takes (which are both costly and time-consuming) and instead let the camera roll non-stop; leaving the piecing together of a performance which was coherent until the editing phase.

Logan's final verdict on the film is worth noting, since it seems to sum up the ambivalence felt by everyone who worked on the project. '[In this film] I thought [Marilyn Monroe] was a combination Greta Garbo and Charlie Chaplin, because to me she had the beauty of

Garbo and this comic, pathetic thing that I had only really seen in perfection before from Chaplin. But Marilyn had that ability to make you feel sorry for her and laugh at her at the same time, and she did it many times in my film. I think *Bus Stop* turned out to be a smallish picture but a perfect one.'

Sheilah Graham considered the role of Cherie in *Bus Stop* to be amongst the best things Marilyn did, finding hidden parallels between the nomadic waif and Monroe's own personality. 'In *Bus Stop* . . . she was like a little fawn . . . so hurt, so used. She was bullied, threatened, used by everyone since she was a baby. It isn't true that she only loved herself. She loved the people who loved her. She was looking for direction and she never really found it. Marilyn was lost somewhere between birth and death.' Film critic Alan Brien, however, taking the other side, carped: 'In *Bus Stop* she had never looked less glamorous. The blue saucer eyes are chipped at the edges. The soft yellow hair is as synthetic and springy as oak shavings. And her voice has the flat whine of a Liverpudlian film fan doing a bad imitation of Shirley Temple.'

As deep as Logan's admiration was for Monroe, he still evinced ambivalence when she became ill with bronchitis and was laid up in hospital for fifteen days whilst they shot around her. In a desire for authenticity, Monroe chose to shoot the snow scene in sub-zero weather wearing only a thin dress and Bo's brown leather jacket. As a result, she was admitted to hospital in Los Angeles by the Fox studio physician, diagnosed as suffering from a virus, exhaustion, overwork and acute bronchitis. Logan rather consciously referred to her as 'looking genuinely sick'. Why 'genuinely'? Perhaps she 'looked' well, but 'was' sick. Would that have made any difference? It is reminiscent of the Preminger incident where they thought she was faking a fracture. Once again, it seems surprising that there were no precautions taken to protect Monroe's tenuous physical condition, since the delicacy of her constitution was well known.

During the fifteen days that she remained in hospital, Monroe had but one visitor: Mrs Josh (Nedda) Logan, whose recollection is that Monroe didn't have so much as a blanket for when the nights grew cold. Monroe is reported, however, to have had billings and cooings, which sometimes lasted for an hour, with Arthur Miller, who had gone to Reno to file for divorce from his wife of fifteen years, Mary Slattery. He camped out in a rustic cabin at Pyramid Lake (a natural lake on an unspoiled stretch of land belonging to the Piute Indians), 45 miles from the carnival-like atmosphere of the Nevada gambling centre of Reno. It was something which he and Monroe would share, she having gone there ten years previously to divorce Jim Dougherty. Later, Miller would write about the transience of people who come to Reno to obtain their divorces in *Misfits*.

Miller stayed there for eight weeks, six of them necessary to fulfil the residency requirements, and spent most of his time in the cabin writing. Before he had left for Reno, he was like a kid about Marilyn, friends recall that 'He acted like a kid in love. No one who had ever known him had ever seen this kind of ebullience in him. It was almost as if he was dancing a jig.' An ecstatic beginning for what would become one of the most notoriously tragic Hollywood marriages of all time.

22
'Mr Sir' and the Showgirl

Nine days after Miller's divorce from Mary Slattery was finalized he was summoned to appear before the HUAC (House on Un-American Activities Committee) on 21 June 1956. Caught up in what became known as the McCarthy witch-hunts, Miller, in common with many other American writers and artists, was suspected of being Communist and of subversively promoting the overthrow of a constitutional government through propaganda purveyed in articles, books and plays.

Recalling the atmosphere at the time, Jan Sterling remembers the suspicion and mistrust which existed amongst people and how fearful they were of being secretly denounced for anything that could be considered liberal in sympathy. 'I had to sign a thing at MGM. They had documentary lists of what you had done and they said that my mother had voted Communist in Chicago. My mother was living in South America. I had only four little things. People had stacks of stuff against them. If your name was ever quoted in a newspaper that was "off-white" you had to say "why" that name was quoted.'

She pauses: 'We lived on 57th Street, across from the Millers after they had married, and I remember seeing Arthur the day he was cited for contempt of Congress [on 31 May 1957, for refusing to name names of people

witnessed by him at Communist Party meetings] come
out of his flat with his son [Bobby] and get on a bike
and pedal down 57th Street. I thought: "That's a good
way to take being cited for contempt of Congress."'
She goes on: 'Marilyn was courageous. She married
Miller knowing that he would be in contempt of Congress. She admired him for his principles. I think that
the marriage was fine when he was the hero fighting the
government. I think that later on when he became "Mr
Monroe" that is when the trouble started. He didn't
write anything during that time.'

The contempt citation was ratified by a vote of 373 to
9, and sent on to the Justice Department for prosecution,
where the judge ruled that the Congressional Committee
did have the right to demand that Miller inform on his
friends and on 19 July 1957 Miller was fined $500 and
given a suspended one-month jail sentence. The leniency
of the sentence was, to a large extent, irrelevant; having
a criminal record, however, meant Miller would be
restricted in where he could travel.

The sentence was later reversed by the Supreme Court
in August 1958, but the two years of protracted litigation
which dominated Miller's life affected both his marriage
and his work. Two years after the Supreme Court
reversed the contempt citation, Miller separated
from Monroe; it was nine years, however, before he
wrote another play, *After the Fall*, which was staged
on 23 January 1964 in New York's Lincoln Center
theatre.

I have always thought it odd that merely a decade
after the Nazi menace was subdued, the American
government chose to mobilize a campaign that was not
dissimilar from Hitler's own law-and-order crusade.
It seems quite apparent, both then and now, that the
interrogation of a Pulitzer prizewinning playwright
whose work was being produced internationally was a
petty and jealous intrusion of privacy and a violation of

human rights. It also seems odd that there was no great
outcry from intellectuals in other parts of the world
similar to today's protests against the persecution of
Soviet dissidents.

On a lighter note, poet Norman Rosten remembers
Monroe going to Washington with Miller for his appearance on 21 June, and recalls that 'she sat in the front row
of the gallery when he was testifying' smiling, waving
and being deliriously supportive. Miller referred to Monroe's appearance in a recent documentary that the Canadian Broadcasting Corporation produced, and describes
'Congressman Walter [asking] if he could take a photograph with Marilyn [in which case] he would call off the
hearing'.

But generally speaking, the hearings were unpleasant,
Miller confronted by men of both enormous sanctimony
and power, who justified their actions by claiming that
they were the guardians of the public. It is worth noting
the degree to which religious prejudice was internalized
into political policy, for whilst non-Jewish intellectuals
were freely allowed to express their opinions without
incurring restrictions on travel, Miller had difficulty
for years in obtaining travel visas, even before he was
summoned to appear before Congress. When he accompanied Marilyn to England in 1956 where she filmed
The Prince and the Showgirl, his passport was only renewed for six months instead of the then normal two-
year period.

Whilst friends attribute the breakup of their marriage
to the effect of political persecution on Miller's creative
output and emotional stability, it is also possible that
Monroe's discovery of what it meant to be married to a
'Jew' in terms of the handicaps and prohibitions could
have been a contributory factor. She may have perceived
Miller as Abe Lincoln, and the world may quite rightly
have seen him as a prophet of his time, but the image
and living with the reality inevitably caused problems.

Monroe's reaction, understandably, was one of irritation at having her own movements curtailed by Miller's limited mobility; housekeeper Lena Pepitone recounts: '"We can't go anywhere!" she complained to me one time.'

Transcripts of the hearings would be funny if they weren't so deadly serious. Miller was asked a number of questions dealing with his opinions of subjects ranging from the Communist Party, to Red China, the Smith Act, Congressional Committees, specific playwrights and novelists, his own work, and the position of the writer in America.

'Have you ever made application for membership in the Communist Party?'

'In 1939 I believe it was, or in 1940, I went to attend a Marxist study course in the vacant store open to the street in my neighbourhood in Brooklyn. I there signed some form or another.'

'That was an application for membership in the Communist Party, was it not?'

'I would not say that . . . I am here to tell you what I know.'

'Tell us what you know.'

'This is sixteen years ago . . . I understood then that this was to be . . . a study course . . .'

'Who invited you to attend?'

'. . . it was a long time ago.'

'Who was there when you walked into the room?'

'There were writers, poets, as far as I could see, and the life of a writer, despite what it sometimes seems, is pretty tough. I wouldn't make it tougher for anybody.'

'The record shows . . . that these were Communist Party meetings . . .'

'I understood the participants to be Communist writers who were meeting regularly . . .'

Given ten days to respond to the question asking him to name those he saw at the meetings, Miller was advised that he would risk a possible contempt citation if he failed to comply.

It is in this atmosphere of gloom that Miller dropped the bombshell that he and Monroe were to marry on 29 June and that he would accompany his wife to England where for fourteen weeks she would be involved in filming *The Prince and the Showgirl* with Sir Laurence Olivier. This public announcement of an engagement which had been private since April sent publicist Rupert Allan into a rage. He contends that Miller used Marilyn to get himself off the political meat hook. 'If Miller was such a prince, how do you explain that he would go to Washington about the Hollywood Ten business and announce to the press that he and Marilyn were engaged without ever having asked her? If you need to marry anybody and you need to get back into the public image, why not marry the all-American girl?'

Prior to the wedding, Monroe stayed with Miller and his parents at the nine-room 17th-century farmhouse in the village of Roxbury, Connecticut, which Miller had purchased in 1948 with wife Mary. This gave her the chance to study Judaism with Rabbi Robert Goldberg; but it was from Miller's mother that she learned the most important thing about being a Jew – how to cook! Mrs Miller taught Marilyn how to make traditional dishes such as gefilte fish, borscht, chicken soup with matzoh balls, chopped liver, *tsmimis* and potato *pirogen*.

Having first been married in a civil ceremony on 29 June at the White Plains City Hall by City Judge Seymour Rabinowitz, the couple were again wed (in the Jewish faith) on 1 July by Rabbi Goldberg at the nearby home of Miller's agent, Kay Brown. Miller's sister recalls her impressions of that memorable day: 'It was a very hot July day. Everyone was warm from waiting a lot. Then everybody took off their jackets because it was very hot and it was outside. There was a lot of sun that day. It was an excited and exciting afternoon.'

'Everyone' in this instance was confined to twenty-five family members and close friends: the Greenes; Hedda and Norman Rosten; Lee and Paula Strasberg; Bobby and Jane (Miller's children from his first marriage); Miller's parents; his sister Joan and her husband; his brother Kermit and his wife; and Miller's cousins, the Morton Millers.

'I remember that she was *late* for the wedding. They were driving down from Roxbury. She was late and kept everybody waiting. She arrived in jeans or something. Afterwards she came out of the bedroom dressed in beige – wearing a beautiful off-white beige veil.' What Monroe would wear was kept as secret as any royal wedding, the designing house smuggling the dress by station wagon to the country house where the couple were staying. Enveloped in three yards of rich champagne-coloured chiffon, Marilyn wore matching slippers, an off-the-face tiny halo hat, and carried orchids, which she clasped in one hand. The simple ceremony was followed by a wedding supper which was held in the garden under a marquee.

'There was always a low-grade fever amongst all of the spectators whenever [Marilyn] was around which was titillating,' recalls Copeland. 'You always felt excited when you were around her. That day she was absolutely and incredibly radiant. She was like a "bolt of moonlight" walking into the room. Although it was daytime, she was all aglow. She was some sort of vision and she always seemed to have a halo around her. You know those creatures from outer space – how the atmosphere around them shimmers? Well, that was how Marilyn looked, her whole body glowed from within. She had the most incredible translucent kind of skin – almost alabaster in colour.'

The clannish world of the Millers was far removed from anything Marilyn had previously known. 'I remember when Arthur and Marilyn would come to my parents' home when I was there, which would be on occasions like Mother's Day or Thanksgiving or something like that. The family would all be there. She'd fit in quite well. She adored my father. She was comfortable with my father and he adored her. He was not judgemental. I don't think she felt she was being watched by him. I think she felt she could tell him anything and if she said, "I'd like this to be between you and me" it would only be between her and him. After mother died he lived with me, and although he died after Marilyn he'd go out with her to some fancy place for dinner. I am sure she confided things in him but he never would tell us. Sometimes he would be her date at a big party.'

Press reaction to the marriage was coy; a British journalist penning what has to be the funniest putdown of all. Entitled 'Highbrowarthur's Honeymoon', it begins: 'And he murmured soft endearments. And she talked of Dostoyevsky.' Asked about love at first sight, Monroe said: 'The greatest thrill of my life was at a cocktail party when my hand accidentally brushed Arthur Miller's ankle.' Whilst Miller was unusually celestial when asked what it felt like to marry Monroe, sighing: 'Her beauty shines because her spirit is forever showing itself.'

Thirteen days later Monroe, accompanied by Miller, left for London to begin work on *The Prince and the Showgirl*, which was scheduled to start shooting on 30 July 1956. They took twenty-seven pieces of luggage (three of which belonged to Miller) and were joined by acting coaches Lee and Paula Strasberg; producer Milton Greene and his wife Amy; two film publicists (Arthur Jacobs and Jerry Juroe); makeup man Whitey Snyder; Marilyn's personal hairdresser; and her secretary, Hedda Rosten. (Since the British Eady Plan prohibited the employment of more than a couple of foreigners one wonders how Monroe managed to circumvent the ban.)

Olivier was in a difficult mood throughout filming,

and seemed generally unimpressed by the fact that Monroe owned the film and was in a superior business position to him. She was treated like a freak by many Pinewood Studio personnel, who complained that she failed to bid them good-morning or good-night. Others, however, recall her behaviour at the time as being typically and exceedingly polite. The inclement weather, routine nervous pains, and intermittent ulcer attacks gave her legitimate cause for illness, none of which mattered to Olivier who was often bad-tempered.

The years have not altered Olivier's opinion of the encounter. It is also worth noting that when Monroe left Britain, she vowed never again to return. The press, who she described as a pack of sex-starved schoolboys, were disappointed by her failure to be seen in society. They failed to understand that the 'Marilyn' whose image they coveted was a manufactured film one whose creation took a great deal of concentrated preparation and work. They were critical, too, of the money she lavished on having her dressing room re-done and the purchase of a caravan, into which she moved when she discovered that the noise and distractions at Pinewood interfered with her level of concentration.

It was no one incident, but an accumulation of several which widened the gap with Olivier. Whilst Monroe reacted by removing herself from social intercourse, Miller's approach was more sophisticated. A political animal, he sensed trouble on the horizon, and struck out not at Olivier, whose antipathy was undermining his wife's equilibrium on her first independent production, but at Monroe, since it was of paramount importance to him to keep the peace in Britain, a country where his plays were widely acclaimed and regularly produced. The conceptual differences which put the superstars at artistic loggerheads evolved over differences on two major points: 1) whether they were merely filming the play, or making a movie; and if they were making a movie, why Olivier declined to allow her scope to develop her performance with her own nuances and mannerisms, and 2) why he insisted upon getting an equal share of the close ups when the film was entitled 'The Prince' *and* 'the Showgirl'? Marilyn clearly thought they had agreed about the concept when Olivier took on the film and that his generous percentage disposed him to exploiting what was exploitable. When it became apparent this was not so, problems inevitably arose.

Miller was accused by the British press of being manipulated by Olivier ('lumbered by English upmanship, he secretly respects Sir Laurence much too much') and it was his surprisingly tendentious stand which probably planted the seeds of doubt in Monroe about her marriage. Several people have described to me how that once you had double-crossed Marilyn you were off her list for good. A person capable of enormous feeling and great intimacy she reacted emotionally to Miller's betrayal and sought comfort in both liquor and pills. Her dependency on these increased on the occasions Arthur Miller removed himself from the set. Although, ostensibly, he returned to New York to nurse his sick daughter, and whilst we may assume that the litigation with Congress required sporadic appearances on his own behalf, the real reasons behind the absences are recounted by his sister, Joan Copeland:

'Arthur came back a couple of times from London. Apparently there was trouble on the set with Olivier. He really did not want to talk too much about it, because it was a volatile situation and every day it would change. Some days it would be wonderful and some days it would not be so wonderful . . . apparently she felt besieged whilst he felt undermined. But when you look at the film, it is apparent who won the battle and it wasn't Olivier.'

A foretaste of the problems which were later to ensue with Olivier and the crew at Pinewood occurred upon her arrival in the country, when she found herself in the centre of a row with a society hostess who complained that her Berkshire mansion had been thrown over in preference for another which the Millers intended instead to let in Surrey. Although she had been paid in full for the let, the woman angrily maintained that she had been caused public embarrassment, since she had appeared on television and given interviews about her prospective tenants. Monroe's press agent, Arthur Jacobs, a living Coca-Cola advert, who consumed bottles of the stuff, drank another glass and shrugged his shoulders.

Nor, for that matter, was Monroe's reception by Lady Olivier (Vivien Leigh) particularly sunny. Her comments when asked by the press about Monroe were chilly and she cautioned one reporter for his presumption in thinking that the Millers would be staying with the Oliviers for the duration of their stay. 'Marilyn *will* not be staying with us. She will weekend with us sometimes at our country home [Notley Abbey] in Buckinghamshire . . . Miss Monroe desires vacant possession of her little bit of England . . .'

The socializing Monroe did in England was limited to appearances at a Royal Film Performance; a special preview of Miller's play *A View from the Bridge*, which was banned by the censor; and a housewarming thrown for her by playwright Terry Rattigan at his Sunningdale Georgian country house in Berkshire, one of the most glorious parts of the Thames valley. Hosted by Leigh and Olivier, the party, an after-theatre supper dance, was the highlight of the social season, and invitations were highly coveted. Guests included the US Ambassador and Mrs Winthrop Aldrich; Dame Margot Fonteyn; the Duke and Duchess of Buccleuch; Lady Diana Cooper; Sir Terence and Lady Nugent; Dame Sybil Thorndike and Lewis Casson; Sir John Gielgud; Mary and John Mills; Alan Webb; and Douglas Fairbanks, Jr.

When, only recently, I asked both Gielgud and

Casson's nephew, Sir Hugh, what their impressions of
Monroe had been, they replied that they had only the
barest memories. Gielgud had nothing to say, and Sir
Hugh recounted that his aunt (who co-starred in the film
with Marilyn) had said that she was tedious. All of which
confirms my view that she was treated shabbily by the
English who betrayed the very worst aspects of both
class and national snobbery by refusing to recognize the
genius of a working-class American girl. Marilyn was
right, the English did perceive her as a freak, a misfit, a
waif – someone to be either patronized or avoided.

Her attempts to fit in were derided. When she arrived
at the party at 10.45 p.m., wearing a film reject designed
by Beatrice ('Bumble') Dawson – a tight-fitting ball
gown of white chiffon with a pale blue ribbon below
the bust line – Olivier grimaced, compelling Monroe to
explain 'It's a reject, Larry. It was made for the film, but
you're not using it now.' The chill persisted throughout
the evening. 'I think he hated me. He gave me the dirtiest
looks, even when he was smiling,' Monroe recounted
to Lena Pepitone, adding that she tried to flirt with
Olivier at parties when she was wearing tight, revealing
gowns as she thought these might help him to overcome
his English reserve. '"He looked at me like he had
just smelled a pile of dead fish," she said. "He'd say
something like, 'Oh, how simply ravishing, my dear.'
But really he wanted to throw up. I just felt like a little
fool the whole time!"'

Anthony Quayle, who was cast as the Brooklyn long-
shoreman Eddie in Miller's play, *A View from the Bridge*,
whose love for his niece leads to a campaign to get
deported the Italian immigrant who is his rival for her
affections, was similarly abrupt. In response to a compassionate remark Marilyn had made about animals, he
eyed her floor-length mink coat and scolded: 'And what
about the poor little animals whose skins you're wearing
on your back?'

Following a buffet of lobster curry (at which Monroe only nibbled), there was dancing in the large drawing room accompanied, not by a band, but gramophone records cranking out such sentimental favourites as George and Ira Gershwin's 'Embraceable You'. Any feeling that she was wrong and that really he liked her was quickly dispelled when Olivier declined to ask her to dance. Marilyn instead clung to Miller, but for occasional lapses with (hairdresser) Sidney Guilaroff and Terence Rattigan, who she joined in a mean Charleston (the twenties motif became the central one for Monroe when she made her next film *Some Like It Hot*). The hands-off policy suggests that the prevailing belief was that she was what the film's cinematographer, Jack Cardiff, described as 'schizo'; one hopes it wasn't someone in Monroe's own contingency who started the rumour.

The party wound down at about 4 a.m. with Monroe complaining how much she wanted to take a bike ride, but that she couldn't get out of the house with all those people crowding outside the mansion gates. Leigh said little to her in the course of the evening, possibly she was still smarting at being considered 'too old' for the role of the showgirl. 'I suggested that [Marilyn] star in the film . . . and I added that I might be too old for the part,' she said at the time. 'They believed me, and Terry Rattigan and Larry went crazy over Monroe and when I changed my mind and suggested I might play the part after all, they said, "Oh, but you're too old."'

Whilst her retinue stayed at a hotel in nearby Windsor, Monroe and Miller based themselves in Lord Moore's country estate, Parkside House, in the rolling Surrey countryside close by to Pinewood Studios. An eleven-bedroomed white elephant of a mansion, lacking in some amenities, it was cold, damp and draughty and thus contributed to the viral infection which laid her low on several occasions during production. Recounts Whitey

Snyder: 'Marilyn didn't like Lord Moore's house. There was a long hallway leading to a room, and when Marilyn asked him about it, this old boy said, "I don't go down there any more. The walk is so boring."'

Few efforts appear to have been made to make the place more hospitable. The cook and butler tried to organize the Miller's lives with an exactitude which drove Marilyn up the wall and they were finally sacked. Before they left they made some snide remarks about the honeymooners not sleeping together (which was only partly true, since when it was suggested that she wear a hair net to bed Marilyn replied: 'I've only been married for a month!'). They did, I believe, have separate bedrooms, since Monroe was required to awaken each morning at 5 a.m., but they made up for it in the evenings when Miller went in their chauffeured limousine to fetch his wife from the studio at the day's end. In the evening they'd stroll together in the garden before taking their evening meal – just they two (or three): Marilyn, Arthur and a Scotland Yard gumshoe with the amusing surname of Hunt, whose job, along with five other policemen, was to ensure her safety during her stay in Britain. Monroe described the security as 'airtight', even their guard dog couldn't get past the double white gates which had been fitted with new locks.

When she arrived, Monroe was the ultimate Anglophile. She had read almost everything she could about Britain and the British and she had even purchased a pair of Ferragamo walking shoes which she intended to use for country walks. Her initial delight in things British was recounted to friends to whom she wrote: 'Compared to California, England seems tiny and quaint with its little toy trains chugging through the miniature countryside . . . I am dying to walk bareheaded in the rain. I want to eat real roast beef and Yorkshire pudding as I believe only the English can cook it. I want to buy a tweed suit that fits me – I have never worn a tailored suit in my life. I want to ride a bicycle, and I'd like someone to explain the jokes in *Punch* – they don't seem funny to me.'

When she got the chance to go shopping in Regent Street, a fabulous Regency arcade in London's West End, Monroe went on a spree and bought all kinds of sensible clothes – tweed suits, camel hair coats, cashmere sweaters in 'lovely English autumnal shades' and a couple of Oxford dictionaries for Miller.

Since *The Prince and the Showgirl* set was to be closed to all press, Olivier held a press conference at the Savoy Hotel, where 200 newsmen laughed and cheered Monroe who came up with some earthy rejoinders in spite of looking every bit the mindless fool in a skin-tight black sheath with a diaphanous midriff. It is worth noting that the conference got greater coverage than those of either John Foster Dulles or Harry Truman; and that actress Ava Gardner, a tremendous personality herself, passed unnoticed through the hotel lobby during the course of the event.

The questions varied little from those asked on the other side of the Atlantic:

'Now that you are married to Arthur Miller, are you going to change your name to Marilyn Miller?'

'What do you wear when you go to bed?'

'Chanel No. 5 – oops wrong country – Yardley's English Lavender!'

Marilyn created a bad impression with the media since she arrived about 40 minutes late. Although this was not her fault – she was unavoidably detained when her car was mobbed by 300 villagers outside the gates of Lord Moore's country house – many thought it was intentional.

By the time filming had finished, quite a lot of fuss had been made about the explosive situation with Olivier and how the great one had to be coaxed into seeing her off. 'Miss Monroe's a wonderful person. She's been really poorly since she's been here, but I'd make a film with her again,' he said.

Monroe's lack of sincerity was equally transparent: 'I want to thank everyone for our treatment when we were in Britain.' Miller's silence was Pinteresque.

Whilst Monroe didn't have a chance to meet most of her neighbours in Surrey, she did meet one – a rather famous one residing in Windsor Great Park. When she heard that she would meet Queen Elizabeth II at the Royal Film Performance at the Empire, Leicester Square, Monroe was told by Fred Karger's mother to look her straight in the eye, whilst thinking: I am just as pretty as you are! The Queen, on the other hand, was apparently fascinated by Monroe and she reputedly asked Sir Terence Rattigan what she was like; the playwright compared Marilyn to a shy exhibitionist – a Garbo who likes to be photographed.

Publicist Rupert Allan recounts: 'That would have been a big challenge to meet the Queen – but here again, she was late. As long as I knew Marilyn I had to wait for her to prepare herself. It could be an hour – she would re-do her hair and her face. She was never perfect, never right. She told me about it. Olivier and Vivien Leigh were annoyed to hell with her. So was Arthur Miller. That would drive someone like Olivier who was very professional crazy. Somebody from the theatre is never late.'

Marilyn wore a dress designed by Bumble Dawson, which whilst it lacked the simplicity of Travilla's garments, was, nonetheless, distinctive in its ostentation. Similar to the hell-raising gown Marilyn wore to the *Photoplay* awards, this one was also of gold lamé, but instead of clinging simply to her shape it encumbered the body, dropping over the bust and falling to the ground in floor-length Greek folds.

When finally they met, the Queen joked about their being neighbours (which Marilyn missed entirely, as she failed to realize that Windsor Great Park was a royal park). 'How do you like your home at Windsor? . . . You are neighbours of ours.' Momentarily uncertain, Monroe quickly rallied. 'We love it and as we have a permit my husband and I go for bicycle rides and walks in the Great Park.'

What made Rattigan's 'occasional fairy tale' work as a stage play was the conceit of a silly, adolescent showgirl sowing her wild oats with the Prince Regent of the mythical kingdom of Carpathia. Had the character been other than virginal there would have been no story. Jamesian in conception, Rattigan's Elsie exhibits all the wonder and euphoria of an innocent abroad. What is wrong with the film is Olivier's attempt to subvert the subtext of the script, changing things round so that the girl appears little better than a strumpet. By reversing the conceit he eliminates the guts of the piece, leaving us to wonder at the Prince's preoccupation with a woman whose morals are little better than those of a prostitute; and to query, too, an ending which has them falling deeply, but unrequitedly, in love.

Playwright Rattigan confirms that his vision of the piece was sympathetic to Monroe's. 'The play is about a man who has been asleep – at least his emotional side; but little by little a relationship builds up between him and this American chorus girl. He begins to stir in his sleep. But he is a married man.' Initially concerned that Olivier would romanticize the man too much (here, after all, was an actor whose performance had succeeded in glamorizing Richard III), Rattigan was reassured when he discovered that Olivier intended to conceal his emotions behind a panoply of armour penetrable only by an A-bomb. Olivier's Prince was the most arrogant, opinionated, sexist, racist, chauvinist pig that ever there was; and to get across the point that he held the girl in complete and utter contempt, he employed all kinds of theatrical conventions ranging from speech to costume.

One of the most esoteric bits of camp was his Oxford pronunciation of English slang, which would have been offputting for any actress, but for Monroe, it must have created an unsurmountable mental block.

Echoing his own surprise at Olivier's decision to de-romanticize the Prince, Rattigan says: '. . . Where I had feared that my "Prince Uncharming" would inevitably become "Prince Utterly Irresistible", those fears were forever laid to rest when . . . I went into his dressing room . . . to be confronted by a rather dull-looking little man, with an anaemic complexion . . . a thin, prissy, humourless mouth, hair parted in the middle and plastered repulsively downwards over his ears, and a sad-looking monocle glued over his right eye.'

Perhaps if Olivier had allowed Monroe to share the joke, if together they agreed that the man was an old goat whose appalling treatment of the girl showed him to be nothing more than a patronizing tyrant, it might all have come right. As it was, the unsatisfactory relationship which existed between Olivier and Monroe prevented this.

Norman Rosten's wife Hedda accompanied Monroe to England, assuming the temporary role of a secretary. Recalling the general attitude of the British toward the American company, she told Norman '. . . that their first important vibration was bad. It occurred on the opening day at the studio where the cast gathered with director Olivier preparatory to the beginning of shooting . . . Olivier formally welcomed the company . . . He then introduced Marilyn. He remarked that it would be a new experience for her and would probably take her a while to get accustomed to their way of doing things. He was outwardly polite and gracious, but his slight smile, his change in tone from that of clubby professionalism when speaking to the rest of the cast . . . to one of careful, almost elementary explanation when speaking to Marilyn . . . came across to her as patronizing. He was talking down to her, she was just another Hollywood Blonde.'

Cinematographer Jack Cardiff, who has worked with many legendary actresses queries Olivier's behaviour. According to Cardiff, Monroe was 'impeccable and fastidious in every possible way. She was always to me "clean" – if you know what I mean. The average film star (and I have worked with many) were hooker types in their language (they'd swear and stuff). You knew from the way they talked that they were Hollywood types, and that they had slept all over the place. From Marilyn I can never once remember hearing a four-letter word. On the set she was professional. She never burst into tears or rows.'

And yet, in spite of this, there was the presumption that she was 'schizo', which contributed to Olivier's firmly entrenched prejudice that she didn't know beans about anything. ★Explains Cardiff: 'Larry's position at one time in England was that he was like a kind of God. He ruled the theatre world. And when it was proposed that he would work with Marilyn Monroe, it tickled the press. What a combination – Laurence Olivier, the great Shakespearean actor working with this American cream puff.

'Another thing was that he had already been a success. The play had been a success. He had had Vivien. And Vivien was there (she appeared twice on the set, both times when Monroe was absent). That was another factor. Subconsciously he had formulated a concept of the way she would play it based on his wife's success in the play and based on his performance which was natural

---

★ This might be accounted for because during production a woman claiming to be Marilyn Monroe's lover kept phoning the set. Monroe said that she did not know who the woman was. Subsequently the lady, a society woman, committed suicide. This information was disclosed to the author following hardback publication of the book by someone who worked on the 'Showgirl' set.

enough. When she started to use her Method acting and to question everything – the reason, the motivation – this was a difficulty for him.

'It was the most dreadful experience of [Olivier's] life. He had greatness. And all that greatness went right up against a stone wall when he was working with Marilyn. It was two personalities which didn't get on because she wouldn't listen to him. She doubted his wisdom about how to play the part. She wanted to play it the way she felt and the way her coach had told her.'

Classically trained, Olivier believed that acting consisted of saying a line and executing a movement, nothing more. When Monroe stared at him in confusion when he told her what to do, he became cross. Recounts Cardiff: 'She'd stare at him with a blank expression. She either understood the gist of what he was talking about but didn't agree with it or simply didn't understand. I don't think Larry was silly enough to talk above her. She had this Method coach [Paula Strasberg] on the sidelines. When Larry would finish, Marilyn would go over to Paula and speak for about 20 minutes while Larry would stand there. It was embarrassing.'

Method versus Classicism. The stories about the clashes are legendary, neither side giving way in what was to become known as the Olivier–Monroe holy wars. Monroe couldn't, since she was not a RADA-trained actress and was incapable of playing the role with classical precision. And Olivier wouldn't, although he was perfectly capable of star acting, judging from his memorable film performances in both *Rebecca* and *Wuthering Heights*.'

Roy Baker, who directed Marilyn in *Don't Bother to Knock*, was also at Pinewood when Monroe was making the film, and observed the difficulties she encountered: 'She was delightful in *The Prince and the Showgirl* but she had no sense of period. She was nowhere near the period. She looked modern. She played it modern. She had no

sense of costume at all. She didn't know how to wear
the clothes. There is a way of walking about in a long
skirt which young girls today do not know. They have
to be trained at RADA so that they can play classical
parts.'

Olivier's refusal to simplify the text in everyday terms
so that they could play it like human beings sent Monroe
into panic; crew members remember seeing her scrib-
bling notes about the role in two tiny notebooks –
one red, one blue. Constantly agitated, she patted her
fingertips on the outer arches of her eyebrows or pulled
nervously at her hair whilst concentrating – her hairdresser continually had to right it. 'She was a genius!'
says Cardiff, who had the chance to observe her over a
four-month period. His candid photographs of the actress (which were favourites of Miller's) captured in the
adult the mind and soul of a four-year-old sex maniac.
'Some people say that Chaplin had it. I am not so sure
about that. Marilyn had a genius for being so different
from most people – a quality. She had this magic on the
screen. We were watching the rushes. I said what a
marvellous actress I thought she was. An actor said:
"How dare you say she is a great actress?" I said, "I am
not saying she is a *great* actress. I am saying she is a
genius!" You can get hundreds of girls in Hollywood
with the same bust measurements. She had something
the others haven't got. She had "quality" which came
out on the screen and Larry saw that.'

The laboriousness of the shoot has been well documented, several actors recounting instances where
Monroe delayed production for hours, searching for
motivation. Actor Paul Hardwick, cast in the film as the
Major Domo, recalls Monroe's difficulty in completing
a very short scene in Westminster Abbey – a five-second
take which required her to raise her eyes and appear
strongly moved. 'She simply couldn't do it,' he recalls.
'Larry had a record of "Air on a G String" playing for

a good hour . . . trying to coax that look out of her. At the end of the hour he . . . said "You love 'Air on a G String', don't you?" "Yeah," [Monroe] said. "But I think I could do it better if I had 'Danny Boy'."'

'I was there when Olivier told Monroe to "Be sexy!"' says Jack Cardiff. 'It was a terrible row because she took it very badly. Well, she was sexy. She was sexy in everything. She sort of looked sexy. Marilyn was sexy in her facial movements. And in her vulnerability which came over.'

This incident had horrendous repercussions, since it highlighted not only differences in approach, but Olivier's insupportably patronizing attitude towards Monroe. Coach Paula Strasberg objected: 'I never told [Marilyn] how to say a line. You don't have to teach her to be sexy. She *is* sexy. You don't have to teach her how to be American. She *is* American.'

Susan Strasberg adds: '[Olivier's] wife, Vivien Leigh, had done the part of the showgirl in the London production of the play. She was a wonderful actress but miscast as the sexy, naïve American showgirl, a part for which Marilyn was perfect. Marilyn could play this role with her eyes closed, but Olivier seemed to feel that she should play it like Miss Leigh and he was infuriating her with his exacting and specific direction . . . Olivier [was] resentful of my mother's presence on the set. He was unable, however, to establish any rapport with Marilyn as some of her other directors, like George Cukor or Josh Logan, had done. This was obvious when he asked her to "Come into the room and act sexy." There was a long, heavy silence. Marilyn looked at him. "Larry, I don't have to act sexy. I am sexy."'

In order to get round the vast number of re-takes occasioned by Monroe's exactitude, Olivier constructed a movable set which eliminated the lengthy time lapses needed to re-set the camera. This way the entire set could simply be switched round to photograph the scene from another angle. Whilst there were still delays, they were infinitely less protracted. But that was Monroe.

Recalls columnist Radie Harris: 'I happened to be on the set . . . when Marilyn had to say just four words: "Oh, you poor Prince." . . . First she conferred with Larry, then with Terry Rattigan, and then with Paula to find out the motivation of the word "poor". Finally, in desperation Larry said, "For God's sake, Marilyn, there is no motivation! Just say the word and let's get on with this scene."'

The famous 'caviar' scene took two days, thirty–forty takes and twenty jars of caviar at $8 per half-jar to get right, since Monroe was unable to summon up the proper reaction to the delicacy, looking more ill than euphoric. This is the scene where she is required to nibble on something while the Prince ignores her, engrossed in conversation with his Ambassador. Finally, Paula Strasberg is supposed to have coached 'Think of cold sausages and Coca-Cola!'

Reducing everything to the pedestrian level of a grunt or a burp was understandably discouraging for Olivier. The irony, however, is that it worked; and whatever Monroe used to make a connection with her character should not be discounted. 'Her system was spontaneity,' said Cardiff. 'The system of searching the subconscious was the thing which Monroe employed. So there was a complete clash. She didn't trust anything but herself and her Method acting. It is like asking a Catholic to forget about the Virgin Mary. She was dedicated to Method acting where she had to dig deep into every single thing she did.'

Fanatical about things which might seem incidental to others, Monroe was concerned that her costume, hair and makeup should be right and it was not unusual for her to hold up production for hours until she was ready. (Always obsessive and neurotic about her looks, Olivier didn't help when at the start of production he said something about Monroe's teeth looking a bit yellow in the rushes and hinted that baking soda and lemon would whiten them. She was furious.) A supporting actor recalls: 'There was often a hold-up while Miss Monroe's hair had to be fixed over – and then fixed all over again, because she did not like it . . . but then towards the end of the day when the beads had been stitched on and the lights were up and the hair was right, Marilyn Monroe sat down and sang a snatch of song for the film . . . And in five takes, surprisingly short for a film song, the scene was shot.'

Looking right in front of the camera was of paramount importance, since Monroe was, if nothing else, a *visual* comedienne – communicating meaning with a smile, a wink or a nod. Consequently it was not exceptional for Monroe to take the day off if she felt she was not looking physically fit. 'She had a fantastic inferiority complex,' says actress Vera Day, who played one of Monroe's friends. 'She got so nervous about everything that she just locked herself in her dressing room and refused to come out.'

Problems would ensue when Olivier had organized a very complicated scene and had got the other actors ready and into their costumes. There is one tragi-comic exchange between Monroe and Dame Sybil Thorndike who plays the Queen Dowager. Actor Douglas Wilmer recounts: 'Monroe was always late, and one day when we were shooting the Coronation scene it meant that Dame Sybil was kept waiting for ages in her heavy robes. Sir Laurence told her, "Don't you think you ought to apologize to Dame Sybil?" And Marilyn exploded. "Apologize!" And she turned on her heels and flounced off. But she was good enough about half an hour later to apologize very nicely and Sybil said very grandly: "Not at all, my dear. I'm sure we're all very glad to see you. Now that you *are* here."'

Amazing as it may seem, the result was quite an

interesting film. Set against Carmen Dillon and Roger
Furse's Regency sets, Cardiff's romantic cinematogra-
phy, and Beatrice Dawson's elegant costumes, Monroe
is the all-American Dream Girl besotted by the splendour
and elegance of European traditions: the Prince, the
country (England) and the coronation of a monarch.
Maybe she doesn't know how to walk in period clothing
and perhaps her expression in Westminster Abbey is
rather dazed, but maybe it all is true for her. The be-
mused smile that creases her face in the Coronation scene
brilliantly captures the reverence and awe such a girl
would feel at suddenly finding herself in such magnificent surroundings. Although she did not get much help
from Olivier, she managed to flesh out a character that
in reality was terribly sketchy and her performance won
Italy's David di Donatello award for Best Foreign Actress.

Ironically, it was not Monroe's professional lapses
with Olivier but her frenetic marriage to Miller which
threatened to bring the film to a crashing halt. Midway
through production she suffered a nervous breakdown.
The breakdown was hushed up, but it is nevertheless
true that her New York analyst Dr Marianne Kris flew
to England on several occasions to patch things up so
that Monroe could continue.

The cause of Monroe's collapse has been attributed to
Miller's growing disenchantment over the manner in
which she comported herself with Olivier and the way
she failed to show up for work if she felt that she looked
less than superb. Although she knew that the tensions
with Olivier placed a strain on him, she begged Miller
not to get involved, assuring him that whilst they might
lose money by going overschedule, they stood to lose a
lot more if she looked awful and the film flopped.
Incidentally, it was mentioned to me by one of the
actors that although Miller may have privately voiced his
objections about delays, it was he who often caused

them by coming along to the set in the middle of the afternoon with some review of his play or other bit of news which he'd communicate to Monroe whilst everyone else stood around waiting.

What threw Marilyn in turmoil, however, was the discovery of a diary Miller was keeping about their marriage which, according to Susan Strasberg, 'spoke in a very denigrating, condescending way about her. She had been devastated and her reaction lapped over into her work and, of course, placed an additional strain on mother.'

David Conover quotes the passage exactly: '. . . I thought you were an angel, but Mary [Miller's first wife] was a saint compared with you. Olivier is right! You are troublesome bitch. What a waste of love! All you want is a flunky. Someone who'll make excuses for you, wait on you night and day, pour out sweet talk to make you feel better and wake you up from the stupor of pills. Well, I'm not up to it. Damn it. I'm not your servant. I'll not bow my head again. Never! You've made love a drudgery. The only one I really love in this world is my daughter.'

Whereas men seem psychologically prepared to cope with insubordination – a non-supportive wife generally gets the sack – women are less inclined to defend themselves, particularly if they are careerists, since they often harbour some element of guilt at being successes in a man's world. Monroe's reaction was typically feminine. Blaming herself for the breach, she sulked until Miller returned from New York, when she returned to work.

In addition to the breakdown, there were other physical ailments: a virus (occasioned by the weather); an ulcer (nerves); and a pregnancy, discovered midway into the fourteen-week shooting schedule. Perhaps the discovery helped to breach the gap with Miller, who came hurrying back to London when he got the news. A London newspaper reported: 'With the stealth of a secret agent, a gynaecologist called to examine Miss Marilyn Monroe at her country home in Surrey yesterday. He arrived before lunch and stayed for about three-quarters of an hour. Afterwards she was on the telephone to America speaking to Arthur Miller, her husband. She seemed bright and cheerful.'

The experience of *The Prince and the Showgirl* so exhausted Monroe that she decided upon her return to the States, in April 1957, to take some time off, both to prepare for the arrival of the baby and to devote herself to the traditional female pursuits of being a wife and mother. The storm clouds cast over their marriage by that ugly episode with the note were temporarily forgotten. Monroe was convinced that the union had every prospect of surviving given half a chance. Without impending business problems setting them against each other, Marilyn figured that she and Miller would settle down together in the manner of an old married couple.

Awaiting the birth of their own child stimulated Monroe's wish to care for Arthur's children by his previous marriage, Bobby and Jane. They all settled into Marilyn's luxurious East Side apartment which she had had redecorated in beige and brown, fixing up a separate study for Arthur where he could write undisturbed. Columnist Radie Harris who visited Marilyn during the sabbatical she took following completion of *The Prince and the Showgirl* found her in superb spirits, and sufficiently Anglicized to have punctuated the interview with a short tea break. Chatting with her in the white living room (it had white walls, white carpet and a white couch), Harris found her 'deliriously happy in her new role of housewife.' 'I know it's considered chic for a husband and wife to have separate bedrooms, but I'm an old-fashioned girl who believes a husband and wife should share the same bedroom and bed,' Marilyn told the columnist. Adds Harris: 'She showed off their king-size bed and love seat [telling me that] Arthur has his own study, where he does his writing . . . but I never intrude except to bring him a second cup of coffee . . .'

Empty days were filled with idle pursuits. Monroe spent her time going for long rides along the East River with their bassett hound (Hugo), bicycling up Second Avenue or window shopping at the antique shops along Third Avenue. Bloomingdales was the department store she preferred to Saks, because of its excellent household department, where she could 'go . . . mad buying furniture, garden implements, seeds for birds and clothes for Arthur. I also take care of his laundry,' she told Harris. 'I definitely don't approve when a man who has to go out finds he has no clean shirts to wear because his wife is off somewhere playing bridge.'

When she wasn't fussing about Miller, she was planning some fun things to do with Bobby (nine) and Jane (twelve). Miller's children, now adults, maintain a tremendous affection for Monroe. Whatever were her problems she never allowed them to interfere with her plans for the group. Given her tremendously creative spirit, she could always be counted upon to be fun! Publicist Rupert Allan recalls: 'His kids adored Marilyn. And Marilyn was good to them and adored them. She always wanted to have children . . . The boy was aged eleven when she gave him the first birthday party he ever had. She gave this birthday party for him and invited his friends up. They parked their bicycles in the lobby of their apartment building.'

Whilst plans were being formulated for them to spend a long, lazy summer vacation in Amagansett, a peaceful hamlet on the eastern end of Long Island Sound, Monroe did some hard thinking about the future of Marilyn Monroe Productions. Her relationship with Greene could on occasion be tense, but she was nonetheless aware that he was a definite asset, her dreams would have remained unrealized had it not been for him. He was enterprising, but he was also pushy. When they were in Britain Greene had placed an advert in one of the London newspapers soliciting for scripts. Encouraged by Arthur Miller, who felt that the relationship was not mutually productive, Monroe began legal proceedings to dissolve the company. She bought back 49.4 per cent of Greene's stock, which she did at an unrevealed price, thereby depleting much of her own cash flow.

David Conover recalls: 'In February, at Miller's urging, Marilyn cast Greene adrift. She had no heart for it. She told me later: "In the lawyer's office, I couldn't face him. I just broke and ran out the door. After all, he was responsible for the two best pictures I've ever made."

'"Why did you give in to Arthur?"

'"He was always hounding me. I couldn't stand it any more . . . I felt you know, I have to keep peace!"'

Greene's removal from Monroe's life did not solve their problems, however. Miller discovered that being married to a megastar interfered with his concentration. What was more, he found her world intruding upon his, and that he unwittingly became involved in business matters relating to her career. Monroe began to distrust Miller's involvement in her affairs, but was unable to alter the situation. 'It was a bad time,' recalls Robert Slatzer. 'He simply couldn't stand having a more famous wife and I believe became hostile (and intrusive) toward Monroe in consequence.'

Whether Miller's citation for contempt of Congress placed an additional strain upon the marriage, or whether much of the aggression directed against Monroe would better have been directed elsewhere, theirs was not a happy marriage, and the problems which had surfaced during their British sojourn lingered.

Recounts Rosten, an Amagansett neighbour: 'One evening, we gave a dinner party at our cottage. After food, there was dancing and quite a bit of merriment. Marilyn left the room at one point without a word to anyone. I followed several moments later and discovered her on the porch sobbing quietly.

'"What is it, dear?"

'"I can't tell you. I feel terrible. Maybe it's the weather."'*

Superficially, however, life went on routinely, Monroe relishing the chance to be 'normal' for the first time in her life. Wearing old khaki shorts and a man's white shirt, she enjoyed being completely idle – swimming, fishing or simply walking arm in arm on moonlight evenings with Miller. According to David Conover, 'She . . . baked bread, weeded the garden and went into the village shopping whilst her husband laboured at the typewriter.' Rosten paints a similar picture: 'She loved being "Mrs Miller". She shopped at the local supermarket, cleaned the house and cooked the meals while Arthur wrote his plays.'

Then on Thursday morning, 1 August, as she was weeding her garden, Arthur heard her screaming. Recounts biographer Zolotow: 'He rushed out to find her

---

* Suicidal moods were commonplace to Monroe and so I asked Jan Sterling, neighbour to Miller and Monroe in New York City, about the reputed suicide attempts. She said that the only ambulance calls she could remember were for miscarried pregnancies (about which she read in the morning newspapers) I could find nothing in the newspaper files alleging to suicides; but it is possible that the stories were covered up by the studios.

Rosten's account of this telling incident, which belies comprehension, seemingly has nothing to do with Miller, or anyone else close to Monroe. It brings again to my mind the subject of voodoo. For it is possible that in a newspaper or on TV Monroe read or saw something personal in an impersonal context, which made her cry. I shall offer my own example. The Post Office left a note for a man who lives in my block of flats. His name is "Jimmy". The slip was made out simply to Jimmy; but the handwriting is *identical* to the script of that on the move marquee for the film entitled "Jimmy Reardon". When I glimpsed the identical script on the marquee, I had a singular heart palpitation. It is this kind of thing which terrifies and can produce sobs, or whatever.

doubled over in pain. He carried her into the house and laid her on the couch. It took four hours to get her to hospital.'

Driven 100 miles by ambulance from their summer home in Long Island, Monroe was carried by stretcher into New York City's Doctors Hospital. Attended by her East Coast physician Dr Hilliard Dubrow, she awoke through a haze of sedatives to hear the shattering news that she had lost her baby. Miller took a room at the hospital to be on hand. He said she had been digging for clams and swimming but he could not recall any incident, such as a fall, which could have brought on the miscarriage.

Optimistic about the future, Monroe fully intended that she and Arthur would have other children. 'A baby makes a marriage, it makes a marriage perfect. But doctors have assured me that I *can* have children. Oh, I'm looking forward to having a family of my own.'

It would be another year before Monroe would return to work. In July 1958 she agreed to co-star in a crazy Marx Bros–type comedy set in the roaring twenties about two jazz musicians in drag (played by Tony Curtis and Jack Lemmon) who, on the run from the mob, join an all-girl band where they meet and befriend a misused jazz baby named Sugar (played by Monroe). Directed by Billy Wilder, the film was to be the first independent production financed by the Mirisch Bros, for which Monroe, on a first-time basis, was to get a percentage instead of the flat fee she usually received. Since the film cost $2.8 million (it went a little over budget) but grossed over $14 million in its first run, Monroe did very well. However, since most of the money came in after her death, it was her estate which benefited mostly.

Years later, Harold Mirisch still shudders when Monroe's name is mentioned, since it was during this film that Monroe became pregnant again and it was gravely doubted both that she would do the stunts and finish the picture. Unfortunately, having done both she had another miscarriage, losing her second child.

Prior to her screen comeback, the Millers decided that they needed a bigger country house and so they decided to purchase a 100-acre holding on which Miller had had his eye for years. According to Robert Slatzer the place was completely uninhabitable. Marilyn helped Miller refurbish the interior, and build him a cosy summer house where he could do his writing without interruption. 'I think she spent about $30,000 all together; but when they divorced, she was too proud to ask for any share of community property.'

Columnist Radie Harris who visited Monroe on the farm, recounts her enthusiasm for the undertaking. 'All our friends agreed the land was beautiful, but they said the house was just uninhabitable. I looked at it and thought how it had been standing there, weathering everything for more than one hundred and eighty years. And I just hated the idea of its being torn down or even left unoccupied. So Arthur and I ignored everybody's advice and got to work. We modernized the back part, put in sliding glass doors, built a garage and a separate one-room studio for Arthur. But in the house itself, we left all the old beams and ceilings intact.'

Equipped with a wing they christened the 'nursery', it was obvious there was every intention both that the marriage should survive and she should have another child. 'Since I lost my baby, my last baby, I couldn't bring myself to hope any more, but I do now, all the time.'

Spring 1958 was a successful time for both Miller and Monroe; the United States Supreme Court reversed his conviction for contempt of Congress, whilst Hollywood beckoned Monroe back to the screen with an offer she could not refuse. When an interviewer described the generous terms of the deal as tantamount to mutiny at an asylum, with the inmates running things, Monroe responded with the literalness which identifies her intelligence: 'I don't understand the line. It is just some incompetent executive seeing how daring a slogan he can find . . . The public makes a star . . .'

23
The Last Eccentric

Two full months of pre-production were consumed
with colour tests, costume fittings, and music rehearsals,
Monroe hitting the proverbial ceiling when she discovered that *Some Like It Hot* was to be shot in black
and white, when her contracts plainly called for *all*
of her films to be made in colour. Recounts Wilder
biographer Tom Wood: 'If the picture was made in
colour, Wilder knew that he'd be laying himself open to
charges of transvestism if their makeup was light and
vulgarity if it was heavy. He finally won his point with
Marilyn by shooting some colour tests of the actors in
their girls' outfits and makeup. Even she was appalled
by the gruesome, unwholesome results and she gave in
– though not with good grace.'

Actually, the monochromatic colour scheme worked
very effectively. Photographed with a resplendence
which suggests use of a double Obie spot, Monroe
shimmers in light. In other respects, too, she glowed:
her hair was dyed platinum blonde; her makeup was
purposefully iridescent; and her costumes tended to be
made of glittering, glimmering fabrics which were also
exceedingly revealing. Whilst there were battles about
how far they should go, it appears from the results –
since in some sequences Monroe appears naked – that
she won; her Oscar-winning costume being 'very, very

tight, slashed very low in front and very low behind'. The real attention-getter is the bare-backed number she wears in the seduction scene with Tony Curtis. Made of sequins, tulle and silver fringing, it was responsible for the film's 'X'; the objection seemed not to reside with the transvestism of the male leads but Monroe's dress, which was considered by the censors to be 'obscene'.

Some Like It Hot is considered by many to be Monroe's best film and one of the reasons for this are the terrific musical numbers which she delivers not with her normally gentle purr but with a loud roar. It appears that Monroe was coached by none other than the most spectacular musical talent ever to be produced in Hollywood: Judy Garland. Choreographer Jack Cole, who himself coached Garland through her superb comeback role in *A Star is Born*, made the introductions hoping that Judy would consent to teach Monroe the ropes. The meeting between the two is legendary. Monroe met Garland at a party and followed her from room to room. 'I'm scared,' she confided to Garland, who herself coped for years with ghosts of one sort of another. 'I'm scared, too. We're all scared, Marilyn.'

Because of Garland's help, Monroe's timing and phrasing are among her best, but the results were difficult to come by. Sound editor Eve Newman remembers Monroe's difficulties: 'She had six weeks to two months rehearsal before shooting started. She had had enough rehearsal. She should have been able to have gotten it clean. But she couldn't concentrate. Do you know how many takes "Running Wild" is made up of to get it so fantastic? About sixty-four! I pieced her performance together. I'd take something from Take 64 and put it with Take 18 and so on.

'And you couldn't watch Marilyn – or she'd get shook. I'd be making notes and she'd ask me to turn my back. So I'd hide behind a potted palm to get out of her line of eye contact. It made her self-conscious to be watched when she rehearsed.'

Monroe had no self-consciousness, however, about the way she looked during rehearsals. Newman confirms producer Rubin's account of the antipathy she engendered by the sloppy way she'd arrive for rehearsals in Capri pants and a torn T-shirt. 'I know that word came down from the head office to Miss Monroe that if she knew she was going to appear on stage before seventy musicians, she should be more careful in her appearance.'

When Marilyn and Arthur Miller arrived in Hollywood after two and a half years on the East Coast, producer Harold Mirisch gave them a dinner party, with some eighty persons invited at 7 p.m. for cocktails followed by dinner at 9 p.m. Monroe arrived at 11.20 p.m. when the party was breaking up. Perhaps she suspected what would happen when Miller met Hollywood's wild bunch; the gag men lampooning Miller's pomposity with their devastating wit. Having known I.A.L. (Iz) Diamond, the film's co-screenwriter, when he was a Fox contract dialogue writer on *Love Nest*, *Monkey Business* and *Let's Make It Legal*, it was logical that he should have been among the first to congratulate the newlyweds. 'Arthur Miller put one arm around Billy [Wilder] and one arm around Iz as Marilyn looked at the trio apprehensively,' an observer recalls. 'Then Miller said, in a pedantic tone: "The difference between comedy and tragedy is . . ." He spoke for several minutes. He was impressive. He was profound. Wilder doesn't remember a word he said. Diamond remembers. He did not wish to repeat it.'

When Miller finally separated from Monroe in 1960 he blamed not her, but Hollywood as having caused the rupture in their marriage. 'I've had it with Hollywood!' he said. The seeds of the inevitable discord were perceived by columnist James Bacon when he first met Miller on the film set of *Some Like It Hot*. 'Miller was a

jealous type. When we were introduced Marilyn said:
"Jim and I used to be real close." Miller just stared. He
didn't even shake hands.'

In the same way that *The Seven Year Itch* used Monroe
in a way which best exploited the talents that were
uniquely hers, *Some Like It Hot* was also a film that very
few other people could have done. 'Marilyn was not
versatile at all,' observes director Roy Baker. 'She could
only play Marilyn Monroe which she did brilliantly. I
couldn't find a subject for Marilyn which I wanted to
do, although I hoped to work with her again and talked
with her about it when she was in England filming *The
Prince and the Showgirl*.'

Some Like It Hot is another of director Wilder's adult
fairy stories, the psychological dream nightmare in this
instance being safety and security, underscored by the
Chicago 1929 St Valentine's Day massacre. Based on the
old German picture, *Fanfares of Love*, where a couple of
unemployed musicians alternately dress up as gypsies,
blacks and women to fit the venues, Wilder's re-creation
takes the conceit one step further, placing the guys in
drag not out of choice but necessity. In the surreal
world of tragi-comic peril envisaged by Wilder, the
predicament becomes infinitely more complex, locking
the characters into a situation from which there is no
escape. Confirms Wilder's writing partner, Iz Diamond:
'We had to find the hammerlock. We had to find the
ironclad thing so these guys trapped in women's clothes
cannot just take the wigs off and say: "Look, I'm a guy."
It has to be a question of life and death. And that's where
the idea for the St Valentine's Day murder came. If they
got out of the women's clothes, they would be killed by
the Al Capone gang. That was an important invention
. . . The two men were on the spot and we kept them
there until the end.'

Played off against the reality of the band's lead singer,
Sugar, the guys in drag are a sort of symbolic double-

cross; their sexual ambiguity the very metaphor for those
deprivations of love, men, marriage and family she has
experienced throughout her life. Release from the mad
world of insane contradictions comes not at the film's
end where the happy trio go off together with a psychotic
millionaire, gleefully played by Joe E. Brown, but when
we (the audience) leave the theatre, casting a cheerful
eye at our own reasonably sane and normal lives.

Ultimately grossing over $22 million, the film is an
acknowledged success and one of Monroe's most tri-
umphant portrayals. There is something in the way she
plays it, something she brings to the character that makes
it a classic; some long, lost bit of regret at finding herself
bystander in a mad, chaotic masculine world of murder,
madness and greed. It is a film I have seen at least fifty
times and in which, each time I see it, I notice some
fresh bit of insight. It is a film which there is talk of
re-making, but I think it would be impossible, since
so much of the intellectual core comes from Marilyn
Monroe.

In the way he dehumanized the characters to accentu-
ate their mythical attributes, Wilder was far ahead of the
European New Wave directors in evolving a psychological never-never land. Sugar and the musicians are joined
in their quest for existential reality by a host of other
misfits which include George Raft, parodying the gang-
ster roles for which he was noted; pugilist Abe Simon
as a mobster; and Joe E. Brown as the hideous (but rich!)
Florida businessman idly whiling away his retirement
years in a bachelor's paradise of sun, stars and sea
maidens. Even Tony Curtis played his role in Cary
Grant drag, a double metaphor, since Wilder had tried
and failed to procure the services of Cary Grant on
numerous occasions.

Originally conceived as a Marx Bros-type comedy,
for Jack Lemmon and Tony Curtis, Wilder was surprised
when Monroe accepted the part after having read a

five-page précis. 'It's the *weakest* part, so the trick was to give it the strongest casting.' Although scenes were written very much as they went along (Wilder living in peril of plagiarism), he discussed the concept in greater detail with the actress. 'She gets the point right away,' said Wilder at the time. 'She is exceptionally keen.' When the distribution company, United Artists, heard that Marilyn Monroe was interested, they didn't care about Lemmon, since they already had the assurance of 'bankability'. Lemmon, however, was keen to participate; so much so that in order to get his release from Columbia Pictures (where he was under contract) he agreed to do four more pictures for them, three more than he was obliged to. Curtis, on the other hand, needed a bit of persuasion since initially he was disinclined to dress up as a woman. '[But] we were in drag because we were trying to save our lives, not because we wanted to swish around the set!' he told *Time Out* magazine. Why the Cary Grant impression? '. . . A few days before we started the shoot they told me that I had to play a very sophisticated English gentleman, so I had to come up with an idea. How did I talk English, except like Cary Grant? So I did it for Billy Wilder, and it became a great joke . . . [There is] that line when Jack Lemmon comes up in the bathroom, and says, "Nobody talks like that!" . . . Billy showed Cary the movie [and he said] "I don't talk like that!"'

A bit of the madness spilled over into the working environment, not least in the erratic behaviour of Marilyn Monroe. Billy Wilder said some very nasty things following her death, which Iz Diamond maintains twenty-five years later: that she was mean – the meanest little seven-year-old he had ever met; that he was both too rich and too old to work with her again; and that whilst she lost her baby he suffered from bursitis. So they were even.

An examination of what really went on during the

marathon shoot puts everything in a somewhat different perspective. Monroe was a genius, but not one, it seems, whose genius was often understood or catered for by Wilder. It hardly takes an Einstein to notice that much of the success of Monroe's films depends upon the way she looks: full-bodied; wholesome; appealing, relaxed. She was, as is stated in the script, 'every red-blooded American male's dream of college humour'. It has by now been established that unlike the Cary Grants of this world, whose personal mannerisms were identical to his screen image, Monroe was altogether different off camera. Since her sex life was often lousy and her professional existence was characterized by incessant quarrels, it took a good deal of time and trouble to put herself together to face the camera. It was not unusual for her to spend a couple of hours relaxing, cat napping or merely fussing about with her hair and face. Since she had a profit share in the film one wonders what the big deal was about her lateness.

It amused me when I discussed the subject with Iz Diamond that he immediately (and defensively) ascribed lateness on Monroe's part to an attempt by the star to throw around the power she had gained following the Fox walk-out. 'Having reached the top she was paying back the world for all the rotten things she had had to go through,' says Diamond. 'There were mornings when 9 a.m. rolled around and Marilyn was *not* on the set. 10 a.m. comes – no Marilyn. She is now in makeup. She is now in hairdressing. 10.45 a.m. she walks on. Everybody has been waiting all morning. Not a word of greeting. Not a word of apology. She just walks straight through to her dressing room. She is carrying a copy of Thomas Paine's *Rights of Man*, presumably given to her by Miller, and walks into her dressing room. Billy waits another 15 minutes. Finally he sends the assistant director to the dressing room to knock on the door and she says: "Screw off" or some such invective.'

Perhaps Diamond can't hear himself, but the intense contempt in which he holds Monroe is highlighted by his reaction to the identical situation in reverse. It was considered neither unique nor eccentric for either Wilder or Diamond to behave in ways that an observer would consider creatively idiosyncratic. Diamond, for instance, was a fastidious screenwriter; so much so that if an actor messed up *one* word, even a syllable, he would request that Wilder ask them to do it again. Wilder biographer Zolotow writes: 'Iz [Diamond] drives the actors berserk. If there is a deviation from holy script, no matter how minuscule, Iz saunters over to Billy and finks on the actor, who must do the scene over.'

Wilder is a perfectionist; and if *he* personally feels that an actor can improve upon a scene, he will request that they do it again.

In essence, then, the conflict was between the 'auteur' director and the star for a controlling voice in the film, each protagonist using the weapons they had to hand. There were, for example, several occasions when Wilder called a lunch break following Monroe's delayed arrival; sound editor Eve Newman recounts one such instance: 'Do you remember the scene in Coronado on the beach where the scene opens up and you see the palm trees, golden sands and the ocean; and the music is playing "By the Sea"? Well, the day we shot that scene Marilyn had a 9 a.m. call when she should have been out of makeup and wardrobe and on the set. It got to be 10.30 a.m. and we have 150 extras standing around and Billy was getting very uptight. At 11.30 a.m. they called and said, "Miss Monroe's car has just driven up." They told Billy and he said: "Fine." He turned around to the company and then said, "Lunch."'

Columnist James Bacon offers another perspective: 'I was on the set one day when Wilder was complaining that Marilyn was late, and that the film was going over budget. I said, "Billy, the public doesn't go to see a film because it is under or over budget. They go to see what is on the screen. She is worth waiting for . . ." Marilyn is peculiar. If she wasn't satisfied with a scene, she wouldn't wait for the director to yell: "Cut." She'd say: "Oh, that's not right. Let's do it again." And they'd have to do it again. In other words, she would terminate her own scenes.'

Eager to re-shoot something when it pleased him, Wilder was alternately unwilling to yield to Monroe's whims. An indication of just how right her thinking was becomes clear when we consider that it was she who insisted that Wilder re-do the opening steam train sequence when the puff of smoke blows her away and we watch (in envy) as Monroe's satin gilded torso sways and bobs in an attempt to keep herself on balance. 'I'm not going back into that fucking film until Wilder re-shoots my opening. When Marilyn Monroe comes into a room, nobody's going to be looking at Tony Curtis playing Joan Crawford. They're going to be looking at Marilyn Monroe.'

Co-star Jack Lemmon recounts: 'Marilyn would drive everybody crazy just psyching herself up for a performance. Even after everything was set and the cameras were rolling, Marilyn would be flapping her wings and screwing her head around like a chicken on a block. She must have wasted $250,000 worth of film doing that.'

Adds Lemmon: 'Whenever she wanted, she'd just walk off in the middle of the scene. She never bothered to wait for the director to shout: "Cut."'

Wilder confirms: 'Once when I tried to suggest tactfully just how I wanted her to read the next line, she snapped back: "Don't talk to me now. I'm thinking about how I'm going to play this scene."'

Whilst there was less physical description of Sugar's character than that of the two musicians, which means that Monroe's performance was that much tougher, her attempts to give substance to the amorphous role were derided. Biographer Wood recounts: '. . . Billy and the company waited and waited, whilst she communed with her soul and listened to mood music . . . When Marilyn, radiant at last and ready for the camera, swept on to the set at about quarter past six, she found it deserted.'

Tony Curtis' notorious comment comparing kissing Marilyn to being akin to kissing Hitler was occasioned by the amount of repetitions upon which she insisted. What is more, according to Henry Ephron, Monroe tended to French kiss Curtis when Miller was around to make him jealous.

The kissing scene is, of course, that corrosively decadent encounter where Monroe, disguised as an overstuffed nymphet wearing a gown of peau-de-soie (backless and frontless) practises a bit of 'lay therapy' by attempting to seduce an impotent millionaire to cure him of a fixation which eluded even the genius of the venerable Dr Freud. Biographer Wood recounts: 'In selecting the shots of the love scenes between her and Tony Curtis, Wilder had prints made of both the early and late takes. In the early ones, Tony looked great but Marilyn was weak. But as she warmed up to the scene she got better and better, and in the late ones she looked wonderful. But by now, Curtis looked tired. As the director . . . Billy had to go with Marilyn . . . because when she was on the screen the audience couldn't keep their eyes off her. Tony blew his stack when he learned this. He later got back at her when an interviewer asked him what it was like to kiss Marilyn in a love scene. "It's like kissing Adolf Hitler," he declared vehemently.'

The remark, when it reached Monroe's ears, hurt her deeply. Recalls her publicist Rupert Allan: 'We discussed what Tony Curtis had said. Marilyn said: "I don't understand that. That is a terrible thing to say about anybody. I don't understand it either because every morning he would stick in his head and say how beautiful I looked and how wonderful it was and how exciting." The only thing she did wrong, she recalls, was saying when the film wrapped to Jack Lemmon: "Yes, it was wonderful too working with you, Jack. The only thing is that instead of Tony Curtis, I should have ended up with you."'

Twenty-five years later Curtis is no less charitable in his opinions about Monroe, having told *Time Out*: 'She was a 600-pound gorilla, y'know. About 680 pounds, actually . . . And she was like a mean six-year-old girl. She would come and tell *me* that I was funnier than Jack Lemmon, then she'd tell Jack she wished she were ending up with *him* at the end of the movie. It got to the point that nobody wanted to talk to her.'

A 600-pound gorilla? Maybe. When Marilyn saw the rushes at the end of the day the only thing she could relate to was her own imperfection and the gargantuan image she saw burgeoning out of designer Orry-Kelly's chic, skin-tight party dress. On one occasion she rushed out of the projection room after seeing some of the footage screaming 'You're all trying to ruin me.'

'What did she expect?' carps Eve Newman. 'She *was* fat. She was pregnant!'

The delay occasioned by Monroe's hospitalization, which prefaced her second miscarriage and sent the film $800,000 over budget, combined with the trauma of coping with the lady's generally bad habits, elicited Wilder's famous (and well publicized) remark that she was 'the meanest woman I have ever met'. It is significant that neither she nor Miller were invited to the wrap party thrown for the cast by Billy and his wife, Audrey; Billy saying at the time that having finished with Marilyn he once again could look at his wife not wishing to strike her because she was a woman. On a slightly more cordial note Wilder added that 'he had never met anyone as utterly mean nor as utterly fabulous on the screen.' Marilyn could not help but be offended by the part about not wishing to work with her again, and it was publicist

Rupert Allan who decided to ring Wilder to enquire precisely what he meant by the remark. 'I said, "Will you talk to him?" She said, "I would love to work with him again." I said, "Billy, I am having lunch with Marilyn at Romanoff's. She said that you said you didn't want to work with her again because she had read something about that in the papers." He said, "For God's sake, you don't believe that shit they put in the papers." I said, "Some is true. Some isn't. You never know." He said, "Of course not. I would love to work with her." I said, "Shall I put her on? She is here with me now." I put Marilyn on. They had a marvellous conversation. She roared with laughter.'

Wilder did not, however, work with Marilyn again, choosing instead to headline films in which Monroe would have been ideal, with Shirley MacLaine. 'Perhaps Wilder didn't want to put himself to the trouble. But then, why should he?' asks director Roy Baker. 'He could make films without Marilyn Monroe.'

Although Monroe's physical screen presence is uniformly tender, innocent and wistful, she was the only performer who never seemed to have any *fun* doing a role. 'She studied for hours, even days, to perfect a segment that lasted only two minutes on film,' says David Conover. 'She worked harder than any other player on the set and the strain eroded her precarious emotional balance and drew out all her bitchiness.'

Meantime, her marriage to Miller suffered. Monroe depended upon him for reassurance, love and attention; while there is no doubt that his presence on the set gave her enormous support, there is also no doubt that the conflicts which ensued caused trouble between them. Described as an oddball, awkwardly standing around, watching his wife work, Miller was actually once again mortified by her unprofessional behaviour. 'Arthur was concerned about something,' recounts Maureen Stapleton who visited the set when she was filming *Lonelyhearts* at the same studio. 'I wasn't getting the signals then whatever was going on; I couldn't figure out why he looked so worried. She seemed to be having trouble and I couldn't figure out why.'

Midway through the film, when she discovered she was pregnant, Monroe implored Miller to speak to Wilder about easing up on the number of re-takes in some of the scenes which demanded physical exertion. According to Monroe's biographer Zolotow, '. . . Miller went to see Wilder. He said, "My wife is pregnant. Would you go easy with her, Billy, please?" Wilder blazed up. "Look Arthur . . . It is now four o'clock. I still don't have a shot. She didn't come on the set until 11 a.m. and she wasn't ready to work until 1 p.m. I'll tell you this . . . you get her here at nine . . . and I'll let her go at noon."'

Predictably, five days before the film wrapped on 6 November 1958, Monroe collapsed on the set and was taken to Cedars of Lebanon hospital where she was heard to sob: 'I don't want to lose my baby again.'

Why did Marilyn choose to take such a risk when plain common sense demanded a quiet restful life? Perhaps Billy Wilder offers an insight into the actress's psyche when he was quoted at the time as having said: 'She insisted on going on until we were ready to finish.' In short, she saved the film, but lost her baby.

Diamond recounts: 'We had not yet written the ending when Monroe took sick and we suddenly found ourselves having to shoot around her, and there was very little in the picture that we could do without her . . . Now, if you recall the picture, when you go to the close-up of Lemmon and Brown in the front seat of the motorboat, you don't see Tony and Marilyn behind. You don't see her because she was not on the set that day. What we did ultimately when we shot her and Tony is, he kisses her and bends her out of the shot to justify the fact that you can't see her in the next scene

. . . Jack Lemmon says: "I'm not a girl, I'm a man."
And Joe E. Brown says, "Well, nobody's perfect."'

Upon her return to the East Coast Monroe was advised to avoid any strenuous activities; she took up painting and did not go out. She did not want to run any risks. But in December 1958 the inevitable occurred; sixteen months after losing her first baby Monroe suffered her second miscarriage. Biographer Zolotow says: 'Her heart was almost broken with the shock.' Aged thirty-two, Monroe issued a statement through her press agent that she and Miller still hoped to have children.

It was at this juncture, adding insult to injury, that director Wilder made his now notorious comments. When Monroe heard about the interview she insisted that her secretary get the paper and read the interview to her. Housekeeper Lena Pepitone recalls: '. . . She couldn't believe that Billy Wilder would make fun of her in public, not after what she had just gone through. "I made *him* sick! . . . I made *him* sick!"' Adds Pepitone: 'Despite her doctor's orders to rest, she leaped out of bed and ran into Mr Miller's study. "It's your fault! . . . *Say* something! Now everybody in the world'll take me for a fool. You've got to say something. People'll listen to *you*. *You've* got respect."'

The Wilder–Miller debates are a classic of their kind:

Wilder: 'I have discussed this project with my doctor and my psychiatrist and my accountant and they tell me I'm too old and too rich to go through this again.'

Miller: 'You were officially informed by Marilyn's physician that due to her pregnancy she was not able to work a full day. You chose to ignore this fact . . . and . . . avoided mentioning it in your attack on her.'

Wilder: 'I am deeply sorry that she lost her baby but I must reject the implication that overwork . . . was in any way responsible . . . If you took a quick poll among the cast and crew on the subject of Marilyn you would find a positively overwhelming lack of popularity.'

Miller: 'The simple truth is that whatever the circumstances she did her job and did it superbly, while your published remarks create the contrary impression without any mitigation.'

Having the last word, Wilder conceded: 'I hereby acknowledge that good wife Marilyn is a unique personality and I am the beast of Belsen but in the immortal words of Joe E. Brown quote Nobody is perfect end quote.'

Rallying to her defence, publicist John Springer says: 'Now Wilder goes around saying how marvellous she was and how important she was; but he should have said it then. The things he said about Marilyn hurt her a lot but I guess that was what you did. You talked about how difficult she was and how impossible she was . . . Marilyn was fair game by then . . . If you want to blame someone for your problems, blame Marilyn. Marilyn was an easy scapegoat.'

It was upon Miller, however, that she unleashed her fury and frustration at being bullied by Wilder, castigating him for his inability to stand up for her from the start. Recalls Pepitone: 'Once she had an argument with Mr Miller about *Some Like It Hot* before it was released. She kept complaining about it. He tried to praise her for being funny. "Fuck you!" she shouted. "I don't want to be funny . . . I look like a fat pig. Those goddamn cocksuckers made me look like a funny fat pig. A freak. Funny! Shit!" . . . Marilyn . . . ran into her bedroom, crying.'

By the time they returned to the East Coast in the winter 1959 the couple had discovered that they were birds of dissimilar feathers, which made any kind of cohesive lifestyle difficult. When she was working, Monroe was as remote as a Martian. When at home during those precious intervals between films, she wanted to unwind and live it up, which was difficult since she was married to a writer hidden away either in his den at their New York flat or the summer house she had built for him on the 100-acre farm in Roxbury, Connecticut.

Pepitone recounts: 'At the farm, the routine was very much the same as in New York. Mr Miller would work – alone on his writing, walk the dog, tend the garden. Marilyn would stay in the bedroom, drink champagne or sleep.'

Joan Copeland confirms this. 'His business was writing. I think there were times when she wanted to go out when he couldn't, or wouldn't go out. I think there were times when he wanted to go out and she wouldn't go out of her room.' In short, they were mismatched; each needing what the other couldn't or wouldn't provide.

Says Robert Slatzer: 'He put her down mentally. He almost broke her. She built him a summer house on the estate, which he never appreciated. She had a fridge installed. She would knock on the door every other day and he wouldn't answer it. She'd fix a nice lunch and he wouldn't speak to her. He beat her to death mentally. The fact is that after a while he would ignore her and they were no longer close. After a while, there was no sex whatsoever. They seemed to lose communication. She had feelings. He lost interest in her. She felt rejected. He would get angry. He claimed he couldn't write; that they were always arguing. That's why she kept her 57th Street flat, while he lived on the farm. But he would come into the city and spend a week or two and then go back to the farm. It was a refuge for her to get away from him. They had arguments there. She liked to drink, so she'd drink herself into a stupor. He accused her of seeing Jack Kennedy while they were married. She was – but not that much. Her treatment by Miller increased the frequency of visits to Dr Kris.'

24
All About Yves

Although Monroe did not consume alcohol or drugs to excess, as the marriage to Miller began to wind down she increased her dependency upon artificial substitutes. Miller's sister Joan Copeland recalls a conversation with Monroe when she boastingly told her: 'I'm so proud. I only took two sleeping pills last night.' The growing estrangement in his marriage elicited the wry comment from Miller that he was grateful to whoever could put a smile on his wife's face – the 'whoever' in this instance being Yves Montand, the French actor whom Monroe wanted as her co-star in *Let's Make Love* when it was announced that Gregory Peck was unable to fulfil the obligation because of a prior commitment.

Written and produced by Norman Krasna and Jerry Wald whose intelligent manipulation of the nude calendar gaffe transformed disaster into victory, the film is a standardized Fox comedy, circa 1959, which Monroe did to get another of her irksome Fox commitments out of the way. The film cast Monroe in the role of a poor–but–honest chorus girl who falls for the French hoofer who has thrown in his lot with their off-Broadway theatrical company, never for a moment suspecting that he is a famous billionaire who is in fact in hot pursuit of her affections. It gave Monroe the opportunity to say lots of nasty things about rich people.

The script was doctored by Arthur Miller who injected it with working-class sentiments when he took over as writer in the wake of a protracted Writers Guild strike that brought production to a halt.

Although Monroe's advisers from the Strasbergs on down suggested that someone of Cary Grant's sophistication would be better cast in the role, Monroe plumped for Montand and spent days on the phone pushing for Yves, using, to advance her cause, the acclaim his one-man show had received when it opened at New York's Henry Miller Theater that year.

Miller knew the Montands as they had starred in the French production of his play *The Crucible*, so he was in the audience with Marilyn the night Yves opened in New York. Of that heroic occasion, Radie Harris wrote: 'On the star-studded opening night, Simone [Signoret, Montand's wife] walked down the aisle to her front row seat and there was a spontaneous burst of applause from the audience. Yves, peeking through the keyhole to see who was causing all the commotion, later confessed to Simone that he thought it was Garbo, at least!'

Whether Miller suspected that he was throwing away his marriage by encouraging his wife's desire to see Montand cast in the role, is impossible to say, but when the two met, the inevitable happened and they fell in love. The circumstances of the Millers' failure to communicate, which prefaced their final marital breakup whilst filming *Misfits*, are recounted both by Robert Slatzer and David Conover. According to Slatzer, 'Miller couldn't stand Montand. He was dashing, educated and conversant – everything Miller was not . . . Miller was never a good conversationalist. He was a quiet person. Marilyn used to tell me that they'd sit for hours in the same room and he wouldn't say anything. He'd turn and look at her and look away. When she'd see him looking, it made her self-conscious. Was she doing something wrong? Should she say something? She was confused!'

In conversations with Conover at around the same time, Monroe is quoted as having expressed doubts about whether the marriage would survive. 'It started out so beautifully,' she told him. 'I was terribly in love. I wanted children, a happy home, a loving husband. It all seemed so simple and possible, like a birthright given to everyone. Now . . . there's nothing left between us . . . Oh, God, if we could only break up . . . But . . . there's still *Misfits* to do . . .'

Whilst it would be some months before the affair would be consummated, Monroe's feelings for Montand were evident from the start. 'Marilyn was not promiscuous,' says Conover. 'She never stepped out on a man unless the affair was over.' She trusted Montand to do the right thing. '"Yves won't let me down . . . He loves me. That's all that counts," she told me.'

The Montand saga of seduction and betrayal, culminating in Monroe's committal into the Payne Whitney Psychiatric Hospital the following year is one of the ugliest in the nightmare series of escapades which caused her pain.

When it was announced that Montand had secured the role of billionaire Jean-Marc Clement, the Montands and the Millers were put up by Fox at the swank Beverly Hills hotel in adjoining bungalows, where they were quoted as making a congenial foursome 'sharing spaghetti dinners and drinking Chianti'. Although a successful European actor, Montand was not what you would call a 'bankable' Hollywood star, unlike Monroe whose anticipated gross receipts in any country ran into the hundreds of thousands of dollars. Getting cast in a film opposite Monroe was no mean accomplishment, and both Simone and Montand were no doubt aware of this and anxious to keep her good will for the duration of the shoot. Whether he purposefully exploited what he

later (in an appalling Hedda Hopper interview) referred
to as 'a schoolgirl crush' is uncertain. Whatever he might
have led her to believe at the time is also unclear,
although in the aftermath Montand's wife Simone was
quoted as having said something about American girls
expecting a man to marry them, whilst Europeans accept
a man's affection for his mistress without expecting him
to leave his wife. Even if he hadn't promised to marry
her, there is something rather shabby and dismissive in
the way that both Yves and Simone dealt with Marilyn.
(It is ironic that whilst Monroe was not even nominated
for her performance in *Some Like It Hot*, Simone won
an Oscar for her role in *Room at the Top*, prompting
columnist Hedda Hopper to protest that having seen the
Award go to an avowed Communist, she intended to
resign from the American Motion Picture Academy.)

In other words, it was the old Anti-myth surfacing
again: that Monroe was some sleazy, little tramp whose
self-absorption was so great that she fancied every man
in pants to be in love with her. It is this facet that the
papers picked up on when the published account of their
romance hit the headlines. Monroe, it was claimed,
entered Montand's bungalow wearing nothing but a fur
coat and propositioned him.

Outraged by the factual misrepresentation which
places Monroe in the role of aggressor and therefore (by
implication) responsible for what ensued, publicist John
Springer argues: 'It wasn't all on Marilyn's side. It wasn't
Marilyn going after Yves. That was only how the press
made it seem when they related that awful story about
the fur coat seduction. Yves had a lot of girls on the
string – a lot of very famous ones.'

Particularly gullible at the time, it is quite possible
(even probable) that Monroe did not realize she was
being 'had'. Although according to Maureen Stapleton,
'She almost got Montand, but Simone's hold was too
strong. She had bet everything on Miller – on that turn

of the wheel. If she went with Montand, she wanted
"out" of the Miller marriage.'

The Montand episode is baffling on two accounts:
firstly, because Simone and Yves were reputed not to
have had a love marriage but rather one of convenience
where each pursued their own lifestyle. Why the press
chose to misrepresent their marriage and in so doing to
create an impression that Monroe, once again, was a
homewrecker, is confusing. Secondly, if Monroe had
been Montand's mistress his manner of dealing with her
was not only an improper way to treat a superstar, it
was an improper way to treat a flower girl.

Columnist Radie Harris characterized Simone's hasty
departure for Paris 'as the last stand of an outraged wife
watching the foundation of her marriage falling apart.'
Yet having won the Oscar, Signoret would have done
well to have stuck around for a while to consider the
Hollywood offers that were bound to come along. It is
worth noting, however, that it was Simone, not Montand, who ended the affair; she rang Monroe from Paris
to tell her that Yves would not be coming to New
York following the *Misfits* wrap. When she writes about
Monroe in her autobiography there is an unmistakable
undertone of contempt, mingled with the sympathy
which, I think, characterizes what she must have felt
about the star. '[Marilyn] never knew to what degree I
[never] detested her; and how thoroughly I had
understood . . .'

Recounts Harris: '. . . Simone was so hurt and humiliated by all the publicity linking Yves with Marilyn that
she decided to go back to Paris and sue for divorce.
Jimmy Woolf, who produced *Room at the Top* . . . drove
her to the airport. He told me that he begged her not to
leave. "Simone you are making the most foolish mistake
of your life . . . Yves isn't in love with Marilyn. It's just
his male ego that has been inflated. You should know
by now how secure your marriage is or you would have

tried to compete long ago with all the glamour women who are constantly throwing themselves at Yves. You wear no makeup. You have allowed yourself to get fat because Yves loves you as you are."'

But, frankly, I doubt if there ever was any chance of a divorce, although I am sure Montand *did* allow himself to fall in love with Marilyn; and if one believes *her* accounts of the affair, there was every certainty on her part that they *would* marry.

Ironically, the Montands were invited to the opening night of *After the Fall*, Miller's epitaph for his late wife, joining others in this final send-up of a superstar.

After a while they must have felt some remorse, for when columnist James Bacon sought an interview with Montand in Paris he recounts that the actor jabbered on in French (which Bacon doesn't speak). Says Bacon: 'I was in Paris when Fox had a picture opening and they wanted a story on Montand. I knew Simone, so I went over to their apartment – a wonderful place. When I came in Yves lapsed into rapid French and would not speak one word of English. Simone comes out and says: "I must apologize for my husband. He is afraid that you are going to ask him about Marilyn Monroe."'

Bacon laughs, finding the remark humorous, since he knew about their affair from the start, having been tipped off by a waiter at the Beverly Hills hotel who had just served Montand and Monroe breakfast in bed – in the same bed! 'He said, "I just served breakfast to Marilyn Monroe and Yves Montand in Bungalow 5 and they are both naked in bed!" So *I* called Bungalow 5 and Montand answered and I said, "What are you doing in bed naked with Marilyn Monroe?" He started speaking the most rapid French I have ever heard in my life (I don't understand a word of French). Then he hung up. Fifteen minutes later I get a call from Marilyn's press agent. She said that Marilyn and Yves were discussing a script. I said, "That's nice. A good way to discuss a script –

naked in bed!" I didn't use it at the time, in deference to Marilyn whom I liked very much.'

Columnist Earl Wilson embellishes upon the story by having Miller discover the couple in bed together, accidentally having returned to their suite in search of his pipe or glasses. 'Returning to their bungalow . . . he found her already in bed with Yves Montand. "Let's straighten it out and get the work done," he said grimly.'

Whilst Miller was acknowledged to be the jealous type, whose sexual interest could be aroused by her interest in other men, on this occasion he was not provoked. Norman Rosten, friend of both Marilyn and Miller, visited Simone whilst in Paris, in an effort to discover just how serious the romance was. Did the Montands intend to divorce? '[Simone] was very charming,' recalls Rosten. 'She remembered our meeting in New York . . . Like any worldly woman, the possibility of a brief affair did not unduly upset her. What bothered her was the thought that the man she loved would do something foolish and hurt their marriage. She was concerned also about his career. She was, in short, a wife who did not want her husband to suffer any unnecessary consequences . . .'

Whether Rosten's visit with Simone clarified things for Miller is unlikely, since he kept a watchful eye on the affair until Yves was safely out of the country: Monroe rang him from Idlewild Airport at regular intervals prior to the plane's Paris departure. Several of Monroe's friends feel that Miller wanted *out* of the marriage and purposefully removed himself from her presence to write a screenplay of *Misfits*; to take meetings with director, John Huston; and to scout locations. Written for Marilyn following her first miscarriage in August 1957, the film was set to begin shooting in Reno, Nevada, following completion of *Let's Make Love* in July.

David Conover reports: 'Marilyn told me: "[Arthur] knows how much I need him when I work. I think he did it to hurt me . . . turning on the screws . . . he's getting back at me."'

Publicist Rupert Allan concurs: 'I think he was being selfish. Yves Montand has a great deal of charm. He is Continental and he set after [Marilyn] for two reasons: one, she was a very attractive person; and two, he had no holds barred in that Simone was a different kind of relationship. He had many other affairs.

'[Yves] was Europe to her and everything. He told her how marvellous Italy was (he left it when he was a boy – about aged two). He had her thinking he was from Tuscany so she decided she'd go to Tuscany.

'The irony was that they had met Yves Montand and Simone Signoret in New York when Yves did his first concert there. They were taken to meet by mutual friends and they fell madly in love . . . Then Simone had to go back to Paris and work. She was a great friend of mine. It was a very unpleasant time for me. More so because Arthur made it difficult for me. When two people are around each other all day long, whether or not they are filming – waiting around, talking – it is a silly thing for a husband (he isn't a child) to know that if he went to [New York] he was risking his marriage. But he did his own reading and writing and locked Marilyn out of his life.'

If Miller left his wife defenceless, it is Montand whom Allan cites for unfair play in the game of love. Word of the affair, he claims, had been leaked to the press by Montand himself. Allan recounts: 'Montand announced it to Hedda Hopper himself. She rang him up one afternoon and she asked him to come and have tea. He said, "Fine." Why would he say: "Fine." There was no word out about this romance. The lead story in Hedda Hopper the next day was that Marilyn had "a schoolgirl crush" on Yves Montand. Hedda Hopper used that very word,' concludes Allan incredulously.

Perhaps Allan never saw the other things which

Montand said about Monroe: '. . . I'm a vulnerable man. We're going to work together and I don't want the responsibility. She's not well. Anyone can see that. I'm really in a spot.' Expanding upon the comment, Montand later confessed, 'Marilyn is a simple girl, without any guile. I once thought she was sophisticated like some of the other ladies I had known. Had Marilyn been sophisticated, none of this ever would have happened.'

The film which, in Allan's words, was a bit of 'artsy-craftsy junk in which Monroe should not have worked', was the one occasion where the delays were occasioned not by her absences, but the Screen Actors Guild strike over residual rights payments for films made years earlier that were currently being shown on television. Relieving Miller of his role as therapeutic wet nurse, Montand had an energizing effect upon Monroe: his affection dispelling the usual preoccupations of self which beleaguered Monroe during filming. 'We'd hold hands, and stuff,' she told a friend. 'And Yves would scold me for drinking too much coffee, saying, in his wonderful French accent: "Cherie, it will make you too nervous."'

Choreographer Jack Cole, who coached Monroe through the dance sequences, received, in addition to an inflated salary for consenting to work with a lady whom others wouldn't touch with a ten-foot pole, a $2,000 gift from Monroe. He acknowledges, however, the prevailing view of others that she was a pain in the ass: 'She'd (usually) come to the studio with the line that she was sick, because the one thing she counted on was the way she looked. If she had a line on her face she would not be photographed. (Things were better on *Let's Make Love* where she was a lot more relaxed.)'

The only day she skipped work is recounted by Simone in her autobiography. It illustrates the sophistication of Montand in dealing with women's foibles. Apparently the two left together at 7 a.m. every morning for the studio in a limousine provided by Fox. One morning when Monroe didn't show up she received the following note from Montand. 'You can do whatever you like to Spyros Skouras and the Fox studio if that's what you want. But next time you decide to hang around too late listening to my wife tell you stories instead of going to bed, because you've decided not to get up the next morning and go to the studio, please tell me! Don't leave me to work for hours on end on a scene you've already decided not to do the next day. I'm not the enemy. I'm your pal and capricious little girls have never amused me. Best, Yves.'

Making the movie was an ordeal from start to finish, not so much because of their affair, but because the effect that the Screen Actors Guild strike had upon production. The Screen *Writers* Guild also went on strike in sympathy with the actors. Producer Jerry Wald persuaded Arthur Miller to finish the job. In the words of columnist Sidney Skolsky he prevailed upon 'the big liberal – the man who always stood up for the underdog, to ignore the Screen Writers Guild strike and rewrite the final scenes in the script. Arthur did it silently, at night, for his wife, of course . . .'

Paid $25,000 for the chore, it nonetheless must have been demoralizing for a Pulitzer prizewinning playwright to be bossed about by a man of Wald's earthy sensibility. Used to working without commissions Miller found that writing to specifications was encumbered with problems; he often found himself besieged by Wald, demanding: 'Arthur, where are those pages?'

Whilst Miller remained an ivory-tower intellectual, whose success accrued as a result of gentlemanly intercourse, he was heroic in Monroe's eyes. When circumstances changed and he assumed the role of script doctor, entrapped in the political dragnet which Monroe despised and from which she sought respite when she moved to New York, he became less heroic. Skolsky is right when he claimed that 'While Miller's stature was shrinking, Yves Montand's was growing in Marilyn's eyes.'

If the script was off, so too were the costumes. Dorothy Jeakins designed a look that was more suited to a bohemian or rock performer. 'Dorothy Jeakins was a different kind of designer, but not for Marilyn,' says Rupert Allan. 'In *Let's Make Love* she had to wear a heavy woollen sweater in a dance sequence. She had to rehearse in it, and it almost came down to her knees. What you paid your money to see Marilyn in on the screen you would never see in that sweater with those tights underneath it. She rehearsed in it and every time she wore it, it got another inch longer. There was not a second sweater. They had to shoot around it until they had another one knitted in the west of Ireland.'

Whilst this was only Monroe's first time around working with director George Cukor, it appears that even at this stage the vibrations between them were so bad that Cukor communicated with her through a third party: choreographer Jack Cole. In conversations with John Kobal, Jack Cole admits that Cukor '. . . used to use me to get things done because of my effect on Monroe . . . We were doing one scene where [Monroe] . . . looked uncomfortable and I said, "What's the matter, darling?" She said, "I don't have anything to do" . . . I had been through this thing for about six months. The script was a mess. I was making up numbers as we went along . . . So I said . . . "Do you want me to give you something to do? . . . Then stick a finger up your ass" . . . Monroe went white and started with the tears and Paula glowered at me . . . Cukor looked at me as if to say, "Could you please hold on. We only have one month to go" . . . We finished the picture and it was really a terrible ordeal for everybody. Cukor was not crazy about Marilyn for a number of reasons. He was not good for her . . .'

When the film wrapped, her publicist and friend Rupert Allan threw a splendid party to celebrate her thirty-third birthday in his Benedict Canyon villa (which Marilyn loved because of its superb views overlooking Beverly Hills). Allan recounts: 'Marilyn was very sweet. She said, "Why not get a piano and that will be fun? Since I am going to pay for it." I said, "No, you are not. It's my treat. And we can't have a piano because it wouldn't fit." Then she said, "Why don't we have it in the courtyard and set up a marquee?" I said, "No, you're not giving this party. *I* am giving it. I can't afford a tent and all this" . . . She was looking down the guest list the day before the party and said, "It will be a disaster. None of these people know each other." I said, "No, they don't. That is why it will be a good party. They all know you and they want to come and they'll be interested in meeting one another." That night she looked great. Of course she had a marvellous time and she moved around. These were her friends, so she wasn't worried about them. She arrived *early*. Some of them left at 12.30 a.m. or 1 a.m., but most people stayed on into the early hours of the morning.'

Conspicuously absent, Miller was in New York and it appears that there was no attempt to ask him to fly in on either Allan's or Marilyn's part. 'If Marilyn didn't like the wife or the husband she'd just invite that person, and they were free to bring who they wanted. She was honest and direct. She didn't want to invite people she didn't like . . . Montand was the only one invited from the film. Acting coach Michael Chekhov and his wife both were invited. We asked Nabokov [the Russian writer] and whoever he wanted to bring (I told Marilyn that there was a "Mrs" Nabokov. When I rang I got Mrs Nabokov on the telephone and I asked to speak to Mr Nabokov. I didn't know him. I said, "I would like to give him an invitation to Marilyn Monroe's birthday party I am planning." She said, "Indeed not. He is working very hard. He doesn't need distractions like that."

'Jack Lemmon couldn't come. He was doing a film in San Diego and thought he could get finished in time. Marlon Brando declined. Actor Jimmy Stewart and his wife, Gloria, cancelled at the last minute. He had accepted another dinner party two weeks before. He was furious because he wanted to come very badly. "That damn Gloria always does something like that," grumbled Stewart. Actor Gary Cooper and whoever he would like to bring. I said, "Come on, Marilyn. Rocky [his wife] is here in town." She said, "Well, just ask him. If he wants to bring Rocky, he can bring Rocky." Lotte Goslar, Marilyn's mime coach, was there. So was writer Clifford Odets who stayed until 4.30 a.m. reading palms. Composer Sammy Cahn and his then-wife (a very pretty girl), and that was it. Since the most I could have for dinner was 20.'

It wasn't long thereafter, and before she left to return to the East Coast, that Marilyn was again invited to Allan's house, this time to meet playwright Tennessee Williams, who had expressed a desire to make her acquaintance. The attraction between them is understandable; Monroe was born to play roles in *Streetcar Named Desire* and *The Sweet Bird of Youth*. She was the perfect Williams' heroine – brittle, neurotic and self-obsessed. 'Tennessee was a close friend, and whenever he was in town he'd come for dinner. (He loved the house.) Once he said, "I know that you are a close friend of Marilyn Monroe. If it is at all possible, I would love to meet Marilyn Monroe." When I told her that she was very excited. She said, "Of course, I would like to meet him. I can't tell about his plays what his humour is, but it is a more sophisticated intellectual humour depending upon how they are played and read."

'It was a small gathering – just the Williams family (his mother and brother) and us. It was a great success. He wanted to meet her. He was a great fan of hers. She had a great sense of humour. So did he. It is an L-shaped house with a cocktail bar and a table. They laughed so hard they almost fell off the couch roaring. Just like a house on fire . . .'

The end of the Montand affair was, in effect, pure Williams tragi-comedy. Monroe arranged a surprise rendezvous at New York's Idlewild Airport, which turned out instead as a surprise for her when Montand appeared with his press agent, a Fox PR man and a couple of reporters and photographers in tow.

'He tried to be tender and sweet,' she sobbed to David Conover. 'But he said that he couldn't possibly leave Simone . . .'

But it was to housekeeper Pepitone that she unburdened herself. 'Marilyn was nearly hysterical when she described how all her plans were fouled up. First of all, several press agents and reporters were already at the airport, asking far too many snoopy questions . . . Secondly, Yves himself didn't want any part of going to the hotel with Marilyn. He wanted to get back to Paris and Simone . . . He said he hoped [she] had enjoyed [herself] with him and told [her] what a "nice time" he had had. "Lena [she told me], I was in love and he was just having a 'nice' time . . ."'

Montand's publicist, Marilyn Reiss, recalls that the situation was reduced to the level of a slapstick comedy, everybody chasing everybody else, and all of them fleeing from the press. 'I went to the airport to meet Mr Montand's incoming Los Angeles plane, and to get him on the flight to Paris. (I could never bring myself to call him "Yves" – it is too feminine.) But because of a bomb scare, there were 10 million people milling about in a large quonset hut. (This was before TWA built their new terminal.) In those days you could go out and meet the plane on the runway. I saw Audrey Meadows get off and Mr Montand was following directly behind her. I said we could go to the VIP lounge where we could wait until things settled down.

'As we walked from the enclosure toward the VIP room, a woman jumped out from behind a pillar dressed all in beige, wearing a head scarf and dark sunglasses. It was Marilyn. She said, "I have a limo, a chauffeur, and caviar." She had with her her secretary May Reis. I said, "We'll get it shipped. We'll go to the International Hotel and wait. (We had to wait on account of the bomb scare.) We drove over to the hotel which was three minutes away. I put the champagne under my raincoat and May Reis carried the caviar. I asked Marilyn to wait in the limo. I preferred it if she did not walk in with us. Montand had a look on his face – more shock than horror! Out stepped Monroe from the elevator. I said, "I told you to wait in the car." She laughed, since it was such an old line.

'We had a four-hour wait: Montand asking me, "What is she doing here?" I said, "I thought *you'd* know the answer to that one." He tried to joke about it: "Marilyn Reiss, May Reis and Marilyn Monroe. Very confusing." I sat there chatting. I kept checking with TWA . . . Every few minutes Marilyn went into the bedroom to call Arthur telling him there was a bomb scare and that the plane had been delayed.

'A Fox colleague had brought a photographer and a reporter (the invincible Vincent Canby, then a reporter for the trade newspaper, *Variety*) and they wanted to interview Montand during the lay-over. They thought that the Blonde in the back room was Kim Novak. I said, "Ditch them." He said, "Why?" He then tried to kill it with Canby and the photographer. (Later Canby nailed me because I was rude to the Fox guy.)

'When I got a TWA phone call, we drove back and I made sure that Yves got on the plane . . . Marilyn waited and drove me home . . . Years later I worked with Yves. "Why do they keep asking me about her? It would not be like this in Paris. In Paris to have a fling doesn't mean a thing."'

Reiss muses: 'I have a feeling Marilyn Monroe expected Montand to marry her. Her mind was not European. But I don't believe that she divorced Miller because of Montand.'

Not having seen the press interviews Montand had given, Monroe sincerely (but wrongly) believed that the affair would rebound when Yves returned to Los Angeles to re-record or 'dub' portions of the film's soundtrack. In addition to the Hopper interview, Montand had given out other press stories which characterized Monroe as 'a sick lady having thrown herself at me'. Montand's sex mastery is evident in the level of excitation sustained by Monroe throughout *Misfits* until her return to New York. Failing to communicate with him in Los Angeles, it is only when she received the phone call from Simone in New York telling her that Yves would not be coming to town, that she knew it was over. The realization that the Montand affair was over catapulted the lady into a mental depression which prefaced committal into New York's Payne Whitney Psychiatric Hospital for Highly Emotionally Disturbed Patients.

25
Lady Genius

Seventeen days after *Let's Make Love* wrapped, Monroe reported for work in the blistering 100 degree temperature of Reno, Nevada, to begin filming Arthur Miller's *Misfits* – purported to be the love poem he wrote for her following the miscarriage of their first child.

Originally drafted as a short story, the piece evolved into a screenplay and in that state underwent revisions. Whilst Miller denied that he wrote 'character', which is to say that he attempted to create fictional people along the dimensions of stars, he *did* in fact use a great deal of the personalities of Marilyn (his wife), Monty Clift (a pal) and Eli Wallach (another friend) when writing *Misfits*.

The piece briefly deals with a divorcee living out the required six-week residency period in Reno to obtain a divorce who meets up with three cowboys whose livelihood is supported by selling mustangs to dealers for horse meat. Marilyn is cast as divorcee Roslyn, a corrupt, hard, transient woman sustained through life by a combination of pills, liquor and sex; Clift plays Perce, a unisex mama's boy who the actor believed represented emerging American manhood and felt should have got the girl in the end; Wallach portrays Guido, a religious obsessive, hysterically sublimating carnal passion into orthodox experience. Thelma Ritter plays Isabelle (or 'Iz') whose irritation with Monroe's character seems ready to erupt into homicidal antipathy. Whilst Miller had no idea of who they would get to play Gay, the lead cowboy whose 'machismo' is as transparent as cellophane, both he and Marilyn agreed that Gable would be superb (Marilyn had always wanted to co-star with the King). Gable, whose last couple of films hadn't done too well, was discouraged from taking the offbeat part by friends who pointed out that 'he was no actor', and he complained about the interminable waits occasioned by working with someone of Monroe's temperament. In consequence, he asked for, and got, an incredible deal – $750,000 plus 10 per cent of the gross; in addition, he was to be paid at an overtime rate of $48,000 per week.

Although director John Huston uses Monroe in an interesting way – exploiting both the addictions and sado-masochism which increased in consequence of the problems within the Miller marriage – to get a terrific rendition of one strung-out lady, the role does nothing to enhance either Monroe or her career. The character is not only downbeat, she is thoroughly dislikeable: insincere, egocentric, rude, spoiled and patronizing. A great deal of what Iz Diamond told me about Monroe's behaviour on the *Some Like It Hot* set comes through in the Roslyn characterization, causing me to wonder if Miller had listened to gossip. Diamond, who liked Monroe during her starlet days, found her unpleasant later on, claiming 'she bossed people about who could not defend themselves. She was awful to her secretary, May Reis.' However, since Monroe included Reis in her will and since the secretary witnessed (among other fiascos) Marilyn's brutal rejection by Montand, it is unfair to imply that she lorded it over Reis, or to characterize her relationships as a *need* to feel physically and emotionally superior to people.

From the beginning, Monroe was unhappy with the

screenplay and she hoped that Miller would both change it and *improve* (humanize) her character. She consistently referred to it as 'weird', predicting that it would fail (which it did). Whilst she could have backed out of the project (particularly since her marriage to Miller was over – they were only staying together for appearances' sake, while they finished the film) Monroe stayed because she had made a commitment. Her dissatisfaction with the Roslyn role went back to the script's inception when Monroe complained to Norman Rosten about inconsistencies in characterization, protesting that the heroine was too 'passive'. Rosten recounts: '[I told her] "Look, it's a draft. I'm sure there'll be more work on it. I mean it's not final, is it?" Miller responded listlessly, "It's a draft." "Maybe that section can be trimmed. If Marilyn has specific objections!" "I object to the whole stupid speech," she said, "and he's going to re-write it!"'

Prior to the start of production when Miller still had failed to humanize the character, things between the couple became strained to the point of outright hysteria. Presumably Monroe's 'minders', the Strasbergs (loathed by Miller because he felt, according to Joan Copeland, that 'they protected [Marilyn] too much') also objected to the characterization, suggesting that she should get Miller to re-write it. Housekeeper Pepitone recounts: 'She believed that [Miller would] never hurt her, but now she lost her faith . . . She stormed through the living room and began pounding on the study door, which was locked. Mr Miller refused to come out . . . Marilyn kept screaming. "It's not *your* movie, it's *ours*. You wrote it, but you said you wrote it for *me*" . . . Marilyn kicked over some tables, banged down the keys on the piano, and grabbed another champagne bottle from the kitchen. When she returned to her room, I heard a terrible crash. She had thrown the bottle against the mirror behind her bed. Her sheets were covered with glass, and she kept slamming her body against the closet door . . . Mr Miller did not sleep in the apartment that night or any other night before they left for Nevada.'

The changes that were made, by both Miller and Huston, conspired to create a film which focused not upon the *woman's* character (although Monroe's name was the undoubted box-office draw), but that of the three men, conferring upon Miller the accolade of writing the very first anti-machismo stag film. But for Monroe it was a disaster, primarily because she was forced to play a part which she disliked and, worse, to accept the characterization as a valid assessment of her own character, Miller having adopted the roles of analyst and priest. Secondly, she was portraying someone antipathetic to the Monroe Myth – someone she feared (and rightly) that her fans would not like either. Publicist Rupert Allan observes: '[Marilyn] was miserable playing herself in Miller's eyes . . . Roslyn was written about Marilyn. Her dialogue. Her lines. That's why it was difficult for her. She had to play herself. Her vision. I think she got trapped into that film. The producer (an erudite guy) promised her a lot of things that were not forthcoming.'

The producer, a friend of Miller's, was commissioned by Monroe because she believed that he would produce her husband's script with the restraint it deserved. Frank Taylor had done a couple of films in Hollywood years before, but he was by no means a top-flight producer so it was an extremely generous gesture on Marilyn's part. That he subsequently attempted to prevent her coaches, the Strasbergs, from seeing the rushes or a final cut of the film is regrettable. His complete and utter disregard of Monroe's bankability, and converse indulgence of the whims of both Huston and Miller confirms my belief that no one seemed to care whether the film made money or not.

Baiting Monroe had become quite a popular sport – the consensus being that she was fair game. She was on the way out the theory went, 'her age, her track record of being an expensive troublesome person to work with, and her coterie of nagging advisers making her just not worth the risk'; the irony, of course, is that she has maintained her international popularity years after her death, all of which indicates that her career could have sustained for at least another ten or twenty years.

Neither Taylor nor his wife Nan seemed to realize that it was Marilyn and not Huston, Miller or Gable who earned them their bread–and–butter. Nan Taylor has been quoted in print on several occasions as expressing concern not for Monroe but Miller. '. . . Nan Taylor . . . had heard that Marilyn had spent an especially bad night, but she was *even more distressed* to see what it had done to Miller . . . He is taken care of in his pain by the [two] women. "Perhaps we can't solve Marilyn's problem this morning," Nan Taylor will say, "but we can do something about you."'

Once the contracts were signed Monroe was cast as shrew and Miller as pet. Monroe knew it, and told her housekeeper Pepitone that her incentive to see through the commitment was both a fancy for Monty Clift (whom she tried to seduce) and an infatuation with Clark Gable – the great cinematic father figure. It is testimony to her affection for him and what he represented as a deity that (without batting an eyelash) she paid him a fee which had no real bearing on what he was worth on the market at the time.

In spite of the theatrical display of political *macho*, Miller seems intimidated by the 'jock' antics men use to get power. When Taylor and Huston took sides against Monroe, he was all too willing to join them. Curiously Miller doesn't seem to have known when he was being tested. On several occasions he allowed himself to be placed in the invidious role of Monroe's adversary – judging and questioning his own wife's professional behaviour. He never detected that John Huston was having him on when he suggested that since it was the picture, and not the star, which mattered, he should strengthen the male parts, leaving Monroe but to play a supporting role. (In other situations the front office would have interfered, but this film was being released by United Artists, where the *director* has final cut.) A supremely *macho* male, known both for his liking for women and gambling, Huston (like Olivier) was testing Miller's mettle; and Miller, failing the test, took Monroe down with him in a pile of rubble. It was this realization, that produced Monroe's scathing attack upon Miller in front of both Robert Slatzer and John Huston: 'As soon as this film is over, I'm going to divorce that sonofabitch,' she shouted.

During filming, Marilyn came across a draft of the play, *After the Fall*, which probably accounts for Monroe's regular weekend sojourns in Los Angeles where she saw her psychiatrist. On one occasion, recounts publicist Allan, 'Marilyn was coming into Los Angeles for the weekend. Paula and Marilyn and I were at the airport in Reno and Eli [Wallach] was there. He was waiting for a plane to San Francisco. He came over and was playful with Marilyn. She said, "Where are you going?" He said, "To San Francisco, just for the weekend." She said, "Going alone?" He said: "Yeah." She said, "Why didn't you ask me? I'm just going with two friends. I have no plans at all. If you had asked me I would have gone with you." Eli said, "You would, Marilyn." She nodded: "Yes." That was one of the few times I thought she was cruel. She would never have gone to San Francisco with him. I know she wouldn't have. But she thought it would have been fun to flirt.'

During the day Miller was both critical and obstructive; whilst at night he was angry and passive. Their sex life was fraught; Miller unable or unwilling to share himself, assuming instead the neutral role of night nurse. Whilst I have little doubt that Monroe was swept off her feet by Montand's advances at a time when her sex life with Miller was nil, it is worth noting that she remained immensely attracted to him. Fiercely jealous of other women, she is recounted as having asked the script girl: 'Are *you* sleeping with Arthur?'

It had been hoped that their marriage would rebound during the interval they spent together in Reno working on Miller's first original screenplay; everyone seemed optimistic when Miller took Monroe in his truck to scout locations along the Piute Indian trails. However, when he began going out alone, the prognosis became less so. It was thought that perhaps what they needed was privacy and so the Millers moved out of the historic Mapes Hotel and into the Holiday Inn, where they distanced themselves from other cast members.

'It was an unfriendly situation,' recounts Allan. 'Miller and she were through at that time. One night Miller had a lot of re-writes to do for the next day. There was a complete power failure in the town or city of Reno. They had generators for the lights and had hooked one up to the line on his floor. So he had lights to work until 2 or 3 a.m. There was a tremendous criticism of her by everyone in the town saying that of course she got lights when the hospital didn't get lights and there were people dying. Arthur Miller did not do one thing to explain to the people that it was he who had the lights since he was working.'

Shortly thereafter Miller and Monroe took separate rooms, since it was apparent to them both that their emotional problems were of such intensity that a marriage in those circumstances was impossible.

Makeup man Whitey Snyder, who witnessed both the evolution and the decline of their relationship, was there on the *Misfits* set when things hit rock bottom. 'When Marilyn was staying at the Mapes, she'd come down to my room and sit there with her black maid [Harriet]. I'd say: "Marilyn, come on, we have to go back to your room." I took her back and put her into bed. The first time I did it I opened the door and thought she was alone. And there is Miller standing looking out the window. He didn't seem to care then either.'

Whitey pauses: 'Miller was fine at first and then not so fine. Marilyn went down to live in Connecticut and turned to be a Jewess. Then she came back. He started out fine but after months and months and months he was against her. He wrote the script. The story was pretty good. But the script kept getting changed until Gable and his attorney sent a letter to the company which read: "Clark Gable will not accept any more script changes."'

According to Snyder, the end of the Miller marriage came when Miller 'started going with somebody else. He just turned against [Marilyn].' The 'somebody else' in this instance is the lady whom Miller refers to as 'the first adult I ever married' and whom he wed on 7 February 1962, when she was aged thirty-eight. When they met, Ingeborg Morath was a tall, attractive, Austrian-born, freelance photographer, journalist and critic, working for the Magnum Group as a protégé of photographer emeritus Henri Cartier-Bresson. A year and a half later they had a daughter, whom they named Rebecca. The Millers are still married twenty-five years later. The success of Miller's marriage to Morath and the birth of their only child has no real relevance to Marilyn's death, since she was not a suicide. However, given the profound emotional investment she had made in her marriage to Miller, it is reasonable to assume that news of his marriage and birth of their child contributed toward the great chasm of pain in which she spent the last years of her life.

Ironically, Morath took some highly sensual photographs of Monroe, which were exhibited (along with her other work) in New York City in November 1986 at the Gotham Book Mart's gallery. Although the two women were 'rivals', they got on well. Perhaps Monroe felt that Morath wasn't Miller's type or maybe she felt physically superior to the lady. Maybe she just didn't understand Miller. In any event, although Marilyn suspected others, it was Morath who caught Miller's fancy. Rupert Allan who arranged for the photographer to come on to the set, recounts: 'I knew the third wife in Europe. When I was with *Look*, we worked with the Magnum Group. She had been married once and had had a disastrous marriage. She was an attractive-looking woman – a nice person – and had been through quite a lot of tragedy. She was very talented. Maybe that is what Miller wanted. Because it has lasted.'

Maureen Stapleton, who knew Arthur during all three of his marriages to Mary, Marilyn and Inge, was filming *A View from the Bridge* when Miller was courting Morath. It was only after they were married and living in Connecticut that she got to visit, however, when residing nearby at a rest home which she had entered in an attempt to wean herself from a dependency upon pills. Whilst Stapleton does not reveal any astute observations about either the marriage to Morath or Miller's lingering feelings about Monroe, there is something in their friendship which has been disturbed neither by the divorce nor Marilyn's death that helps me to understand how the playwright had the presumption to write that shocking account of his life with Marilyn in *After the Fall*. He was, in the final analysis, not victimizer but victim, an assessment shared by most people but for a few loyalists to Monroe's memory such as publicist John Springer.

Whilst I assume that die-hard Monroe fans will perceive *Misfits* as an oddity, it is nonetheless a strangely climactic film where Anti-Myth devastates Myth; Monroe emerging as a representation of all the terrible things people were saying about her. As hard as she tries to infuse the part with a woman's sensibility – her own sensibility – she cannot; and whilst the nudity and sensual

Method seduction of a tree, along with bits and bobs of porno Monroemania tacked upon her closet door, attempt to do a Billy Wilder in terms of suggesting Freudian fixations, the reality is that Huston and Miller together prove insurmountable; they successfully conspire to make an anti-Monroe film which frustrates her at every turn. From start to finish, the mythology is against her. The film risked being released without the Legion of Decency seal of approval, the reason had nothing to do with the nudity but the ending which implied that the lady was forced to exist within the confines of a loveless marriage. The nudity, as conceptualized by Huston, does nothing to enhance Monroe's part, since it is moribund and in consequence without any hint of seduction. The scenes where Monroe attempts to make some connection with the character's subconscious are ridiculed by Huston, who allows her histrionics to go over the top without imposing any restraint upon camerawork or editing, to allow her to save face. And then, she looks awful – the impact of those sleepless nights when she'd awaken screaming is visible in the frustration lining her face. The monochromatic black and white photography seems rather evil, leaving us to wonder about Huston's justification for not having shot in colour.

Since Monroe never finished *Something's Got to Give*, *Misfits* was the last complete film she made. Thus John Huston, who was trapped into casting Monroe as Angela in *Asphalt Jungle*, was also responsible for the film that ended her career. Whilst Huston couldn't help but be amazed by Monroe's growth in terms both of the focus and the depth of her performance (in *Asphalt Jungle* she moved like a zombie throughout), their working relationship was not significantly different. Summoning up a façade of conviviality, Monroe told writer Jim Goode: 'John has meant a great deal in my life. Nobody would have heard of me if it hadn't been for John

Huston. It's sort of a coincidence to be with him ten years later.'

But it was to those close to her that she confided her real concerns about Huston. Sensing that she was not Huston's favourite – that he did not 'react' to her, she blamed Miller for filling Huston's ears with misrepresentations. She told housekeeper Pepitone: 'I bet Arthur complains to him about everything he thinks is wrong with me. That I'm crazy and all. That's why he [Huston] treats me like I'm an idiot. "Honey, this" and "Honey, that". Why can't he treat me like a normal actress?'

She expressed similar sentiments when she talked to David Conover: '. . . It was to be "our" movie. But . . . all [Arthur] wanted was to use me to regain his prestige. I'll never forgive him. Never . . . Arthur changed the script. She's not like me at all. All he cares about are the men . . . She's almost an incident to the story . . . He's letting Huston ruin the film.'

If the intention was to make a film which sent up Monroe's image by suggesting it was narcissistic and anti-male, Miller had found a friend in Huston. 'I think he's arrogant and rude,' she told Conover. 'Women to him are just brainless creatures to be put up with. He calls me honey just to irritate me. I get so mad sometimes. I could kick him in the balls, but what can you expect. He's in Arthur's camp.'

'Camp' is the operative word; Monroe's experiences read like a prisoner of war diary. In addition to her complaint that Huston talked down to her, she argued that it was too hot in Nevada; the food was awful; and that she couldn't sleep in the suite she had to share with Miller. Rupert Allan, who visited Monroe on the set whilst they were filming, says that Huston 'kept Marilyn waiting for hours in that hot Nevada sun making her wait for the re-writing which he occasioned. She had the skin which couldn't take being in that hot weather.'

Six weeks into production, Monroe was admitted into

Los Angeles hospital for treatment for 'acute exhaustion', the result of having worked for several weeks in 95–100 degree heat. She is quoted as having insisted upon a speedy return to work after only a 24–hour period of recuperation, but she was overruled by her internist, Dr Hyman Engelberg, who said that she needed a complete rest, for ten days. Recalls Allan: 'When Marilyn was committed to that La Cienega hospital, I went with her and so did Lee and Paula Strasberg. It was agreed that she would be able to make one call out a day only. No calls could come in. She decided that I would be the one to take all calls for her. She would call me once a day and return any calls she wanted to. So I got to know who really were interested in her as friends loyal to her and who sent flowers. Marlon Brando and Frank Sinatra called regularly.'

The significant exception was Montand, whose lack of solicitude was missed. Although in town completing the incidental dubbing on *Let's Make Love*, he was nonetheless unavailable to Monroe when she rang his suite at the Beverly Hills Hotel. Marilyn was visited by Miller, but she was cynical about his expression of concern, recounting to housekeeper Pepitone: 'He is visiting me not as a husband but as a spy for John Huston. They don't want anything to happen to their precious movie.'

Never once in the entire duration of the filming did Gable attempt to criticize or scold Monroe. His response, congenially male, appreciated the care she took with her appearance so that their love scenes would be funky, natural and spontaneously fun; even if it meant waiting an entire afternoon in temperatures which spiralled upwards of 104 degrees. And whilst Monroe was savagely criticized for having caused Gable's death (the day after the film wrapped) by having kept him waiting for hours in the hot sun, the reality is that Gable died as the result of an oversized 'virility complex'. He felt compelled to compete with stunt men in completing some devilishly fierce horse roping sequences crucial to the film.

A friend of mine, who covered the Hollywood beat in the fifties, and met Monroe a couple of times, told me that she and Gable had had a one-nighter when she was a starlet, although nothing came of it. If Monroe attempted to show him how far she had come in fifteen years, it may explain the guilt she felt when Gable died of a heart attack on 16 November 1960. Recounts Pepitone: '. . . Somehow she got it into her head that she was responsible for Gable's heart attack. The awful nightmares started. Then it became impossible for her to sleep . . . she even lost her appetite. For days, she would lie on the bed, her eyes bulging out, wringing her hands in frustration.'

Columnist Skolsky adds that Monroe's guilt had something to do with a psychological perception that she was getting back at her father for having abandoned his child at birth (Gable reminded her of a photo Monroe's mother kept on the bureau).

'Was I punishing my father? Getting even for all the years he's kept me waiting?' she asked Skolsky.

Columnist Bacon, who was on the *Misfits* set the day the film wrapped, also remembers her grief. 'The last day of *Misfits* I went over to see Gable. He is an old friend of mine. I am sitting there with Gable and Marilyn is about five hours late. Monday morning Gable had a fatal heart attack and died a couple of days later. I went to the hospital with Gable when he died.

'Marilyn had a guilt feeling. She thought it was unprofessional to be late. Gable was on the set every morning at 9 a.m., knew his lines and was ready to leave at 5 p.m. Sometimes Marilyn wouldn't show up until 4 p.m. She was insecure – always unsure of herself.'

Whilst Miller and the others implied that Monroe in one way or another had caused Gable's death by the strain she placed upon his endurance, Kay Gable believed

otherwise, and said so publicly following the birth of
Gable's son, John Clark, on 20 March 1961. Recounts
Rupert Allan: 'Kay Gable didn't think that Marilyn
caused his death. They were friends until the end. She
didn't think so. And Gable didn't think so. "If we stick
together they can't make us do it," he said about that
last scene (which Miller kept re-writing). She told me
that she felt it was wrong for him.

'The night Gable died, I was staying in New York at
my brother Chris' apartment. The telephone rang at 4
a.m. and Chris said, "It's Marilyn. She wants you." She
was crying and sobbing and said she had been awakened
by the press who wanted her to give a statement on his
death. How awful to awaken somebody in the middle
of the night. I said, "Say what you feel about Gable, but
that you don't want to talk now. You can't. Don't be
rude but don't talk to them unless you have to or want
to." She immediately called Kay Gable and they had a
long talk. I saw Kay a number of times after that and
she told me how fond she was of Marilyn. She liked
Marilyn. Clark liked her.'

The one sweet dream that never went sour, Gable's
affection for Monroe sustained throughout the rigours
of filmmaking. It was an infatuation which harked back
to *The Seven Year Itch* at the famous wrap party where
Gable asked her to dance. 'Marilyn worshipped Gable,'
says David Conover. 'They had met years earlier at a
Hollywood party, and as they danced that evening she
had told him that he was the father she had always wished
she had. Gable was flattered and loved her frankness. A
man of considerable compassion, he took a paternal
interest in Marilyn all through the film.'

He adds: '[When I asked her how she] and Gable hit
it off, she beamed: "He's so kind and sweet and patient,
and so modest . . . a perfect gentleman."'

Although there is very little of Rhett Butler in Gable's
portrayal of Gay, and he appears to be what he is – a

man riding for his last roundup – there is still something in the timing, in the nuance, in the glance, that confirms Gable's label as the King. Very much in the Hollywood tradition of a man playing himself on the screen, Gable's off-camera personality did not differ greatly from what you saw on the screen. His ability to jolly Monroe along was unlike any other person's. He sympathized with her menstrual cramps; he objected to the exploitation of her time by the PR people; and he bridled at Miller's unremitting re-writes which finally, and in tandem with Monroe, he refused to do. What is more, he coped with her legendary lateness with a wink or a quip: 'Why are sexy women so late?' Other times, he'd give her a little squeeze on her fanny and call her 'chubby' or 'fatso'.

Recounts Pepitone: 'She loved being around him . . . [she told me] "He never got angry with me once, for blowing a line or being late, or anything. He never raised his voice, lost his temper. Not like Tony Curtis. He was a gentleman, the best."'

The famous nude scene which, in the European version at least, allows Monroe to fulfil her dream of going topless, was shot several times, with Gable kissing her good morning. 'On one take, Marilyn told me that she was so electrified by Gable's kisses that she let the sheets drop and he accidentally placed his hand on one of her breasts,' says Pepitone. What did it feel like? '"I got goose bumps all over . . ."'

Ironically, *Misfits* was the ultimate film for both Monroe and Gable, and one of the last for Monty Clift who died four years later in 1966. '*Misfits* was not a happy film,' says John Springer. 'Monty was having problems. Gable was having problems. Huston was having problems. And so was Marilyn. But whatever the problems were it wasn't Marilyn's fault. Marilyn was a very convenient scapegoat for a lot of things. But she got the rap.'

He continues: 'That the newspapers implied that she

was in any way to blame for Gable's death [was absurd]. She had such respect for Gable. She and Monty were very close. John Huston gave her a bad time. He gave Monty a bad time. She and Monty were two lost souls together. She had great respect for Gable and he was very sweet to her. Those accusations after his death were completely unfounded but they hurt her very badly.'

Following the completion of *Misfits* in November, Monroe languished in the expectation of seeing Montand at Christmas; strung out by hopes of their reunion, fully supposing that he would marry her. It is obvious that Montand had no intention of marrying Monroe, or if he did, the idea had long since been abandoned. That he ended the affair ignominiously had a devastating effect upon Monroe's stability. Combined with the other disappointments she faced that year: the failure of *Misfits*; the breakup of her marriage to Miller; and the premature death of Clark Gable, that disaster prompted Monroe to ask psychiatrist Dr Marianne Kris to admit her into a rest home for a couple of weeks R&R (Rest and Relaxation). The rest home to which Kris had her 'committed', however, was New York's Payne Whitney Hospital, a psychiatric hospital for Highly Disturbed Mental Patients.

Recounts Susan Strasberg: 'I saw her face just after she had been released from a . . . mental institution to which she had committed herself upon the advice of her doctor. Either by accident or deliberately she had been placed in a locked ward.

'It took three days to get her released and afterwards there was an expression of amazement on her face as she talked about her experiences . . .'

'Marilyn,' says Robert Slatzer, 'didn't know it was a psychiatric clinic. She thought it was a sanitarium where she'd have a week's rest cure. Instead it was a psychiatric place with a padded room. They took everything away from her and put her in a hospital gown.

'Afterwards it came out that Lee Strasberg was
worried. He thought she'd have a mental collapse and
should be confined for an interminable period of time.

'Marilyn attacked Dr Kris and was told by Kris that
Strasberg had recommended it. Strasberg was calling
the shots. Dr Kris was a beneficiary. She told Marilyn
Monroe up front that it was a prim and proper hospital
where she'd have a week's rest.

'But it was a psychiatric hospital. Marilyn Monroe
was afraid Lee Strasberg would commit her to a mental
institution. She was single and had nobody. She trusted
Strasberg enough to walk into the hospital of her own
accord. She never trusted him after that.'

According to Monroe biographer Anthony Summers,
Monroe scribbled a note which she sent to Strasberg
begging to be extricated. He didn't respond. The only
person who did was Joe DiMaggio, who she located in
Florida. He used all his influence to see to it that Monroe
was transferred to the Columbia Presbyterian Medical
Center where she remained for three weeks. From here
on in, however, things would only go downhill. Monroe
would begin work on *Something's Got to Give*, but would
never complete it. And the breakup of her romance with
John F. Kennedy would lead first to her fourth (and
final) abortion, and then to her death.

Epilogue

What happened to Marilyn Monroe is an outrage – not merely the events surrounding her bizarre death, but the pattern of her entire life.

The degree to which she was victimized is something we may never fully know, but at the very least we may infer that she was victim of the most elementary kinds of sex, class and race prejudices.

Some small measure of satisfaction may come if, in view of the mounting pressure to have it re-opened, the Los Angeles Police Department do decide to take another look at the case, since it would mean a disavowal of the suicide myth.

But the greater lesson may be in accepting the agony of Monroe so that we can endeavour to see that others agonize less, and in so doing, in some small way mitigate the ignominy of Marilyn's suffering. I hope that this is so.

Sandra Shevey, 1987

Bibliography

Capell, Frank A., *The Strange Death of Marilyn Monroe*, Herald of Freedom Press, Zarephath, New Jersey, 1969

Conover, David, *Finding Marilyn: a Romance*, Grosset and Dunlap, New York, 1981

Dougherty, James E., *The Secret Happiness of Marilyn Monroe*, Playboy Press, Chicago, 1976

Gourlay, Logan, *Olivier*, Weidenfeld and Nicolson, London, 1973

Graham, Sheilah, *My Hollywood*, Michael Joseph, London, 1984

Graham, Sheilah, *Scratch an Actor*, W. H. Allen, London, 1969

Greene, Milton, *My Story: Marilyn Monroe*, W. H. Allen, London, 1975

Guild, Leo, *Zanuck: Hollywood's Last Tycoon*, Holloway House, Los Angeles, 1970

Guiles, Fred, *Norma Jean*, W. H. Allen, London, 1969

Guiles, Fred, *Norma Jeane* (Revised), Granada, London, 1985

Harris, Radie, *Radie's World*, W. H. Allen, London, 1975

Kobal, John, *People Will Talk*, Aurum Press, UK, 1985; Alfred A. Knopf, Inc., USA, 1986

Lambert, Gavin, *On Cukor*, Putnam, New York, 1972

Logan, Joshua, *Movie Stars, Real People and Me*, Delacorte Press, New York, 1978

Martin, Ralph, *A Hero for Our Time*, Macmillan, New York, 1983

Pepitone, Lena and Stadiem, William, *Marilyn Monroe Confidential*, Sidgwick & Jackson, London, 1979

Romero, Gerry, *Sinatra's Women*, Manor Books, New York, 1976

Rosten, Norman, *Marilyn: An Untold Story*, The New American Library, New York, 1973; Millington, UK, 1973

Skolsky, Sidney, *Don't Get Me Wrong, I Love Hollywood*, Putnam, New York, 1975

Slatzer, Robert F., *The Life and Curious Death of Marilyn Monroe*, Pinnacle Books, USA, 1975

Summers, Anthony, *Goddess*, Gollancz, London, 1985

Warren, Doug, *Betty Grable: The Reluctant Movie Queen*, Robson Books, London, 1982

Welland, Dennis, *Miller the Playwright*, Methuen, London, 1979

Wilson, Earl, *The Show Business Nobody Knows*, Cowles Books, Chicago, 1971; W. H. Allen, London, 1972

Wood, Tom, *The Bright Side of Billy Wilder, Primarily*, Doubleday, Garden City, 1970

Zierold, Norman, *The Hollywood Tycoons*, Hamish Hamilton, London, 1969

Index